Communication Ethics

Critical Intercultural Communication Studies

Thomas K. Nakayama
General Editor

Vol. 12

PETER LANG
New York • Washington, D.C./Baltimore • Bern
Frankfurt am Main • Berlin • Brussels • Vienna • Oxford

Communication Ethics

Between Cosmopolitanism and Provinciality

EDITED BY
Kathleen Glenister Roberts
and Ronald C. Arnett

PETER LANG
New York • Washington, D.C./Baltimore • Bern
Frankfurt am Main • Berlin • Brussels • Vienna • Oxford

Library of Congress Cataloging-in-Publication Data

Communication ethics: between cosmopolitanism and provinciality /
edited by Kathleen Glenister Roberts, Ronald C. Arnett.
p. cm. — (Critical intercultural communication studies; v.12)
1. Communication—Moral and ethical aspects.
I. Glenister Roberts, Kathleen. II. Arnett, Ronald C.
P94.C5717   175—dc22   2008009789
ISBN 978-1-4331-0325-4 (casebound)
ISBN 978-1-4331-0326-1 (paperback)
ISSN 1528-6118

Bibliographic information published by **Die Deutsche Bibliothek.**
Die Deutsche Bibliothek lists this publication in the "Deutsche
Nationalbibliografie"; detailed bibliographic data is available
on the Internet at http://dnb.ddb.de/.

Cover design by Joni Holst

© 2008 Peter Lang Publishing, Inc., New York
29 Broadway, 18th floor, New York, NY 10006
www.peterlang.com

Printed in the United States of America

Contents

■ ■ ■

Introduction

Cosmopolitanism and Provinciality: [Exploring] Communication Ethics

KATHLEEN GLENISTER ROBERTS
& RONALD C. ARNETT

This book, *Communication Ethics: Between Cosmopolitanism and Provinciality,* comple-
ments a book selection in the field very specifically: it is the second title in
Communication Ethics to be published with Peter Lang Publishing. The first was
Exploring Communication Ethics: Interviews with Influential Scholars in the Field,
edited by Pat Arneson, containing interviews with leading scholars from the Eighth
National Communication Ethics Conference (2004). *Communication Ethics: Between
Cosmopolitanism and Provinciality* continues the conversation from the Ninth National
Communication Ethics Conference (2006). As was the case with Arneson's edited
volume, we anticipate that this book will be an excellent resource for instructors in
Communication and could be used for upper-level undergraduate courses in
Communication. Because of its focus on cosmopolitanism, *Communication Ethics*
would be especially appropriate for Intercultural Communication classes.

This project invites a dialogue of major authors in the field of Communication,
engaging a conversation of cosmopolitanism and provinciality from a communication ethics perspective. There is no consensus on what constitutes communication
ethics, cosmopolitanism, or provinciality. This work does not attempt to provide an
action plan for bringing communication ethics to the public forum. Our task is both

more modest and diverse. The charge of this work began with the following question of major authors in the field of communication ethics: "What does the bias of your work suggest or offer for understanding the theme *Communication Ethics: Between Cosmopolitanism and Provinciality?* Using the notion of *Communication Ethics: Between Cosmopolitanism and Provinciality* as a hermeneutic entrance into your own scholarship, please respond to the insight of the theme not with authoritative knowledge, but with acknowledgment of your own work." We cannot invite cosmopolitanism without provinciality; engaging this unity of contraries is perhaps our best hope—a dialogic hope that begins not with proclamations about cosmopolitanism or provinciality alone, but small glimpses from the center of our own bias, engaging the necessity of the urban and the different.

This project assumes that *Communication Ethics: Between Cosmopolitanism and Provinciality* offers no answers, but invites a conversation that is more akin to a beginning, a joining, an admission that there is more than "me," "us," or "my kind" of people, theory, or wisdom. Perhaps one could call communication ethics that embraces the unity of cosmopolitanism and provinciality, ironically, a smart contribution that knowingly begins with ignorance—what we do not know. In the words of Hans Georg Gadamer, advancing knowledge rests with bias, not knowing, and the meeting of questions significant to a given historical moment.[1] Such is the reason for *Communication Ethics: Between Cosmopolitanism and Provinciality.*

Communication Ethics: Between Cosmopolitanism and Provinciality will most likely complement the selection of books on communication ethics, cosmopolitanism, and provinciality, but there are few books that would "compete." A similar edited work is Martha Nussbaum's *For Love of Country?,* wherein a number of philosophers and essayists respond to Nussbaum's position on cosmopolitan education in the United States. However, our work takes a broader view of the topic of cosmopolitanism by placing it in tension with provinciality. Its contributors also have had free rein to connect cosmopolitanism to their own work, rather than respond to issues raised by another author. Finally, this is the only book within the field of communication that addresses cosmopolitanism.

The evolution of this text and the scholarly articles that follow demonstrate communication ethics at work. The first question raised in the course of the project was the use of the term "globalization" within the original manuscript. At the request of Walter Fisher, a distinguished scholar within the field of Communication as well as a contributor to this project, the editors considered the term "cosmopolitanism" in opposition to the term "globalization." As we examined essays for this particular volume, the term "cosmopolitanism" took on greater significance through the voices of Fisher and our keynote at the communication ethics conference, John Stewart. In honor of our colleagues, and in our articulation of a legitimate position within the field, the term "cosmopolitanism" became one of the two centers of this work.

It was decided that the term "cosmopolitanism" held greater implications for the emergent biases of the scholars within this work than did the term "globalization." The editors admit, however, that questions remain about the distinction between "globalization" and "cosmopolitanism," which we articulate in the Afterword and in the essay by Roberts.

The authors within this work engage the ongoing debate between cosmopolitanism and provinciality from their own standpoints. Accordingly, the term "provinciality," or locality, joins this volume. Authors as distinguished as Martin Heidegger[2] and Alasdair MacIntyre[3] have pointed to the importance of local soil in decision making. The work of Seyla Benhabib[4] reminds us over and over: the particular matters. Provinciality is indeed the ground of the particular. And without the particular, without provinciality, what we normally call "pluralism" loses its face. The irony is that provinciality is the dwelling place of multiple pockets of provinciality, lending to a larger gestalt known as pluralism.

This work does not attempt to offer a conclusion to the questions revolving around the polar terms of "cosmopolitanism" and "provinciality." Rather, it attempts to recognize, in a postmodern age of multiplicity of narrative and virtue structures, that polar realities are to be expected, penned perhaps more eloquently by Martin Buber as the "unity of contraries."[5] This work seeks not to settle the argument, just to give a public space for the reminder of the importance of both sides of the conversation.

Additionally, this work which began with the framing of dialogic ethics moved into the more common vernacular of communication ethics for one basic reason: not all ethical orientations are dialogic, nor should they be. In the dialectical tension between cosmopolitanism and provinciality, we are more often likely to find monologic proclamations than dialogic renderings of the other's side of the argument. Dialogue foisted upon the human community quickly morphs into monologic telling. The permission, the invitation, the appreciation of monologue makes the possibility of dialogue ultimately possible. Communication ethics is the home of the I-Thou and the I-It; sometimes life is more akin to putting one foot in front of another and going on in the revelatory hope of dialogic insight.

This book on communication ethics is an effort to make the possibility of dialogue possible, beginning not with a dialogic presupposition but with the monologic presupposition. People right now are fighting for opposing positions on how the human community ought to organize itself. Such an argument is not new. But indeed, such an argument matters. Cosmopolitanism and provinciality remind us of the big and the local. Hannah Arendt[6] reminds us that an "enlarged mentality" is less likely to embrace either in isolation. The following essays take us into conversation about cosmopolitanism and provinciality; the conclusion takes us to projects that have emerged from this one. The conversation does not end; this book simply brings before us two primary metaphors that shape our life together around the question of communication ethics: cosmopolitanism and provinciality. The editors would also like to account for the random distribution of essays within this work. Cosmopolitanism and provinciality do not live in neat linear categories. And neither are the articles presented as such. We deliberately, as editors, withhold comment about the following essays and instead invite you, the reader, into the conversation. The answer to the question of the global and the local has been, is, and most assuredly will be yes and no, no and yes—such is the way we learn, not from argument, but from long-standing substantive difference.

NOTES

1. Gadamer, *Truth and Method* (London: Continuum Publishing Incorporated, 1994).

2. Heidegger, *Being and Time* (Oxford: Blackwell, 1962).

3. MacIntyre, *After Virtue: A Study in Moral Theory* (London: Duckworth Publishers, 1981).

4. Behabib, *The Reluctant Modernism of Hannah Arendt (Modernity and Political Thought)* (Thousand Oaks, California: Sage Publications, 1996).

5. Buber, *The Knowledge of Man: A Philosophy of the Interhuman* (New York: Harper and Row, 1966), 111.

6. Arendt, "Truth and Politics" in Peter Lanslett and W.G. Runicman, eds. *Philosophy, Politics and Society,* 3rd series (Oxford: Blackwell Publishers, 1967), 115.

■ ■ ■

Universals and the Human

CLIFFORD G. CHRISTIANS

My perspective on provinciality and the universal is philosophical anthropology. For my framework, I identify the characteristics common and unique to human being. The status of philosophical anthropology is controversial within the classical philosophical disciplines at present: epistemology, metaphysics, and ethics. Its agenda typically has been taken over by the philosophy of mind or eclipsed by analytical philosophy in the North Atlantic. Therefore, while working out of the necessary and sufficient conditions of the human species, my perspective is more exactly "anthro-ontological":

> For one thing, language presupposes corporeality for vocal utterances to be articulated and pronounced. For another, language necessarily refers to a world perceptible to the senses and common to the speaker; it implies their common being-in-the-world.[1]

I've appealed to only a pentad—Descartes, Cassirer, Freire, Jonas, and Wiredu—but this is at least a general framework for the way philosophical anthropology addresses the particular and global in dialogic ethics.

RENE DESCARTES

The elephant in the room is Rene Descartes. In coming to grips with the nature of the human in dialogic theory, we must establish the alternatives contrary to Descartes. For him, the father of modernist philosophy, human subjects are interiorized mental substances. Human bodies are subject to the laws of mechanics, but human minds are private and metaphysical. The essence of the self is thinking substance.

In his *Meditations On First Philosophy* (1641/2), Descartes seeks an absolute proof that I exist. What concerns him is distinguishing illusion from reality. He realizes our brain could be activated by an evil genius. Perhaps reality is disjointed and horrible rather than regular and benevolent. Is my nightmare or daily routine the reality? I fall asleep and dream of an igloo at high noon. I wake up and it is dark night in Urbana. Presuming I must pass the most strenuous tests of skepticism, it is still true I must perceive in either case. Whether dreaming appearances or negotiating the real world, my mind is necessary. Therefore, my thinking capacity is indubitable, even if I doubt everything. *Cogito, ergo sum*—I think, therefore I am. Human rationality reigns supreme. But notice the minor premise on which this model is constructed. Descartes insisted on the noncontingency of starting points, unconditioned by circumstance. He presumed clear and distinct ideas, objective and neutral, apart from anything subjective. Imagine the very conditions under which *Meditations II* was written. The Thirty Years War in Europe brought social chaos everywhere. The Spanish were ravaging the French provinces and even threatening Paris. But Descartes was in a room in Belgium on a respite, isolated literally from actual events. And his *Discourse on Method* (1637) elaborates this objectivist notion in more detail. Genuine knowledge is built up in linear fashion, with pure mathematics the least touched by circumstances. Two-plus-two-equals-four was lucid and testable, and all valid knowledge in Descartes's view should be as cognitively clean as arithmetic.

Descartes contended, in effect, that one could demonstrate truth only of what she could measure. The realm of the spirit was beyond such measurement, a matter of faith and intuition, not truth. The physical became the only legitimate domain of knowledge. Descartes's spiritual world was left to speculation by the divines, many of whom shared the Cartesian bias that theirs was an ephemeral pursuit. Science gained a stranglehold on truth. A split between facts and values was bequeathed to the Western mind, in fact, a radical discontinuity between hard facts and subjective values. It is the hallmark of Enlightenment materialism in all its forms that reason is isolated from faith, knowledge from belief. No one sketched the modern intellectual terrain more decisively that Descartes, and in terms of philosophical mapmaking, entire regions of human interest which had engaged the intense efforts of earlier cultures and non-Western peoples, simply ceased to appear.

BEING-IN-THE-WORLD

The essentialist paradigm rooting our humanness in linear rationality has had its detractors, of course, within modernity itself. An example is chosen from each of the three Enlightenment centuries.

COUNTER-ENLIGHTENMENT

Giambattista Vico contended against Descartes that philology ought to preoccupy philosophers because language was the central human activity. Mathematics, in his view, was a form of knowledge appropriate to the natural order. As a professor of rhetoric at the University of Naples for four decades (1699–1741), his magnum opus was the expansive *New Science* (1725) though his *Study Methods of Our Time* (1709) is a testimony to his genius also. *New Science* was a detailed account of the history of language and cultural customs in which Vico argued that the mind coheres in imaging, not in rational linearity. The distinctive human power to give imagistic form to experience he labeled *fantasia*. He thereby placed the image over the concept, the mythopoetic over the fact, and language over logic. He redefined science, not as an examination of external events, but as the power of imagination to create reality and give us an inside perspective on it. His highly original theory of imaginative universals remains an ideal of humanists even now.

Hegel's successor at Berlin, Wilhelm Dilthey, illustrated the ongoing concern in the 19th century for a holistic understanding of our humanness, contrary to the mathematical foundation for humanity in Descartes. He considered *New Science* "one of the greatest triumphs of modern thought"[2] and believed with Vico that inside understanding (*Verstehen*) was the illuminating and inescapable issue. Dilthey put *Verstehen* into the framework of lived experience (*Erlebnis*), with *Erlebnis* becoming the ultimate basis and givenness of knowledge for him. *Erlebnis* is not epiphenomenal in Dilthey, but an irreplaceable and immediate grasp of meaning that underlies reflexive thought. This lived experience is an ever-flowing stream. The relations of life are historical in nature rather than rational first of all. Our forms of consciousness and expression are determined by history, he argued: "Life contains as the first categorical definition, fundamental to all others, being in time."[3] He defined the problem of understanding as recovering a consciousness of our historicality (*Geschichtlichkeit*).

For a Counter-Enlightenment voice in the 20th century, explicitly opposed to *animale rationale* in the context of social science, one can hardly improve on the framework presented by C. Wright Mills in *The Sociological Imagination* (1959). In Cartesian science, one inevitably lives on the deductive/inductive, rationalist/empiricist seesaw—sometimes emphasizing the subject and developing grand theory and at other times focusing on the object and generating abstract empiricism. Mills's eloquent plea for the sociological imagination, which avoids both errors, stands squarely on the shoulders of the Counter-Enlightenment. Lying between abstracted empiricism and grand theory, humans through their sociological imagination formulate classic problems in terms of cultural, social, and historical structures. "This is the key point," Mills wrote, "taking up substantive matters on the historical level of reality" and interpreting the issues in terms appropriate to their substance.[4] Instead of limiting humans to rationality in grand theory or to biological sense data in empiricism, Mills activates the interpretive capacity, that is, the sociological imagination. As with *fantasia* and *verstehen,* he insists on humans as creative beings who build worlds of meaning in their particularity and complexity. He recognized along with Vico and Dilthey, that for all the Enlightenment's puffery about the human species, Descartes, in effect, had defined humans away as unnecessary. Overestimating the rationalist-scientific mode of thinking, the Enlightenment sought to grasp the essence of nature completely apart from persons.

MARTIN HEIDEGGER

While broadening our definition of human beings beyond Cartesian rationalism, the concept of essential human nature prevailed. Insisting on moral discernment beyond the rational faculty, and emphasizing *fantasia, verstehen,* and the sociological imagination did not in themselves deny the notion of essence that is central to the tradition of rational being. It was the mega voice, Martin Heidegger's existentialism, that contradicted Cartesian essentialism at its core.[5] "Calculative thinking," he called it, through which our authentic humanness is closed down.[6] From Heidegger's early classic *Being and Time* (1927) through his last major book in 1958 (*What is Philosophy?*) his philosophical preoccupation was being. Human being, *Dasein* our concrete intentional existence, distinguished people from all other entities. Human beingness is not a static substance but radically contextual. The human species actualizes the presence of Being, and Being can show itself only through humanity. Humans alone are the beings to whom all things in the world can reveal themselves as meaningful. Phenomena disclose their is-ness through the human opening. Human beings are "the clearing of Being." Humans are in the peculiar position of raising the problem of Being through their unique self-consciousness. Human beingness is not a static substance, but a situated existent receiving and expressing the significance of things. There is no subject-object dichotomy whatsoever. "The disclosure of things and the one to whom they are disclosed are co-original."[7]

Human action is not self-originating, but guided by a historical play of language and concepts not under any one person's control.

Man (*sic*) can indeed conceive, fashion, and carry through this or that in one way or another. But man (*sic*) does not have control over unconcealment itself, in which at any given time the real shows itself or withdraws.[8]

"Beings or entities thus appear only against, from and within a background or opening, a framework. But the opening or clearing within which they take the shapes they assume, is itself structured."[9] Our actions are not inventions, but emerge within the claims that the natural and cultural worlds lay on us. Being as such is never simply given; beings come to presence in a definite way that depends on the total field of revealing in which they are situated. Our cultural and technological products appear ontically in terms of civilizational givens that are taken for granted, or, in other words, that stipulate for us what is true.[10] Our mode of being has specific features, deriving from an era's pretheoretical commitments, "something like deeply held, dynamic but enduring traditions, historical but no more easily thrown over than one's own deepest character or personality."[11]

HUMANS AS CULTURAL BEINGS

This body of work opposed to Descartes's rational being sets the context for the most productive trajectory into the universal and particular. Within this philosophical framework of being-in-the-world, the specific definition of humans as cultural beings is the best pathway to a dialogic ethics.

ERNST CASSIRER

Ernst Cassirer's *Philosophy of Symbolic Forms* (1923–1929/1953–1957/1996) opens this arena brought to fulfillment in Paulo Freire's ontological vocation.[12] In Cassirer's view, "we are language-using and culture-incorporating creatures whose forms of experience, conduct, and interaction take shape in linguistically and culturally-structured environments, and are conditioned by the meanings they bear."[13] His four-volume work in the 1920s brings to completion the symbolic tradition established by Ferdinand de Saussure's *Course in General Linguistics* (1916). For Cassirer, symbolization is not merely the hallmark of human cognition; our representational capacity defines us anthropologically. Cassirer (1944) titled his summary monograph, *An Essay on Man*. He identified our unique capacity to generate symbolic structures as a radical alternative both to the *animal rationale* of Descartes' modernity and to the biological being of evolutionary naturalism. Arguing that the issues are fundamentally anthropological rather than epistemological, Cassirer's creative being is carved out against a reductionism to intellectus and disciplined thinking on one hand, and a naturalistic neurophysiology and biochemistry on the other.

In *animal symbolicum*, Cassirer collapsed the presumed differences among human symbolic systems. Music, art, philosophical essays, mathematics, religious language, and Bacon's scientific method are placed on a level playing floor. Symbol is the critical concept. What atom is to physical science and cell to biology, symbol becomes for communications. Cultures are interconnections of symbolic forms—those fundamental units of meaning expressed in words, gestures, and graphics. Realities called cultures are inherited and built from symbols that shape our action, identity, thoughts, and sentiment. Communication, therefore, is the creative process of building and reaffirming through symbols, and culture signifies the constructions that result.[14]

The symbolic realm is considered intrinsic to the human species. Humans alone of living creatures possess the creative mind, the irrevocable ability to reconstruct, to interpret. From this perspective, communication is the symbolic process expressing human creativity and grounding cultural formation. Culture is the womb in which symbols are born and communication is the connective tissue in culture building. Symbol is the basic unit that carries meaning, thus anchors the communicative capacity, which in turn is central to our humanity, and humans are culture builders.

Communication is the catalytic agent, the driving force in cultural formation, and if cultures are sets of symbols that orient life and provide it significance, then cultural patterns are inherently normative. Assuming that culture is the container of our symbolic capacity, the constituent parts of such containers are a society's values. As ordering relations, values direct the ends of societal practice and provide implicit standards for selecting courses of action. Our concern then is to articulate the appropriate use of language, the ends communication should serve, and the motives it should manifest. With standards recognized as inherent in the concept of symbolic environments, we can begin putting content into the normative, asking what authentic social existence involves.

In the shift from rational being to cultural being, language is not a vehicle of private meaning and subjectivism but belongs to a community where it is nurtured in reflection as well as action. Communities are knit together linguistically; however, the lingual is not neutral but value laden, so our social bonds are moral claims. Ernst Cassirer represents an integrated view of the human as whole being—body, mind, spirit—humankind, the species which creates and maintains through language the value-centered world we call culture.

REALISM

Symbolic language has meaning only in contrast with the nonsymbolic. Make the concept "symbol" all-embracing and it has been rendered contentless. Analogously, if all the universe expanded simultaneously and in exact proportions, how could we know of such expansion? So the symbolic realm as well must be limited by something unsymbolic. At least one statement must be literal, communicating directly and properly, without pointing beyond itself. In a celebrated dispute with William Urban over Paul Tillich's[15] totally symbolic system, Tillich concluded that as a matter of fact all knowledge and experience cannot be of symbolic character. He points to a God who is ground of being. As a result, all mental functioning remains finite. Beginning with some non-negotiable ultimate claim, he establishes the possibility of interpreting all other activity symbolically. As Aristotle validated for all cognition, infinite regression is impossible. In a causal chain, there must be an unmoved mover with which we begin. We have come to recognize that Aristotle was correct for the ages: without a starting point our thinking is incoherent.

As cultural beings we enter a world always and already meaningful. In learning a language we find a world. It is language that discloses a world to us already disclosed. When we learn a language we are schooled in a culture that embeds its own presuppositions, a worldview. Participation in a cultural heritage is a precondition of all thought including critical reflection. The presuppositions of human existence are the centerpiece of the way humans arbitrate their presence in the world. Contrary to Rene Descartes for whom facts are distinct from values—our cultural formation is grounded in first beliefs. There are presuppositions to which we are committed inescapably. One cannot proceed intellectually without taking something as given. The theoretical models humans create are grounded in first beliefs, not in objectivist absolutes. Scholarship is encompassed by its presuppositions. Scientific naturalism and humanism are faith-based in the same formal sense as theism. A faith commitment is the very condition through which human cognition is intelligible.

Humans-as-cultural-beings entails realism, not nominalism—ontological realism. There are enormous issues here in philosophical anthropology contra Descartes's mathematical reasoning in which the mind alone knows. But in terms of realism, our cultural formation operates within an intelligible universe. Physical reality is not an undivided monad, not raw material or undifferentiated energy. A complex network of relations binds the universe into a cosmic oneness. Vegetables are ordered to people as food. Rocks are ordered to trees as the foundation for the soil in which they are to grow. Some kinds are hierarchical, sub-species within species and species within genus. But relations among humans are horizontal. No slave race serves a master race. Nature is a given totality which forms the presupposition of historical existence. The human species will not transmogrify into something else. The natural order is history's source, its beginning, an intelligible order that makes history intelligible. The temporal extension of a coherent and meaningful order cannot by definition be random and meaningless flux.

Human creative ability works within an intelligible order. For humans there is no *creatio ex nihilo*. The eternal Creator of all things is the source and norm of all truth about everything. Nature as a coherent whole affirms that truth is knowable and ultimately makes sense. Humans as intelligent beings can hope to understand in measure an intelligible world made by, in my terms at least, the supremely intelligent being.[16]

Instead of appealing to rational abstractions, humans-as-cultural-beings is an ontological paradigm rooted in animate nature. The Age of Science defined nature as spiritless materiality. This reductionism to matter and motion enabled the technological revolution to prosper. Material reality as inert substance could be manipulated at will. In Cartesian terms, we were considered masters and possessors of nature. But this view cannot account for the purposiveness of life itself. Humans-as-cultural-beings see the natural world in contradiction to the Age of Science. Living nature gives evidence of one determinate goal, its own reproduction. This reverence for life on earth is the philosophical foundation of the moral order. It is an ontological ethics that makes no appeal to essentialist human nature or to universal reason. It presumes only that without a starting point, ethical imperatives are always indeterminate. If moral claims are assumed to be presuppositionless, the possibility of doing communication ethics at all is jeopardized.

ONTOLOGICAL VOCATION

In Paulo Freire's *Pedagogy of the Oppressed* (1970), dialogue is the means for emancipation and the dialogic concept forms its intellectual core. Following the work of the Spanish philosopher Eduardo Nicol (1965), Freire makes dialogue the distinctive element in his emancipatory strategy. Without dialogue, Freire argues, there is conquest, cultural invasion, manipulation, and imprisonment in antagonistic relationships. He takes the Martin Buber tradition full strength, embracing its basic presupposition regarding human relationships as *a priori*.[17] With Buber he categorically rejects all dualisms between selves and culture. Society is macroanthropos rather than microcosmos, and dialogue is therefore the only morally acceptable tool for liberation. The goal is revolutionary cultural transformation from the dehumanization of a non-dialogic existence.

As the ground of his model, Freire establishes for empowerment and social transformation a definition of the human species as a being of cultural praxis. In his terms, it is our ontological vocation as creative subjects to act upon the world while being critical of it and transforming it to suit our purposes. Freire[18] presumes an explicit anthropology—conceiving humans as existing not only in the world but with the world, constructing it but through symbols separating from it in our consciousness: "Consciousness neither precedes the world nor follows it." Humans are able to adopt postures ranging from nearly undifferentiated response, to a critical attitude that entails a conscious process of intervention, even objectifying themselves through existential experience. While analyzing Freire's epistemology opens some interpretive windows, his philosophical anthropology is actually the determinative issue. As with the dialogic tradition generally, Freire sweeps epistemology into his anthropology. He declares that we have understood reality when we have gotten inside the self-in-relation. He presumes a philosophy of culture with the radically human as the meaning-center.

And the vehicle through which we exercise our humanity is communication. Communication simultaneously stands in a necessary relationship to our humanness and our liberation. In analyzing dialogue as a human phenomenon, for example, the word is understood as the essence of dialogue itself. But, given his anthropology, Freire contends that the word is more than just an instrument which makes dialogue possible. It has two constituent elements—reflection and action—in continual tension. "There is no true word that is not at the same time a praxis. Thus to speak a true word is to transform the world."[19] Or in terms more Habermasian, liberation is a process of self-reflection achieved in dialogue through communication free of domination.

The uniquely human capacity of "speaking a true word" is Freire's veranda on the socio-historical process in which thought and language are existentially experienced. For him, "thought and language, constituting a whole, always refers to the reality of the thinking subject. Authentic thought-language is generated in the dialectical relationship between subjects and their concrete historical and cultural reality."[20] Thus, in the case of dependent or culturally alienated societies, thought-language is itself alienated since it is cut loose from the action entailed by authentic thought. It generates only false words, not true words. Freire argues that the fundamental right of the Third World, for example, is exactly that of its own voice, the right to pronounce its own word. Without our voice, we cannot be the subject of our own choice.

In his essay, "Cultural Action for Freedom," Freire is even more explicit about the meaning he attaches to the idea of naming the world:

> Learning to read and write ought to be an opportunity for men (*sic*) to know what speaking the word really means: a human act implying reflection and action. As such it is a primordial human right and not the privilege of a few. Speaking the word is not a true act if it is not at the same time associated with the right of self-expression and world-expression, of creating and recreating, of deciding and choosing and ultimately participating in society's historical process.[21]

For Freire the cultural dimension of dialogue—the transformation of culture by naming it—belongs to the very nature of human beings. In that light, he argues, "human existence cannot be silent, nor can it be nourished by false words, but only by true words with which men transform the world. To exist humanly is to name the world to change it."[22] The goal is conscientization. A countermyth or moral outrage is insufficient; while analytically rigorous of concrete reality, conscientization for Freire also entails "authentic points of departure" as evidence of uncoerced praxis.[23]

In Freire's framework, culture is a created reality which establishes a meaningful cosmos; it is not just a derivative of social forces. Thus a revolution in our language (conscientization) is an integral component in the process of human liberation. Freire confronts the evils of starvation, poor housing, environmental abuse, unemployment, health hazards, and a lack of essential commodities. But these problems cannot be solved in a culture of silence. In the absence of a true word about human dignity and the existential condition, a word which enables us to decenter the reality in which we live, no transformation is possible. Symbolic forms are thus a critical element in our total humanization. Until we have an adequate language, we will only allow dominant myths to control the future.

Freire makes an elementary distinction between absolute and total depravity, contending that while oppression reaches totally to the boundaries of human existence it is not absolute. He never loses hope, while insisting on reflecting only what he has actually experienced. Our ontological vocation, in other words, is "of history-making creation and self-assertion which seek to unmask the 'inevitabilities' of fate, myth, magic, and the given structures."[24] But unmasking is a moral imperative for him, not an existential reality. In the face of a culture of silence, he insists on a theory of our universal humanness, not as romanticism but as a barrier against nihilism. While tearing down our idols and rejecting evil structures, Freire refuses to condemn all our cultural creations. His program of resistance ruptures our situated experience, while retaining a redemptive ambience through a language of possibility.

SYMPATHETIC IMPARTIALITY

Cultures are formed in terms of a differentiated universum. Agriculture imposes order, but is not an artifice outside the seasons and nature's givens. In music we discover a harmony that's there. In Michael Polanyi's tacit knowledge, laboratory work on frogs presumes a concept of animal in general and frogness specifically. The electromagnetic spectrum has always existed, but we didn't find it until the 19th century and then built our electronic media systems within that spectrum. And in this discovery mode, contrary to constructionism, we identify within nature the purposiveness of life.

PURPOSIVE NATURE

Nature insists on the propagation of life. Natural reality has a moral claim on us for its own sake and in its own right. The Enlightenment worldview, reflecting Descartes, assumed that humans alone are conscious and purposeful and that nature is spiritless. Hans Jonas contradicts this dichotomy. In his perspective, purpose is embedded in the animate world and its purposiveness is evident "in bringing forth life. Nature evinces at least one determinate goal—life itself."[25] Thus, he concludes, "showing the immanence of purpose in nature,... with the gaining of this premise, the decisive battle for ethical theory has already been won."[26] When new life appears, the forbears have a natural duty to preserve it, an obligation "independent of prior assent or choice, irrevocable, and not given to alteration of its terms by the participants."[27] Parental duty to children is an archetype of the natural accountability Jonas thus establishes—an *a priori* ought, grounded ontologically, one that is timeless and nonnegotiable.

Jonas gives the preservation of life a taken-for-granted character. Concrete human existence is embedded in the vitalistic order as a whole, and in cultural terms we sacralize it. Natural reality has a moral claim on us for its own sake and in its own right. Our human identity is rooted in the principle that "human beings have certain inescapable claims on one another which we cannot renounce except at the cost of our humanity."[28] Human responsibility regarding natural existence contributes the possibility of intrinsic imperatives to moral philosophy. Reverence for life binds us into a universal human solidarity and is the pre-theoretical given of the moral order. In other words, there is a fundamental commitment that precedes reification into ethical principles. The moral order is positioned in the creaturely and corporeal rather than in the conceptual of Descartes. The sacredness of life, evident in natural being, grounds a responsibility that is global in scope and self-evident regardless of cultures and competing ideologies.

Reverence for life on earth establishes a level playing floor for cross-cultural collaboration on the ethical foundations of responsible communication. Various societies articulate this protonorm in different terms and illustrate it locally, but every culture can bring to the table this fundamental norm for ordering political relationships and such institutions as the media. It represents a universalism from the ground up. Master norms are of a universal order conceptually speaking; they reflect our common conditions as a species. Yet human beings enter cultures through the immediate reality of geography, ethnicity, and ideology. We distinguish between the universal and particular as with a window pane, knowing there is a decisive break yet recognizing that the universal realm is only transparent in the local.

In contrast to the rest of the animal kingdom, humans are not only situated in the natural world but live alongside the it. Their symbolic capacity separates them from other life forms through their consciousness. Thus different cultural traditions affirm the sacredness of life in a variety of ways, while presuming that all human beings have sacred status without exception. Native American discourse is steeped in reverence for life, an interconnectedness among all living forms so that we live in solidarity with others as equal constituents in the web of life. In communalistic African societies, *likute* is loyalty to the community's reputation, to tribal honor. In Latin American societies, insistence on cultural identity is an affirmation of the unique worth of human beings. In Islam, every person has the right to honor and a good reputation. In Judeo-Christian theism, all humans are made in the image of God and therefore special status equally. In Confucius, veneration of authority is necessary because our authorities are human beings of dignity. Humans are a unique species, requiring within itself regard for its members as a whole.

From this perspective, one understands the ongoing vitality of the Universal Declaration of Human Rights issued by the United Nations General Assembly in 1948. As the Preamble states it, "Recognition of the inherent dignity and of the equal and inalienable rights of all members of the human family is the foundation of freedom, justice and peace in the world"[29] Every child, woman, and man has sacred status, with no exceptions for religion, class, gender, age or ethnicity. This common sacredness of all human beings, regardless of merit or achievement, is the universal commitment out of which we generate particular adaptations and expansions. This diversity in turn enriches the primordial universal.

KWASI WIREDU

Our cultures are constituted by language, and Kwasi Wiredu enables us to understand how human beings rooted in culture are also trans-cultural. Wiredu was Head of the Philosophy Department at the University of Ghana for 23 years until his retirement in 1999.[30] His philosophy of language is anthro-ontological and provides a theoretical argument for integrating universalism with particularism consistent with the Cassirer to Jonas tradition. In his words, "human beings cannot live by particulars or universals alone, but by some combination of both." Their incompatibility in philosophy and anthropology is illusory. "Without universals intercultural communication must be impossible," while our natural formulations are in the vernacular.[31]

Wiredu's argument can be summarized this way: All 6,000 known languages are equally complex in phonetic and phonemic structure. All humans learn languages at the same age. All languages enable abstraction, inference, deduction and induction. All languages serve cultural formation not merely social function. All languages can be learned and translated by native speakers of other languages; in fact, some human beings in every language are bi-lingual.

In Wiredu's terms, as cultural beings we are sympathetically impartial to other cultures. "Human beings do have a basic natural sympathy for their kind," the difficulty being that this "sympathy is often quite sparse and...easily extinguishable."[32]

> The survival of human society is possible in the face of quite a lot of defaults and defections from the observance of the ethical principle, but unless it held a certain minimum of sway in the thought and action of some individuals at least, there would be a collapse of human society. This necessary connection of the principle with the survival of the group and, by and large, of the species, invests it, as in the case of non-contradiction, with the status of an evolutionary force.[33]

Universals are not epistemic, but a mosaic of cultural habitats which we engage sympathetically and impartially at the same time. My solidarity with the human race is activated by intra-cultural engagement, but when humans are defined as cultural beings, there is no individuated subjectivity. We embrace an Other with deep personal sympathy, and simultaneously universalize impartiality—wishing conceptually that the whole human race were like the Other, and defining the Other as the universal ideal.

CONCLUSION

Dialogic ethics rooted in humans as cultural beings is normative morality and not metaethics. Normative ethics orients our lives within cultural formation. It is not Cartesian formalist theory within a contained circle. Normative dialogic ethics does not fall prey to the fallacy of rationalist ethics where reason determines both the genesis and the conclusion. Normative ethics is an intrinsic morality in radically different terms than an abstract rationalism. The domain of the good is not extrinsic, but rather calibrated by formal rules that autonomous moral agents must apply consistently and self-consciously to every choice.

This normative ethic works within the general morality. Rather than developing prescriptions for agents external to society and culture, the preoccupation is the normative moral dimension of everyday life. I have appealed to only a pentad-- Descartes, Cassirer, Freire, Jonas, and Wiredu--but this is at least a general framework for the way philosophical anthropology addresses the particular and global in dialogic ethics.

NOTES

1. Henrici, "Towards an Anthropological Philosophy of Communication," *Communication Resource* 1 (1983): 2.

2. Dilthey, *Gesammelte Schriften*, Vol. 14 (Leipzig & Berlin: Tuebner, Goetingen, Vandenhoeck & Ruprecht, 1966), 2.

3. Dilthey, *Gesammelte Schriften,* Vol. 6, 192.

4. Mills, *The Sociological Imagination* (New York: Oxford University Press, 1959).

5. Heidegger's stellar reputation has been sullied by his commitment to German national socialism prior to and during World War II. As Rector of the University of Freiburg in 1933–34 and as a prominent intellectual during the war years, he refused to condemn Nazism and offered no apology before his death in 1967 at 87. While not excusing this grotesque failure, his philosophical project has been important for hermeneutics, postanalytical philosophy, critical theory, poststructuralism, and deconstructionism. Jean-Paul Sartre was his most famous student, along with Georg Gadamer and Hannah Arendt. The smaller scale controversy over his four-year affair with Arendt has also complicated an assessment of his philosophical stature.

6. Heidegger, *Discourse on Thinking* (New York: Harper and Row, 1966), 56.

7. Hood, "The Aristotelian Versus the Heideggerian Approach to the Problem of Technology." *Philosophy and Technology: Readings in the Philosophy of Technology* (New York: Free Press, 1972), 353.

8. Heidegger, *Discourse on Thinking,* 18.

9. Idhe, "Heidegger's Philosophy of Technology." *Technics and Praxis* (Dordrecht: The Netherlands, D. Reidel, 1979), 105.

10. Idhe, *Existential Technics* (Albany: State University of New York Press, 1983), 11.

11. Idhe, "Heidegger's Philosophy of Technology," 201.

12. Cassirer (1960) has developed the most systematic treatment to date of the nature of the cultural sciences. See especially his "Naturalistic and Humanistic Philosophies of Culture" (1960, pp. 3–38) and "Nature-Concepts and Culture-Concepts" (1960, pp. 117–158). This book is particularly valuable in the context of this essay, since Cassirer self-consciously acknowledges his indebtedness to Dilthey. Cassirer referred to Vico's humanism throughout his career, beginning with his first book in 1902, *Leibniz' System.* For a summary, see his "Descartes, Leibniz, and Vico" (Cassirer, 1979, pp. 95–107).

13. Schacht, "Philosophical Anthropology: What, Why, and How." *Philosophy and Phenomenological Research* 50 (1990): 155–176.

14. I appropriate here a semiotic definition, which stands in contrast to anthropology where culture refers to entire civilizations as complex wholes, and in contrast to common parlance where culture is identified as refined manners. Most definitions of culture are expansive, encompassing under the term virtually all human activity. Culture is thus said to involve technologies, customs, arts, sciences, products, habits, political and social organizations which characterize a people. Others such as Jacob Burckhardt (1943) find the broad definition inchoate and distinguish culture from political and social structures, from direct efforts to understand nature (such as chemistry, physics, astronomy), and from religious institutions. Culture thus becomes essentially people's communicative activities and refers primarily to the products of the arts and language. The term is used here in Burckhardt's sense.

15. Tillich, *Theology of Culture* (New York, Oxford University Press, 1959).

16. For elaboration of this realism rooted in natural reality, see Christians (2003).

17. Freire, *Pedagogy of the Oppressed* (New York: Seabury Press, 1970), 67.

18. Ibid., 69.

19. Ibid., 75.

20. Freire, "Education as the Practice of Freedom" and "Cultural Action for Freedom." *Harvard Educational Review* 1 (1970): 210.

21. Ibid., 212.

22. Ibid., 213.

23. Ibid., 47.

24. Freire, "Paulo Freire: Notes of a Loving Critic," *New Catholic World* 15: 84.

25. Jonas, *The Imperative of Responsibility* (Chicago: University of Chicago Press, 1984), 74.

26. Ibid., 78.

27. Ibid., 95.

28. Peukert, "Universal Solidarity as the Goal of Communication," *Media Development* 28.4 (1981): 11.

29. Universal Declaration, 1988, 1.

30. Wiredu's first major book, *Philosophy and an African Culture* (1980), deals with African philosophy in terms of the folk thought preserved in oral traditions and critical reflection using modern conceptual techniques. He contends that philosophical work is culture-relative but can be universal too. African philosophy uses historical resources and engages them in indigenous languages but then actually does philosophy. As editor-in-chief of the Blackwell *Companion to African Philosophy* (2004) he provides comprehensive coverage of African philosophy across the ages—including Ancient Egypt, North African thinkers, pre-colonial philosophy, and African political thought in the 19th and 20th centuries. His "sympathetic impartiality" adopted here is developed systematically in his *Cultural Universals and Particulars: An African Perspective* (1996).

31. Wiredu, *Cultural Universals and Particulars: An African Perspective* (Bloomington: Indiana University Press, 1996), 9, 1.

32. Ibid., 41.

33. Ibid., 41.

BIBLIOGRAPHY

Boston, B. "Paulo Freire: Notes of a Loving Critic," *New Catholic World* 15 (1973):82–93.

Burckhardt, Jacob. *Force and Freedom: Reflections on History,* New York: Pantheon, 1943.

Cassirer, Ernst. *An Essay on Man: An Introduction to the Philosophy of Human Culture.* New Haven: CT: Yale University Press, 1944.

Cassirer, Ernst. *The Philosophy of Symbolic Forms.* Trans. R. Manheim and J. M. Krois. Vols. 1–4. New Haven, CT: Yale University Press, 1953–57, 1996). [Original work published 1923–1929]

Cassirer, Ernst. *The Logic of the Humanities.* Trans. C. S. Howe. New Haven, CT: Yale University Press, 1960.

Cassirer, Ernst. "Descartes, Leibniz, and Vico." In *Symbol, Myth, and Culture: Essays and Lectures of Ernst Cassirer, 1935–1945,* Ed. D. P. Verne. New Haven, CT: Yale University Press, 1979.

Christians, Clifford. "Cross-cultural Ethics and Truth." In J. Mitchell and S. Marriage, Eds., *Mediating Religion: Conversations in Media, Religion, and Culture.* London: T. & T. Clark, 2003. 293–303.

Descartes, Rene. *Discourse on Method.* Chicago: Open Court Publishing, 1938. [Original work published 1637]

Descartes, Rene. *Meditations on First Philosophy.* Trans. John Cottingham. Cambridge: Cambridge University Press, 1996.

Dilthey, Wilhelm. *Gesammelte Schriften.* (19 vols). Leipzig & Berlin: Tuebner, Goetingen: Vandenhoeck & Ruprecht, 1914–1982.

Freire, Paulo. "Education as the Practice of Freedom" and "Cultural Action for Freedom." *Harvard Educational Review* and the Center for the Study of Development, Series No. 1, Cambridge, MA, 1970.

Freire, Paulo. *Pedagogy of the Oppressed.* New York: Seabury Press, 1970.

Freire, Paulo. *Education for Critical Consciousness.* New York: Seabury Press, 1973.

Heidegger, Martin. *What Is Philosophy?* New York: Twayne Publishers, 1958.

Heidegger, Martin. *Being and Time.* Trans. J. Macquarrie and E. Robinson. New York: Harper and Row, 1962. [Original work published 1927]

Heidegger, Martin. *Discourse on Thinking.* New York: Harper and Row, 1966.

Henrici, Peter. "Towards an Anthropological Philosophy of Communication," *Communication Resource* 1 (March 1983): 1–4.

Hood, W. F. "The Aristotelian Versus the Heideggerian Approach to the Problem of Technology." In C. Mitcham and R. Mackey, Eds., *Philosophy and Technology: Readings in the Philosophy of Technology.* New York: Free Press, 1972. 347–363.

Idhe, Donald. "Heidegger's Philosophy of Technology." In *Technics and Praxis.* Dordrecht: The Netherlands: D. Reidel, 1979.

Idhe, Donald. *Existential Technics.* Albany: State University of New York Press, 1983.

Jonas, Hans. *The Imperative of Responsibility. (Macht oder Ohnmacht der Subjektivat? Das Lieb Seele Problem im Vorfield des Prinzips Verantwortung)* Chicago: University of Chicago Press, 1984.

Mills, C. Wright. *The Sociological Imagination.* New York: Oxford University Press, 1959.

Nicol, Eduardo. *Los Principios de la Ciencia. (The Principles of Knowing).* Mexico City: Fundo de Cultura, 1965.

Peukert, Helmut. "Universal Solidarity as the Goal of Communication," *Media Development* 28.4 (1981): 10–12.

Schacht, Richard. "Philosophical Anthropology: What, Why, and How," *Philosophy and Phenomenological Research* 50 (Fall 1990): 155–176.

Tillich, Paul. *Theology of Culture*. Ed. Robert C. Kimball. New York: Oxford University Press, 1959.

Vico, Giambattista. *On the Study Methods of Our Time*. Trans. Elio Gianturco and Donald Phillip Verene. Ithaca, NY: Cornell University Press, 1990.

Vico, Giambattista. *The New Science of G. Vico*. Trans. T. G. Bergin and M. Fisch. Ithaca, NY: Cornell University Press, 1948. [Originally published 1725]

Wiredu, Kwasi. *Philosophy and an African Culture*. Cambridge, UK: Cambridge University Press, 1980.

Wiredu, Kwasi. *Cultural Universals and Particulars: An African Perspective*. Bloomington: Indiana University Press, 1996.

Wiredu, Kwasi, ed. *A Companion to African Philosophy*. Oxford, UK: Blackwell, 2004.

Aesthetic Love and Romantic Love in Close Relationships

LESLIE A. BAXTER AND CHITRA AKKOOR

For interpersonal communication scholars interested in close relationships, "love" is a core concept. Scholars view it as prerequisite to relationship formation and essential in partner satisfaction and relationship success. However, communication scholars privilege the Western construct of romantic love, or romanticism. Spanier captures the essence of romanticism in his claim that it is "a general disposition an individual has towards love, marriage, the family, and with relationships involving male-female interaction in which the affective component is regarded as primary and all other considerations are excluded from conscious reflection."[1] From the perspective of romanticism, self "seek[s] entry into a state of emotional, erotic, and social fusion" in which the other is "idealized as unique, the epitome of everything that is beautiful and virtuous."[2] Parties experience an acute intensity of feelings, including a "pining for merger" in a risky enterprise in which the parties experience a loss of emotional control exemplified in the common metaphor of "falling in love."[3] As Hendrick and Hendrick note, "Romanticism has much to do with mythmaking, and the romantic love belief system has definite, predictable components."[4] Key components of romanticism include these beliefs: (1) we should follow our heart over other more practical concerns when choosing a partner; (2) love can strike at first sight; (3) there is only one "true love" for each person; (4) the object of one's love will be perfect; (5) love conquers all; and (6) love will not fade but will last forever.[5]

The discourse of romantic love is a cultural motif of contemporary U.S. society. Bachen and Illouz refer to it as "an obsessive theme"[6] that proliferates in all imaginable cultural sites, from fairy tales and popular songs to prime-time television. Moore refers to it as the "romantic tyranny" of American society.[7] A number of scholars concur, arguing that romantic love is a powerful cultural discourse through which interpersonal practices are produced and evaluated.[8]

Scholarly research reproduces this ideology of romantic love in a number of different ways. In this essay, we employ Mikhail Bakhtin's theory of dialogism as a theoretical framework by which to assess critically the scholarly discourse of romantic love. Our central argument is that romantic love, as conceptualized by researchers, is monologic in nature. We argue the value of opening up the scholarly discourse of love to include a dialogic conception of love and describe Bakhtin's concept of "aesthetic love." The essay is organized in three major sections. The first section introduces Bakhtin's theory of dialogism and the features of monologue around which a dialogic critique is oriented. This section also presents the dialogic concept of "aesthetic love." The second section presents a critical summary of the romantic love research with a goal of explicating its monologic bias. The third and final section of the essay discusses the implications of opening up discursive space to include a dialogical conception of love, using arranged marriage as a specific example.

BAKHTIN'S THEORY OF DIALOGISM

Mikhail Bakhtin was a prolific Russian philosopher of language whose writings span the fifty-year period from the 1920s to the 1970s. Although Bakhtin's scholarly work addresses a range of specific topics, Holquist[9] argues that the concept of "dialogue" is the master key that brings coherence to the whole. In its most general sense, dialogue is the simultaneous fusion and differentiation of perspectives. Dialogue is "constructed not as the whole of a single consciousness, absorbing other consciousnesses as objects into itself, but as a whole formed by the interaction of several consciousnesses, none of which entirely becomes an object for the other."[10] Contrasted against dialogue is monologue, where "Everything capable of meaning can be gathered together in one consciousness and subordinated to a unified accent…. Semantic unity of any sort is everywhere represented by a single consciousness and a single point of view."[11] Throughout his career, Bakhtin was critical of the "monologization" of the human experience that he perceived rampant in the dominant philosophical, linguistic, literary, political, and social theories and practices of his time. His intellectual project was a critique of those efforts that reduced the unfinalizable, open, and varied nature of social life in determinate, closed, totalizing ways. To Bakhtin, social life is not a closed, univocal monologue in which only a single voice (consciousness, perspective, world view, ideology) can be heard; instead, social life is an open dialogue characterized by multivocality and the emergence of meaning when those multiple voices interpenetrate.

Although the concept of dialogue is the conceptual strand that integrates Bakhtin's corpus of work, two distinct phases can be identified in Bakhtin's career and writing.[12] During the first phase of the early 1920s, Bakhtin's energies were concentrated on aesthetics, the creative act, consciousness, and ethics. By the end of the 1920s and for the remainder of his career, Bakhtin's work evidenced a distinct "linguistic turn." The critique of romantic love advanced in this paper is positioned, for the most part, in the early Bakhtin period.

Bakhtin's early writings circulated in the broader neo-Kantian philosophical discussions of his intellectual times. Bakhtin's early articulation of his theory of dialogism centers around two key arguments: (1) the need to decenter the sovereign self, and (2) the necessity of the aesthetic and ethical deed of answerability. Elaboration of both of these points provides us with a framework from which we can view critically the ideology of romantic love.

DECENTERING THE SOVEREIGN SELF

The first claim shifts the site of knowing from an autonomous mind to the dialogic site between consciousnesses. As Holquist usefully summarizes this key Bakhtinian claim:

> Bakhtin's thought is a meditation on how we know, a meditation based on *dialogue* precisely because, unlike many other theories of knowing, the site of knowledge it posits is never unitary…. In dialogism, the very capacity to have consciousness is based on otherness… In dialogism, consciousness is otherness.[13]

Thus, Bakhtin argued that consciousness is impossible without Other. Persons can never see themselves as a whole; Other is necessary to give us—to author—our consciousness. As Bakhtin stated in often fragmented notes he had recorded for purposes of revising his book, *Problems of Dostoevsky's Poetics:*

> Non-self sufficiency, the impossibility of the existence of a single consciousness…. The most important acts constituting self-consciousness are determined by a relationship toward another consciousness…. Separation, dissociation, and enclosure within the self as the main reason for the loss of one's self. Not that which takes place within, but that which takes place on the *boundary* between one's own and someone else's consciousness, on the *threshold*. And everything internal gravitates not toward itself but is turned to the outside and dialogized, every internal experience ends up on the boundary, encounters another, and in this tension-filled encounter lies its entire essence… *To be* means to communicate.

> Absolute death (non-being) is the state of being unheard, unrecognized, unremembered.…
> A person has no internal sovereign territory, he is wholly and always in the boundary;
> looking inside himself, he looks *into the eyes of another* or *with the eyes of another.*[14]

Consciousness at the threshold is positioned in marked contrast to the prevailing view of self that dominates Western thought since the Enlightenment, a view of the individual as "a coherent, integrated, singular entity whose clear-cut boundaries define its limits and separate it from other similarly bounded entities."[15] This monadic or sovereign self is, according to Bakhtin, "a hermetic and self-sufficient whole, one whose elements constitute a closed system presuming nothing beyond themselves, no other utterances."[16]

The ideology of the sovereign self is an assumptive pillar of the Euro-American ideology of individualism in general and psychologically informed scholarly approaches to interpersonal communication in particular. The dominant approach to communication begins with a pre-formed, sovereign self, complete with internal needs, motives, goals, attitudes, and beliefs. From this perspective, communication is deployed in response to these internal states; it represents a speaker's internal attitudes and beliefs and is strategically used to accomplish goals and meet needs. By contrast, the dialogic self envisioned by Bakhtin aligns itself with the constitutive approach to communication, which in general asks not how communication transmits or represents a speaker's internal states and beliefs but instead inquires how communication between persons creates, or constructs, the social world, including our selves and our relationships.[17]

What is it about Otherness that is so crucial to consciousness? Simply put, Other is difference. In early Bakhtinian work, difference is conceptualized as the unique excess of seeing, or outsideness, that characterizes human embodiment. A person is a concrete, embodied being who exists in the given temporal moment in a given spatial location (geographic as well as social). Thus, each person has a unique perspective, always outside another's perspective. Bakhtin describes this excess of seeing in the following oft-quoted passage:

> For at each given moment, regardless of the position and proximity to me of this other human being whom I am contemplating, I shall always see and know something that he, from his place outside and over against me, cannot see himself: parts of his body that are inaccessible to his own gaze (his head, his face and its expression), the world behind his back, and a whole series of objects and relations, which in any of our mutual relations are accessible to me but not to him.[18]

Such outsideness privileges difference, not similarity, as the key constitutive element in the process of consciousness. This stands in marked contrast to monologic approaches to communication, in which reproduction, commonality, and similarity are privileged. In prevailing traditional approaches to interpersonal communication, the goal of communication is minimally information transmission with a goal of fidelity of transmission; that is, the reproduction of meaning from a speaker's mind to a listener's mind. Beyond fidelity of transmission is a goal of consensus, in which the speaker's goal is to identify commonalities or similarities with another or to persuade the listener to conform to one's own beliefs and attitudes. By contrast, Bakhtin's concept of excess of seeing serves to underscore the inherent value of difference to the communication project. It is through mutual difference that consciousness (and every other constructed meaning) is created.

The quoted excerpt above from Bakhtin's fragmented notes underscores that consciousness is not a passive process, in which one person is passively positioned as an object to be infused with Other's perspective. The construction of consciousness is not reducible to receiving a hypodermic needle of Otherness in which self becomes a mirror-like reflection of others' views of us. Consciousness is located *between* persons; it involves a two-fold process of exposure to Other's unique perspective *and* exposing Other to one's own perspective simultaneously. Exposing Other to one's own excess of seeing is the process of authoring, in Bakhtin's terms.[19] Authoring brings us to the second argument central in understanding Bakhtin's early articulation of dialogism: answerability.

ANSWERABILITY AS AN ETHICAL AND AESTHETIC ACT

Central to consciousness is not only being authored by Other, but additionally, authoring Other. Consciousness can thus be viewed as a mutual process of authoring, an ongoing dynamic of joint action. The act of authoring another—sharing one's excess of seeing—is what Bakhtin refers to as *answerability,* and he viewed it as the ethical obligation of being human. Bakhtin's reference to the "non-alibi in Being"[20] captures the responsibility associated with mutual authoring. In essence, Bakhtin's position is that our very consciousness as human beings depends on answering an Other—giving the Other the "gift" of our excess of seeing. We have no alibi from co-participating with another in the mutual process of constructing one another's consciousnesses:

> I, too, participate in Being in a once-occurrent and never-repeatable manner: I occupy a place in once-occurrent Being that is unique and never-repeatable, a place that cannot be taken by anyone else and is impenetrable for anyone else. In the given once-occurrent point where I am now located, no one else has ever been located in the once-occurrent time and once-occurrent space of once-occurrent Being.... That which can be done by me can never be done by anyone else. The uniqueness or singularity of present-on-hand Being is compellently obligatory.[21]

Thus, argues Bakhtin, it is the unique positionality each of us occupies at a given temporal-spatial moment that denies us the alibi not to author an Other: No one else can do the task for us, and our very humanity rides on our ethical acts of ongoing answerability.

However, not all forms of responsiveness are equal. The act of authoring is aesthetic to Bakhtin when a person acts toward the other as a whole being. However, Bakhtin readily admits that in living everyday life, we often respond only to bits and pieces of the other. Louie, the neighbor boy who is hired as the lawn mower, is greeted at the end of his task with a $20 bill and a gracious expression of thanks and perhaps some polite chit-chat about the humidity of the afternoon, but the whole of his being is not addressed. And so it goes with many of our everyday interpersonal encounters. As Bakhtin indicates,

> In life, we are interested not in the whole of a human being, but only in those particular actions on his part with which we are compelled to deal in living our life and which are, in one way or another, of special interest to us. In the work of art, on the other hand, the author's reactions to particular self-manifestations on the part of the hero [the other] are founded on his unitary reaction to the *whole* of the hero [other].... What makes a reaction specifically aesthetic is precisely the fact that it is a reaction to the *whole* of the hero [Other] as a human being.[22]

When we respond to the whole of another person, we have shifted from the prosaic answerability of much of everyday life to the artful domain of aesthetic activity. Another term that Bakhtin used to describe this aesthetic answerability was aesthetic love, and we describe it next in order to provide a point of conceptual contrast to the ideology of romantic love.

AESTHETIC LOVE

Bakhtin conceives of aesthetic love not "in a passive psychological sense."[23] It is not a concept organized around internal feelings of sexual attraction or feelings of sentiment. Rather, it is "above all a concentration of attention."[24] It is, in other words, an act of answerability characterized by an all-encompassing attention to the whole of an Other. As Bakhtin articulates the concept,

> Only un-self-interested love on the principle of "I love him not because he is good, but he is good because I love him," only lovingly interested attention, is capable of generating a sufficiently intent power to encompass and retain the concrete manifoldness of Being, without impoverishing and schematizing it.... Lovelessness, indifference, will never be able to generate sufficient power to slow down and linger intently over an object, to hold and sculpt every detail and particular in it, however minute. Only love is capable of being aesthetically productive; only in correlation with the loved is fullness of the manifold possible.[25]

Several constituent qualities are marked in Bakhtin's description of aesthetic love. First, love is not predicated on the other's "goodness" or sources of attraction as rewarding to oneself; rather, love is answerability predicated on an orientation of respect for the other, "a confirmative acceptance"[26] of the other's whole being. Second, it is not an internal feeling state; instead, it is an action of answerability, of lingering attention. Third, it is an act addressed not to a part of the other (e.g., other's physical qualities) but rather to the whole of the other's Being, "however minute." Fourth, because of the aforementioned qualities, aesthetic love is capable of being "aesthetically productive." This last feature merits additional elaboration.

Answerability is aesthetically productive to Bakhtin if it functions to consummate the other. Consummation is an act of answerability that functions to complete the other, to somehow make him or her more whole, more than the other's consciousness was prior to the consummating interaction. Consummation might appear quite monologic on first blush, because it appears to privilege unity and wholeness. Bakhtin's position is that consummation is a fleeting moment, an act of punctuation in what is an ongoing, indeterminate process of creation. Bakhtin views all of social life as a fragmented, disorderly, and messy interplay of difference; such ongoing fragmentation precludes finalizability of all kinds: "Complete chaos still holds sway…in the aesthetics of verbal art…. At every step, one encounters indiscriminate mingling of different points of view, different levels of approach, different principles of evaluation."[27] Consciousness is never finalizable; instead, it is always a "yet-to-be."[28] If a person acted toward the other as finalized, by definition this would evidence the absence of aesthetic love, for it would be a response that ignored the fact that a person's self is "never at rest and never coincides with its given, presently existing makeup."[29] Consummation is thus not an act of finalizability but a fleeting "aesthetic moment"[30] of wholeness.

But how are aesthetic moments of consummation accomplished? Bakhtin answers this question by reminding us that attention is an act of answerability located in one's particular excess of seeing. Aesthetic activity is a three-part process in which unity and difference are at play. The first action is one of unity: empathy. As Bakhtin states, "I must experience—come to see and to know—what he experiences; I must put myself in his place and coincide with him as it were."[31] The second action is located in difference, a return to one's position of outsideness: "My projection of myself into him must be followed by a return into myself, a return to my own place outside…for only from this place can the material derived from my projecting myself into the other be rendered meaningful."[32] The last action interanimates unity and difference in the aesthetic act of answerability, in which the other is somehow consummated. It is, of course, artificial to present these three phases sequentially, for, as Bakhtin observes, they are "ultimately intertwined and fuse with one another."[33]

Against the theoretical backdrop of Bakhtin's theory of dialogism, we turn next to a critical review of the literature on romantic love that informs scholars of interpersonal communication. Our central argument is that the ideology of romantic love is monologic in nature.

THE MONOLOGUE OF ROMANTIC LOVE

Although a number of different approaches and typologies of love have been developed by various scholars in an attempt to show that love is multidimensional, an overarching monologic orientation prevails. First and foremost, these conceptualizations of romantic love have a strong individualistic bias in which love is conceptualized as an internal emotional or attitudinal state. Second, romantic love is oriented toward the individual's self-interests; the love object is serviceable to the individual's needs. Third, love is conceptualized as a finalized end-state that precedes relationship formation; a relationship lasts to the extent that love can be maintained.

The most common conceptualization of romantic love views it as an internal emotion. Zick Rubin, widely credited as the author of the first empirical measurement of love, developed a scale of love by contrasting it with liking. Whereas liking was conceptualized as feelings of warmth, closeness, and admiration of the Other's positive qualities, loving was conceptualized as emotional attachment, a motivation to care for the Other, and intimate feelings toward the Other. Rubin's basic distinction between liking and loving has been sustained by others. For example, Walster and Walster distinguish companionate love and passionate love, respectively. What is common to this body of work on companionate-passionate love is a conceptualization of love as an internal emotional state of an individual.

Others have advanced conceptualizations of love that make even finer emotional distinctions. Lee[34] argued for six styles of love: Eros (passionate love), Storge (friendship or companionate love), Ludus (self-gratifying, recreational or game-playing love low in commitment), Mania (possessive love), Pragma (practical love), and Agape (selfless love). Hendrick and Hendrick[35] developed an empirical measure of these six love styles, known as the Love Attitudes Scale, underscoring that love was conceptualized as a set of dispositional beliefs and attitudes held by a person. Relatedly, Sternberg's Triangular Theory of Love[36] posited a three-component structure for love: Passion (passionate love), Intimacy (companionate love), and Commitment (a feeling of loyalty toward Other). Although these multidimensional approaches appear to identify elements of aesthetic love (especially Agape love and Commitment), it is important to note that these are conceptualized as internal feeling states of individuals, in contrast to the emphasis on action that is centered in Bakhtin's notion of answerability.

Additional approaches to romantic love appear to highlight an Other-orientation similar to Bakhtin's aesthetic love. In her prototype approach to love, Fehr[37] has argued for a broader conceptualization of love that includes companionate love, unconditional love, giving love, and altruistic love. Sprecher and Fehr[38] recently proposed a scale to measure compassionate love based on measuring empathy and Other-orientedness. Although these approaches emphasize an Other-orientation more so than prior work, they still display a conceptualization of love as an internal state of an individual; in the end, love is an internal attitude held toward another.

When love is conceptualized as an internal emotion or feeling (regardless of its dimensionality), communication is positioned as a representational device: its function is to transmit internal feelings of love to others. Communication is a conduit by which one's love for another becomes known and understood to others.

Some contributions to the romantic love literature take an evolutionary approach based on biological conceptualizations of love.[39] For example, attachment theory conceptualizes romantic love as an internal need based in the nervous system and serving the important function of survival of the species through reproduction.[40] Conceptualized as a hard-wired need, this approach to love still locates it inside the individual.

One approach in evolutionary theory that moves from internal emotions and needs to external actions is Buss's conceptualization of love acts.[41] Buss makes the argument that too many theories focus on psychological aspects of love (internalized feeling states) to the relative neglect of love as acts. He developed a typology of love acts, including such behaviors as love expressions (e.g., saying "I love you"). Although Buss's work is important in shifting the attention from internal states to actions, his conceptualization of love acts differs substantively from Bakhtin's discussion of aesthetic love, not the least of which is the mutual obligation to act toward the Other from one's positionality of difference. Furthermore, communication is positioned as a representational device, a way of expressing an internal feeling state driven by genetically programmed needs.

Marston and Hecht[42] have similarly attempted to focus on love as action. These scholars sought to determine the types of feelings and behaviors that occur when people experience love, including felt physiological changes that occur when "in love." They also sought to identify how parties communicated love to one another. Despite the focus on behavior and actions, this program of research still positions love as an internal state. Actions are not constitutive of love, but rather ways to express, or represent, those internal feelings to the Other.

In sum, the first argument we are advancing is that existing scholarship on romantic love is monologic in its conceptualization of love as an internal emotional or attitudinal state. Such an approach is predicated on the monadic or sovereign self, an autonomous individual replete with a variety of internal feelings, beliefs, and needs. Efforts to externalize love by focusing on love acts still conceptualize love as an internal state; the act is merely an expression or representation of what already exists inside the person.

Our second claim is that existing work on romantic love is organized around a logic of individualistic self-interest. A person "falls in love" with another because of an attraction to him or her based on reward potential. For example, evolutionary approaches to love emphasize attraction for purposes of propagation of the species. Attachment theory emphasizes attraction based on ability to fulfill one's needs for secure care-giving. More generally, attraction scholarship has identified three key bases of interpersonal attraction: physical attraction, social attraction, and task attraction.[43] Physical attraction holds obvious reward potential for sexual activity. Social attraction refers to a person's perceived potential to provide social rewards such as caring and closeness. Task attraction refers to a person's perceived capacity to provide instrumental rewards; for example, Pragma love might be based on perceived ability to earn money in a high-status occupation.

In the attraction literature, substantial scholarly attention has been given to similarity between persons—demographic similarity (e.g., similarity with respect to age, ethnicity, social class); attitudinal similarity; similarity in abilities; similarity in communication styles; and similarity in physical attractiveness. Similarity is widely accepted as the love currency that crosses all bases of attraction. Similarity between parties is generally accepted as a prerequisite to romantic love, and difference is positioned as a deterrent or barrier to love. For example, Felmlee[44] argues in her research program on "fatal attraction," that parties can sometimes be attracted to differences but that it often backfires on them, jeopardizing love to the point of relationship dissolution.

A notable exception to the privileging of similarity comes from Aron and Aron's[45] conceptualization of love as a process in which the self expands by including the Other, "integrating to some extent, others' resources, perspectives, and characteristics into the self."[46] The basic premise of their Self-Expansion Theory is that people seek self-expansion through Others. Thus similarity is not a pre-condition to love because Other's difference actually increases the potential for expansion: a self has no resources with which to expand if the Other is but a mirror image of oneself. Although this theory embraces difference more than other work in the romantic love tradition, it still differs markedly from Bakhtin's notion of aesthetic love. First, the work of self-expansion is located inside a monadic person rather than between persons. Second, difference is framed hedonistically as a source of personal gain.

The attraction-love association that prevails in the romantic love literature evidences what Bellah and colleagues refer to as the therapeutic ideal of love: "The therapeutic attitude reinforces the traditional individualism of American culture, including the concept of utilitarian individuals maximizing their own interests."[47] For those enthralled with the therapeutic attitude, "obligation of any kind becomes problematic in relationships."[48] In the therapeutic ideal of love, love exists so long as it is rewarding to the individual; love ends when it ceases to be individually serviceable.

To summarize our second claim, the self-interest bias that prevails in scholarly discourse about romantic love reserves no conceptual place for obligation. The Other is eligible as an object of love to the extent that he or she is rewarding to self. It privileges similarity as the foremost mechanism of attraction, the precursor to love. In marginalizing difference and in centering self-interest, romantic love evidences its monologic bias.

Our third, and final, argument is that romantic love presupposes finalizability. The Other is finalized as a person whose rewarding qualities are worthy of love, and love is finalized as an outcome of attraction. Love is thus positioned outside of, and prior to, the formation of a committed relationship. As the old adage has it, "First comes love, then comes marriage." Of course, the reality of relating is that partners do not stay the same; over time, they inevitably change. The object we fall in love with is a perpetually moving target, thus challenging the stability of love. Of course, relationship parties, in their efforts to achieve the romantic love idealization of perfection, embrace this potential malleability in their attempts to extinguish the partner's flaws. In fact, Dillard has argued that "close relationships may be the social arena that is most active in terms of sheer frequency of influence attempts,"[49] especially concerning efforts to change lifestyle patterns. If the cost-benefit ratio changes and the Other ceases to be rewarding, then love ceases to exist. Interpersonal communication researchers recognize that the form of love can change over time; for example, passionate love can decline in long-term married couples whereas their commitment to love may increase. However, it is foreign to the ideology of romantic love to imagine a relationship satisfying unless it were formed on a bedrock of romantic love. Sternberg's choice of labels is quite revealing: a relationship in which parties have commitment but lack passion and intimacy is "empty love."[50] The ideology of romantic love is predicated on the belief that love can endure all challenges if it is "true." That is, if partners truly love one another, they can roll with the punches, including modifying the form of their love from passionate to companionate. However, romantic love is the prerequisite condition for relationship formation and success.

From an American standpoint, grounded in the ideology of romantic love, marriage based on anything but romantic love is something "to be looked on with pity or even moral condemnation."[51] Relationships that are not based on romantic love thus get marginalized by the discourse of romantic love. One such relationship is the arranged marriage. Scholarly labels are most revealing in referring to this kind of marriage. For example, Hatfield and Rapson contrast "love marriages" with "arranged marriages,"[52] semantically positioning the latter as non-love marriages. Other scholars have perceived love as a phenomenon unique to "industrialized and technologically advanced countries like the U.S. and Europe" concluding that "closeness and intimacy between marital partners" is generally lacking in cultures with arranged marriages.[53] Our argument is that arranged marriages might well be "love marriages," but with a different conception of "love," one which Bakhtin's concept of aesthetic love might help to render intelligible. We turn next to arranged marriages among those socialized in Indian culture as a case study by which to examine the heuristic value of a dialogic conception of love. If Bakhtin's concept of aesthetic love opens up discursive space to allow us to understand arranged love as a coherent ideology of love, then it has demonstrated heuristic value.

INDIAN ARRANGED MARRIAGES: AN EXAMPLE OF A MARGINALIZED RELATIONSHIP

The idea of arranged marriage evokes images of loveless and choiceless unions in which people, more often women, are forced into marriage. Scholars have noted that contrary to popular Western beliefs, there are different kinds of arrangement: ones in which parents arrange the entire process; a second kind in which the young people meet and interact with family members present; and a third kind in which marriage follows a getting-acquainted period.[54] Regardless of stereotypes, arranged marriages in some form are still the norm in many if not most countries, including India which is often considered the vanguard of arranged marriages.[55] Despite Western influences and popular media images, an estimated 95% of the marriages in India are still arranged. Western anthropologists have found the continuity of this practice quite remarkable.[56] One anthropologist captures nicely the Western reaction to the resiliency of arranged marriage:

> When I first came to India, this [arranged marriage] astonished me. I knew arranged marriage was standard among many villagers, and the rural poor, but I did not expect that an Indian man who had lived in the United States would come home after years of dating American women to marry someone he had met only three times. I did not expect college women in big cities to gladly give their parents the task of finding them good husbands. I was more amazed when some would say yes to a prospective groom after a half-hour meeting.[57]

Other studies have noted that many young people in India consider the practice of arranged marriage to be both "sensible"[58] and "desirable."[59]

Although the ideology of romantic love forecloses positive outcomes in relationships not based on romanticism, research shows that arranged marriages are stable, long-lasting, and based on long-term commitment.[60] Comparative studies between arranged marriage couples in India with those in romantic-love marriages in the United States have found no differences in satisfaction levels between the two groups,[61] and in some cases even higher satisfaction in the arranged marriage situation.[62] In an interview study of largely unmarried Indian men and women, Sprecher and Chandak asked participants to assess the advantages and disadvantages of arranged marriages and romantic love marriages. Both forms of marriages were characterized by advantages and disadvantages. The advantages of arranged marriage included perceived support and approval from families and society, the quality and stability of the marriage, the compatibility and desirability of partner backgrounds, and release from the pressures of meeting a partner. Disadvantages of the arranged marriage included unfamiliarity of the partner upon marriage, family problems, and interpersonal problems.

In the mate selection process of arranged marriage, arranged love is seen as something that follows marriage.[63] Love before marriage is generally discouraged because romantic love is seen as a blinding emotion that has the potential to lead a person into making a wrong choice of partner, one who is not suited to the family as a whole.[64] Love is not an outside precursor but something crafted from the inside of marriage.

The arranged marriage structure is embedded in an ideology of familial obligation. Thus, the arranged marriage is "an alliance between two families rather than a mere union of two individuals,"[65] including parents, in-laws, aunts, uncles, cousins, and other kin. According to Gupta, "marriage is an ideal, a duty, and a social responsibility"[66] that seeks to foster mutual support between the individual and the collective. Interdependence is an important value taught early in life that promotes integration with and emotional investment in the family.[67] Arranged marriage is a central means of maintaining the integrity of the immediate and extended family.[68]

Although existing research on the Indian arranged marriage provides us with a general sense of how it contrasts with romantic-love marriage, we lack specific insights into what "love" means from the perspective of Indians who are in arranged marriages. In an attempt to illuminate what "love" means to insiders of arranged marriages, we conducted a small-scale exploratory study, using an open-ended survey distributed through snowball sampling to Indian-American social-network members known to the second author, who were in arranged marriages. For our purposes in this chapter, we focus only on responses to the first survey question: "How would you describe 'love' in an arranged marriage?" Of the 45 distributed surveys, 19 were returned from 10 women and 9 men. Ages of participants ranged from 28 to 70, the number of years of marriage ranged from 2 to 41, and the number of years in the U.S. ranged from 5 to 43. The time period the participant had known the spouse prior to marriage ranged from 0 to 6 years.

These exploratory surveys were analyzed inductively for themes of meaning, organized around Spradley's[69] semantic relationship of Attribution ("X is an attribute (characteristic) of Y," where "X" was a coded theme and "Y" was "love in arranged marriage").

Although our sample size was small and precludes generalized claims beyond our immediate sample, the insider-identified characteristics of arranged love suggest that Bakhtin's concept of aesthetic love holds potential to render intelligible this form of love. We will address the dominant themes that emerged in our informant discourse on the meaning of love in arranged marriage.

LOVE AS THE ONGOING ACCOMPLISHMENT OF RESPECTFUL ATTENTION

Notably absent from our participant responses was an articulation of arranged love as an internal, affective emotion directed toward Other. The passion of romantic love was not salient in our informants' discourse. Instead, and more compatible with Bakhtin's focus on aesthetic love as a mutual action of answerability, was a theme of *love as the ongoing accomplishment of mutual attention*. Ongoing accomplishment repositions love as action, not feeling. In particular, it is caring-centered responsiveness to the other, and it is expected to be mutual. As one male informant, married for 35 years, expressed it, "They [the spouses] may or may not have common interests; they may not even be always together. But regardless of the circumstances, they have to know that one is always there for the other if and when needed." A female informant, married for 31 years, mirrored this sense of love in telling us "My description of love is…being there for him in need and always." Another female informant, married for 43 years, echoed the same theme: "Love between husband and wife is understanding, mutual respect, genuine interest in each other and their welfare and compromise."

Key to the ongoing responsiveness of arranged love is its grounding in mutual respect; the other is accepted on his or her own terms. One male informant, married for 40 years, told us that love is "a gradual process of acceptance, caring, maturing, accommodating, mutual sharing, enhancing opportunities for the partner to excel in special aptitudes." Evident in this quotation is its underlying tone of respectful attentiveness to the other—action embedded in acceptance of the other. A female informant, in an arranged marriage for 31 years, also reflects love as respectful of the Other: "Love is…respecting him/her, his ideas, opinions and not trying to change him…. Never insulting or putting him down…. Accepting minor faults." The theme of this woman's conception of love is oriented toward answerability predicated on respect for the Other, a respect that accepts the whole of the partner, "minor faults" included. Another male informant, married for 35 years, addressed the same theme of respectful attention to the Other in his statement that "They [the spouses] have to accept each other as they are or as they evolve. They should not try to change the other person just because they think that is what is best for him/her."

Several features of Bakhtin's dialogic concept of aesthetic love render intelligible an articulation of *love as the accomplishment of respectful attention*. First, love is positioned as a joint action between partners, not an individualized internal state of each person. Thus, love is not psychologized but constituted through partner actions. In particular, partners must engage the Other in caring and respectful ways, accepting both the strengths and limitations of the partner. The correspondence with Bakhtin's notion of answerability is evident. The romantic love rejoinder to our analysis might be that marriages based on true love ideally involve acts of caring and respect, thus suggesting that romantic love and aesthetic love are not that different after all. Our response is that the accomplishment of respectful attention is not an outcome of an internal passion-based emotional state of the individual. Rather, love is constituted in the accomplishment. The significance of this distinction becomes evident in conjunction with the next theme that emerged in our informant articulations of "love."

LOVE AS AN EMERGENT PROCESS

Our informants indicated that love was not something that preceded marriage; rather love emerged over time in the process of living the relationship with the spouse. One male informant, married for 42 years, told us quite directly that arranged love was "not love at first sight. It has to grow/develop gradually." A female informant, married for 34 years, told us that "In arranged marriage, husband and wife try to get to know each other over the first few years. Slowly they build up mutual understanding.... It gets stronger and stronger after they have children. Gradually, these understandings, trust, and care turn into love for each other." Another female informant, married for 33 years, echoed the same theme: "The love between the two develops through various experiences and understandings about each other. Sometimes, there may be disappointments and unexpected events in the arranged marriage life, but I think that it's through all of these good and bad experiences...their mutual love grows (almost) unnoticed day by day! Somehow, they become dependent on each other...this dependency...[is] love for each other."

The theme that weaves throughout these informant excerpts is the belief that love is not a finalized precursor to marriage but rather is something that grows inside the relationship, as parties live an interdependent life. One male informant, married for 4 years, summarized this theme well for us in noting that love in arranged marriages is "created during the marriage.... It is a commitment for life." This theme departs from the sense of "love first" that prevails in the ideology of romantic love, and is quite compatible with the sense of love as lingering attention in Bakhtin's concept of aesthetic love; love emerges from ongoing—lingering—mutual attentiveness. But such lingering attentiveness is far from easy, which segues to the third theme that emerged in our informant articulations of arranged love.

LOVE AS ONGOING EFFORT

In idealized romantic love, the partner is selected for maximum reward value, driven on the principle of similarity; if the partner and the relationship cease to be rewarding, love either was not "true" to begin with or it has ended. By contrast, our informants' conceptions of love include effort as part of love, not a threat to it. This effort was expressed in terms of the importance of compromise to arranged love. One male informant, married for 12 years, told us that love is "the understanding and appreciation that one must learn to live with his or her spouse as a life-long companion." Another male informant, married for 41 years, told us that in arranged marriages, "Both enter the relationship not knowing each other very well and also knowing that they must please their partner. As such each is more receptive to the opinions and desires of the other and is willing to accommodate the partner's views/desires. Hence there is greater flexibility and a desire for compromise.... 'Love' between husband and wife is a basket full of compromises and a strong desire to make each other happy." A female informant, in a marriage of 14 years' duration, echoed this same theme of compromise in telling us "As we were conscious of the fact that we were starting together as strangers, there was the willingness to accept and accommodate each other. Over the years this has helped us appreciate one another for who we are in spite of the differences of opinions and personalities."

Compromise is rooted in the realization, often the appreciation, that arranged marriage is constructed through the differences of the two parties. Compromise is also rooted in a sense of obligation to the institutional structure of the extended family. As one male informant in a 12-year marriage wrote, "Love, respect, and obedience towards the family are intertwined in Indian traditional culture." Another male informant, married for 33 years, told us that "Both husband and wife live together because they knowingly or unknowingly strongly believe in the institutions of marriage and the family." One female informant, married for 33 years, wrote in a way suggesting that marriage is a union with the entire family, not just the spouse: "The first few months are full of excitement and totally new experiences and (mixed) feelings, apprehensions about the new environment and time spent in the attempt to understand the new family members and new household."

The sense of compromise and familial commitment that characterize our informants' arranged marriages undermine an ideology of love that privileges self-interest. The willingness to please the partner, and the family, is not positioned as a threat to self-interest (and love), but rather integral to the very conception of love. Such an ideological belief clearly bears resemblance to the dialogic conception of love conceived by Bakhtin. Difference holds a prominent place in arranged love, and parties do not attempt to extinguish it. Consistent with the concept of answerability, parties are committed to the effort that it takes to construct a life-long relationship. In part, this commitment is grounded in familial obligation and the realization that the boundary of the partner does not end with him or her as an individual but includes, as well, his or her entire family. Thus, the partner's whole being includes his or her family of origin.

The romantic-love rejoinder might be that U.S. married couples, especially long-term married couples such as many of those in our sample, understand and value the importance of compromise and effort to a healthy marriage. Thus, a conception of *love as ongoing effort* might not appear incompatible with the ideology of romantic love. Our response to this position is that effort is occupying a different discursive place in the ideology of romantic love in contrast to the ideology of arranged love. Compromise in an ideology of romantic love is conceived as a diminution of rewards, perhaps a practical necessity, but a cost nonetheless. In the ideology of romantic love, a partner is entitled to abandon feelings of love, and the relationship, should compromise become an ongoing relational motif. By contrast, the ideology of arranged love does not position compromise as a cost that legitimates relationship dissolution. Rather, compromise is inevitable and an expectation of love rather than a violation of it.

In sum, our admittedly small sample of Indians, in arranged marriages for a varying number of years, articulated a conception of arranged love that bears remarkable similarity to Bakhtin's aesthetic love. Arranged marriages are not without love; love is simply calibrated along more dialogic lines than the ideology of romantic love common in the U.S. Of course, we make no claims about all Indian arranged marriages, or arranged marriages more generally. Further, our informants provided us with conceptions of arranged love that probably were idealized, just as our discussion of romantic love captured the idealized form of that ideology. Actual marriages, whether based on romantic love or arranged love, may or may not approximate the ideal. Thus, we make no claims about how satisfying arranged marriages are, compared to marriages of choice; however, as we noted above, existing research has not located major differences in overall satisfaction between these types of marriage.

CONCLUSION

In the globalized times in which we live, it is important that scholars of interpersonal communication appreciate that concepts such as "love" are not culturally neutral.

Arranged marriages probably are more common in the societies of the world than are marriages of choice. Rather than viewing arranging marriages as somehow love deficient, and thus inferior to marriages of choice, we argue for a more culturally sensitive approach to love. Bakhtin's concept of aesthetic love might prove fruitful in giving us a conceptual frame for making sense of arranged love that legitimates its integrity as a coherent system of meaning.

In addition, scholars of interpersonal communication should ask whether other love-based relationships in the U.S. could benefit from the aesthetic love framing. For example, stepfamily relations are often strained because stepfamily members, excluding the married couple, often fail to have strong feelings of "love" for their step-relations.[70] But the conception of "love" that stepfamily members use might hold them hostage in unfortunate ways. If "love" is conceived as an internal state of affection, rooted in similarity, finalized prior to relationship formation, and evaluated according to a metric of self-interested reward, then it is easy to see why stepchildren and stepparents report that they do not "love" one another. If, instead, scholars could open up discursive space to imagine other kinds of understandings of love, it might be easier for family members to construct loving relationships. From the perspective of aesthetic love, for example, love is not a precursor but something that inherently emerges over time, through much effort. It is based on respect and lingering attention, rather than "instant" affection. Although both romantic love and aesthetic love are challenging to achieve and sustain, each affords us a different discursive logic by which to gauge success. We think that aesthetic love holds much potential for relating parties, even in our provincial everyday lives in the U.S.

In more general terms, aesthetic love positions communication differently from how it is framed in the ideology of romantic love. Because romantic love is conceptualized as a psychological construct, communication is positioned as a conduit—a way to transmit to the Other one's feelings of love. Communication is also positioned as a conduit that transmits essentialized selves to prospective Others, so they can assess one's potential for reward. By contrast, aesthetic love positions communication as constitutive. It is through communication between persons that love—mutual, lingering attention—is constituted.

NOTES

1. Spanier, "Romanticism and Marital Adjustment." *Journal of Marriage and the Family* 34 (1972): 481–482.

2. Lipset, "Modernity Without Romance? Masculinity and Desire in Courtship Stories Told by Young Papua New Guinean Men." *American Ethnologist* 31 (2004): 205.

3. Ibid.

4. Hendrick and Hendrick, *Romantic Love* (Newbury Park, CA: Sage Publications, 1992), 61.

5. Hendrick and Hendrick, *Romantic Love;* Knee, "Implicit Theories of Relationships: Assessment and Prediction of Romantic Relationship Initiation, Coping, and Longevity." *Journal of Personality and Social Psychology* 74 (1998): 360–370; Sprecher and Metts, "Development of the Romantic Beliefs Scale and Examination of the Effects of Gender and Gender-Role Orientation." *Journal of Social and Personal Relationships* 6 (1989): 387–411.

6. Bachen and Illouz, "Imagining Romance: Young People's Cultural Models of Romance and Love." *Critical Studies in Mass Communication* 13 (1996): 279.

7. Moore, "Love and Limerence with Chinese Characteristics: Student Romance in the PRC." *Romantic Love and Sexual Behavior* (London: Praeger, 1998), 264.

8. Varenne, *Americans Together: Structured Diversity in a Midwestern Town* (New York: Teachers College Press, 1977),189, 204.

9. Holquist, *Dialogism* (New York: Routledge, 2002), 15.

10. Bakhtin, *Problems of Dostoevsky's Poetics* (Minneapolis: University of Minnesota Press, 1984), 18.

11. Ibid., 82.

12. Baxter, "Mikhail Bakhtin and the Philosophy of Dialogism." *Perspectives on Philosophy of Communication.* West Lafayette, IN: Purdue University Press. In press.

13. Holquist, *Dialogism,* 18.

14. Bakhtin, *Problems of Dostoevsky's Poetics,* 287.

15. Sampson, *Celebrating the Other: A Dialogic Account of Human Nature* (San Francisco: Westview, 1993), 17.

16. Bakhtin, "Discourse in the Novel." *The Dialogic Imagination: Four Essays by M. M. Bakhtin* (Austin: University of Texas Press, 1981), 273.

17. Craig, "Communication Theory as a Field." *Communication Theory* 9 (1999): 119–161.

18. Bakhtin, *Art and Answerability: Early Philosophical Essays by M. M. Bakhtin* (Austin: University of Texas Press, 1990), 22–23.

19. Ibid., 8.

20. Ibid., 40.

21. Ibid.

22. Ibid., 5.

23. Bakhtin, *Toward a Philosophy of the Act* (Austin: University of Texas Press, 1993), 64.

24. Emerson, "Solov'ev, the Late Tolstoi, and the Early Bakhtin on the Problem of Shame and Love." *Slavic Review* 50 (1991): 665.

25. Bakhtin, *Toward a Philosophy of the Act,* 64.

26. Bakhtin, *Art and Answerability,* 90.

27. Ibid., 8.

28. Ibid., 16.

29. Ibid.

30. Ibid., 67.

31. Ibid., 25.

32. Ibid., 26.

33. Ibid., 27.

34. Lee, *The Colors of Love: An Exploration of the Ways of Loving* (Don Mills, Ontario, Canada: New Press, 1973).

35. Hendrick and Hendrick, "A Theory and Method of Love." *Journal of Personality and Social Psychology* 50 (1986): 392–402.

36. Sternberg, *A Triangular Theory of Love: Intimacy, Passion, Commitment* (New York: Basic Books, 1988).

37. Fehr, "Prototype Analysis of the Concepts of Love and Commitment." *Journal of Personality and Social Psychology* 55 (1988): 557–579.

38. Sprecher and Fehr, "Compassionate Love for Close Others and Humanity." *Journal of Social and Personal Relationships* 22 (2005): 629–651.

39. e.g. Harlow, *Learning to Love* (New York: Jason Aronson, 1974); Mellen, *The Evolution of Love*, (San Francisco: Freeman, 1981).

40. Hazan and Shaver, "Romantic Love Conceptualized as an Attachment Process." *Journal of Personality and Social Psychology* 52 (1987): 511–524.

41. Buss, "Love Acts: The Evolutionary Biology of Love." *The Psychology of Love* (New Haven: Yale University Press, 1988), 100–118.

42. Marston and Hecht "Love Ways: An Elaboration and Application to Relational Maintenance." *Communication and Relational Maintenance* (New York: Academic Press, 1994), 187–202.

43. McCroskey and McCain, "The Measurement of Interpersonal Attraction." *Speech Monographs* 41 (1974): 261–266.

44. Felmlee, "Fatal Attraction." *The Dark Side of Close Relationships* (Mahwah, NJ: Lawrence Erlbaum Associates, 1998), 3–32.

45. Aron and Aron, *Love and the Expansion of the Self: Understanding Attraction and Satisfaction,* (New York: Hemisphere, 1986).

46. Aron, Paris, and Aron "Falling in Love: Prospective Studies of Self-concept Change." *Journal of Personality and Social Psychology* 69 (1995): 1103.

47. Bellah et al., *Habits of the Heart: Individualism and Commitment in American Life* (Berkeley: University of California Press, 1985), 104.

48. Ibid., 101.

49. Dillard, "Types of Influence Goals in Personal Relationships." *Journal of Social and Personal Relationships* 6 (1989): 293.

50. Sternberg, *Triangular Theory of Love*, 54.

51. Moore, "Love and Limerence with Chinese Characteristics: Student Romance in the PRC." *Romantic Love and Sexual Behavior* (London: Praeger, 1998), 264.

52. Hatfield and Rapson, *Love & Sex: Cross-Cultural Perspectives* (Boston: Allyn and Bacon, 1996), 51.

53. Medora, Larson, Hortacsu and Dave, "Perceived Attitudes Towards Romanticism: A Cross-Cultural Comparison of American, Asian-Indian, and Turkish Adults." *Journal of Comparative Family Studies* 33 (2002): 165.

54. Seymour *Women, Family, and Child Care in India* (Cambridge, UK: Cambridge University Press, 1999); Zaidi and Shuraydi, "Perceptions of Arranged Marriages by Young Pakistani Muslim Women Living in a Western Society." *Journal of Comparative Family Studies* 33 (2002): 495–514.

55. Seymour, *Women, Family and Child Care in India*.

56. Bumiller *May You Be the Mother of a Hundred Sons* (New York: Random House, 1990); Mitter, *Dharma's Daughters: Contemporary Indian Women and Hindu Culture* (Piscataway, NJ: Rutgers University Press, 1991).

57. Bumiller, *May You Be the Mother*, 26.

58. Boyle, *Daughters, Brides, and Devoted Wives: Changing Perspectives of Hindu Women* (Unpublished doctoral dissertation, University of California, 1999),54.

59. Seymour, *Women, Family and Child Care in India*, 213.

60. Singh and Kanjirathinkal, "Levels and Styles of Commitment in Marriage: The Case of Asian Indian Immigrants." *Handbook of Interpersonal Commitment and Relationship Stability* (New York: Plenum, 1999), 307–322.

61. Myers, Madathil and Tingle, "Marriage Satisfaction and Wellness in India and the United States: A Preliminary Comparison of Arranged Marriages and Marriages of Choice." *Journal of Counseling and Development* 83 (2005): 183–190.

62. Yelsma and Athappilly, "Marriage Satisfaction and Communication Practices: Comparisons among Indian and American Couples." *Journal of Comparative Family Studies* 19 (1988): 37–54.

63. Medora, "Mate Selection in Contemporary India: Love Marriages Versus Arranged Marriages." *Mate Selection Across Cultures* (Thousand Oaks, CA: 2003), 209–230.

64. Blood, *Love Match and Arranged Marriage: A Tokyo-Detroit Comparison.* (New York: Free Press, 1967); Rao and Rao; Sastry, "Household Structure, Satisfaction and Distress in India and the United States: A Comparative Cultural Examination." *Journal of Comparative Family Studies* 30 (1999): 135–152.

65. Rao and Rao, 433.

66. Gupta, "Love, Arranged Marriage, and the Indian Social Structure." *Journal of Comparative Family Studies* 7 (1976): 79.

67. Seymour, *Women, Family and Child Care in India*.

68. Sodowsky, Kwan and Pannu. "Ethnic Identity of Asians in the United States." *Handbook of Multicultural Counseling* (Thousand Oaks: Sage, 1995), 123–145.

69. Spradley, *The Ethnographic Interview* (New York: Holt, Rinehart and Winston), 111.
70. Baxter, Braithwaite and Nicholson, "Turning Points in the Development of Blended Families." *Journal of Social and Personal Relationships* 16 (1999): 291–313.

BIBLIOGRAPHY

Aron, Arthur, and Elaine Aron. *Love and the Expansion of Self: Understanding Attraction and Satisfaction.* New York: Hemisphere, 1986.

Aron, Arthur, Meg Paris, and Elaine Aron. "Falling in Love: Prospective Studies of Self-concept Change." *Journal of Personality and Social Psychology* 69 (1995): 1102–1112.

Bachen, Christine, and Eva Illouz. "Imagining Romance: Young People's Cultural Models of Romance and Love." *Critical Studies in Mass Communication* 13 (1996): 279–308.

Bakhtin, Mikhail. *Art and Answerability: Early Philosophical Essays by M. M. Bakhtin.* Ed. Michael Holquist and Vadim Liapunov. Trans. Kenneth Brostrom. Austin, TX: University of Texas Press, 1990.

———. "Discourse in the Novel." *The Dialogic Imagination: Four Essays by M. M. Bakhtin.* Ed. Michael Holquist. Trans. Caryl Emerson and Michael Holquist. Austin, TX: University of Texas Press, 1981. 259–422.

———. *Problems of Dostoevsky's Poetics.* Ed. and Trans. Caryl Emerson. Minneapolis: MN: University of Minnesota Press, 1984.

———. *Toward a Philosophy of the Act.* Ed. Vadim Liapunov and Michael Holquist. Trans. Vadim Liapunov. Austin, TX: University of Texas Press, 1993.

Baxter, Leslie. "Mikhail Bakhtin and the Philosophy of Dialogism. *Perspectives on Philosophy of Communication.* Ed. Pat Arneson. West Lafayette, IN: Purdue University Press. In press.

Baxter, Leslie, Dawn Braithwaite, and John Nicholson. "Turning Points in the Development of Blended Families." *Journal of Social and Personal Relationships* 16 (1999): 291–313.

Bellah, Robert, et al. *Habits of the Heart: Individualism and Commitment in American Life.* Berkeley, CA: University of California Press, 1985.

Blood Jr., Robert. *Love Match and Arranged Marriage: A Tokyo-Detroit Comparison.* New York: Free Press, 1967.

Boyle, Corinne. *Daughters, Brides, and Devoted Wives: Changing Perspectives of Hindu Women.* Unpublished doctoral dissertation, University of California, 1999.

Bumiller, Elisabeth. *May You Be the Mother of a Hundred Sons.* New York: Random House, 1990.

Buss, David. "Love Acts: The Evolutionary Biology of Love." *The Psychology of Love.* Ed. Robert Sternberg and Michael Barnes. New Haven: Yale University Press, 1988. 100–118.

Craig, Robert. "Communication Theory as a Field." *Communication Theory* 9 (1999): 119–161.

Dillard, James. "Types of Influence Goals in Personal Relationships." *Journal of Social and Personal Relationships* 6 (1989): 293–308.

Emerson, Caryl. "Solov'ev, the Late Tolstoi, and the Early Bakhtin on the Problem of Shame and Love." *Slavic Review* 50 (1991): 663–671.

Fehr, Beverly. "Prototype Analysis of the Concepts of Love and Commitment." *Journal of Personality and Social Psychology* 55 (1988): 557–579.

Felmlee, Diane. "Fatal Attraction." *The Dark Side of Close Relationships.* Ed. Brian Spitzberg and William Cupach. Mahwah, NJ: Lawrence Erlbaum Associates, 1998. 3–32.

Gupta, Giri Raj. "Love, Arranged Marriage, and the Indian Social Structure." *Journal of Comparative Family Studies* 7 (1976): 75–86.

Harlow, Hary. *Learning to Love.* New York: Jason Aronson, 1974.

Hatfield, Elaine, and Richard Rapson. *Love & Sex: Cross-Cultural Perspectives.* Boston: Allyn and Bacon, 1996.

Hazan, Cindy, and Phillip Shaver. "Romantic Love Conceptualized as an Attachment Process." *Journal of Personality and Social Psychology* 52 (1987): 511–524.

Hendrick, Clyde, and Susan Hendrick. "A Theory and Method of Love." *Journal of Personality and Social Psychology* 50 (1986): 392–402.

Hendrick, Susan, and Clyde Hendrick. *Romantic Love.* Newbury Park, CA: Sage Publications, 1992.

Holquist, Michael. *Dialogism.* 2nd ed. New York: Routledge, 2002.

Knee, C. Raymond. "Implicit Theories of Relationships: Assessment and Prediction of Romantic Relationship Initiation, Coping, and Longevity." *Journal of Personality and Social Psychology* 74 (1998): 360–370.

Lee, John. *The Colors of Love: An Exploration of the Ways of Loving.* Don Mills, Ontario, Canada: New Press, 1973.

Lipset, David. "Modernity Without Romance? Masculinity and Desire in Courtship Stories Told by Young Papua New Guinean Men." *American Ethnologist* 31 (2004): 205–224.

Marston, Peter, and Michael Hecht. "Love Ways: An Elaboration and Application to Relational Maintenance." *Communication and Relational Maintenance.* Ed. Daniel Canary and Laura Stafford. New York: Academic Press, 1994. 187–202.

McCroskey, James, and Thomas McCain. "The Measurement of Interpersonal Attraction." *Speech Monographs* 41 (1974): 261–266.

Medora, Niluffer. "Mate Selection in Contemporary India: Love Marriages Versus Arranged Marriages." *Mate Selection Across Cultures.* Ed. Raeann Hamon and Bron Ingoldsby. Thousand Oaks, CA: Sage, 2003. 209–230.

Medora, Niluffer, Jeffrey Larson, Nuran Hortacsu, and Parul Dave. "Perceived Attitudes Towards Romanticism: A Cross-Cultural Comparison of American, Asian-Indian, and Turkish Adults." *Journal of Comparative Family Studies* 33 (2002): 155–178.

Mellen, Sydney. *The Evolution of Love.* San Francisco: Freeman, 1981.

Mitter, Sara. *Dharma's Daughters: Contemporary Indian Women and Hindu Culture.* Piscataway, NJ: Rutgers University Press, 1991.

Moore, Robert. "Love and Limerence with Chinese Characteristics: Student Romance in the PRC." *Romantic Love and Sexual Behavior* . Ed. Victor de Munck. London: Praeger, 1998. 252–265.

Myers, Jane, Jayamala Madathil, and Lynne Tingle. "Marriage Satisfaction and Wellness in India and the United States: A Preliminary Comparison of Arranged Marriages and Marriages of Choice." *Journal of Counseling and Development* 83 (2005): 183–190.

Rubin, Zick. *Liking and Loving*. New York: Holt, Rinehart and Winston, 1973.

Sampson, Edward. *Celebrating the Other: A Dialogic Account of Human Nature*. San Francisco: Westview, 1993.

Sastry, Jaya. "Household Structure, Satisfaction and Distress in India and the United States: A Comparative Cultural Examination." *Journal of Comparative Family Studies* 30 (1999): 135–152.

Seymour, Susan. *Women, Family, and Child Care in India*. Cambridge, UK: Cambridge University Press, 1999.

Singh, Raghu and Matthew Kanjirathinkal. "Levels and Styles of Commitment in Marriage: The Case of Asian Indian Immigrants." *Handbook of Interpersonal Commitment and Relationship Stability*. Ed. Jeffrey Adams and Warren Jones. New York: Plenum, 1999. 307–322.

Sodowsky, Gargi Roysircar, Kwon-Liem Karl Kwan, and Raji Pannu. "Ethnic Identity of Asians in the United States." *Handbook of Multicultural Counseling*. Ed. Joseph Ponterotto. Thousand Oaks, CA: Sage, 1995. 123–145.

Spanier, Graham. "Romanticism and Marital Adjustment." *Journal of Marriage and the Family* 34 (1972): 481–487.

Spradley, James. *The Ethnographic Interview*. New York: Holt, Rinehart and Winston.

Sprecher, Susan, and Rachita Chandak. "Attitudes about Arranged Marriages and Dating Among Men and Women from India." *Free Inquiry in Creative Sociology* 20 (1992): 1–11.

Sprecher, Susan, and Beverly Fehr. "Compassionate Love for Close Others and Humanity." *Journal of Social and Personal Relationships* 22 (2005): 629–651.

Sprecher, Susan, and Sandra Metts. "Development of the Romantic Beliefs Scale and Examination of the Effects of Gender and Gender-Role Orientation." *Journal of Social and Personal Relationships* 6 (1989): 387–411.

Sternberg, Robert. *A Triangular Theory of Love: Intimacy, Passion, Commitment*. New York: Basic Books, 1988.

Varenne, Herve. *Americans Together: Structured Diversity in a Midwestern Town*. New York: Teachers College Press, 1977.

Yelsma, Paul and Kuriakose Athapilly. "Marriage Satisfaction and Communication Practices: Comparisons among Indian and American Couples." *Journal of Comparative Family Studies* 19 (1988): 37–54.

Zaidi, Arshia and Muhammad Shuraydi. "Perceptions of Arranged Marriages by Young Pakistani Muslim Women Living in a Western Society." *Journal of Comparative Family Studies* 33 (2002): 495–514.

Glimpses of Hope

Rhetorical and Dialogical Discourse Promoting Cosmopolitanism

WALTER R. FISHER

*"Working toward seemingly unreachable goals requires hope."**

The theme of this essay was prompted by the invitation to contribute to this volume. It was the word "hope" that caught my attention in the initial letter of invitation to participate in this project. It reminded me of a conversation I had some years ago after presenting a paper at the University of Utah. Several of us, faculty and students, got together to discuss what I had said. The conversation went amiably until an intense faculty member looked at me and declared: "You're an optimist, aren't you?" I was somewhat taken aback; thought about what she asked; and then said "no." She insisted. I reflected for a minute or two and then came up with something I had not realized about myself until then. I said: "Actually, I am a romantic cynic. I dream dreams, but I am fully aware of the obstacles to their realization. I am not optimistic, but I have hope."

Maintaining hope in these tumultuous times is not easy. However, I have found sustenance to continue to hope from a remarkable exchange of views between Umberto

---

* The epigraph for this chapter comes from Paul Rogat Loeb's *Soul of a Citizen: Living with Conviction in a Cynical Time* (New York, NY: St. Martin's Press, 1999), p. 334.

Eco and Cardinal Martini. Their conversation appeared in a series of articles in the Italian newspaper, *La Correra de la Serra,* and later in a book, *Belief or Nonbelief: A Confrontation.*[1] The exchange is more dialogic than confrontational. Their positions are presented in humane, humble, respectful expressions of care and concern. Their comments on hope are most germane here. Eco writes, "Only by having a sense of history's trajectory (even if one does not believe in Parousia) can one love earthly reality and believe—with charity—that there is still room for Hope."[2] Cardinal Martini responds, "In some way, hope has to exist in practice, because believers and nonbelievers can be seen living together in this moment, giving meaning and involving themselves with commitment."[3] Hope may not spring "eternal in the human breast," as Alexander Pope maintained. But contra to Nietzsche, who proclaimed that hope is the "most evil of evils because it prolongs man's torment,"[4] I believe in the thirteenth-century proverb: "If it were not for hope, the heart would break."

Hope may have very different objectives, from hoping for material success to world peace. Whatever its aim, however, it seeks a goal, has an agenda, and has a sense of a way to its realization. It is not a mere wish, a "feeling directed toward something which one believes would give satisfaction if attained, possessed, or realized." Hope carries with it an expectation that through concerted effort enviable ends can be achieved.

The kind of hope I hold is well expressed in Kenneth Burke's subtitle for *A Grammar of Motives: "Ad bellum purificandum.*[5] Early on, the theme of the project, which led to this volume, included the term, "Globalization," I proposed that it be replaced with the concept of "Cosmopolitanism." I am persuaded by Kwame Anthony Appiah's observation that globalization is a "term that once referred to a marketing strategy, and then came to designate a macroeconomic thesis, and now can seem to encompass everything and nothing."[6] He notes two strands in the notion of cosmopolitanism, both of which are germane to ethical communication practices. One strand "is the idea that we have obligations to others, obligations that stretch beyond those to whom we are related by kith and kind, or even the more formal ties of shared citizenship." The second strand "is that we take seriously the value not just of human life but of particular lives, which means taking an interest in the practices and beliefs that lend them significance."[7] Given this conception of cosmopolitanism and Burke's hope of forms of communication that achieve identifications that transcend (but do not ignore) the self-understandings of particular people, the ultimate hope and aim of future theories and practices of rhetoric, dialogue, and conversation could be a world-wide sense of "world citizenship." What is needed is a sense of common humanity. If this is the hope, the questions to be addressed are: What are the obstacles to its realization? What are the roles to be played by rhetorical and dialogical discourse?

RHETORICAL HOPE

From a rhetorical perspective, the specific question to be pondered is: How do people come to be members of a community, or, put another way, how are they induced to recognize that they are, in fact, members of a community? Given urbanization and the breakdown of neighborhoods, given the fragmentation of society and the problems of legitimation, given the renascence of nationalism and fundamentalism, given the struggles among people within and among nations over economic, ecological, and military enterprises, and given the control of media by commercial interests and power elites, the question is: how can dissociated, unhappily associated, or unreflectively entangled people be brought to a sense of interdependence and common fate that leads to joint action, to a realization of community, without individuals being homogenized into conformist or repressive collectivities? One answer, perhaps the dominant one today, is to give up on the idea of community beyond the local and ephemeral, to celebrate diversity, difference, and democracy in their fragile spans of existence.[8]

More hopeful answers are provided by Kenneth Burke and Chaim Perelman. What is called for in Burke's thinking are symbolic actions, words and deeds, that enable individuals to identify with one another in such a way that they can resolve their differences. "Identification," he wrote, "is compensatory to division. If men were not apart from one another, there would be no need for the rhetorician to proclaim their unity."[9] The ground for the generation of such unity is well delineated by Martha Nussbaum. She insists that one need not rely on Plato's notion of "essentialism," that one should consult Aristotle to note the functional commonalities among all humans: we all live in the same world; we die in it; we hunger and thirst; we need shelter; we experience sexual desire and pursue relationships; we try to avoid pain and seek pleasure; we try to use all of our senses and when they fail, we want remedies; we want to live free from repression and oppression, and free enough to realize our own beings.[10] We are, moreover, as I have maintained often, reasoning, valuing, and feeling beings. Each of these attributes is intersubjectively acquired and is susceptible of change through communicative experiences. As such, they are the promise of persuasive attempts to influence beliefs and actions that lead to more peaceful means of resolving differences that inhibit the generation of communities in particular localities and throughout the world.

Because reasoning entails values, because feelings are aroused by values, and because discourses, whether monologic or dialogic are value-laden, it is worth time exploring values at some length. In earlier work, I argued that there is a form of life that is life itself. This is the realm of universal values and the container of ordinary forms of interpersonal life and all sorts of public and professional practices, including law, medicine, science, scholarship, and so on. Its constitutive values are tenets of

Judaism, Christianity, Islam, and other major religions: mercy, compassion, justice, humility, and love.[11] They also include the values celebrated by Socrates and Plato: truth, the good, beauty, health, wisdom, courage, temperance, justice, friendship, and a oneness with the cosmos. And they are explicit in the United Nations' "Declaration of Human Rights," which includes the recognition of each person's dignity, brotherhood, equality before the law, and freedom from governmental oppression. It is well to note that the existence of universal values does not entail a necessity that they be upheld universally or absolutely, or constantly. That they may be used in self-serving or destructive ways is clear. That they can be and are used to advance humane policies and practice is also clear.

At the same time that these values are alive in the world, there are other values that move humanity, not ideal but often more compelling. They are the goods celebrated by Callicles and others of a materialistic or hedonistic orientation: the will to power, success, self-aggrandizement, expedience, strength, self-determination, and pleasure. The rhetorical hope of providing discourse that advances a sense of world community, of common humanity, requires awareness of and adaptation to these two realms of values, the ideal and the so-called "real." The task before us, as Chaim Perelman observed, "is not, as often assumed, to address *either* a particular audience *or* a universal audience, but in the process of persuasion to adjust to and then transform the particularities of an audience into universal dimensions."[12]

To conclude this section on rhetorical hope, it seems appropriate to summarize the conclusion of a chapter that Stephen D. O'Leary and I published in *An Integrated Approach to Communication Theory and Research,* titled: "The Rhetorician's Quest." We were asked to project the future of rhetorical inquiry. We opined that "In a world (at least purportedly) without foundations—God, logic, science, language, history, and so on—rhetorical theory and philosophy can provide guidance for reconstructing reason, reinserting a reconfigured ethics into the fabric of private and public life, and restoring a meaningful, useful conception of the public sphere. A major project for emerging inquiry would be to pursue modes of communication that can ameliorate the conflicts arising out of religious, tribal, ethnic, gender, and economic class differences, which appear to have replaced the foundations that have served to ground notions of self-identity in centuries past. The conflicts arising from clashes dependent on these new senses of self and the worldviews that they entail must be transcended if the conflicts are to be resolved peacefully."[13] The modes of communication required by this project are not only rhetorical, but dialogic and conversational modes as well.

RHETORICAL/DIALOGIC HOPE

This is not the place to argue that dialogic and conversational discourses are rhetorical modes of communication (as a true Burkean might). It is, however, useful to explore certain features that each of these modes have in common. In order for any kind of human communication to occur, participants must share some commonality in symbol systems, some degree of trust, some willingness to engage in the process, some belief in the desirability of the encounter, and some interest (or expectation) of the advancement of self-understanding and/or increased knowledge of the world in which they live.[14] Beyond this, there is a certain kind of recognition of the Other that is essential if communication is to be successful. I learned about this sort of recognition from personal experience and later from reading, especially the writings of Emmanuel Levinas and Knud Ejler Logstrup.

I first learned about this sort of recognition when I was asked to meet with minority students in the late 1960s after they had occupied the office of the university president. The call came on a late December Friday night. The students had been told that I would meet with them on the following Tuesday. I told the Dean that I could not meet with the students unless I had something to offer them. He asked for my suggestion. I said that I wanted to assure them that there would be a major in Ethnic Studies in the fall. (I was aware of the minority students' interest in a BA program from an earlier investigation the Dean had asked me to pursue in regard to locating courses for "Black and Brown" students in the current curriculum.) There was silence. Then, he said go ahead. Thus, I became the architect of the Ethnic Studies program, chairing a committee to develop the program, hiring faculty, and serving as liaison between the administration and the students.

Needless to say, there were many problems to be solved, but the one here concerns communication. It was difficult at times to communicate effectively with Chicano and Asian students, but, it was most difficult, and potentially dangerous, with the members of the Black Student Union. The problem with the last group was that they did not know exactly who they were—Black, Afro-Americans, Pan-Africans, and so on. None of them wanted to be called "Negro." They were in a process of redefining themselves. In addition, individual members of the group were re-naming themselves. So, it quickly became obvious that the only safe and honorable approach I could take was to only address them as they addressed themselves.

This lesson was brought home to me in a searing experience when I went to one of our entrances to greet an African professor from UCLA, whom we were interested in hiring. The gate guard was "Black." I asked him if it was all right for me to wait there for a professor I had invited to the university. He said "Yes." As time went on, I noticed that he was stopping and asking white professional-looking people if they were coming to see me. So, I went to the guard and told him I was waiting for a "black" professor. He looked at me with fire in his eyes and said: "You've been talking to the blankety blank young radical students. They don't know anything about life." I said I was sorry, that I did not mean to offend. He said: "I know. But I was born colored and I am going to die colored." The lesson I learned then was this: Successful communication begins with more than "adjusting ideas to audiences, and audiences to ideas," it requires recognition of an other's self-definition, a sensitivity to how one perceives oneself.[15]

With this lesson in mind, I was better able to understand the occasional difficulties I had communicating with my teenage daughter. It had been somewhat of a mystery to me that once in awhile, I would ask her to do something and she would get huffy and act as though I had offended her. She would say, "Dad, I'm not a child anymore. I'm grown up." At other times, I would address her as though she was indeed grown up, and she would break into tears. Obviously, she was shifting in self-definition from child to adult, and I could not keep up.

The lesson also helped me to better understand the phenomena of charisma and alienation. Charisma arises in situations when a communicator is granted indisputable credibility, is inordinately admired, and can induce an audience to believe and act in extraordinary ways, to sacrifice themselves, even to the point of death. A communicator achieves charisma by projecting an image of audience members that coincides with their own best self-image. They feel not only acknowledged by the communicator but also elevated, esteemed, even loved. Alienation, on the other hand, occurs when a communicator projects an image of an audience that signals manipulation, exploitation, indifference, or a basic misreading of the audience's own understanding of itself. On the simplest level, the alienated person is saying: "You really don't know, respect, or understand me."[16] When I developed narrative paradigm for communication, the lesson led me to the observation, "Any story, any form of communication, not only says something about the world, it also implies an audience, persons who perceive of themselves in very specific ways."[17] This holds true, I believe, whether discourse is monologic or dialogic.

Earlier I made mention of Levinas and Logstrup. Their writings insist that more than sensitivity is required in any communicative encounter that one may participate in, and I agree with them. Meeting the "face" of the Other, Levinas maintains, is "straightaway ethical."[18] "By face," he writes, "I do not have in mind a person's physical or social presence; I have in mind and heart the face's signification without context."[19] This means without specific regard for either what one immediately sees on meeting an other—eyes, nose, chin, forehead, and so on, or what one may learn about a person's familial or professional status. "What is meaningful in the face is the command to responsibility"; it is an impetus to attend to the other without qualification.[20] And that command includes foremost, "Thou shalt not kill." To be ethical is to follow this command, to be responsive and responsible in authentic relationship with any and all others. "Love is a duty before the face of the Other."[21]

Logstrup takes a parallel position to that of Levinas. Rather than "command" or "duty," he argues that what is called for is living up to the "ethical demand" of human encounters. Key to meeting this demand is "trust." "It is characteristic of human life that we normally encounter one another with natural trust. This is true not only in the case of persons well acquainted with one another but also in the case of complete strangers."[22] "Human life," Logstrup affirms, "could hardly exist if it were otherwise."[23] Being ethical from this stance comes down to one taking the risk of laying oneself open to another and protecting the other who has placed his or her trust in our hands.

The upshot of this exploration of the common grounds of monologic and dialogic communication is this: whatever differences there are between these modes of human communication, they are alike in being value-laden, ethical encounters, transactional meetings in which identities are at stake, and in which stories are made and remade that determine who we are and what we can become at our best in relation to others.

DIALOGIC HOPE

The main obstacle to the hope that dialogue can move us to a more humane world is the problem of all "idealized" conceptions of human communication.[24] By "idealized," I do not mean unrealistic or fanciful. As I noted earlier, one need not subscribe to Plato's view of truth being grounded in the noumenal world to recognize the reality of ideals. Love is just as real as evil; compassion as real as hate; generosity as real as greed; and forgiveness as real as revenge. Dialogue requires or desires special qualities from its participants and adherence to certain rules of interaction. My meaning will become more clear as I explore the views of John Dewey, Martin Buber, Jurgen Habermas, and Hans-Georg Gadamer. The guiding argument of this exploration is that conceptions of communication imply forms of community and a dialectical tension exists between ideal conceptions of communication and the realization of ideal community beyond the local and ephemeral. When ideal conceptions are applied to ongoing associations, such as society, communication is seen as distorted and community is seen as a distant dream.

Dewey maintained that there could be "no such thing as community" if people were not interested in others, "in entering into the activities of others and taking part in conjoint and cooperative doings."[25] Because people do have this inclination, along with their private proclivities, community is not only possible, it happens. It comes into being through communication, by which he meant, "a process of sharing experience till it becomes a common possession. It modifies the disposition of both parties in it."[26] The impetus for and realization of communication is understanding. "Society," for Dewey, "not only continues to exist *by* transmission, *by* communication, but it may be fairly said to exist *in* communication."[27] He did not limit the forms of communication that contribute to community. Everyday discourse counted, as did artistic and scientific expressions. He was, however, concerned about the negative character of public debate, comparing it to a "watered-down version of the Hegelian dialectic."[28] Persuasion, in his view, was an inevitable consequence of genuine communication, but such discourse had to be a nonmanipulative form, a mutual, educative experience.

In regard to community, Dewey held two ideas: (1) that a real community already exists by virtue of "the infinite relationships of man with his fellows and with nature"[29]; and (2) that an ideal community only exists in democratic experience. His conception of communication was tied to this ideal. The connection between ideal community and ideal communication is established clearly in this passage from *Problems of Man*:

> What is faith in democracy in the role of consultation, of conference, of persuasion, of discussion, in the formulation of public opinion . . .except faith in the capacity of the intelligence of the common man to respond with common sense to the free play of acts and ideas which are secured by effective guarantees of free inquiry, free assembly, and free communication.[30]

Given this faith, along with common agreement about common ends sought by conjoint action, understanding would follow and democratic community would thrive. "Consensus," Dewey wrote, "demands communication,"[31] and "Democracy is not an alternative to other principles of associated life. It is the idea of community life itself."[32]

Dewey held that democracy was not a mode of nation-state governance but a "mode of associated being, of conjoint communicated experience,"[33] a position similar to that of Martin Buber. The passage captures Buber's vision of community as well as any:

> On the far side of the subjective, on this side of objective, on the narrow ridge, where I and Thou meet, is the realm of the 'between.' This reality, whose disclosure has begun in our time, shows the way, leading individualism and collectivism, for the decision of the future generation. Here the genuine third alternative is indicated, the knowledge of which will help to bring about the genuine person again and to establish genuine community.[34]

Additionally, Buber states: "The real living together of man with man can only thrive where people have the real things of their common life in common; where they can experience, discuss and administer them together, where real fellowship and real work guilds exist."[35] For Buber, genuine community, as an ongoing association, seems to be a commune inspirited by Hasidic and socialist ideals.

It immediately follows from this conception of genuine community that communication cannot be the usual form of monologic discourse. Whenever communication is strictly monologic, whether in debate, in conversations, in friendly chats, or in lover's talk, real relationship is nonexistent. The same applies to technical communication, which Buber ironically writes is "the inalienable sterling quality of 'modern existence.'" On rare occasions, even in the sorts of communication just enumerated, dialogic communication may emerge. Genuine dialogue appears in those encounters "no matter whether spoken or silent—where each of the participants really has in mind the other or others in their present and particular being and turns to them with the intention of establishing a living mutual relation between himself and them."[36]

Consider again the themes that arise from Dewey's and Buber's views. The realization of community in Dewey's thought depends on human intelligence and mutual, educative exchange. The actualization of community in Buber's thinking relies on the human capacity to enter the "in-between," to be genuinely in relation to others through dialogic communication. Since the potential for intelligence and authenticity is rarely achieved, true democratic and socialist communities are seldom in existence. When they do exist, they appear in local and short-lived encounters. As ideal achievements, they serve as standards by which ordinary experience and public discourse must be seen as distorted and counterproductive to life as we would want it to be. Reverberations of these themes recur in the writings of Habermas and Gadamer.

Habermas's notion of an emancipated, rational society has strong conceptual affinities with Dewey's construction of democracy. Like Dewey, Habermas stresses human intelligence, the capacity of people to reason and to be rational. This potential is evident in argumentation, which he defines as "that type of speech in which participants thematize contested validity claims and attempt to validate them through arguments." "An argument," he writes, "contains reasons or grounds that are connected in a systematic way with the validity claim of a problematic expression."[37] The aim of such discourse, in line with Dewey's ideas again, is understanding, or "valid agreement," and consensus. The model underlying Habermas's view of argumentation resembles Buber's notion of encounter. Habermas envisions an "ideal speech situation," a symmetrical and noncoercive transaction. There would be equal opportunity to participate, to criticize, to express personal aims and attitudes, and to perform these acts without regard to power, status, or ideology.[38] The paucity of argumentation based on this model accounts for the lack of an emancipated, rational society, and when the model is used to assess ordinary and public discourse, such discourse must be viewed as distorted.

Gadamer's concept of conversation, like Buber's view of encounter, leads to the same conclusion when applied to everyday discourse. "It is characteristic of every true conversation," he maintains, "that each opens himself to the other person, truly accepts his point of view as worthy of consideration and gets into the other to such an extent that he understands not a particular individual, but what he says."[39] True conversation for Gadamer is dialogue, question and answer, in which there is a "fusion of horizons," an encounter of "transformation into a communion, in which we do not remain what we were."[40] The result of the process is understanding, not necessarily valid agreement.

Gadamer privileges linguisticality rather than intelligence, the capacity for authenticity, or argumentative ability. "Language," he insists, "is not just one of man's possessions in the world, but on it depends the fact that man has a world at all."[41] From this view, communication is a "living process in which community is lived…. All forms of human community of life are forms of linguistic community: even more, they constitute language"[42] Gadamer is talking here about communication and community with their initial "cees" in lowercase. When the "cees" are capitalized, when the stress is on true conversation, ordinary, usual communication and community fall short of the ideal, and, again, we are left with the local and isolated realization of what communication and community can be.

A glimmer of hope exists in each of these writer's views—people do have intelligence, the capacity for authenticity, the ability to argue, and a desire for understanding. There is some measure of hope in the views of certain postmodernists. Theorists such as Michel Foucault, Jacques Derrida, and Jean-Francois Lyotard and feminist thinkers such as Genevieve Lloyd, Annette Bair, Carol Gilligan, and Jane Flax consider ethical conduct as relating to others responsibly. Each author outlined the importance of a disposition to do the right thing in each case; that is, to be authentic, fair, judicious, trustworthy, and loving—to live with integrity.[43]

Foucault saw all human relationships as inflected with power—"it traverses and produces things, it induces pleasure, forms knowledge, produces discourse."[44] Holding that "truth is already power," he advised that it was necessary to detach "the power of truth from the forms of hegemony, social, economic and cultural, within which it operates at the present time."[45] But, he also held that power could be positive as well as negative, and that under the conditions of freedom, self-knowledge, and self-caring that ethical conduct could thrive. Freedom, he believed, was the "ontological condition of ethics."[46] In addition, he insisted, one needs to be reflective and know a "number of rules of acceptable conduct or of principles that are both truths and prescriptions" that are inherited from the time of Socrates and Plato.[47]

For Derrida, all discourse is condemned to totalization through logocentric distinctions that undermine truth claims and marginalize people, ideas, institutions, and so on.[48] Yet, he thought of himself as a cosmopolitan, a "world citizen."[49] In a brief book, titled *On Cosmopolitanism and Forgiveness,* he took the position that the hallmark of culture is hospitality:

> Hospitality is culture itself and not simply one ethic among others. Insofar as it has to do with *ethos,* that is, residence, one's home, the familiar place of dwelling, inasmuch as it is a manner of being there, the manner in which we relate to ourselves and to others, to others as our own or as foreigners, *ethics is hospitality….* [50]

As for forgiveness, in its purest sense, the only one worthy of its name, he maintains, "would be a forgiveness without power: *unconditional but without sovereignty.*"[51]

Lyotard, on the other hand, is more problematic in his views, as he declares the end of all metanarratives—the stories that have aspired to universal application and on which dreams of transcendental community have depended.[52] It seems to me that in declaring the end of metanarratives, Lyotard implicitly affirms a new metanarrative. Rather than a story that accounts for one's being in an ongoing narrative that grounds one's identity in a continuous historical or transhistorical epic, the postmodern story asserts that progressive history is at an end; life is a short story marked by contingency, discontinuity, and accidents of birth, experience, and death; the only ground for one's identity is local circumstance, one's religion, ethnicity, nationality, economic or social class, sexual orientation, ideology, desire and so on. There is little or nothing in this scenario that augers well for cosmopolitan hope.

Consensus, as conceived by Dewey and Habermas, he says, is "outmoded and suspect."[53] Community on any large scale is foreclosed by the fact that communication in society has been reduced, fragmented into local language games. Because this is so, he thinks that "the idea…we need today in order to make decisions in political matters cannot be the idea of the totality, or of the unity, of a body. It can only be the ideal of multiplicity or of a diversity."[54] He insists that "ethics is indispensable," but "we must assume the responsibility to judge reflectively without knowing the rules."[55]

Feminists are diverse in their thinking, but they tend to agree that, by and large, traditional epistemology—conceptions of reason, truth, and knowledge—and ethical thought are fundamentally flawed because of an historical male bias.[56] As Jane Flax observes, feminists generally agree, with other postmodernists, that there is no "essence" that defines a man or woman, that gender is a socially constructed entity. Each person's well-being is ultimately dependent on the development of tolerance, empathy, friendly concern. In short, Flax concludes: we must practice "responsibility without grounds." "To take responsibility is to situate ourselves firmly within the contingent and imperfect contexts, to acknowledge differential privileges of race, gender, geographic location, and sexual identities, and to resist the delusory and dangerous recurrent hope of redemption to a world not of our own making."[57]

Based on her studies of the moral development of young women, Carol Gilligan maintains that females act out of a caring perspective, males out of a justice perspective. She summarizes the distinction as follows:

> Women's construction of the moral problem as a problem of care and responsibility in relationships rather than as one of rights and rules ties the development of their moral thinking to changes in their understanding of responsibility and relationships, just as the conception of morality as justice ties development to the logic of equality and reciprocity. Thus the logic underlying an ethic of care is a psychological logic of relationships, which contrasts with the formal logic of fairness that informs the justice approach.[58]

By incorporating the ethic of caring, she argues, the foundation of ethics "shifts from the Greek ideal of knowledge as a correspondence between mind and form to the Biblical conception of knowing as a process of human relationship."[59] To be ethical, in other words, is not only to be dutiful, but also caring and compassionate.

Annette Bair, on the other hand, surveyed feminist writings on morality and concluded that the most consistent stance was an ethic of love. She held that women theorists needed "to connect their ethics of love with what has been the men theorists' preoccupation, namely obligation."[60] Specifically, she wrote that the critical question to be pursued was: "Who should trust whom, with what, and why . . ."[61] She concluded that "A moral theory...that made trust its central problem could do more than do better justice to man's and women's moral intuitions than do the going men's theories."[62]

To all this—the thinking of pre- and postmodernists alike—our leading neopragmatist, Richard Rorty, says: "We need a redescription of liberalism as the hope that culture as a whole can be 'poeticized' rather than as the Enlightenment hope that it can be 'rationalized' or 'scientized.' That is, we need to substitute the hope that chances for fulfillment of idiosyncratic fantasies will be equalized for the hope that everyone will replace 'passion' or fantasy with 'reason'."[63] This new hope, he hopes, will be kept alive by keeping the conversation of humankind going. Perhaps needless to say, it is not Gadamer's concept of conversation that he has in mind. It is talk that recognizes contingency, irony, and solidarity.

KEEPING THE HOPE ALIVE

For my part, I believe that communities are co-constituted through communication transactions in which participants adopt a story that has coherence and fidelity for the life they would live. One may adhere to a story because it sanctions a life one must live in order to survive or to succeed. This sort of adherence creates communities by concession or conformity. One may also adhere to a story because one senses in it an honored perception of oneself. Such adherence creates communities by election or conversion. From this view, truly transcendental stories are those that show or reveal to ourselves what we are ontologically as human beings; they account for not only what we are, but also what we can be at our best in relation to others.[64]

There is an old axiom in rhetorical lore that stipulates that an audience must be open to persuasion or enlightenment in order for persuasion or enlightenment to occur. A parallel axiom must also exist in the lore of dialogical inquiry. If these axioms are true, it appears that the hope of future rhetorical and dialogical efforts to move people toward recognition of their common humanity requires that people be educated in such a way as to insure a state of mind and heart that makes ethical persuasion and dialogue more possible than it is today. Martha Nussbaum has advanced just such an educational program. With the advice from Karen Armstrong's study of the origins of the axial age of religions and the thinking of Appiah in regard to cosmopolitanism, there is a fountain of wisdom to be gained that can inform future rhetorical and dialogical efforts.

Nussbaum's proposal of "cosmopolitan education" is contextualized by reference to the thinking of such ancient sources as Diogenes the Cynic, who declared, "I am a citizen of the world"; Seneca, who upheld the concept of the "*kosmou polites* (world citizen)"; Plutarch, who maintained that "We should regard all human beings as our fellow citizens and neighbors"; and the Stoics, who believed "We should recognize humanity where it occurs, and give its fundamental ingredients, reason and moral capacity, our first allegiance and respect."[65] Based on this foundation, Nussbaum advances four arguments to support her proposal:

1. Through cosmopolitan education, we learn more about ourselves;
2. We make headway solving our problems that require international cooperation;
3. We recognize moral obligations to the rest of the world that are real and that otherwise go unrecognized;
4. We make a consistent and coherent argument based on distinctions we are prepared to defend.[66]

She insists that to be a citizen of the world does not mean that one must give up on local identifications. "But," she argues, "we should...work to make all human beings part of our community of dialogue and concern...."[67]

Armstrong's detailed study of the Axial Age, the period between 900–200 B.C.E., when Confucianism, Daoism, Hinduism, Buddhism, monotheism, and philosophical rationalism came into existence, lends substance to Nussbaum's proposal. Armstrong believes that today we need to rediscover the Axial ethos, an ethos of compassion. "In our global village, we can no longer afford a parochial or exclusive vision. We must learn to live and behave as though people in countries remote from our own are as important as ourselves."[68] Axial faiths, at their core, she reports, "share an ideal of sympathy, respect, and universal concern." This faith was not based on doctrine or a creed. "What mattered was not what you believed but how you behaved."[69]

This view that behavior is more important than belief is strongly upheld by the Dalai Lama, in his book, *Ethics for the New Millennium*. He thinks that "we humans can fare quite well without recourse to religious faith."[70] Underlying this thought is an important distinction he makes between religion and spirituality. He writes:

> Religion I take to be concerned with faith in the claims to salvation of one faith tradition or another, an aspect of which is an acceptance of some form of metaphysical or super-natural reality, including perhaps an idea of heaven or *nirvana*. Connected with this are religious teachings or dogma, ritual, prayer, and so on. Spirituality I take to be concerned

with those qualities of the human spirit—such as love and compassion, patience, tolerance, forgiveness, contentment, a sense of responsibility; a sense of harmony—which bring happiness to both self and other.[71]

An ethical act occurs, he writes, "where we refrain from causing harm to others."[72]

Appiah provides further support for Nussbaum's proposal and is also in line with Armstrong's position. His view of cosmopolitanism "begins with the simple idea that in the human community, as in national communities, we need to develop habits of co-existence: conversation in its old meaning of living together, association." This does not mean, however, that individuals should be submerged by the "world."[73] In a discussion of "Cosmopolitan Conversation," he insists that "the individual whose self-creation is being valued here is not, in the justly censorious sense of the term, individualist. Nothing I have said is inconsistent with the recognition of the many ways in which we human beings are naturally and inevitably social."[74] Put more directly, he asserts: "Cosmopolitans do not ask other people to maintain diversity of the species at the price of their individual autonomy." What is called for, in short, is dialogue "with others around the world about questions great and small that we must resolve together...."[75]

With world and time enough, with rhetorical and dialogical efforts based on the wisdom we have inherited from such thinkers as Aristotle, Burke, Perelman, Dewey, Buber, and Gadamer, and the inspirations of Nussbaum, Armstrong, the Dalai Lama, and Appiah, I look to the future as I have in the past—as a romantic cynic with hope.

ACKNOWLEDGMENT

I am grateful for the readings of the drafts of this chapter by my friends and colleagues Thomas S. Frentz, Thomas A. Hollihand, Thomas G. Goodnight, Stephen O'Leary, Kenneth K. Sereno, and especially John R. Stewart.

NOTES

1. Umberto Eco and Cardinal Carlo Maria Martini, *Belief or Nonbelief: A Confrontation,* tr. Minna Proctor (New York, NY: Arcada Publishing, 2000).

2. *Belief ...*, p.25.

3. *Beliefs ...*, p. 32.

4. Friedrich Nietzsche, *Human, All-Too-Human,* trs. Marion Faber, with Stephen Lehmann (Lincoln, Neb: University of Nebraska Press, 1984), p. 76.

5. Kenneth Burke, *A Grammar of Motives and A Rhetoric of Motives* (New York, NY: Meridan Books, The World Publishing Co., 1962).

6. Kwame Anthony Appiah, *Cosmopolitanism: Ethics in a World of Strangers* (New York, NY: W. W. Norton and Company, 2006), p. xiii. See also: Kwame Anthony Appiah, "Cosmopolitan Patriots," in *For Love of Country: Debating the Limits of Patriotism: Martha Nussbaum with Respondents,* ed. Joshua Cohen (Boston, MA: Beacon Press, 1996), pp. 21–29.

7. Appiah, *Cosmopolitanism...*, p. xv.

8. See: Walter R. Fisher, "Narration, Reason, and Community," in *Writing the Social Text: Poetics and Politics in Social Science Discourse,* ed. Richard Harvey Brown (New York, NY: Aldine De Gruyter, 1992), p. 214.

9. Burke, *Rhetoric...*, p. 546.

10. Martha C. Nussbaum, "Human Functioning and Social Justice: In Defense of Aristotelian Essentialism," *Political Theory,* 20, 216–222.

11. Walter R. Fisher, "The Ethic(s) of Argument and Practical Wisdom," in *Argument at Century's End: Reflections on the Past and Envisioning the Future,* ed. Thomas A. Hollihan, et al. (Annandale, VA: National Communication Association, 2000), pp. 1–15; and "Reconfiguring Practical Wisdom," in *Proceedings of the Fifth Conference of the International Society for the Study of Argumentation,* ed. Frans H. van Eemerin, et al. (Sic Sac, The Netherlands, 2002), 319–324. On shared values, see: Sissela Bok, *Common Values* (Columbia, MO: University of Missouri Press, 1995); Clifford Christians and Michael Traber, *Communication Ethics and Universal Values* (Thousand Oaks, CA: Sage Publications, 1997); Barack Obama, *The Audacity of Hope* (New York, NY: Crown, 2006); Alan Wolfe, *One Nation, After All* (New York, NY: Viking Press, 1998); *Prospects for a Common Morality,* eds. Gene Outka and John Reeder, Jr. (Princeton, NJ: Princeton University Press, 1993); *Global Codes of Conduct,* ed. Oliver F. Williams, C.S.C. (Notre Dame, IN: University of Notre Dame Press, 2000).

12. Chaim Perelman, "The New Rhetoric and the Rhetoricians," *The Quarterly Journal of Speech,* 70 (1984), 192.

13. Walter R. Fisher and Stephen D. O'Leary, "The Rhetorician's Quest," in *An Integrated Approach to Communication Theory and Research,* eds. Michael B. Salwen and Don W. Stacks (Mahwah, NJ: Lawrence Erlbaum Associates, Publishers, 1996), p. 258.

14. Walter R. Fisher, *Human Communication as Narration: Toward a Philosophy of Reason, Value, and Action* (Columbia, SC: University of South Carolina Press, 1987, 1989), p. 92. This statement appeared as part of a contrast I drew between my view of the underpinnings of human communication and Jurgen Habermas's conception of the "ideal speech situation."

15. The phrase cited here originated with Donald C. Bryant, who wrote: "the rhetorical function is the function of adjusting ideas to audiences and of people to ideas." See his essay: "Rhetoric: Its Functions and Scope," *The Quarterly Journal of Speech,* 39 (1953), 413.

16. See: Walter R. Fisher, "Rhetorical Fiction and the Presidency," *The Quarterly Journal of Speech,* 66 (1980), 125–126.

17. Fisher, *Human Communication...*, pp. 75, 187.

18. Emmanuel Levinas, *Ethics and Infinity: Conversations with Phillippe Nemo,* tr. Richard A. Cohen (Pittsburgh, PA: Duquesne University Press, 1985), p. 85.

19. Levinas, *Ethics…,* p.86.

20. "Emmanuel Levinas," in *Conversations with French Philosophers,* ed. Florian Rotzer, tr. Gary E. Alylesworth (Highlands, NJ: Humanities Press International, Inc., 1995), p. 61.

21. "Emmanuel Levinas,"…, p. 60.

22. Knud Ejler Logstrup, *The Ethical Demand* (Notre Dame, IN: University of Notre Dame Press, 1997).

23. Logstrup, *The Ethical Demand,* p. 8.

24. My understanding of dialogue is derived from an variety of sources, including John R. Stewart, "Foundations of Dialogic Communication," *The Quarterly Journal of Speech,* 66 (1978), 183–201; Ronald C. Arnett and Pat Arneson, *Dialogic Civility in a Cynical Age: Community, Hope, and Interpersonal Relationships* (Albany, NY: State University of New York, 1999); *The Interpretation of Dialogue,* ed. Tullis Maranhao (Chicago, IL: The University of Chicago Press, 1990; *The Human Dialogue: Perspectives in Communication,* eds. Floyd W. Matson and Ashley Montagu (New York, NY: The Free Press, 1967); for an exploration of the relationship between dialogue and "rhetorical conversation, see: Thomas S. Frentz, "Rhetorical Conversation, Time, and Moral Action," *The Quarterly Journal of Speech,* 71 (1985), 1–18.

25. John Dewey, *Democracy and Education* (New York, NY: The Macmillan Company, 1916), p. 24.

26. Dewey, *Democracy…,* p. 9

27. Dewey, *Democracy…,* p. 4

28. John Dewey, *Liberalism and Social Action* (New York, NY: Capricorn, 1935), p. 71.

29. John Dewey, *Human Nature and Conduct* (New York, NY: Modern Library, 1930), p. 330.

30. John Dewey, *Problems of Men* (Totowa, NJ: Littlefield, Adams, 1958), p. 5.

31. Dewey, *Democracy…,* p. 5.

32. John Dewey, *The Public and Its Problems* (Athens, OH: Swallow Press, Ohio University Press, 1954), p. 148.

33. Dewey, *Democracy…,* p. 87.

34. Martin Buber, *Between Man and Man,* tr. Ronald Gregor Smith (New York, NY: The Macmillan Company, 1967), pp. 204–205. See also: Ronald C. Arnett, *Communication and Community: Implication of Martin Buber's Dialogue* (Carbondale, IL: Southern Illinois University Press, 1986).

35. Martin Buber, *Paths to Utopia,* tr. R. F. C. Hull (Boston, MA: Beacon Press, 1958), p. 19.

36. Buber, *Between…,* p. 19.

37. Jurgen Habermas, *The Theory of Communicative Action,* vol. 1, tr. Thomas McCarthy (Boston, MA: Beacon Press, 1981), p. 18.

38. Jurgen Habermas, "Toward a Theory of Communicative Competence," *Inquiry,* 13 (1970), 371. For further information about Habermas's view of ideal speech and ethics, see: Jurgen

Habermas, *Moral Consciousness and Communicative Action,* trs. Christian Lenhardt and Shierry Weber Nicholsen (Cambridge, MA: The MIT Press, 1990); and, Jurgen Habermas, "Discourse Ethics: Notes on a Program of Philosophical Justification," in *The Communicative Ethics Controversy,* trs. Seyla Benhabib and Fred Dallmayr (Cambridge, MA: The MIT Press, 1990), pp. 60–110. The strengths and limitations of Habermas's work are brilliantly explored in Thomas B. Farrell's *Norms of Rhetorical Culture* (New Haven, Conn: Yale University Press, 1993), see especially chapter five, "Universal Pragmatics and Practical Reason: From Deformation to Reformation," pp. 187–229.

39. Hans-Georg Gadamer, *Truth and Method* (New York, NY: The Crossroad Publishing Company, 1982), p. 347.

40. Gadamer, *Truth and Method,* p. 340.

41. Gadamer, *Truth and Method,* p. 401.

42. Gadamer, *Truth and Method,* p. 404. See also: Hans-Georg Gadamer, *Reason in the Age of Science,* tr. Frederick G. Lawrence (Cambridge, MA: The MIT Press, 1981), p. 50.

43. For explorations of postmodern views of ethics, see: Zygmunt Bauman, *Postmodern Ethics* (Cambridge, MA: Blackwell Publishers inc., 1993); John D. Caputo, *Against Ethics: Contributions to a Poetics of Obligation with Constant Reference to Deconstruction* (Indianapolis, IN: Indiana University Press, 1993); Simon Critchley, *The Ethics of Deconstruction: Derrida and Levinas* (Edinburgh: Edinburgh University Press, 1992); Todd May, *The Moral Theory of Postmodernism* (University Park, PA: The Pennsylvania State University Press, 1995).

44. Michel Foucault, *Power/Knowledge: Selected Interviews and Other Writings, 1972–1977,* ed. Colin Gordon; trs. Colin Gordon, Leo Marshall, John Mepham, and Kate Soper (New York, NY: Pantheon Books, 1977), p. 118.

45. Foucault, *Power/Knowledge...,* p. 133.

46. Michel Foucault, *Ethics: Subjectivity and Truth,* vol. 1, 1954–1984, ed. Paul Rabinow (New York, NY: The New Press, 1997), p. 284.

47. Foucault, *Ethics...,* p. 285.

48. See, for instance: Jacques Derrida, *Dissemination,* tr. Barbara Johnson (Chicago, IL: University of Chicago Press, 1981); Jacques Derrida, *Of Gramatology,* tr. Gayatri C. Spivak (Baltimore, MD: The Johns Hopkins University Press, 1976).

49. Jacques Derrida, *On Cosmopolitanism and Forgiveness,* trs. Mark Dooley and Michael Hughes (New York: NY: Routledge, 2001), p. 3.

50. Derrida, *On Cosmopolitanism...,* pp. 16–17.

51. Derrida, *On Cosmopolitanism...,* p. 59.

52. See: Jean-Francois Lyotard, *The Postmodern Condition: A Report on Knowledge,* trs. Geoff Bennington and Brian Massumi (Minneapolis, MN: University of Minnesota Press, 1984).

53. Lyotard, *The Postmodern...,* p. 66.

54. Jean-Francois Lyotard and Jean-Loup Thebaud, *Just Gaming,* trs. Don Barry, et al. (Minneapolis, MN: University of Minnesota Press, 1985) p. 94.

55. "Jean-Francois Lyotard," in *Conversations with French Philosophers...,* p. 76.

56. See: Genevieve Lloyd, *The Man of Reason: 'Male' and 'Female' in Western Philosophy* (Minneapolis, MN: University of Minnesota Press, 1984); Mary Daly, *Beyond God the Father: Toward a Philosophy of Women's Liberation* (Boston, MA: Beacon Press, 1985);Virginia Held, *Feminist Morality: Transforming Culture, Society, and Politics* (Chicago, IL: The University of Chicago Press, 1993); Rosemary Agonito, *History of Ideas on Women: A Source Book* (New York, NY: G. P. Putnam's Sons, 1977); and, of course, Simone de Beauvoir, *The Second Sex,* tr. and ed. H. M. Parshley (New York, NY: Vintage Books, 1974).

57. Jane Flax, "Responsibility without Grounds," in *Rethinking Knowledge: Reflections Across the Disciplines,* eds. Robert F. Goodman and Walter R. Fisher (Albany, NY: State University of New York Press, 1995), p. 163.

58. Carol Gilligan, *In a Different Voice: Psychological Theory and Women's Development* (Cambridge, MA: Harvard University Press, 1982), p. 73.

59. Gilligan, *In a Different Voice…*, p. 173.

60. Annette Bair, *Moral Prejudices: Essays on Ethics* (Cambridge, MA: Harvard University Press, 1995), p. 4.

61. Bair, *Moral Prejudices…*, p. 14.

62. Bair, *Moral Prejudices…*, p. 17. For a more traditional approach to ethics by a woman, see: Iris Murdoch, *Metaphysics as a Guide to Morals* (New York, NY: Penguin Books, 1992); Iris Murdoch, *The Sovereignty of Good* (New York, NY: Routledge, 1999).

63. Richard Rorty, *Contingency, Irony, and Solidarity* (New York, NY: Cambridge University Press, 1989), p. 53. See also: Richard Rorty, *Philosophy and the Mirror of Nature* (Princeton, NJ: Princeton University Press, 1979), p. 394.

64. For a fuller presentation of my views on communication and community, see: Fisher, "Narration, Reason, and Community," in *Writing the Social Text…*, pp. 199–217.

65. See: Martha C. Nussbaum, "Patriotism and Cosmopolitanism," in *For Love of Country…*, pp. 6–7.

66. Nussbaum, "Patriotism and Cosmopolitanism," pp.11–14. See also: Martha C. Nussbaum, *Cultivating Humanity: A Classical Defense of Reform in Liberal Education* (Cambridge, MA: Harvard University Press, 1977), especially chapter two, "Citizens of the World," pp. 50–84.

67. Nussbaum, "Patriotism and Cosmopolitanism," p. 9.

68. Karen Armstrong, *The Great Transformation: The Beginnings of Our Religious Traditions* (New York, NY: Alfred A. Knopf, 2006), p. xiv.

69. Armstrong, *The Great Transformation…*, p. xiii.

70. His Holiness The Dalai Lama, *Ethics for the New Millennium* (New York, NY: Riverhead Books, 1999), p. 20.

71. *Ethics…*, p. 22.

72. *Ethics…*, p. 61.

73. Appiah, *Cosmopolitanism…*, p.xiv.

74. Kwame Anthony Appiah, *The Ethics of Identity* (Princeton, NJ: Princeton University Press, 2005), p. 267.

75. Appiah, *The Ethics of Identity,* p. 271.

BIBLIOGRAPHY

Agonito, Rosemary. *History of Ideas on Women: A Source Book,* New York: G. P. Putnam's Sons, 1977.

Appiah, Kwame Anthony. "Cosmoplitan Patriots" in *For Love of Country: Debating the Limits of Patriotism: Martha Nussbaum with Respondents.* Ed. Joshua Cohen. Boston: Beacon Press, 1996.

———. *The Ethics of Identity,* Princeton, NJ: Princeton University Press, 2005.

———. *Cosmopolitanism: Ethics in a World of Strangers.* New York: W.W. Norton and Company, 2006.

Armstrong, Karen. *The Great Transformation: The Beginnings of Our Religious Traditions.* New York: Alfred A. Knopf, 2006.

Arnett, Ronald C. *Communication and Community: Implications of Martin Buber's Dialogue.* Carbondale, IL: Southern Illinois University Press, 1986.

Arnett, Ronald C., and Pat Arneson. *Dialogic Civility in a Cynical Age: Community, Hope, and Interpersonal Relationships.* Albany: State University of New York Press, 1999.

Bair, Annette *Moral Prejudices: Essays on Ethics.* Cambridge: Harvard University Press, 1995.

Bauman, Zygmunt. *Postmodern Ethics.* Cambridge: Blackwell Publishers, 1993.

de Beauvoir, Simone. *The Second Sex.* Tr. and Ed. H. M. Parshley. (New York: Vintage Books, 1974.

Bok, Sissela. *Common Values.* Columbia, MO: University of Missouri Press, 1995.

Bryant, Donald C. "Rhetoric: Its Functions and Scope." *Quarterly Journal of Speech* 39 (1953): 413.

Buber, Martin. *Paths to Utopia.* Tr. R.F.C. Hull. Boston: Beacon Press, 1958.

———. *Between Man and Man.* Tr. Ronald Gregor Smith. New York: Macmillan, 1967.

Burke, Kenneth. *A Grammar of Motives and A Rhetoric of Motives.* New York: Meridan Books, The World Publishing Company, 1962.

Caputo, John D. *Against Ethics: Contributions to a Poetics of Obligations with Constant Reference to Deconstruction.* Indianapolis: Indiana University Press, 1993.

Carter, Jimmy. *Our Endangered Values: America's Moral Crisis.* New York: Random House, 2006.

Christians, Clifford and Michael Traber. *Communication Ethics and Universal Values.* Thousand Oaks: Sage Publications, 1997.

Critchley, Simon. *The Ethics of Deconstruction: Derrida and Levinas.* Edinburg: Edinburgh University Press, 1992.

Dalai Lama. *Ethics for the New Millennium.* New York: Riverhead Books, 1999.

Daly, Mary. *Beyond God the Father: Toward a Philosophy of Women's Liberation*. Boston: Beacon Press, 1985.

Derrida, Jacques. *Of Gramatology*. Tr. Gayatri C. Spivak. Baltimore: The Johns Hopkins University Press, 1976.

———. *Dissemination*. Tr. Barbara Johnson. Chicago, IL: University of Chicago Press, 1981.

———. *Cosmopolitanism and Forgiveness*. Trs. Mark Dooley and Michael Hughes. New York: Routledge, 2001.

Dewey, John. *Democracy and Education*. New York: Macmillan, 1916.

———. *Human Nature and Conduct*. New York: Modern Library, 1930.

———. *Liberalism and Social Action*. New York: Capricorn, 1935.

———. *The Public and Its Problems*. Athens, OH: Swallow Press, University of Ohio Press, 1954.

———. *Problems of Men*. Totowa, NJ: Littlefield, Adams, 1958.

Eco, Umberto and Cardinal Carlo Maria Martini. *Beliefs or Nonbeliefs: A Confrontation*. Tr. Minna Proctor. New York: Arcada Publishing, 2000.

Farrell, Thomas B. *Norms of Rhetorical Culture*. New Haven, CT: Yale University Press, 1993.

Fisher, Walter. "Rhetorical Fiction and the Presidency." *Quarterly Journal of Speech* 66 (1980): 125–126.

———. *Human Communication as Narration: Toward a Philosophy of Reason, Value, and Action* Columbia, South Carolina: University of South Carolina Press, 1989.

———. "Narration, Reason, and Community" in *Writing the Social Text: Poetics and Politics in Social Science Discourse*. Ed. Richard Harvey Brown. New York: Aldine De Gruyter, 1992.

———. "The Ethic(s) of Argument and Practical Wisdom" in *Argument at Century's End: Reflections on the Past and Envisioning the Future*. Eds. Thomas A. Hollihan, et al. Annandale, VA: National Communication Association Press, 2000.

———. "Reconfiguring Practical Wisdom" in *Proceedings of the Fifth Conference of the International Society for the Study of Argumentation*. Eds. Frans H. van Eemerin, et al. Sic Sac, The Netherlands, 2002.

Fisher, Walter, and Stephen D. O'Leary. "The Rhetorician's Quest." in *An Integrated Approach to Communication Theory and Research*. Eds. Michael B. Salwen and Don W. Stacks. Mahwah, NJ: Lawrence Erlbaum Associates, 1996.

Flax, Jane. "Responsibility without Grounds," in *Rethinking Knowledge: Reflections Across the Disciplines*, Eds. Robert F. Goodman and Walter R. Fisher. Albany: State University of New York Press, 1995.

Frentz, Thomas S. "Rhetorical Conversation, Time, and Moral Action." *Quarterly Journal of Speech* 71 (1985): 1–18.

Foucault, Michel. *Power/Knowledge: Selected Interviews and Other Writings, 1972–1977*. Ed. Colin Gordon. Trs. Colin Gordon, Leo Marshall, John Mepham, and Kate Soper. New York, NY: Pantheon Books, 1977.

———. *Ethics: Subjectivity and Truth*. Vol. 1. 1954–1984. Ed. Paul Rabinow. New York, NY: The New Press, 1997.

Gadamer, Hans-Georg. *Reason in the Age of Science.* Tr. Frederick G. Lawrence. Cambridge: MIT Press, 1981.

———. *Truth and Method.* New York: Crossroad Publishing Company, 1982.

Gilligan, Carol. *In a Different Voice: Psychological Theory and Women's Development.* Cambridge: Harvard University Press, 1982.

Habermas, Jürgen. "Toward a Theory of Communicative Competence." *Inquiry* 13 (1970): 371.

———. *The Theory of Communicative Action.* Vol. 1. Tr. Thomas McCarthy. Boston: Beacon Press, 1981.

———. "Discourse Ethic: Notes on a Program of Philosophical Justification." in *The Communicative Ethic Controversy.* Trs. Seyla Benhabib and Fred Dallmayr. Cambridge: MIT Press, 1990. 60–110.

———. *Moral Consciousness and Communicative Action.* Trs. Christian Lenhardt and Shierry Weber Nicholson. Cambridge: MIT Press, 1990.

Held, Virginia. *Feminist Morality: Transforming Culture, Society, and Politics.* Chicago: The University of Chicago Press, 1993.

Levinas, Emmanuel. *Ethics and Infinity: Conversations with Phillippe Nemo.* Tr. Richard A Cohen. Pittsburgh: Duquesne University Press, 1985.

Lloyd, Genevieve. *The Man of Reason: 'Male' and 'Female' in Western Philosophy.* Minneapolis: University of Minnesota Press, 1984.

Logstrup, Knud Ejler. *The Ethical Demand.* Notre Dame: University of Notre Dame Press, 1997.

Lyotard, Jean Francois. *The Postmodern Condition: A Report on Knowledge,* Trs. Geoff Bennington and Brian Massumi. Minneapolis: University of Minnesota Press, 1984.

Lyotard, Jean-Francois, and Jean-Loup Thebaud. *Just Gaming.* Trs. Don Barry, et al. Minneapolis, MN: University of Minnesota Press, 1985.

Maranhao, Tullis, ed. *The Interpretation of Dialogue.* Chicago: University of Chicago Press, 1990.

Matson, Floyd W., and Ashley Montagu, ed. *The Human Dialogue: Perspectives in Communication.* New York: Free Press, 1967.

May, Todd. *The Moral Theory of Postmodernism.* University Park, PA: Pennsylvania State University Press, 1995.

Murdoch, Iris. *Metaphysics as a Guide to Morals.* New York: Penguin Books, 1992.

———. *The Sovereignty of Good.* New York: Routledge, 1999.

Nietzsche, Friedrich. *Human, All-Too-Human.* Trs. Marion Faber with Stephen Lehmann. Lincoln, NE: University of Nebraska Press, 1984.

Nussbaum, Martha. "Human Functioning and Social Justice: In Defense of Aristotelian Essentialism." *Political Theory* 20: 216–222.

———. *Cultivating Humanity: A Classical Defense of Reform in Liberal Education.* Cambridge: Harvard University Press, 1977.

———. "Patriotism and Cosmopolitanism." In *For Love of Country: Debating the Limits of Patriotism: Martha Nussbaum with Respondents.* Ed. Joshua Cohen. Boston: Beacon Press, 1996.

Obama, Barack. *The Audacity of Hope.* New York: Crown Publishers, 2006.

Outka, Gene and John Reeder, Jr., eds. *Prospects for a Common Morality.* Princeton: Princeton University Press, 1993.

Perelman, Chaim. "The New Rhetoric and the Rhetoricians." *Quarterly Journal of Speech* 70 (1984): 192.

Rorty, Richard. *Philosophy and the Mirror of Nature.* Princeton, NJ: Princeton University Press, 1979.

———. *Contingency, Irony, and Solidarity.* New York: Cambridge University Press, 1989.

Rotzer, Florian, ed. *Conversations with French Philosophers.* Highlands, NJ: Humanities Press International, 1995.

Stewart, John R. "Foundations of Dialogic Communication." *Quarterly Journal of Speech* 66 (1978): 183–203.

Williams, Oliver F., C.S.C., ed. *Global Codes of Conduct.* Notre Dame: University of Notre Dame Press, 2000.

Wolfe, Alan. *One Nation, After All.* New York: Viking Press, 1998.

■ ■ ■

Provinciality and the Face of the Other

Levinas on Communication Ethics, Terrorism —Otherwise Than Originative Agency

RONALD C. ARNETT

This chapter unites the work of a major ethics theorist, Emmanuel Levinas, with an investigation of a term cast into darkness by the Enlightenment—provinciality. With the guiding notion of provinciality, this chapter enters the conversation about terrorism with humility, trembling, and the reality of the complexity and, at times, hopelessness of terrorist acts. Levinas, a Jewish scholar and survivor of Nazi xenophobia, is one of our premier scholars of ethics. Postmodern scholars turn to Levinas, recognizing the heuristic significance of his insights for interpreting otherwise than humanistic agency. Levinas recasts our gaze to a phenomenological reality of "ethics as first principle," rejecting the humanistic assumption that the human is capable of constructing an ethically independent self.[1]

For Levinas, human beings are derivative creatures. They are ethically called out by a precognitive a priori, listening for echoes that call forth a moral conscience.[2] Levinas's work reminds us of this moral echo in the dark that counters terrorism, a communicative act that attempts to impose darkness on another. Ironically, Levinas's work, unlike the social convention of attraction to light whether artificial or not, embraces darkness as a home of an ongoing ethical echo—"I am my brother's keeper." This ethical echo begins within the darkened depths of human existence, and our attentiveness to it begins with a reminder given to us in the face of the Other. This chapter understands the face of the Other as the first human home of provinciality. The human face is the primordial first home; it is the provincial welcome to another.

The human face is a provincial signpost that redirects us to an ethical echo a priori to the Western construct of Being and, in communication ethics, prior to the construction of an autonomous ethical self. The *visage* of another takes us from sight to attentive listening to an ongoing quiet mantra: "I am my brother's keeper."

INTRODUCTION

This chapter follows the spirit of Levinas's ethics project, seeking to understand terrorism through provinciality within a horizon that Levinas referred to as its proper name.[3] Phenomenologically, a proper name attends to the things themselves, tying naming to the temporal act of connecting the "saying" with the "said." This chapter takes Levinas's project into a space of anger that knows no bounds. When events legitimate or not, drive a person to an anger that makes "sensible" violation of conventional norms in order to eradicate "evilZ fostered by an "alien Other," resolutions are messy and void of simple answers. The complexity and depth of such anger recall the reminder of the founder of conflict theory, George Simmel, who offered simple and enduring advice—conflicts fueled by deep anger and hate have no one specific resolution; the rift between persons finds reason in multiplicity, seemingly unlimited webs of discontent.[4]

With the warning of Simmel, this chapter examines the question, "How are we to respond to acts of terrorism from the depth of Levinas's ethic?" Neither Levinas nor any other human being can definitively answer questions that find life from multiple webs of discontent. However, his work has insightful utility in that he begins from a point of origin contrary to conventional attempts at resolution. His commitment to ethics prior to Being and prior to an originative sense of communicative agency offers philosophical and practical tools for understanding and employing a response to terrorism that supplies a challenge to the West, providing a paradigmatic alternative to our current state of seemingly increasing hostility.

Levinas's contrasting stand on the conventional understanding of humanism as encouraging an originative sense of communicative agency provides a hermeneutic clue to implementation of his ethical instruction. Levinas's ethical theory interprets otherwise than conventional thought, pragmatically providing a spirit necessary for understanding terrorism that interprets otherwise than convention He rejects the sanctity of the originative communicative agent, displacing our understanding of ethics grounded in an individual agency attracted to a "bootstrap" ideology, offering instead a derivative sense of "I" responsive to the call to be my brother's keeper.[5] Levinas's contrariness to Western conventions is instructive in understanding the obstinacy of terrorist acts that invoke the gasp of horror—"This is beyond belief." Levinas's work tenders a contrary communication ethic that begins not beyond, but prior to, belief. Levinas points to a dual critique—first, of terrorism that seeks to hold another hostage literally or by fear, and second, of the typical Western view of originative agency that seeks to hold another hostage to one's own will. Both terrorism and the typical Western view of agency—what Tocqueville coined as individualism[6]—seek to stand outside a community or stand above history, unconcerned about the Other's face. The Western worldview connected to modernity has an aversion to the local, to the particular. This aversion to the particular and the local begins with the Enlightenment hope of liberating all from a limited worldview "naively" resting within provinciality of the particular. Terrorism lives within a moment inattentive and hostile to the first home of provinciality—the human face.

PROVINCIALITY

Levinas is one of the premier ethics scholars of the twentieth century, whose work found shape in the crisis of World War II. In the postmodern demands of the twenty-first century, Levinas's project has even more currency. His insights offer a potential contribution to communication ethics, offering assistance in understanding and meeting the major concern of this moment, terrorism. He points to an understanding of provinciality that is prior to ownership of property or self—to the uniqueness of a given human face.

Provinciality is not escapable, no matter what the task or the question. Provinciality is an originative form of standpoint. Sandra Harding's[7] thoughtful reminder of the importance of social-cultural standpoint is a counter to the assumption that provinciality rests merely upon "unsophisticated soil." Differences in class, education, and power are more likely to drive attribution of another's behavior, resulting in pejorative accusation of provinciality. This essay, of course, cannot solve the question of terrorism; the objective is much more modest, to offer a basic reminder—provinciality matters.

Throughout human history, terrorizing of another people, culture, and way of life haunts and continues to disrupt. Our attention to terrorism seems unique, but the reality is that such act brought forth human cries long before us and most likely long after our toil no longer matters. Terrorism works as an active effort to disrupt another's existence or way of life; it is a heightened form of violent graffiti that seeks to deface another.

The corpus of Levinas's project of provinciality and the human face challenges the Enlightenment's discarding of provinciality as "bad faith."[8] He rejects the assumption that provinciality is a fantasy that lost to an evolutionary "better" insight of universal access to truth and rationality. This chapter counters, suggesting that provinciality is not the bane of the human condition; it is the home of difference and learning that welcomes the guest to a world of narrative and virtue contention. Provinciality is both the home of terrorism and simultaneously our best hope.

Postmodern scholarship, closely attuned to Levinas, begins with one major assumption: the death of a universally attainable rational view of truth is a flagellant feature of the Enlightenment project. The moment we take off the table the assumption that a universal truth is attainable, we open the door to a counter proposal—a postmodern revelatory assumption that returns us to the local. It is in the local that we find texture, new insight, and knowledge guided by admission of limits. Postmodernity rejects the hegemony of universal agreement on narrative and virtue direction, not by stating that there is no ground, but by honoring the existence of a sense of a multiplicity of ground(s) and by acknowledging ground other than one's own.

The move from the universal to recognition of multiple locals or places upon which to stand privileges one major action metaphor that defines this historical moment: difference. Postmodernity is the philosophical and practical welcome to difference; it is the home of many locals, the home of multiplicity, and the home of difference. Postmodernity is, on the one hand, the sanctuary of those on the outside of dominance and privilege, and, on the other hand, in the eyes of those fighting to keep the hopes of modernity alive, an illegitimate philosophical offspring vying for the family inheritance. Postmodernity is the moment when those perceived as illegitimate have a claim in the family inheritance within the human community; such a moment suggests that we are the inhabitants of many local homes. In a postmodern age of narrative and virtue contention, communication ethics assumes a pragmatic stance of privileging understanding/learning[9] prior to both description and prescription.

The multiplicity of this moment suggests a pragmatic reality—we assume that the Other wants to protect and promote a communication ethic different than our own. We cannot assume universal agreement on "my" rights and privileges of humanness. Our understanding is local. No matter how much we wish to deny our provinciality, we are tied to a place, an institution, religion, theory, ideology, race, gender, ethnicity and so on. We are creatures of limits, persons who rest within pockets of provinciality, even as we deny the limits of our vision and knowledge, ashamed to think of the modern person as finite, bounded by the limits of our insight, wisdom, and standpoint.

Provinciality, used in its modern sense, offers a pejorative picture of the unsophisticated, the narrow, and the limited. Postmodernity assumes that one cannot stand above history, mired in the limits of habits, traditions, and customs.

Provinciality within modernity has a negative cast, reflecting the local and less than sophisticated and urbane. However, when one follows the scholarly mandate of Levinas—to think otherwise than convention—a first principle question emerges. What is, then, the proper name of provinciality? Levinas's construction of proper names returns us to the "saying" and the "said"; events have a saying that turns to a said, and then the said begins to influence our understanding of the saying. The saying, at times, breaks forth from the said, calling us to reexamine and ask, simply: "What is the proper name of this event?" Levinas states that we are ending an era in which the said, "the word" can trump the saying, ending a time of unending identities, concluding the philosophy of "…the Same, and of immanence, or ontology."[10] A proper name abandons the anticipation of finding the "ideal" that accurately deems a given identity for all time.

The search for the proper name of provinciality deconstructs the Enlightenment's vision, the extermination of provinciality from intersubjective modern reality. For Levinas, the search for a proper name begins with the following coordinates. First, a proper name has limits and begins in the local. Second, a proper name does not identify for all time. Third, a proper name is a phenomenological commitment to uniting "saying" and "said," doing one's best to align revelation with a name with full recognition of the temporal necessity of such a move. This chapter assumes that proper names begin with attentiveness to "saying" in the local, the place that modernity that sought to control identity attempted to displace. The notion of the proper name of provinciality begins in local soil, deconstructing modernity with each hearing that calls into question constructs that do not unite the horizons of saying and said.

The most constructive read of terrorism is that it is a fight for provinciality, a local worldview, put at risk, imagined or otherwise, by an alien Other. As one colleague asked, how does the notion of provinciality fit the acts of an anarchist? The answer reveals the power of provinciality in a modern form. The anarchist fights for the provinciality of modernity, the self, and an individualism that seeks to dismiss, disdain, and destroy whatever other form of local soil might guide a people. It is a form of terrorism that rests in the extreme individualism of modernity, assuming that within every other form of provinciality rests an evil calling to be eradicated. An anarchist celebrates modernity and the freedom of an originative understanding of the self. Levinas points to a rendering of provinciality that is a priori to such a construction.

Accepting provinciality as a given assists in understanding the fight for the particular. The forms of provinciality change, but its power remains. Modernity fights tradition as the curse of the local, only to fall into the same trap of embracing the provinciality of the autonomous human agent. Terrorism seeks darkness for another who, legitimately or not, seeks to protect and promote another provinciality, another local soil, a given virtue structure at odds with those in a given place of power. Levinas points to a recasting of the importance of provinciality, which assumes that we simply cannot see or hear in all directions at once. The phenomenological reality of human sense-making begins with the assumption of limits, a particular ground, and a particular sense of provinciality. To seek to destroy provinciality is to embark on a modernist alchemy of recasting the face of the human being. From an unconventional hermeneutic entrance that unites communication ethics, provinciality, and the face of the Other, "…one can say that the face is not 'seen.' It is what cannot become a content, which your thought would embrace; it is uncontainable, it leads you beyond."[11]

The face of the Other is maiden home of a provinciality that leads us "beyond." A place to begin leads beyond to another place. Terrorism is the act of taking from persons a place to begin that will lead them far beyond; terrorism attacks the phenomenological beginning of provinciality, the face of the Other. With a play on the words of the *Star Trek* theme, the face is a place of provinciality that begins and remains the final frontier of human responsibility. The face is the infinite place of call from the Other, calling one to act otherwise than convention.

OTHERWISE THAN CONVENTION

Levinas's work engages a project otherwise than the convention of the West. He displaces the Western emphasis on Being with ethics as first philosophy. He offers a phenomenological sense of hope that walks with us in the human experience, even in the deepest moments of suffering. His insights proffer conversation with a witness and a scholar who met terror with "ethics as first philosophy."[12] Levinas described a phenomenological world without the primeval assumption of the West that Being is the originative principle of the human condition. Philosophically and practically, Levinas's starting place is profoundly ethical, predating the disclosure of Being. "Preexisting the disclosure of being in general taken as basis of knowledge and as meaning of being is the relation with the existent that expresses himself; preexisting the plane of ontology is the ethical plane."[13] Akin to the otherwise than convention and prior to Being, this inquiry embraces provinciality both in the "saying" and the "said" as the ethical alternative to a Western commitment to the primacy of originative sense of communicative agency.

In an age of diversity, the first communication ethics begins otherwise than convention, forgoing the temptation to tell, in either descriptive or prescriptive form, as first communicative engagement. The author is aware that Levinas utilizes a phenomenological description that is, additionally, prescriptive. Levinas's employment of the terms prescriptive and descriptive offers an understanding that is otherwise than convention, contrasting with a Western emphasis on Being. His description and prescription of ethics is responsive to the face of the Other, meeting and responsiveness to the particular unique face of the Other, prior to the emergence of Being.

Unconventionally, for Levinas it is not Being, but the interplay of an ethical echo, "I am my brother's keeper," recorded within the face of another human being. Levinas begins with an echo and a human face, not with ontology. It is not the one looking or the one looked upon that guides ethics; the face repositions another from the visual to the aural, listening for an ethical echo that is both foundational and uniquely responsive to a particular human face. Levinas does not begin with an originative sense of agency, but with derivative construction of the "I" situated in the response to an ethical echo. The face of the Other offers an echo of human recording that requires our listening. Sight of face quickly gives way to listening in attending to ethics as first principle. With the face as the home of an echo or human recording, Levinas begins to frame an ethics where justice is blind—our liking or disliking of the Other is irrelevant in our responsibility to hear a call to attend to the Other.

The face of the Other demands that one listen to an ethical echo, an echo situated in the originative home of provinciality. One could call terrorism the unwillingness to attend to the face of the Other, attending instead to an ethical echo prior to being. In this historical moment, terrorism is the fulcrum point upon which contrasting understandings of communication ethics divide. For Levinas, an answer lies in an ethical echo and in the human face, not in grand theory or a trust in Being. Levinas brings us an alternative, interpreting contrary to Western ontology. One might go so far as to suggest that we live in a time of ontological terrorism of which its extreme darkness manifested itself in explicit fashion in the destructive hands of the Nazis, continuing today, with its roots deeply entangled in the assumption that ontology, Being, is the primordial constructor of the human condition.

Unless there is an attending to an ethical echo prior to Being, Levinas's project suggests a chilling reality—terrorism is unlikely to be eradicated within a Western understanding of ontology. Even the goal of resolution, itself, takes on a form of violence, imposing a temporal universal in a world of difference—such is the concern of Lyotard.[14] The hope of moving us out of this practical and conceptual bind requires Levinas to redefine the nature of prescriptive and descriptive, for neither comes from the "I," but instead is a calling forth of the "I." For Levinas, prescription and description are derivative of hearing a call that beckons forth an "I" not yet known.

In Levinas's rejection of the Western infatuation with Being, he employs a strikingly unexpected vocabulary, a vocabulary that on first blush is more associated with terrorism and oppression than with a sense of ethics and care for the Other. Levinas deconstructs the Western focus on Being and the originative construction of agency as failed developments. Levinas interprets otherwise than Heidegger's view of the Greeks and of conventional understanding of Enlightenment thought. His vocabulary reveals the "why" of modernity's vulnerability to terrorism. Levinas usurps a vocabulary that invites destabilizing fear of terrorism, offering an alternative to the moral *cul de sac* of the Enlightenment project that rest in belief in the originative power of the self as the fulcrum of human progress.

The uniqueness of Levinas's language explains the effectiveness of terrorism in undermining human routine, leaving us with unspecified fear and suspicion. Levinas's message is that the modern project of the self situated within a metanarrative of progress makes us vulnerable to fear and suspicion. Levinas makes his case by undermining the very foundation of Being as the privileged project for shaping a human being. Instability generated by terrorist acts undercuts a constructed assumption of progress by the enhancement of fear. Fear is the primary tool of instability in the terrorist's arsenal, striking at the heart of the taken-for-granted background of daily routine that offers persons ground from which to engage and meet the possibilities of everyday life. The battleground of terrorism is the shift of focus of attention from the routine to uncertainty and fear.

FOCUS OF ATTENTION

On the one hand, terrorism is one form of provinciality contending against another provinciality. On the other hand, terrorism is a disparate effort of the disempowered to protect a provinciality that grounds a people. Whatever the reading of a terrorist act, it disrupts the focus of attention that permits one unreflectively to appreciate the routine: of work, a beautiful sunset, meals with friends, talk with family, and an evening walk. Terrorism terminates the common and the expected that offer meaningfulness and the stability from which one can meet the inevitable sorrows and disappointments of life. Terrorism alters a focus of attention, taking one from the routine and stability of everyday communicative life. Instability generated by terrorist acts undercuts, alters, dissipates an ongoing focus of attention, disturbing joy, enhancing fear.

Terrorism begins with an invasion of fear and loss of the routine as the primary weapon. Terrorism is partially akin to the act of imperialism in that it storms the beaches of routine life, destroying all that is different. The difference is that imperialism demands substitution and subordination to a "new way of being" consistent with those coming into power. Terrorism destabilizes ground. Unlike imperialism, which gives one something to fight against, something to push against, terrorism seeks to undercut the ground from which one stands and pivots. Traction on a remnant of ground against a new regime permitted a Camus to join the French underground. Terrorism, on the other hand, effectively works to eliminate all places where a foothold is possible. Terrorism generates a fear as the routine erodes from the foothold of everyday assurance.

The loss of routine brings a sense of fear that shifts one's focus of attention from meeting and engaging life to obsessing over the absence of the expectation of hope. Fear tied to loss was a major point penned first by Augustine, who connected fear to expectation of loss.[15] Destabilization of life through disruption of the expectation of hope places anxiety at the center of existence. Levinas cites Heidegger, saying:

> …brilliant analyses…made of affectivity, sentiments, emotion, *Befindlichkeit*. Every emotion has, according to him, what he calls a double intentionality: it is an emotion *before* something and *for* something. Fear is fear *about* what is terrifying and always also fear *for* myself. Heidegger insists on the fact that in German verbs expressing emotions are always reflexive, as in French are the verbs to be moved, to be frightened, to be sad, etc. Anxiety, according to him, is an exceptional emotion wherein the *about* and the *for* coincide: anxiety *about* finitude is anxiety *for* my finitude and, in a certain sense, all emotion, because of this return to the self, goes back to anxiety. It seems to us the fear for the other does not have this return to the self. Is it not in that the emotion of fear of God regains its sense, disengaged from every reference to the idea of a jealous God?[16]

Levinas's understanding of fear is both in agreement with and contrary to that of the modern existential project. Fear connected to finitude makes sense to Levinas; his work critiques totality. Yet, it is fear connected to Being that he rejects. As is his custom, Levinas offers a contrary read to a convention. In this case he counters a conventional view of fear. Levinas connects direction and turning to the question of fear, making that toward which we turn the central weapon against a terrorism of ontology.

Terrorism disrupts the routine of everyday life—making one attentive to the potential of fear, less attentive to the joy of everyday life. Terrorism shifts the focus of attention from the doing of life to the fear of anticipation of loss. Terrorism plays on our fears of expectation and loss. Hannah Arendt provided insight into such fear, experienced as a Jew in Nazi Germany and theoretically framed within her dissertation on Augustine. The dialectic of fear and love (loss and craving) keeps the person from enjoying life with a sense of calm. The future rests in uncertainties, robbing the present of its power. Future anticipation of love and fear (the dialectic of craving and loss) shapes the character of the present. Happiness consists in possession of a given object craved, ever challenged by fear of the safety of a given possession. This picture gives rise to the image of Gollum in *Lord of the Rings,* who loves the ring and fears its loss with the haunting chant of "my precious, my precious." The dialectical movement between craving and fear deconstructs the present.

> Constantly bound by craving and fear to a future full of uncertainties, we strip each present moment of its calm, its intrinsic import, which we are unable to enjoy. And so, the

future destroys the present. Whatever can be taken away from a lasting enjoyment for its own sake cannot possibly be the proper object of desire.[17]

The world of Gollum consists of ever wanting, craving, and fearing, living in constant "need." In contrast, Levinas's world offers the distinction between "need" and "desire"[18] with the former the world of Gollum and the latter—that world of ever meeting anew. Desire goes unfulfilled; it calls forever for another meeting. After the death of a loved one, "need" suggests that one must bring the other back—somehow. "Desire," on the other hand, feels a pain that could not go away even if the other returned. Each meeting is yet a call for another, an unending call that cannot be answered. Ironically, "desire" prepares us for death and "need" moves us further and further into Gollum's cave, a prison of possession.

Terrorism seeks to turn a person into a "Gollum," ever fearing loss and living with the expectation of loss. Without uttering a word, one begins to state, "My precious, my precious." The precious is a sense of safety in routine disrupted by fear of loss. One hears of airlines, then nuclear plants, then schools that "were," "are," and "may be" under attack. One lives in the midst of fear—one's focus of attention goes to the precious, missing the everyday joy of life. Such is the aftermath of such violence. Only when there is "…no death, and hence no future, can men live 'without the anguish of worry [fear of loss].'"[19] Augustine frames an existential reading of life in the following manner: human life as "not yet," "having" as governed by fear, and "not having" as dictated by craving. The human lives within an expected future of cravings and fears—in the "not yet."[20] Only a present without a future is without a sense of menace—for each craving once found then fades into fear and eventual death. Only a present without a future has no foreboding. Only eternity, the loss of fear of death, after death braces one fearlessly against one's own will. Terrorism depends on a turning toward loss, in modern philosophical terms, a loss of an originative sense of Being and its ever-expanding possibilities. Terrorism invokes constant fear, leaving a person within a self-preoccupation framework. Such preoccupation misses alterity/difference that reconstitutes identity. Levinas situates ethics as first philosophy only as the person turns toward alterity outside the self, which shapes and reshapes identity of the self. We find who we are and who we might become outside the confines of the self. Turning toward alterity is the cornerstone of Levinas's rejection of self-preoccupation; such a move places him at the forefront of postmodern critique of agency independent of alterity that offers transcendence and new insight.

TURNING TOWARD AN A PRIORI TO FEAR

Roosevelt's famous phrase was "All we have to fear is fear itself."[21] He understood that that to which we turn, the phenomenon to which we engage, makes all the difference. Levinas sought to turn us differently as he foreshadowed a postmodern questioning of an originative understanding of human agency. He turns us from agency that houses fear due to the originative and control features of this view of human agency to an ethical echo that disarms the weapon of fear. Perhaps it is this sense of turning that permitted Bonhoeffer to walk to his own hanging with a sense of peace that quieted all who watched. Such a turning makes all the difference. Fear relies on our turning to loss.

Levinas's ongoing critique of agency suggests that our image of the human condition, in the midst of everyday toil, depends upon what and where we turn; turning matters. He suggests that human health rests upon an ethical pivoting. The question is: to what do we turn? Martin Buber[22] framed the importance of turning toward the Other as does Levinas. This turning takes one someplace other than self-reflection. For Buber, it is an emergent "between," a temporal answer that calls for one's attention. Levinas begins with the focus on the Other who calls forth a pivot not only to something other than the individual self, but toward an a priori oral ethic. Levinas moves the notion of turning to an ethical responsiveness attentive to an echos of responsibility that predates the object under reflection and consideration. Levinas outlined a phenomenological listening,[23] an attentiveness not dependent upon the object itself. Levinas does not turn toward the Other in a humanistic appreciation of the object of the person, but toward the Other as a reminder of a phenomenological echo that takes one from the face of the Other to a call of responsibility. It is an oral ethical call that directs, not the Other.

How we turn and to what we turn shape the phenomenological reality of life. Terrorism works to turn us in a given direction of self-protection. Levinas recognized that the manner of our turning and toward what we turn shapes the significance and meaning of human life. In the spirit of Levinas, that to which we turn opens our ears to a particular call to responsibility, suggesting the manner of uniting the "saying" and the "said" of a given phenomenon.

Levinas suggests that the subject must separate from direct reflection upon itself. One must turn toward an alterity beyond the self. The alterity of earthly nourishments "…contains a forgetfulness of self."[24] When one turns toward the distant sound of an ethical echo, one turns from the self toward alterity, which offers the irony of transcendence and change within the very self. The self grows, matures, changes and discovers new identity in the meeting of alterity beyond the self to which one turns.

It is Levinas's early foreshadowing of the postmodern condition that displaces the primacy of the agent as an originative point. For Levinas, the agent/self is derivative, a by-product of a primordial call from the Other. The assertion that guides Levinas is "I am my brother's keeper." He begins with a declarative assertion, not a question: "I am my brother's keeper." His work commences from a perceived phenomenological reality—the "I" is derivative of the Other, a derivative sense of alterity. In essence, our identity finds shape from the call of the Other, not from our own self-assertion. For example, suppose a young teenager has a child and becomes the primary caretaker of the child. In the middle of the night, the child cries and a parent-child, who previously could not get up until midday, rises to care for the baby. In that moment, the young caretaker hears an a priori call from the face of the infant, invoking a sense of responsibility that calls for a parent, shifting identity from that of the young person concerned only about "me" and "my" comfort to that of a parent answering the call of responsibility.

Clearly, not all people make the move from self-absorption to parent. In Levinas's terms, when one hears the call of the Other as a reminder of responsibility to act out an oral ethic that "I am by brother's keeper," one's identity shifts, moving one to a "responsive ethical I" that is derivative of a call. Such is the reason Levinas stated that the person who answers the call is held "hostage" by the call of responsibility for the Other. The face of the Other reminds one of a call that continues to echo with an impersonal call to responsibility for the Other. It is not whether one likes another that beckons, but the reminder of an a priori saying of responsibility—a priori to humanistic questions about liking or disliking of the Other—"I am my brother's keeper." This basic move of ethics is a pragmatic response to a phenomenological reality—the Otherness shapes me. I do not shape myself—without the Other, there is no I. For Levinas, we are held hostage by the Other as we turn toward something prior to fear.

THE HOSTAGE

Turning toward alterity offers insight into how one becomes a derivative subject. For Levinas, our phenomenological ethical call comes from the Other, who holds "me" hostage. Levinas, again working otherwise than convention, offers an unusual way of understanding the notion of hostage. He suggests that when alterity of the Other holds us hostage, we are transformed by that responsibility. Again, his insight uses language similar to that of terrorism—reminding us of a turning that recasts identity, a turning toward the Other that results in our own servitude to the Other. A hostage is bound by a fundamental turning toward the Other. Levinas suggests that as we turn toward the face of the Other, we are held hostage by the provinciality of a human face that calls us to attend to an ethical echo.

Terrorism holds both joy and innovation hostage at the feet of survival and fear. Phenomenologically, terrorism shifts the focus of attention from a life of enjoyment and productivity to a life of fear and survival. Levinas, on the other hand, provides an understanding of the hostage that undercuts and deconstructs a conventional understanding of hostage as defined by survival and fear.

The notion of terrorism is almost synonymous with the fear of being a hostage; yet, it is this very term that shapes Levinas's understanding of alterity that transforms the subject. The notion of hostage is the language of a call to responsibility for a particular Other; it is an action that, without reflection, acts with an "I" called into responsible action by the Other—"If not me, then whom?"[25]

> And so I find myself not the center, the ruler, of my life, but accused.... I must now welcome the other, giving the other the very home, food, clothing, etc., that were for my enjoyment. I suffer to relieve the other's suffering, and in so doing become myself in a way that is impossible though my own enjoyable life. I become myself—I become free in responsibility—only when I answer for the other. I am hostage for the other, says Levinas at his hyperbolic best. Thus I am not my own matter, but am substitute for the other. I must take the other's place, and no one may relieve me of my burden to take that place. I am uniquely responsible. No one can take my place—the place before the other—the hostage for the other.[26]

Levinas uses vocabulary that requires a second hearing, an in-depth understanding that bypasses conventional usage. He used terms in constructive fashion that we often associate otherwise—the notion of "hostage," *par example.* Typically, this term does not meet with a positive appraisal. To state in any meeting the positive connotation of the term hostage is to find few in agreement. For Levinas, the fundamentals of the human condition begin with the focus on bondage to another, who holds one hostage by calling forth a responsibility that would not and could not emerge without such a burden.

Levinas rejects any form of communication situated first in comfort. It is burden from another that offers joy, not the effort to escape it. The work of Viktor Frankl based on meaning in the midst of suffering comes close to Levinas's project. But, even Frankl stated that meaning came from what one got from life, gave to life, and one's stand against the inevitable.[27] Levinas goes to the extreme heart of a sense of burden, making it the fulcrum upon which human responsibility and, ultimately, changes in identity rest. It is the hostage who finds his or her identity from the burden called forth by the Other.

Levinas's view of hostage as a call for responsibility comes to life in Ernest Boyer's comment on how underprivileged students succeed. Boyer stated the following. There must be a mom, dad, brother, sister, coach, friend, aunt, uncle, someone who stands and says, "I will not let you do anything but succeed. It is my task to make sure you do." Boyer says that young people who had such a person were simply more likely to be outstanding students.[28] As such, a person takes up a mantle of responsibility; the burden for another; the caregiver becomes the hostage, changed forever.

The conventional view of the agent or the self leads to the hope of freeing the person. Levinas rebukes the hegemony of a modern presupposition of the primacy of the originative self and its need for freedom. He states differently that the person has a desire for burden that transforms the self. "To welcome the Other is to put in question my freedom."[29] This critique of everyday convention about the primacy of freedom as a social good forgoes the temptations to embrace a humanism that privileges the narcissism of image over the transformative characteristics of burden.

A terrorist takes a hostage. Yet, for Levinas, one cannot take a hostage; the Other takes "me" as the hostage. In taking a hostage the terrorist often masks the eyes of the captured, averting eye contact of one person with another. Once again, with contrary intent, Levinas speaks otherwise than convention, detailing a non-humanistic response to burden that is inattentive to the color of the eyes of the Other, ever responsive to the impersonal as a call to burden and responsibility.

One becomes a hostage, responsible for the life of another, attending to the call that emanates from the Other's face and gaining identity through the burden of the call. The face of the Other is both central to Levinas and not a priori sufficient; he reserves this place as for and of no value if one does not attend to an a priori echo. If one reads this move as dependent upon the Other, one misses Levinas's view of the call, an ethical echo. Further clarity warrants completion of this story from a Levinasian perspective. Let us suppose a young person offers thanks for assistance given in the Boyer example in the last section—a hostage simply thinks privately, "Do not take this personally, I could not do otherwise. I was called to this responsibility; now you must do yours." The hostage responding to an ethical echo answers a call irrespective of the person. It is not the Other, but answering a call of an ethical a priori to the face of a reminder to be "my brother's keeper" that converts a person into a hostage. Levinas takes us again otherwise than convention with a different view of mask and the human face.

MASKING THE EYES, AN IMPERSONAL FACE THAT CALLS

Terrorism lives cloaked by a mask. First, the terrorist masks the self, ignoring the face of the Other. Second, the terrorist puts blinders on the recipient of the terror, moving that person to constant fear of loss. When terrorism works, it does not look into the eyes of the victims, and it shifts the vision of those who remain living in the aftermath of an attack. Yet, Levinas tells us to mask the eyes of the Other, moving us from sight of another, friend or foe, to an ethical echo calling forth responsibility.

As Levinas stated: "The best way of encountering the Other is inattention to the color of the Other's eyes! When one observes the color of the eyes one is in social, not ethical relationship with the Other. The relation with the face is often dominated by perception, but what is specifically the face is what cannot be reduced to that. There is first the very uprightness of the face, its upright exposure, without defenses. At the same time, the face is what forbids us to kill."[30] Levinas's focus of attention attends to the Other without regard for the specifics of the Other. Unlike Mr. Rogers's Neighborhood, where "all are special," Levinas reminds us of a focus of attention that is unresponsive to the "special" characteristics of the Other; his understanding of ethics is impersonal and, therefore, more demanding. Who the person is does not define ethical engagement; the face matters no matter who steps forth before us. Again, only differently, Levinas uses the guidance of terrorism that seeks to mask the eyes of another. He understands the necessity of a mask over the eyes, the unique characteristics of another, not to avoid the Other, but to move from the visual to the auditory, attending to a primordial echo—"I am my brother's keeper."

Beware of anyone too eager to detail the good of their actions; hiding the face is not humility, but a respect for a sense of burden that claims and shapes our future identify without our volition. It is right and appropriate that both terrorists and fictional heroes such as Zorro hide their faces—the actions are the same, yet the latter does so out of the burden of protecting others. Appropriately, the television show began with a counter-intuitive theme—"Out of the night comes.... Zorro." Both terrorism and hope come from a darkness that Levinas's ethic embraced.

The burden of Levinas's project is the call of an impersonal face that takes us to an "enlarged mentality" from Kant and Arendt,[31] an attentive call to an echo of an ethical message older than the cry to kill. Levinas points to the provinciality of the face as the primordial reminder of ethical instruction. It is in the face that the "...trace of God is manifested...."[32] There is no answer from Levinas; or is there? Just a reminder of a primordial echo: I am my brother's keeper, regardless of who the Other is. The call begins outside of me, begun by radical alterity in the face of another.

THE AUTONOMOUS MORAL AGENT —A MORAL CUL DE SAC

Levinas's project is a repeated reminder of communicative life that seeks instruction from the Other; the beginning is not a conventional view of the autonomous human agent. Our view of the West begins with the Socratic exhortation to "know thyself."[33]

Levinas begins with the call to know the Other without ever attending to the color of the other's eyes.[34] He begins with an understanding of Other that rests outside a conventional understanding of agency. "The exteriority of the face is extra-ordinary. It is extra-ordinary for order is justice."[35] Levinas turns to the face of the Other, seeking a justice prior to being, prior to epistemology, prior to the reflective turn back upon the self.

Levinas rejects an Enlightenment view of humanism that gives rise to an autonomous communicative agent; he provides us with a theory that masks the eyes of the agent, an act central to terrorism, yet central to an ethic more fundamental to human responsibility than humanism. He reminds us of a phenomenological call to listen to an *a priori* memory that moves Levinas otherwise than terrorism, suggesting an implicit rhetoric for peace in a time of public admission of danger and fear.

Levinas disconnects from humanism because it is not human enough. Levinas understands humanness as linked with burden, not with the picking and choosing of persons and characteristics of which we approve as we pursue self-actualization. Humanism tied to an originative sense of agency is a philosophy/theory that eclipses an originative ethical echo in favor of the rush to remove the mask from the Other's eyes.

Levinas embraced an anti-humanist stance, rejecting the originative nature and power of the subject, which functions as the foundation of Being in the West. Levinas's contrary motion provides an alternative to a humanistic ethic based upon an ethical self who seeks an ever-increasing degree of freedom. The persuasive power of Levinas's ethic does not begin with the communicative expression of freedom, but with the reality of the Other holding one hostage. Levinas rejected the humanism of the West as simply not the proper name for what it means to be a human—we begin with burden. Levinas turns us toward the face of the Other that calls for our unique sense of burden.

Levinas's project is contrary to the assumption that we can construct an autonomous moral agent, requiring a brief outline that discloses his otherwise than convention about the foundation of the human condition. Levinas's phenomenological description of ethics prior to being is complex in texture but straightforward in its storyline. The basic coordinates are as follows: 1) the human face is the ethical keystone that functions as a reminder to listen; 2) the human face is the foundational ethical beginning, a primeval ethical echo; 3) attentiveness to an ethical echo simultaneously makes the face essential and ethically irrelevant; 4) the face points to an echo, a call that is prior to attending to the "color of another eyes,"[36] prior to asking if one likes or approves of the Other; 5) the face functions as a sign that redirects us from the visual to the auditory; 6) the face returns us to listening, attending to an echo of a primordial human mantra—"I am my brother's keeper"; 7) the phenomenological reason for such an ethical message is a human fact—without the Other, there is no "I"; 8) Levinas ties ethics to a non-humanistic assumption that humanism beginning with the "I" or the "Other" is not human enough; it is insufficient.

The fundamental definition of the human doing communication ethics begins with listening attentive to a chant of long ago that reminds us that without the Other there is simply no "I." The ethical charge to take care of another is both a phenomenological fact and a pragmatic necessity. It is the Other that shapes my sense of "I." As penned in another essay, Levinas reminds us of the derivative and responsive calling forth of a sense of "I."[37] Provinciality begins with a human face, connecting one to a phenomenological reality, a primordial urbanity that knows not how to understand the "I" without attending with care to the Other.

Levinas leaves us with a reminder of an ethical echo that is prior to being. He reminds us of mystery that recognizes that "the face is present in its refusal to be contained."[38] We can, additionally, terrorize another when we think we know the face of the Other. The phenomenological fact of a face that refuses containment manifests itself when listening trumps my seeing, when mystery trumps my knowing, and when moral responsibility trumps being, itself. When we think we know the Other, we risk interpersonal terror. Such is the reason Buber called psychologism the demonic of the twentieth century.[39] When we assume we know the reason for our own actions or that of another, we invite a terror between persons. When we conclude we know the truth about the Other and impose it upon that other, we invite a terror of inquiry. When totality trumps infinity, we invite a terror of categories, forgetting that, at times, totality must trump to keep its secondary status. Otherwise, one turns infinity into a totality.

This chapter ends where it began, admitting that one must enter conversation about terrorism with humility, trembling, and a wondering why for the enactment of seemingly hopeless terrorist acts. Yet, one communication ethics offering of advice comes from this conversation with Levinas—terrorism does not live merely in the lives of those who contend against us, but within any effort, including our own, that defaces another. Defacing another, taking that person's empirical face away from us that reminds us to listen to a phenomenological ethical echo, lessening the urge to claim that one knows and the Other works from the wrong motives or ill-conceived ideas.

Levinas calls us to take humanism off the map in order to remind us to attend to the face of all, even those who seek to deface our own, responding to an impersonal call. Levinas reminds us of an ethical call that holds us hostage—"I am my brother's keeper." The phenomenological Levinasian proclamation is that without the Other, the demands and burdens of the Other, the identity of "I" is no more. We live in a moment in which identity finds derivative clarity through an ethical echo that reminds us to listen to music prior to being, music that resounds even more clearly in the dark.

Levinas offers an answer that moves otherwise than convention—the fight against terrorism begins with a willingness to respond to a derivative sense of identity through the burden of responsibility as a hostage to the Other, attending ever carefully to an ethical echo that makes responsiveness to burden a defining characteristic of what it means to be a human being. Perhaps, only a survivor from the concentration camps of World War II has the right to offer such a radical call—attend to provinciality of the face that reminds us to listen to an ethical echo—"I am my brother's keeper." This same brother or sister then holds us hostage. Levinas leaves us with an ironic message. It is the "hostage" that offers the best hope against terrorism—a hostage called forth by an ethical echo that lives not in any theory but is primordially tied to the face of the Other, a burden from another whose eyes we do not meet. Alternatively, we meet the call that the Other makes possible, a call that functions as a two-sided ethical coin, both holding us hostage and giving us a derivative identity that shapes our humanness and moves us from the terror of fear to the possibility of human joy.

NOTES

1. Levinas. *Ethics and Infinity* (Pittsburgh: Duquesne University Press, 1985).

2. Hyde, *The Call of Conscience: Heidegger and Levinas, Rhetoric and the Euthanasia Debate* (Columbia: University of South Carolina Press, 2001).

3. Levinas. *Proper Names* (Stanford: University of California Press, 1996).

4. Simmel, *Conflict and the Web of Group Affiliations* (New York: The Free Press, 1955).

5. Arnett, "Existential Homelessness: A Contemporary Case for Dialogue," *The Reach of Dialogue: Confirmation, Voice and Community* (New York: Hampton Press, 1994).

6. De Tocqueville, *Democracy in America* (New York: Random House, 1972).

7. Harding. *Feminist Standpoint Theory* (New York: Routledge, 2003).

8. Arnett & Arneson, *Dialogic Civility in a Cynical Age: Community, Hope and Interpersonal Relationships* (Albany: State University of New York Press, 1999).

9. Arnett, Arnseon & Bell, "Communication Ethics: The Dialogic Turn," *The Review of Communication*, 6 (2006): 62–92.

10. Levinas, *Proper Names*, 5.

11. Levinas, *Ethics*, 86.

12. Manning, *Interpreting Otherwise Than Heidegger: Emmanuel Levinas's Ethics as First Philosophy* (Pittsburgh: Duquesne University Press, 1993).

13. Levinas, *Totality and Infinity,* (New York, Springer, 2001), 201.

14. Manning, *Interpreting Otherwise.*

15. Augustine, *Confessions,* (New York, New City Press, 2002).

16. Levinas, *Ethics,* 119.

17. Arendt, Love and Saint Augustine, (Chicago: University of Chicago Press, 1996), p. 10

18. Levinas, *Totality and Infinity.*

19. Augustine, *Confessions,* 11.

20. Ibid., 13.

21. Arnett, Arneson & Bell, "Communication Ethics," (in press).

22. Buber, *Between Man and Man* (New York: Routledge, 1993).

23. Arnett, "The Assumptive Roots of Emphatic Listening."

24. Levinas, *Time and the Other* (Pittsburgh: Duquesne University Press, 1987), 127.

25. Arnett, *Dialogic Education* (Carbondale: Southern Illinois University Press, 2003), 115.

26. Gibbs, *Correlations in Rosenzweig and Levinas* (Princeton, Princeton University Press, 1994), 182.

27. Arnett and Arneson, *Dialogic Civility.*

28. Arnett, *Dialogic Education.*

29. Levinas, *Totality and Infinity,* 200.

30. Levinas, *Ethics and Infinity,* 85.

31. Arendt, *Love and Saint Augustine* (Chicago: University of Chicago Press, 1996); Kant, *The Critique of Judgment* (Lawrence, Kansas: Neeland Media LLC, 2006).

32. Levinas, *Proper Names,* 95.

33. Gross, *Socrates' Way: Seven Keys to Using Your Mind to the Utmost,* (New York: Penguin Putnam, 2002).

34. Levinas, *Ethics,* 85.

35. Levinas, *Time and the Other,* 107

36. Ibid., 107.

37. Ibid.

38. Levinas, *Proper Names,* 168.

39. Buber, *Between Man and Man.*

BIBLIOGRAPHY

Arendt, Hannah. *Love and Saint Augustine.* Chicago: The University of Chicago Press, 1996.

Arnett, Ronald C. *The Assumptive Roots of Emphatic Listening: A Critique.* Communication Education 32 (1983): 368–378.

Arnett, Ronald C. *Communication and Community: Implications of Martin Buber's Dialogue.* Carbondale, Illinois: Southern Illinois University Press, 1986.

Arnett, Ronald C. *Dialogic Education.* Carbondale, Illinois: Southern Illinois University Press, 1993.

Arnett, Ronald C. "Existential Homelessness: A Contemporary Case for Dialogue." *The Reach of Dialogue: Confirmation, Voice and Community.* Eds. Rob Anderson and Kenneth Cissna. New York: Hampton Press, 1994.

Arnett, Ronald C. "The Responsive 'I': Levinas' Derivative Argument." *Argumentation and Advocacy* 40.1 (2003): 39–50.

Arnett, Ronald C. and Pat Arneson. *Dialogic Civility in a Cynical Age: Community, Hope, and Interpersonal Relationships.* Albany, New York: State University of New York Press, 1999.

Arnett, Ronald C. and Clifford Christians. *Dialogic Confession: Bonhoeffer's Rhetoric of Responsibility.* Carbondale, Illinois: Southern Illinois University Press, 2005.

Arnett, Ronald C., Pat Arneson, and Leeanne M. Bell. "Communication Ethics: The Dialogic Turn." *The Review of Communication* 6 (January–April 2006): 62–92.

Benhabib, Seyla. *The Reluctant Modernism of Hannah Arendt.* Lanham, Maryland: Rowman & Littlefield, 2003.

Buber, Martin. *Between Man and Man.* New York: Routledge, 1993.

De Tocqueville, Alexis. *Democracy in America.* New York: Random House, 1972.

Gibbs, Robert. *Correlations in Rosenzweig and Levinas.* Princeton, New Jersey: Princeton University Press, 1994.

Gross, Ronald. *Socrates' Way: Seven Keys to Using Your Mind to the Utmost.* New York: Penguin Putnam, 2002.

Harding, Sandra. *Feminist Standpoint Theory.* New York: Routledge, 2003.

Hyde, Michael J. *The Call of Conscience: Heidegger and Levinas, Rhetoric and the Euthanasia Debate.* Columbia, South Carolina: University of South Carolina Press, 2001.

Kant, Immanuel. *The Critique of Judgment.* Lawrence, Kansas: Neeland Media, LLC, 2006.

Levinas, Emmanuel. *Ethics and Infinity.* Pittsburgh, Pennsylvania: Duquesne University Press, 1985.

Levinas, Emmanuel. *Proper Names.* Stanford, California: Stanford University Press, 1996.

Levinas, Emmanuel. *Time and the Other.* Pittsburgh, Pennsylvania: Duquesne University Press, 1987.

Levinas, Emmanuel. *Totality and Infinity.* New York: Springer, 2001.

Manning, Robert. *Interpreting Otherwise Than Heidegger: Emmanuel Levinas's Ethics as First Philosophy.* Pittsburgh, Pennsylvania: Duquesne University Press, 1993.

Saint Augustine. *The Confessions.* Trans. Maria Boulding. New York: New City Press, 2002.

Simmel, Georg. *Conflict and the Web of Group Affiliations.* New York: The Free Press, 1955.

Dialogic Ethics, Cosmopolitanism, and Intercultural Communication

Globalization Matters

KATHLEEN GLENISTER ROBERTS

No doubt the reader is by now familiar with the purpose of this volume and the story of its development. Addenda in other chapters have noted that in its initial stages, this book used the term "globalization" in describing its project. As co-editor, I wholeheartedly supported a change from "globalization" to "cosmopolitanism." Cosmopolitanism accurately conveys the philosophical intent of the National Conference on Communication Ethics, as well as the humanities-based perspectives of contributors to this volume. To some contributors and attendees at the conference, "globalization" is considered a pejorative term because it is rooted in economics and the marketplace.

This latter opinion on the term "globalization" is where my personal contribution to the book speaks a bit more from the provinces, and where my agreement with the change to cosmopolitanism diverges slightly. Globalization does concern itself with economics and the marketplace, but to me that makes it neither pejorative nor terribly disconnected from cosmopolitanism—for three reasons. First, communication scholars educate communication students who enter and deeply impact the marketplace. We ignore that fact at our own peril. Second, and more importantly, economics and the marketplace do matter to cosmopolitanism. One of today's foremost philosophers of cosmopolitanism, Seyla Benhabib, espouses a cosmopolitan federalism that would direct Kantian cosmopolitanism toward practical application.[1] Since identity claims are at the heart of her cosmopolitan federalism, it is worth noting (as I do in detail later in this chapter) that a theory of cosmopolitanism is impossible without attention to the everyday practices—discursive and otherwise—of diverse groups.[2] At least one political philosopher of cosmopolitanism, then, points us in a direction where at least minimal attention should be paid to economic issues such as globalization.

A final reason to revisit the idea of globalization within this volume is most significant to my "province" of intercultural communication. The reason is this: cosmopolitanism is in large part a *Western* project. Other contributors have cited Appiah[3] and Benhabib[4] whose cultural ancestries are non-Western (Appiah's father was Ghanaian, his mother English). Yet it seems reasonable to state that Appiah and Benhabib both theorize from "scholarly ancestries" that are Western. They were both educated in the West and draw on Western philosophies for their respective positions on cosmopolitanism. Benhabib, for instance, might be said to be in a direct line of descent from Hannah Arendt. And where Appiah diverges from rigid cosmopolitanism in the tradition of Martha Nussbaum, he does so by arguing the importance of localities—virtually always using examples from his life in Ghana.[5]

These are just two scholars whose intercultural educational experiences underscore the nature of cosmopolitanism as weighted more toward a Western perspective. My scholarly position is within the field of intercultural communication, which limits my contribution significantly (in other words, I do not make claims to any specialized knowledge, but only a narrowness of focus). It is important that I pay attention to cultural diversity in a response to the call of this volume. And attention to cultural diversity suggests that "cosmopolitanism" is not easily applied to the cultures I have studied.

Globalization, however, has had a clear impact on those cultures. I believe the change to "cosmopolitanism" in other essays in this volume to be sound and worthwhile. But the bias toward economics that the word "globalization" creates can still open up scholarly discourse on dialogic ethics. In intercultural communication—for the moment at least—cosmopolitanism should be taken off the table, because I have not yet concluded whether or not other cultures espouse the same virtues that Western cosmopolitans do (indeed, this question is at the heart of my current research agenda, but is still a work in progress). To be sure, members of other cultures travel; they have extensive knowledge of other cultures; they shape world economies through trade and international education. But these projects are all those of globalization—not necessarily cosmopolitanism.

To that end, I beg the reader's indulgence as I postpone judgment on how dialogic ethics and cosmopolitanism might be applied to intercultural communication. My request—and contribution—is a dose of provinciality. I bracket off cosmopolitanism in order to write from the provinces: from a small area of communication that still finds itself unable to generalize about its subject—the worldviews of Others. This is not to say that philosophical inquiry into the subject is impossible. Indeed that is my project here. In this chapter of the volume, I consider globalization as a factor to be considered in questions of cosmopolitanism and intercultural communication. The essay is situated in Benhabib's[6] call for attention to the lived everyday practices and evaluative practices of marginalized cultures as a way of understanding current identity claims. In particular I will examine the lived practice of giveaway rituals in Native American communities and the evaluative practices of rhetorical performances that accompany those rituals. It is hoped that this microcosmic study can be fused with some general inquiries into globalization and cosmopolitanism. First, I begin with a Modernist identity claim below, then discuss some problems in the study of globalization. Finally, I discuss giveaways in more detail and apply globalization issues to Native Americans in particular and indigenous persons in general. Ultimately, I argue that attention to cultural performance can inform understanding of not just globalization but the potential for cosmopolitanism in non-Western cultures.

MODERNIST APPROACHES TO CULTURE: THE PROBLEM CONTINUES

One of the most significant barriers to understanding in the study of culture is an approach to indigenous cultures as bounded, discrete, and static. But this is not merely the perspective of non-indigenous peoples; a few Native Americans espouse the view as well. For instance, professor and historian Angela Cavender Wilson (Lakota) has argued that the "reclaiming" of indigenous cultures must occur on at least two fronts: the linguistic and the physiological. First, each tribe must relearn their native language as it existed before European contact. Second, to improve the health of indigenous peoples, methods of finding and preparing traditional foods (those consumed before contact with Europeans) must be sought and disseminated.[7]

A perspective on communication—especially within performance studies—may make Wilson's points appear problematic. One should never underestimate the tragic impact of colonization on the world's indigenous peoples. At the same time, one should never *over*estimate the powers of the colonizers in forcing indigenous peoples to assimilate. It is clear from ongoing gift exchanges and other indigenous practices on the Northern Plains that ancient traditions have *not* been lost; they have evolved through dynamic performances to suit the needs of a given historical moment. So even if a particular tribe could recover their indigenous language as it existed before European contact, would such a language reflect the reality of Native lives today? Of course not. Even if it were practical to gather and prepare foods traditionally, would such practices be helpful to this generation of Native Americans in search of ways of living in the postmodern world? Unlikely.

In fact, such practices have the potential to further alienate cultural groups, since they are grounded (however unconsciously) in a nineteenth-century Modern concept of culture. In such a concept, cultures *are* bounded and discrete wholes, and contact with outsiders presents problems rather than opportunities. Such imaginary cultures are static, superorganic, and rather helpless to define their own lived experiences. More perniciously, there is a racist tendency within these perceptions to inaccurately conflate culture with biology. The suggestion that twenty-first century Native Americans should recover their health through the consumption of seventeenth-century foods does not *recapture* culture but instead has the potential to destroy it. The same is true for Wilson's static conceptions of language. As Leslie Marmon Silko (Laguna) has written, "Things which do not grow and change are dead things."[8]

Putting Wilson's perspective into dialogue with others does bring one aspect of globalization into specific relief: postcolonialism. If Wilson's arguments seem to separate indigenous peoples from the larger global context, that may be her intention and, given the horrors of colonization, it would seem to be valid. My intent is not to argue against the reclamation of indigenous cultures by any means, but to emphasize that culture by definition cannot be "preserved." A better way to consider postcolonial efforts would be to state them in terms of the preservation of heritages, not the preservation of cultures. Bracketing off tradition in this way paradoxically allows it to be reincorporated into cultural performances within globalization. While colonization is certainly a breakpoint for indigenous cultures, it is clear that there have been many other breakpoints in the long history of the world. The arrival of the Blackfeet on the Northern Plains, for example, was another disruptive (but ultimately dynamic) breakpoint for all the groups coming in contact with one another at the time.[9]

In this chapter, then, I seek to bring together my previous work analyzing Native American performances with the overall question of globalization and the peculiarities of this historical moment. Again, postcolonial states are deeply significant to any discussion of culture in the current moment. However there has been too much postcolonial work on discourse.[10] If one actually seeks understanding of indigenous peoples in relationship to their global environment and seeks to create a dialogue of cultures, it would be better to examine the lived experiences of postcolonial individuals. *Human beings have the power to enact and perform change, as well as renewal.* As Benhabib[11] writes, there is not much hope for indigenous cultures to survive if they espouse a "preservationist" perspective of culture that seeks to reclaim precolonial practices. Instead Benhabib calls for an understanding of culture that focuses on the evaluative practices that continually renegotiate identity, recognition, and the dialogue of cultures.[12]

While honoring the emic perspective that some indigenous scholars like Wilson would bring to the debate, the following paragraphs attempt to represent an orientation of Northern Plains reservation giveaways as existing within a globalizing context. It is hoped that the beginning of a dialogue of cultures might be set into motion through a survey of some current problems in the study of "globalization," followed by two of its key concepts for indigenous cultures in particular: deterritorialization and the negotiation of cultural identities. First, though, it will be necessary to place globalization within overall scholarly discourse on culture and discuss a few of its challenges.

RECENT CHALLENGES TO THE STUDY OF GLOBALIZATION

Although globalization is often discussed as though it were an anomaly or peculiarity of the postmodern age, it has been in motion far longer. Some scholars point to Christopher Columbus's voyage in 1492 as the beginning of globalization. From my own perspective, as long as cultures in the "known world" were coming into contact with one another, the world has been globalizing. The conflict over trade routes between the Greeks and the Persians 2500 years ago is probably a relatively recent example of globalization, for example. So the first challenge is to recognize our own "chronocentrism"—belief in the uniqueness of special difficulties of our own time as somehow more important than the past—and to fight it as much as possible.

Nonetheless *this current brand of* globalization is significant, and it is different. As I also described above, the current moment of globalization is marked by postcolonization. Postcolonial dynamics must then be taken into account. However, this presents another challenge: for some scholars, there has been too much focus on postcolonial theory—and especially the idea of discourse—within discussions of globalization.[13] Because of the "obsession" with discourse within postcolonial theory, other aspects of cultural negotiation after colonization and within globalization have been neglected.[14]

These neglected areas also problematize the study of globalization in the current moment. The preoccupation with discourse found in most postcolonial theory means that most studies are too media oriented.[15] I argue that while global media is a major influence on the global homogenization of cultures, the process of globalization overall is much more complex. It has to do with interpersonal interaction as well, and sites such as institutions, public performances, and private relationships may be more significant than media to the actual process of globalization and its impact on lived experiences. All of these sites, for example, are crucial to Northern Plains reservation giveaways. There is very little mass media involved at all.

This focus on media also tends to emphasize the flow of globalization as being primarily from the center to the periphery, which exposes another challenge in globalization studies: there are very few examinations of the flow from periphery to center.[16] This dynamic is particularly important because it allows more insight into the dynamics of power and identity. I argue that the particulars of these flows can expose the problems inherent in the "center" cultures of the West. For example, in previous work I discussed the flow of peripheral powwow practices into the cultures of whites who like to "play Indian."[17] But a close examination reveals that this process is not so much "flow" as it is "commodification and appropriation." And, there are philosophical and emotional problems associated with this cooption of cultural practices from the periphery: the alienation and emptiness of whites who take part in such practices have been well documented (Gonzalez).

Some have argued that peoples of European descent are drawn to the practices of indigenous peoples because they are rich in tradition and spirituality, especially compared to the secularization many European cultures have experienced. Here, though, is another gap in the postcolonial and globalization literature: the impact of globalization on nonwestern spirituality has been ignored. It was reported recently that there is work on globalization and spirituality in preparation,[18] but this work has not had a broad impact in terms of *indigenous* religious practices as of yet. There is much more work to be done.

These discrepancies pertain to cultural practices and performances, and overall these have been relatively ignored in the study of globalization. Economics rather than other aspects of culture have been the focus. The question remains, how do people actually respond to globalization? There are two factors to consider here. One is that the obsession with discourse has disrupted the study of lived experience in postcolonial struggles. What are the material and interactive aspects of these realities?[19] But the second is that the method has largely been one of deconstruction. There have been virtually no interpretive analyses of texts or performances.

My call is for an additive reorientation in the study of globalization, not for the abandonment of economy as a major instigator of change. Certainly economic systems have had a broad impact on cultural performances and evaluative practices, and that is the connection that must be made. This is true in the case of contemporary gift exchange rituals in Native American communities. These rituals are in some senses a response to capitalist influences, but since giveaways are rituals, they engage these influences symbolically and sometimes even subversively. James O. Gump cites Lewis Henry Morgan's theory of individual property in the nineteenth century as the beginning of attempts to assimilate Indians into farm-owners.[20] There was a shared general sentiment among most government reservation agents at that time that giveaways detracted from the "modernization" and the assimilation of the Indians.[21]

Some indigenous societies stand on a quotidian basis in opposition to this modern paradigm of the individual attainment of wealth. In a ritualized sense, Northern Plains reservation powwow participants resist Western domination, but more importantly emphasize their own public virtues within a globalized dialogue of cultures. "The giveaway signals Indian affiliation because popular ideology, both Native and Euro-American, contrasts the Indian value of conspicuous generosity with the Anglo-American value of conspicuous accumulation."[22] This debate of "values" regarding economics is a significant one, and it is cultural. There is a need to take cultural characteristics into consideration when talking about economic impact, especially inequality.[23] The same methods should be taken to questions pertaining to globalization overall. Again this is true not merely of indigenous cultures, but for all groups. For instance, it has been argued that in Western capitalist societies, "gift giving is again becoming a social necessity where the economy excludes millions of people...."[24] In this sense, then, gift exchange as a cultural phenomenon becomes highly significant to understanding processes of globalization, both economic and otherwise.

But how *should* we study these things? This is another neglected area in the scholarship on globalization, as I mentioned above. Again, the preoccupation with text has opened the door for many Bhabhaesque meditations on discourses but also for a devastating disconnection from potential interpretive perspectives on the lived experiences of postcolonial and globalizing peoples. The best of these interpretive perspectives, I argue, would be ethnographic and emic, as well as textual. Because postcolonial theory has often been etic and has often canonized ambiguity, there are as yet no pragmatic suggestions that can be made about life in the twenty-first century. The closest recent theorists have come to practical interpretations is the assertion that neither hybridity nor particularism can characterize this historical moment; instead we require "a variety of interrelated models of identity, positionality and cultural/critical practice."[25] However, no suggestions have as yet been made in terms of what these "interrelated models" might actually be.

Given the well-documented historical precedence for creative responses to intercultural contact and economic disruption on the Northern Plains, it is possible that a reorientation toward interpretive studies of globalization may yield greater understanding of these phenomena. Globalization is yet another challenge to identity and belief. The list of these has been long and much more violent. This is not to say that globalization does not present unique challenges to continuities in the performances of public virtues. The remainder of this chapter discusses two of the challenges—deterritorialization and hybridity—in greater detail.

CULTURE AND DETERRITORIALIZATION

Deterritorialization is accelerated in the current moment of the globalization process and has been increasingly significant for the past several decades. Deterritorialization recognizes that identity is no longer supported by the places we inhabit and vice versa. The relationship between place and identity is disrupted.[26] And this process does not just refer to emigration, but the effects of immigration as well: those who stay in their native places are consistently in contacted with the representatives of other cultures and also by the growing "global culture."

Once again it is important to note that the process of intercultural contact is not new, since "natives, people confined to and by places to which they belong, [and] groups unsullied by contact with a larger world, have probably never existed."[27] But in the past this has largely been a move of center to periphery. Now, as noted above, the opposite kind of flow may be equally common. And while the people of the periphery (including indigenous peoples) may have more commonly stayed in their places of birth, Arjun Appadurai argues that the new global cultural economy "cannot longer be understood in terms of existing center-periphery models."[28]

Instead Appadurai employs a discourse of "scapes" (mediascapes, ideoscapes, ethnoscapes, and the like) to engage the current significance of imagined or even "virtual" worlds. The powwow might be thought of as one such "ethnoscape" or "ideoscape," since so much of the emic literature and data pertaining to powwows posits them as "homecomings" even in a metaphorical sense. One Salish powwow participant explained that his students at the job corps center in the Flathead Nation—in spite of their diverse tribal identities—enjoyed the powwows a great deal because "it reminds them of home."[29] Despite their deterritorialization through economy—they have come to Montana from Arizona in order to find work—they do engage in a different kind of connection to "land(ethno)scape."

But the engagement of these "scapes" is more complex in the overall globalizing context. So, while the powwow offers one example of an evaluative practice that indigenous people may employ to negotiate their "territory," it may not necessarily be translatable to the experiences of other indigenous groups. Deterritorialization is disproportionate, complex, and unpredictable. It is crucial to recognize that patterns of inequality are often reproduced in deterritorialization.[30] The powwow, thus, has positive effects for some Indians but may be seen as a "desacralization" by others.[31] Deterritorialization will also be a far more painful and agonizing process for indigenous peoples than it would for those groups (especially Europeans) who do not have a connection to the land that is as strongly spiritual as well as material.[32] Not all territories are equal!

Arif Dirlik considers this fact and suggests "We need to think in terms not just of places and holisms but also of translocal or transplace interactions that mediate the relationships between places and imperial centers, national or global."[33]

One such interaction may include the particular problems of identity and discrimination indigenous peoples suffer in the cities. For example American Indians are a "minority among minorities" in American urban centers, meaning they unfortunately find themselves marginalized by recognition that is directed toward African and Hispanic Americans rather than Natives.[34]

While the move to the cities has marked a paradigm shift in the cultural negotiations and evaluative accounts performed by Native peoples in America, deterritorialization is also textured by the existence of reservations. On the Northern Plains in particular, Indians have shown a marked resistance to migration away from their traditional lands.[35] Reservations may then represent a particular dynamic of "return to home" for indigenous peoples around the world, but the different systems need to be interrogated. James Hamill has pointed out that tribal identities remain distinct for Natives in the Southwest because there is no history of removal. In contrast, on the Plains, an "Indian" identity has emerged alongside tribal ones because of shared history and confinement to reservation areas that problematized the traditional homes of the tribes.[36] This is just one example of how complex deterritorialization can be, even for groups that initially appear to have the same economic and cultural concerns in the globalizing context.

Considering the territory of "nation" beyond the reservation is also complicated. Mary Brayboy and Mary Morgan point out that "Native Americans are nations of people living within a nation."[37] There are multiple disruptions in identities through intermarriage, migration, and the spread of intertribal symbols and performances. The "many nations" comprise just one part of the process, however. "The indigenous idea of community directly challenges the claims of the nation as 'community,'"[38] but this political reality is also an interpersonal one. The lived interactions with others outside of the reservation and Indian spheres will then result in difficult identity negotiations. In short, "Being Indian can mean living uneasily with white people."[39] Understanding this fact is key to another factor in the current moment of globalization, wherein individuals live within two or more worlds. This phenomenon (when applied to globalization with recognition of the complexity of identity negotiation as a process) is captured within concepts about "hybridity," and I discuss it in the next section.

HYBRIDITY: CULTURE, IDENTITY, AND PERFORMANCE

Arjun Appadurai argues that cultural identity is challenged in globalization. In its current form, he writes, globalization's two challenges of media and mass migration have caused identities to become unstable.[40] I add to this that not merely mass media but also interpersonal communication, participation in institutions, and encounters of Other public cultural performances all also influence identity. The "instability" to which he alludes may not fully capture the complexity of the process either. The mass media and other institutions, as well as the lived experiences to which I refer above, cause identity to be *hybridized* rather than destabilized. I make this argument because again, these influences have existed for much longer than just the last three decades or so that have garnered the attention of postcolonial theorists. We need to put globalization in a much larger temporal frame, and to actively investigate its impact on lived experiences. Are most people actually at a "loss" for what their identity is today? Or are they simply caught in a dialectic between two or more identities? This state of being is hybridity, and it more accurately describes the dynamics of cultural identities in a globalizing context.

Hybridity is not a new phenomenon either, so this moment is simply one where there is an *increase* in—or greater significance of—hybridity. Homi Bhabha claimed this process of hybridity was natural and even pure, but to understand its impact on identity it is necessary to considers the *conditions* of hybridity.[41] It has been argued that Bhabha's postcolonial theory is insufficient because of his inability to 1) clearly describe lived experiences of hybridity beyond text and 2) move away from the "cult of ambiguity"[42] where material, economic, and moral realities were irrelevant. If one actually considers the conditions of hybridity, one outcome may be the revelation that *all* cultures, and not just postcolonial ones, are marked by hybridity.[43]

Thankfully, some systematic studies of these "lived experiences" of the negotiation of identities (including hybrid ones) have begun. The main characterization of hybridity is the tension between globalization and identity, the global and the local. The global end of the dialectic may be thought of as "flow," and the local is "closure." Some scholars argue that people are aware of the "flow" of globalization and their affirmations of local identities produce "closure." This means there is always a flux in this process.[44] In short, there is always hybridity.

Although hybridity may apply to all peoples, and it certainly defines individuals as well as larger groups,[45] indigenous peoples in particular will inevitably face the question of hybridity in that globalization typically makes life in at least two "worlds" necessary. The topic of indigenous identity has been an increasingly important one in the study of current globalization issues, mainly because the metaphor "indigenous" has been highly useful in some cases of nation-making. Surprisingly then indigenism seems like it should be a "primordial" concept, but it is actually a postmodern one.[46] Indigenism is also significant to globalization debates in that it implicitly critiques deterritorialization: indigenous cultures are typically marked by their "absolute attachment to place understood concretely."[47] The dynamics of "return to home" that reservations—and especially public reservation performances like the powwow—provide is just one example of this kind of attachment.

I say that the powwow is "just one example" though because it is all too easy to exaggerate the homogeneity of indigenous views of nature, society, and other aspects of worldview.[48] Even within one regional focus on indigenous peoples of America, the Northern Plains, there are marked differences from tribe to tribe. The "hybrid identities" scholars seek to identify and understand should be approached at least in part through performances. Part of the "culture" that needs to be addressed in the study of globalization is the *performance* of culture, because performance is capable of capturing the emergent structures that continually respond to the dynamics of culture. Few other cultural artifacts or evaluative processes have this capability—least of all the text, which has remained the canonized focus of most postcolonial theory.

In situating powwow participants within the "hybrid" identities they inevitably encounter and the globalized contexts in which they live, it is hoped that the "public virtues" of giveaways come into specific relief. "Hybridity" does not mean relativization, ambiguity, or fragmentation. Hybridity is specific to the historical, interactional, economic, and communal circumstances in which the individual finds herself. Performances such as giveaways are capable of capturing all of these. As Jonathan Friedman writes, the search for self-identity "does not occur in a vacuum, but in a world already defined."[49] The impact of globalization was thus clear at the rituals I observed for this research, especially in 2005. For instance there were many verbal allusions and symbolic references to the current war in Iraq, ranging from princess' prayers for the soldiers to the carrying of veterans' shields during memorial giveaways.

Like globalization itself, this process of creativity has existed for people on the Northern Plains for many centuries. Howard L. Harrod has argued that the malleability of oral traditions and other cultural discourses among Northern Plains groups allowed them to adapt to changing conditions. Their flexibility is what allows Northern Plains Indian cultural identities to thrive.[50] And this quality is not unique to the Northern Plains. In a cross-cultural study of indigenous responses to colonization in Africa, the United States, and New Zealand, James O. Gump noted that "One of the most striking patterns of the colonial conquest is the resilience of the indigenous peoples of these regions."[51] As I stated in the opening paragraphs of this conclusion: one should not underestimate the tragic consequences of colonization, but neither should one overestimate the cultural influences of the colonizers—especially compared to the persistence of indigenous cultural legacies.[52]

These conclusions are significant to the process of the "dialogue of cultures" put forth by Benhabib.[53] Culture in her perspective is the horizon where two accountings of culture meet: first the narratives or accounts themselves, and then the evaluative practices (which she calls "second order narratives") that bring meaning to those accounts. In ethnographic research on cultural performances, many participants offer their "evaluative practices" that point to broad and incisive issues of hybridity and identity. Especially in light of the critiques that have been levied at Bhabha's "discourse obsession" in postcolonial theory, it is possible to enhance this dialogue of cultures through interpretive performance studies. At the very least, discourse should not be considered the unique loci of value in any cultural performance, but especially gift exchange.[54] In bringing together words and objects, it is hoped that postcolonial theory's neglect of material realities and lived interactions may be bridged somewhat. "Words being in the realm of the worldly, it follows by the very nature of the case that any words designed to describe a realm by definition transcendent must be inadequate to their real or supposed subject matter."[55] Discourse is limited, but dance and ritual as seen in the powwow and giveaways may yet mitigate those limits and open up greater possibilities for understanding the evaluative practices in which indigenous groups can engage in a globalizing world. These evaluative practices seem especially important for indigenous groups, since Benhabib has cautioned against the temptation to engage in a preservationist discourse regarding culture and recognition.[56] It remains to be seen whether giveaways will remain one of these evaluative practices and accountings of culture that allow for flexibility and the dialogue of cultures.

Cultural performances, then, need to be incorporated further into scholarship on the influence of globalization on cultural identities and deterritorialization. There is hope for this process, for Clyde Ellis has written that it is not the *form* but the *idea* that is paramount in these studies of cultures on the Plains.[57] For this particular moment and in this particular dialogue, ideas can and do emerge in the performances of gifting—both public and private. The ideas that I have termed "public virtues" performed in giveaways and other gifting events on the Northern Plains include narrative, kinship, competition, representation, perpetuation, revalorization, and sacrament. Watching these evolve in the context of increasing hybridity and globalization—as well as cosmopolitanism—will depend on a recognition of culture as dynamic, emergent, and transcendent beyond discourse.

NOTES

1. Benhabib. *The Rights of Others: Aliens, Residents and Citizens* (Cambridge: Cambridge University Press, 2004).

2. Benhabib. *The Claims of Culture: Equality and Diversity in the Global Era* (Princeton: Princeton University Press, 2002).

3. Appiah. *Cosmopolitanism: Ethics in a World of Strangers* (New York: W.W. Norton, 2006).

4. Benhabib, *The Rights of Others;* Benhabib, *The Claims of Culture.*

5. Appiah, *Cosmopolitanism.*

6. Benhabib, *The Claims of Culture.*

7. Wilson. "Reclaiming Our Humanity: Decolonization and the Recovery of Indigenous Knowledge." Devon Abbott Mihesuah and Angela Cavendar Wilson (eds). *Indigenizing the Academy: Transforming Scholarship and Empowering Communities* (Lincoln: University of Alaska Press, 2004), 69–87.

8. Silko, *Ceremony* (New York: Penguin, 1997), 132.

9. Kelton, "Visions of a Lost World" in *American History Illustrated,* 27(6)(1993): 50–59.

10. San Juan, *Beyond Postcolonial Theory* (New York, St. Martin's Press, 1998).

11. Benhabib, *The Claims of Culture.*

12. Ibid.

13. San Juan, *Beyond Postcolonial Theory.*

14. Ibid.

15. Ibid.

16. Nurse, "Globalization and Trinidad Carnival: Diaspora, Hybridity, and Identity in Global Culture," *Cultural Studies* 13.4 (1999): 661–690.

17. Roberts, "Emotivism and Pseudocultural Identities" *The Howard Journal of Communications* 14.4 (2003): 295–308.

18. Collins, "Review: *Spiritual Perspectives on Globalization (Rifkin),*" *Library Journal* (January 2003): 120.

19. San Juan, *Beyond Postcolonial Theory.*

20. Gump, "A Spirit of Resistance: Sioux, Xhosa, and Maori Responses to Western Dominance, 1840–1920," *Pacific Historical Review* 66.1 (1997): 21–52.

21. Ellis, "'We Don't Want Your Rations, We Want This Dance': The Changing Use of Song and Dance on the Southern Plains," *The Western Historical Quarterly* 30.2 (1999): 133–154; Kracht, "Kiowa Powwows: Continuity in Ritual Practice," *American Indian Quarterly* 18.3 (1994): 321–348.

22. Kehoe, "The Giveaway Ceremony of Blackfoot and Plains Cree," *Plains Anthropologist* 25.87 (1980): 24.

23. Mushinski and Pickering, "Inequality in Income Distributions: Does Culture Matter? An Analysis of Western Native American Tribes," *Journal of Economic Issues* 34.2 (2000): 403–413.

24. Godelier, "Some Things You Give, Some Things You Sell, but Some Things You Must Keep for Your Selves: What Mauss Did Not Say about Sacred Objects," in Edith Wyschogrod, Jean-Joseph Groux, and Eric Boynton, (eds.) *The Enigma of Gift and Sacrifice* (New York: Fordham University Press, 2002), 21.

25. Moore-Gilbert, *Postcolonial Theory: Contexts, Practices, Politics* (London: Verso, 1997), 203.

26. Tomlinson, *Globalization and Culture* (Oxford and Cambridge: Polity Press, 1999).

27. Ibid, 129.

28. Appadurai, *Modernity at Large: Cultural Dimensions of Globalization* (Minneapolis: University of Minnesota Press, 1996), 32.

29. Brazill, "The Powwow for Me Is a Very Religious Experience," in Johnny Arlee(ed.) *Over a Century of Moving to the Drum* (Helena, Montana: Montana Historical Society Press, 1998), 86.

30. Tomlinson, *Globalization and Culture.*

31. Ruml, "The Desacralization of the Powwow? Some Initial Observations," *Papers of the Algonquin Conference* 31 (2000): 333–338.

32. Dirlik, "Globalization, Indigenism, and the Politics of Place," *Ariel* 34.1 (2003): 25.

33. Ibid, 26.

34. Fenelon, "Discrimination and Indigenous Identity in Chicago's Native Community," *American Indian Culture and Research Journal* 22.4 (1998): 273–303.

35. Archer and Lonsdale, "Geography of Population Change and Redistribution within the Post-Frontier Great Plains," *Great Plains Research* 13 (2003): 56.

36. Hamill, "Being Indian in Northeast Oklahoma," *Plains Anthropologist* 45.173(2000): 291–303.

37. Brayboy and Morgan, "Voices of Indianness: The Lived World of Native American Women," *Women's Studies International Forum* 21.4 (1998): 348.

38. Dirlik, "Globalization, Indigenism, and the Politics of Place," 21–22.

39. Lincoln, *Native American Renaissance* (Los Angeles: University of California Press, 1983), 185.

40. Appadurai, *Modernity at Large.*

41. Tomlinson, *Globalization and Culture.*

42. San Juan, *Beyond Postcolonial Theory.*

43. See also Kraidy, "The Global, the Local, and the Hybrid: A Native Ethnography of Globalization," *Critical Studies in Mass Communication* 16.4 (1999): 456–476.

44. Meyer and Geschiere, *Globalization and Identity: Dialectics of Flow and Closure* (Oxford and Malden: Blackwell Publishers, 1999), 2.

45. Kraidy, "The Global, the Local, and the Hybrid."

46. Dirlik, "Globalization, Indigenism, and the Politics of Place."

47. Ibid, 16.

48. Ibid, 22.

49. Friedman, "The Past in the Future: History and the Politics of Identity," *American Anthropologist* 94.4 (1989): 837.

50. Harrod, *Becoming and Remaining a People: Native American Religions on the Northern Plains,* (Tucson: University of Arizona Press, 1995).

51. Gump, "A Spirit of Resistance," 50.

52. Dirlik, "Globalization, Indigenism, and the Politics of Place," 17.

53. Benhabib, *The Claims of Culture.*

54. Keane, *Signs of Recognition: Powers and Hazards of Representation in an Indonesian Society* (Berkeley: University of California Press, 1997).

55. Burke, "What Are the Signs of What? A Theory of 'Entitlement,'" *Anthropological Linguistics* 4.6 (1962): 18.

56. Benhabib, *The Claims of Culture.*

57. Ellis, "We Don't Want your Rations, We Want this Dance."

BIBLIOGRAPHY

Appadurai, Arjun. *Modernity at Large: Cultural Dimensions of Globalization.* Minneapolis: University of Minnesota Press, 1996.

Appiah, Kwame Anthony. *Cosmopolitanism: Ethics in a World of Strangers.* New York: W.W. Norton, 2006.

Archer, J. Clark, and Richard E. Lonsdale. "Geography of Population Change and Redistribution within the Post-Frontier Great Plains." *Great Plains Research* 13 (2003):43–61.

Benhabib, Seyla. *The Claims of Culture: Equality and Diversity in the Global Era.* Princeton: Princeton UP, 2002.

Benhabib, Seyla. *The Rights of Others: Aliens, Residents, and Citizens.* Cambridge: Cambridge UP, 2004.

Brayboy, Mary E., and Mary Y. Morgan. "Voices of Indianness: The Lived World of Native American Women." *Women's Studies International Forum* 21.4 (1998): 341–354.

Brazill, Brian. "The Powwow for Me Is a Very Religious Experience," in Johnny Arlee (ed.) *Over a Century of Moving to the Drum.* Helena, Montana: Montana Historical Society Press, 1998.

Burke, Kenneth. "What Are the Signs of What? A Theory of 'Entitlement.'" *Anthropological Linguistics* 4.6 (1962):1–23.

Collins, William P. "Review: *Spiritual Perspectives on Globalization (Rifkin)*," *Library Journal* (January 2003): 120.

Dirlik, Arif. "Globalization, Indigenism, and the Politics of Place," *Ariel* 34.1 (2003): 15–19.

Ellis, Clyde. "'We Don't Want your Rations, We Want this Dance': The Changing Use of Song and Dance on the Southern Plains," *The Western Historical Quarterly* 30(2) (1999): 133–154.

Fenelon, James V. "Discrimination and Indigenous Identity in Chicago's Native Community," *American Indian Culture and Research Journal* 22.4 (1998): 273–303.

Friedman, Jonathan. "The Past in the Future: History and the Politics of Identity," *American Anthropologist* 94.4 (1989): 837–859.

Godelier, Maurice. "Some Things you Give, Some Things you Sell, but Some Things You Must Keep for Yourselves: What Mauss Did Not Say about Sacred Objects," in Edith Wyschogrod, Jean-

Joseph Goux, and Eric Boynton (eds.). *The Enigma of Gift and Sacrifice.* New York: Fordham UP, 2002. pp. 19–37.

Gump, James O. "A Spirit of Resistance: Sioux, Xhosa, and Maori Responses to Western Dominance, 1840–1920," *Pacific Historical Review* 66.1 (1997): 21–52.

Hamill, James. "Being Indian in Northeast Oklahoma." *Plains Anthropologist* 45.173 (2000): 291–303.

Harrod, Howard L. *Becoming and Remaining a People: Native American Religions on the Northern Plains.* Tucson: University of Arizona Press, 1995.

Keane, Webb. *Signs of Recognition: Powers and Hazards of Representation in an Indonesian Society.* Berkeley: University of California Press, 1997.

Kehoe, Alice B. "The Giveaway Ceremony of Blackfoot and Plains Cree." *Plains Anthropologist* 25.87 (1980): 17–26.

Kelton, Elmer. "Visions of a Lost World," *American History Illustrated* 27.6 (1993): 50–59.

Kracht, Benjamin R. "Kiowa Powwows: Continuity in Ritual Practice," *American Indian Quarterly* 18.3 (1994): 321–348.

Kraidy, Marwan M. "The Global, the Local, and the Hybrid: A Native Ethnography of Globalization," *Critical Studies in Mass Communication* 16.4 (1999): 456–476.

Lincoln, Kenneth. *Native American Renaissance.* Los Angeles: University of California Press, 1983.

Meyer, Brigit, and Peter Geschiere. *Globalization and Identity: Dialectics of Flow and Closure.* Oxford and Malden: Blackwell Publishers, 1999.

Moore-Gilbert, Bart. *Postcolonial Theory: Contexts, Practices, Politics.* London: Verso, 1997.

Mushinski, David W., and Kathleen Pickering. "Inequality in Income Distributions: Does Culture Matter? An Analysis of Western Native American Tribes," *Journal of Economic Issues* 34.2 (2000): 403–413.

Nurse, Keith. "Globalization and Trinidad Carnival: Diaspora, Hybridity and Identity in Global Culture," *Cultural Studies* 13.4 (1999): 661–690.

Roberts, Kathleen Glenister. "Emotivism and Pseudocultural Identities," *The Howard Journal of Communications* 14.4 (2003): 295–308.

Ruml, Mark F. "The De-sacralization of the Powwow? Some Initial Observations," *Papers of the Algonquian Conference* 31 (2000): 333–338.

San Juan Jr., E. *Beyond Postcolonial Theory.* New York: St. Martin's Press, 1998.

Silko, Leslie Marmon. *Ceremony.* New York: Penguin, 1997.

Tomlinson, John. *Globalization and Culture.* Cambridge and Oxford: Polity Press, 1999.

Wilson, Angela Cavender. "Reclaiming Our Humanity: Decolonization and the Recovery of Indigenous Knowledge," in Devon Abbott Mihesuah and Angela Cavender Wilson (eds.). *Indigenizing the Academy: Transforming Scholarship and Empowering Communities.* Lincoln: University of Nebraska Press, 2004. pp. 69–87.

■ ■ ■

Cosmopolitan Communication Ethics Understanding and Action

Religion and Dialogue

JOHN STEWART

As I reflect on this volume's theme, "Communication Ethics: Cosmopolitanism and Provinciality," three recent experiences stand out for me. One began several months ago as I learned about some potentially serious problems in my university's Hong Kong MBA program. We were in the middle of serving our third cohort of Chinese students when we began receiving complaints about the private Hong Kong college that had recruited most of them. Some students who were having difficulties in our courses reported that they were unfamiliar with some content because, as it turned out, they had been enticed to purchase, rather than earn their baccalaureate degrees. Our review of these students' transcripts supported our suspicions. There was surprisingly little difference among the courses or grades reported on these students' apparently phony academic records. We contacted two other universities who had worked with this Hong Kong institution and each expressed concerns about its integrity, but neither felt certain enough to take any action. When I met with the president of the Hong Kong college, a reserved and evasive Chinese businessman, I got little from him other than denial and stonewalling. At that point, my university terminated its working relationship with his institution, which meant that we had to give up the opportunity to provide services to these students, forego the income stream, and that we had to report our suspicions to our accreditors, who, thankfully, were very supportive.

The second event began when our university emerged from a year-long search for a director of our Center for Character and Ethics Education with a finalist who has a very impressive resume. This person earned a philosophy Ph.D. at a prominent university, teaches at a respected institution where he has experienced considerable success, has authored several books, one of which is widely used in character and ethics courses across the curriculum, chaired a national working group on educational reform, and speaks broadly on character and ethics issues. Our president offered him the position, and the troubles began. Initially, he wanted much more money. Then he wanted less teaching. Then he wanted his administrative power more centralized. Put off by the escalating demands, the president decided that we had made a mistake and terminated negotiations, whereupon our apparent paragon of ethical rectitude sent emails threatening legal action, made abusive telephone calls, and generally acted very unprofessionally.

A third experience that helps shape this chapter occurred over several months in the summer of 2005. With the help of my recommendation, one of our faculty members who teaches ethics was granted tenure by our Board of Trustees, to be effective fall 2005, and appointed to a special character and ethics professorship. Apparently unaware of the fact that the decision had to be confirmed by a signed fall term contract, this person began behaving as he seemed to think a tenured professor could behave, by asking to be among the highest paid faculty at the college, demanding the removal of a provision that is a part of every faculty contract, and refusing to collaborate in the college's response to a colleague charged with plagiarism. In several meetings, this professor exhibited the kind of hubris that, frankly, scares administrators. He insisted that he alone accurately understood the ethical dimensions of the plagiarism case, that he should be able to apply university sanctions, and that he should have special financial and procedural status. The University determined that his demands constituted a counter-offer and did not re-offer the tenure contract that he had been asked to sign. It did offer another tenure-track contract, at which point this ethics professor signed and falsely dated the original tenure contract. When the University refused to honor the altered contract, the professor sued.

As I continue to live through each of these experiences, I have reflected on what the events display about the people involved. It seems apparent that the president of the Hong Kong university has built a system that entices vulnerable Chinese students to buy their way into an American MBA program. Obviously, the students are also at fault; they should not have paid him. But the ethical problems here seem to begin either with the culture or with the greedy Chinese businessman. The case of our choice to head the ethics center appears clearly to be one where the professor doesn't practice what he preaches. He has an inflated view of himself; for some reason he can't see the irony of his unethical demands. In the third case, the un-tenured ethics professor also appears to suffer from a serious case of hubris. From his vantage it's "my way or the highway"; nobody but him knows how to act ethically, and since we don't see the error of our ways, he's suing us.

All of this is part of what I conclude when I ask what each of these events *displays* about the people involved. But I am finding as I live through these events that there is a much more important question, a question that connects me directly with the theme of this volume. Rather than focusing on what these events *display* about the people involved, it has been much more fruitful for me to notice what the events *are asking* of me. Every self-righteous bone in my body is comforted by my inferences, attributions, and speculations about the character and ethics *displayed* by the Chinese businessman, the famous author, and the colleague. AND in the process, I learn virtually nothing about Communication Ethics and Culture. Insights about this theme only emerge when I move beyond blaming to serious reflection about how to *understand* what has happened in these three cases and how to *choose or act in response* to them.

In this essay, I want to offer for your consideration one suggestion about how to understand ethically problematic communication situations and one suggestion about how to act in response to them. Those of you who are familiar with the literature of ethics and communication will probably be able to categorize my suggestions as consequentialist, utilitarian, deontological, naturalist, or some other option. But I want to emphasize practice rather than philosophical analyses or labels. I want mainly to offer, as my extended turn in this conversation, two suggestions that have so far proved helpful for me as I have worked to cope with these three very practical and very concrete ethical challenges and others like them.

FROM GLOBALIZATION
TO COSMOPOLITANISM

The first drafts of many of the reflections that make up this volume prominently featured the term "globalization." As the project developed, our language evolved to what is now evident: This book's title and four of the chapter titles feature "cosmopolitanism," and "globalization" appears in a chapter title only once. This shift in conceptual label began for me with a conversation with my friend and mentor, Walt Fisher. Walt recommended that I read Kwame Anthony Appiah's 2006 book: *Cosmopolitanism: Ethics in a World of Strangers.* As is usual with Walt's book ideas, this turned out to be an excellent suggestion. Appiah argues that "cosmopolitanism" is a more functional term than "globalization" because, as he puts it, "globalization" began as a term that "referred to a marketing strategy, and then came to designate a macroeconomic thesis, and now can be seen to encompass everything, and nothing."[1] If you are not persuaded by Appiah's point, remember that communication scholar and teacher Barnett Pearce introduced the term "cosmopolitanism" into the communication discipline's vocabulary in the 1980's, when he contrasted it with "ethnocentrism."[2] It appears to me that Pearce's meaning very nicely complements the direction of this volume.

Another reason that the term "cosmopolitanism" is attractive is that, as Appiah notes, there are two strands that intertwine in the notion of cosmopolitanism, and parallel strands intertwine in the two suggestions I want to make. One strand is global and the other is local. As Appiah explains, the first strand of cosmopolitanism is the idea that we have obligations to others, obligations that stretch beyond those

> to whom we are related by the ties of kith and kind, or even the more formal ties of a shared citizenship. The other is that we take seriously the value not just of human life but of particular human lives, which means taking an interest in the practices and beliefs that lend them significance. People are different, the cosmopolitan knows, and there is much to learn from our differences.[3]

The global strand, which parallels my suggestion about understanding, draws on the realization that humans and cultures are profoundly similar. As Appiah notes in the second sentence of his book, if a normal baby girl born forty thousand years ago were kidnapped by a

> time traveler and raised in a normal family in New York, she would be ready for college in eighteen years. She would learn English (along with—who knows?—Spanish or Chinese), understand trigonometry, follow baseball and pop music; she would probably want a pierced tongue and a couple of tattoos. And she would be unrecognizably different from the brothers and sisters she left behind.[4]

These fundamental similarities across time and cultures provide a rationale for anchoring understanding in a global perspective or fundamental orientation. And this general orientation is not enough. To respond fully to ethical challenges like the ones I've outlined, we need both global insight and local action. This is the operational definition of cosmopolitanism.

SUGGESTION #1: INHABIT A RELIGION
TO ENHANCE UNDERSTANDING

My first suggestion parallels the global dimension of cosmopolitanism. The suggestion is to inhabit a religion to enhance understanding. I am convinced that individuals and groups can cope more effectively with ethical challenges when we enhance our understanding by inhabiting a religious perspective.

Now there are at least three immediate reasons to reject this suggestion and another that would qualify the suggestion. The first reason to reject it is the scientistic or positivist claim that religion is an unverifiable construction of idealistic dreamers. I have to say with respect to this claim that, if you really believe that the world is made up wholly of facts, that values do not exist because they cannot be empirically verified, and hence that one cannot move from an 'is' to an 'ought,' and if you believe that, since nobody has ever proved that God exists, She does not; then you will not want to follow this suggestion. On the other hand, if you acknowledge the self-contradictions inherent in an objectivist world view, and acknowledge the truth of the aphorism, "There are no atheists in foxholes," this perspective will not automatically dissuade you from at least an openness to the possible validity of a religious perspective—any more than it dissuades the vast majority of the world's population.

A second reason to resist religion is historical and cultural. This argument insists that it is unwise to take the risk of applying a way of understanding that has historically brought humanity the Crusades, the Inquisition, the Ku Klux Klan, skinhead fascism, and Al Qaeda. The response to this challenge can only be another historical argument: it does not make sense to reject either science or religion because of its mistakes. In both cases, the inherent social (and hence self-critical) features of the enterprise legitimate not throwing out the baby with the bathwater. Moreover, it has to be significant that every recorded human culture across time has embodied in its artifacts, death practices, and language the acknowledgement of some kind of higher power. Historically, humans seem to acknowledge universally that if life is a ride on a tandem bicycle, humans are not in the front seat.

A third reason to reject religion out of hand is rooted in the claim by Jean-Francois Lyotard and other postmodernists that there can be no efficacious meta-narrative.[5] The first problem with Lyotard's claim is that it embodies a performative contradiction because it offers yet another metanarrative—"There are no metanarratives"—in the place of the ones it attempts to negate. More constructively, postmodern western theologians such as Mark C. Taylor,[6] Robert P. Scharlemann,[7] and David Tracy[8] have proposed accounts of religion in general and Christianity in particular that are informed by Nietzsche, Heidegger, Foucault, and Derrida. Tracy's account,[9] for example, prominently features such terms as "pluralism," "analogical language," and "dialogue," and affirms the global-plus-local analysis that Appiah[10] outlines. So the postmodern criticism of theological systems has not eliminated the usefulness of ethical guidelines that continue to make up important parts of contemporary religious traditions.

The primary challenge to qualify my suggestion is anchored in the distinction between a spiritual program and a religion. Huge percentages of respondents to many recent surveys in this and other countries affirm spiritual interests, while membership in many religious organizations continues to fall. On the one hand, I believe that the benefits that result from following this suggestion occur because of the doctrinal and liturgical elements that mark traditional religions, and from the experiences of community that are equally important. I do not mean to suggest that a vague sense of spirituality will suffice. On the other hand, twelve-step programs would fit my definition of "religion." There is enough liturgy and community in them to provide the benefits that give this suggestion traction.

The Dalai Lama affirms this distinction between spirituality and religion and argues that spirituality is enough.[11] Importantly, he does so from a position solidly within a rich and nuanced religion, and his preference can be understood as a tenet of his religious commitment, not just his spirituality. Moreover, the consequentiality and impact of the values that he affirms—"love and compassion, patience, tolerance, forgiveness, contentment, a sense of responsibility [and] a sense of harmony"[12]— come largely from the teachings, ritual, prayer, and practices that make up the various *religions* that humans inhabit. In other words, one reason to mistrust vague spirituality is that it is difficult to connect with concrete ethical practices.

You notice, of course, that this suggestion about understanding does not prescribe that one's religion must be Judeo-Christian. Every established religious tradition includes prominent ethical components, and writers as diverse as C.S. Lewis and John Hick have demonstrated how similar they are in many significant ways. In a classic essay, for example, Hick collected ten expressions of what he calls "the silver rule and the golden rule" from Hinduism, Buddhism, Jainism, Confucianism, Taoism, Zoroastrianism, Judaism, Greek philosophy, Islam, and Christianity.[13] Unfortunately for contemporary readers, the idea that these eternal verities might actually be true in some cross-culturally and non-relativist way has been rendered offensive by writings authored by the likes of James Dobson and William Bennett. But Hick and Lewis offer considerably less ethnocentric versions of this idea that, when it is expressed as describing a readily observable feature of many historically prominent sacred texts, is difficult to deny.

Whether one references the eight-fold path of Buddhism, the Decalogue of the Old Testament, the beatitudes of Christianity, or the five pillars of Islam, it is clear that overlapping religious frameworks have played a prominent role in developing and enhancing human ethical understanding. From our contemporary vantage, the practices that these understandings have promoted do not all make sense. Today, animal sacrifice seems both quaint and economically ill-advised, and human sacrifice is universally viewed as a perversion. There also continue to be gray areas and importantly ambiguous cases. Suicide bombers can find textual support in the Koran just as those who bomb Planned Parenthood offices can point to isolated verses in the Bible, reminding us that religious involvement clearly involves ethical risk.

But the vast majority of Westerners and Easterners, Northerners and Southerners, readily distinguish between mainstream religious practices and the radical fringes. All but the most obstinate observer can clearly recognize the similarities among—and the existential luminescence of—the Dalai Lama, the Pope, the Patriarch of Constantinople, and many—though not all—rabbis, ministers, pastors, nuns, and priests. In other words, in the majority of cases, for the majority of the people involved, traditional organized religions offer considerable solace, support, confirmation, insight into the human condition, and, most important for my purposes, guidelines about how to recognize and to make ethical decisions and take ethical actions. As Gordon Allport put it in the middle of the last century, "The developed religious sentiment…is not a mere matter of dependency or of reliving the family or cultural configuration…. These and many other factors…form a comprehensive attitude whose function is to relate the individual meaningfully to the whole of Being."[14] This is a main reason why I suggest that it is easier to cope with and respond to an ethical challenge from inside a religious perspective than from outside any religious orientation—if that stance is even possible.

There is a second, equally important way that religion can enhance ethical understanding, namely, by emphasizing the fundamentally tensional nature of human being. The simplest way to think of this idea is with the help of the familiar yin-yang or Tai-Chi symbol. This symbol has come to express the interrelatedness of all nature and the presence in each element of the world of aspects of its opposite or counterpart. As one author puts it, "Yang is like man. Yin is like woman. Yang wouldn't grow without Yin. Yin couldn't give birth without Yang."[15]

The European-American philosopher of history Eric Voegelin also argued that this tensionality is the fundamental feature of human being. As he puts it, "The super-constant above the constants is…the experience of the paradoxic tension in formative reality."[16] From both these viewpoints—the ancient Chinese and the contemporary western—reality is tensional. This means that humans inhabit an in-between reality. In between what and what? Well, the danger of this follow-up question is that it encourages hypostatization, because it turns the poles that co-constitute the tension into things or objects and deforms the tension into a feature of the objective world.

At the risk of falling into this kind of trap, let me try to clarify this claim about tensionality with the help of two pretty familiar polarities: growth/deterioration and immanence/transcendence. The caveat, though, is that this clarification will also introduce some distortion.

After scratching your forearm, there will be dead cells under your fingernails. Part of the truth of humans is that our cells are continually dying. We are deteriorating, even as I write and you read. At the same time, our bone marrow is producing cells. It is literally the case that human bodies—along with other beings—are simultaneously deteriorating and growing. What it means to be growing can only be understood in relation to our deteriorating. What it means to be deteriorating can only be understood in relation to growing. These two events occur, and can only be understood, as tensional. Growth is what it is only in relation to deterioration, and deterioration is what it is only in relation to growth.

Consider a second polarity. If cut, a human bleeds. Each of us is embodied, and human bodies are finite, limited, and mortal. And that is not all there is to us. We are also social and cultural beings. Humans experience dreams that link us to other places, times, and peoples. Across time, humans have buried our dead, often with artifacts, rituals, and prayer. All humans are finite, and in addition, virtually universal human practices implicate a fundamental awareness of elements beyond and independent of materiality. In other words, humans are both immanent and transcendent. Human immanence is understandable only in relation to human transcendence, and vice-versa. Humans live in this tension, too. Immanence-and-transcendence is another part of the tension of human existence.

At one point in the Christian Bible, the apostle Paul poignantly reminds his readers how each of us can be confounded by concrete examples of this tensionality. "For I do not do what I want, but I do the very thing I hate," Paul writes, and "I do not do the good I want, but the evil I do not want is what I do" (Romans: 7.15 & 19). [17] Martin Buber's interpretation of both Psalms and Arabic scriptures similarly reveals that these ancient civilizations historically understood humans to be tensional amalgams of good and evil.[18] And from a fourth perspective, Buddhism teaches that the path to the cessation of suffering is the way between the two extremes of self-indulgence and excessive self-mortification.[19]

I am convinced that cosmopolitan understanding of an ethical challenge can be significantly enhanced by the ethical guidance and the tensional insight that emerge when one inhabits a religious tradition. Importantly, my understanding of ethical challenges is also inherently incomplete. This is part of a tensional understanding, too. Even after I have carefully done my self-reflective and empirical homework, my strongest stance should never be more final than what Allport termed "half-sure yet wholehearted."

SUGGESTION #2: OPEN A SPACE FOR DIALOGUE

As I mentioned, the first element of cosmopolitanism is global and this second element is local. In Appiah's words, this second element takes "…seriously the value not just of human life but of particular human lives, which means taking an interest in the practices and beliefs that lend them significance. People are different, the cosmopolitan knows, and there is much to learn from our differences."[20] I suggest that a useful local move that is consistent with Appiah's analysis is to open a space for dialogue.

My "open a space" language echoes aspects of David Bohm and his interpreters Peter Senge, William Isaacs, and others.[21] I appreciate their reminder that there is no technology or series of steps that can guarantee dialogue's emergence, and that there are decisive communicative choices that can materially increase the probability that dialogue will occur.

So what is the shape of this local move toward dialogue? It is described in a book that Martin Buber wrote over 80 years ago, a book that has been translated into over twenty languages and become one of the world's most widely read ethical texts. *I and Thou*[22] is notable partly because it was one of the first works to challenge the subject-object analysis of the human world established as truth by Descartes and other Enlightenment writers. Alongside, and in tension with subject-object analyses, Buber identified and described a way of contacting things, persons, and God that is (in its pure form) objectless. This way of contacting or relating—he called it "dialogue"—is grounded in the particularity that Appiah identifies as the second element of cosmopolitanism. As Buber put it, this "fold" of the human's twofold orientation to what surrounds him or her begins as the human

> encounters being and becoming as what confronts him[or her]—always only *one* being and every thing only as a being…Nothing else is present but this one, but this one cosmically. Measure and comparison have fled…The world that appears to you in this way is unreliable, for it appears always new to you, and you cannot take it by its word. It lacks density, for everything in it permeates everything else. It lacks duration, for it comes even when not called and vanishes even when you cling to it. It cannot be surveyed: if you try to make it surveyable, you lose it. It comes—comes to fetch you…. It does not stand outside you, it touches your ground…. [23]

Thus for Buber, dialogue is the label for a quality of contact that begins from the acknowledgement of uniqueness and develops as the people involved are willing and able to talk and listen in ways that maximize the presence of the other features that make them persons—immeasurability, presentness, reflectivity, and addressability.

In the years between the publication of *I and Thou* and his death in 1965, Buber wrote hundreds of books, chapters, articles, and talks that unpacked both the philosophical anthropology and the practical advice that are outlined in *I and Thou*. I have spent a good part of my career working to understand Buber's insights, increase their accessibility, connect them with works from other dialogic traditions, and to support the efforts of dialogue practitioners inside and outside the communication discipline. I have done this because I believe that Buber points toward concrete and practical ways to cope with the singularity of ethical challenges.

The two crucial parts of Buber's philosophical anthropology that do this are his identification of "the between" as a "primary category of human reality"[24] and his description of the defining feature of human being—uniqueness—and its correlates:

immeasurability, reflectivity, addressability, and presentness.[25] Humans can learn and can choose to attend to the between, and we can also, to greater or lesser degrees, make present or absent in our speaking and listening the features that constitute human being. As I've noted, dialogue consists of communication that maximizes the presence of these features of the personal; dialogue occurs when the people involved are able to let the other happen to them while holding their own ground.[26]

Now, one could move from this descriptive, definitional effort to an ethical stance by simply equating dialogue with "good communicating." Some of my early writing left itself open to this interpretation, which has led some critics to characterize as naive my work and the writings of other dialogue theorists and teachers. As these critics justifiably and accurately point out, the move to equate dialogue with "good communicating" ignores, among many other things

- The human functionality of Burger King cashiers, ticket takers, and food line servers;
- The complicated means-ends relationships in some stages of negotiation that argue for the appropriateness of strategic ambiguity, over-and under-statement, and even some forms of deception;
- Cultural features that limit the appropriateness of dialogue, such as gender relationships in some Latin and Arab cultures and age relationships in some Asian cultures.

All these features of human and social complexity contextualize my suggestion to open a space for dialogue. But, as important as these caveats are, it would be halfhearted to stop with them. At this point in my understanding, I would describe the communicative "should" that follows from this practical suggestion in three parts. First, one should develop the competencies to open a space for dialogue in the situations you encounter. Second, one should identify and engage our default dialogue index, and third, one should pursue dialogic uptake. I will take each of these in turn.

The first competency is *conceptual clarity.* One should develop a clear understanding of the important distinctions that have been made by dialogue theorists and practitioners. Critical distinctions from Buber include the duality of being and seeming, the distinction between imposition and unfolding, the practice of imagining the real of the other, the difference between the social and the interhuman, the quality of spokenness, the tension between maxim and situation that "demands not our obedience but ourselves,"[27] the connection between distance and relation, and the nature of the between. Also useful are Gadamer's distinction between *Erlebnis* and *Erfahrung,* his use of *Die Sache* and "world," and his notion, "fusion of horizons."[28] Bakhtin contributes centripetal/centrifugal forces and the responsive feature of all communicative actions.[29] Bohm's treatment of dia-logos is valuable, as are his characterizations of fragmentation and proprioception.[30] It is also important to learn, for example, to identify the questioning practices that have been tested and refined by dialogue practitioners at the Public Conversations Project,[31] the dialogue strategies and tactics explored by the Public Dialogue Consortium,[32] and distinctions among critical, empathic, and dialogic listening.[33]

The second competency is *willingness*. It will not work to try to make spaces for dialogue because somebody else wants you to. One has to genuinely want to promote dialogue. Willingness or motivation without conceptual clarity, practical competence, and reflection generates little more than empty enthusiasm. But conceptual clarity and competence without genuine motivation create manipulation. If one's written and oral conversations with dialogue authors and practitioners do not ring true with one's experience, keep doing the research. In my judgment, one should only pursue this quality of communicating in one's own life if you genuinely believe in the possibility of dialogue and the possibilities for dialogue.

The third competency is *skills*. One experiences the distinction between conceptual clarity and practical ability. Despite one's understanding of eye behavior in one's culture, where does one actually gaze while talking and listening? What do sound recordings reveal about the rate, pitch, volume, and vocal quality of your voice? How does one manage space? How quickly or slowly, smoothly or abruptly does one move? How does one's awareness of the impact of time and timing affect how long one pauses after asking a question? How close is the fit between one's interpersonal intent and the effects of your speaking and listening? Some people develop practical interpersonal skills in their acculturation; others benefit from the help of a teacher, tutor, mentor, or coach; and others never quite get there. Part of what it takes to open a space for dialogue, however, consists of concrete behaviors skillfully adapted to the cultural context.

The fourth competency is *reflection and adjustment*. Opening a space for dialogue also takes constant quality improvement. As contemporary conversation analysts demonstrate, dialogue can be facilitated and extinguished by micro-momentary shifts in word choice, eye behavior, vocal tone, and gesture. This quality of contact is continually emergent, at the edges of temporal and spatial limits, ongoing and processual. As a result, it requires constant attention and nurturing. Skilled practitioners of dialogue are continually—although often mindlessly—self-monitoring and adjusting to maintain this quality of contact in the midst of the myriad of changing elements that make up the communicative flow. Responsible dialogic engagement, I believe, requires all four of these competencies.

The second element of opening a space for dialogue is consistently to engage one's default dialogue index. I mean this to be a playful way of suggesting that one might choose aspects of dialogic communicating as our default mode of relating and might assign to this mode a probability or appropriateness index that shifts with the contexts we encounter. So I might strive, roughly eighty percent of the time, to choose first to speak and listen in ways that maximize the presence of the personal, and to let the other happen to me while holding my own ground. Part of my resolve is to hold my communicative feet to this fire. I have already described briefly several reasons why it is unwise to attempt to open a space for dialogue in every communication situation. But it is important for me to be committed to doing my part to enhance the probability of dialogue's occurrence in as many of my communication experiences as possible. This is the rationale for this second element: First, understand and then initiate dialogue as often as you can, or as Buber[34] put it, "*quantum satis.*"

The third requirement of opening a space for dialogue is to pursue uptake. In other words, when one's efforts at initiation strike a promising chord, continue to maximize the presence of the personal and to let the other happen to you while holding your own ground. You may be mistaken about the other's willingness and ability, and sometimes one will encounter a brick wall. But, no pain, no gain; no risk, no reward. If dialogue is going to be a real possibility in one's life, I believe that you will need to help it happen.

CONCLUSION: THE POSSIBILITY OF DIALOGUE, THE POSSIBILITIES FOR DIALOGUE

As I inhabit a religious tradition and open a space for dialogue, I am led to several tentative conclusions. First, the key question in each case is not, "What ethical system is operating here?" or even "What ethical choices have others made?" but the key dialogic question requires my response—"What does this situation ask of me?"

It is much easier to think systematically about communication ethics and to offer guidelines and suggestions than it is to respond effectively to the demands of concrete ethical challenges. Nonetheless, I personally find that I am helped most when I can bring to bear the combination of my religious understanding and my commitment to dialogue.

NOTES

1. Appiah, *Cosmopolitanism: Ethics in a World of Strangers* (New York: W.W. Norton, 2006), xiii.

2. Pearce, *Communication and the Human Condition* (Carbondale: University of Southern Illinois Press, 1989), 120.

3. Appiah, *Cosmopolitanism,* xv.

4. Ibid., xi.

5. Lyotard, *The Postmodern Condition: A Report on Knwledge* (Manchester, IN: Manchester University Press, 1984).

6. Taylor, *Erring: A Postmodern A/Theology,* (Chicago: University of Chicago Press, 1987); Taylor, "The End(s) of Theology," in Sheila Greeve Davaney (ed.) *Theology at the End of Modernity* (Philadelphia: Trinity Press International, 1991).

7. Scharlemann, *The Reason of Following: Christology and Ecstatic* (Chicago: University of Chicago Press, 1991).

8. Tracy, *Plurality and Ambiguity: Hermeneutics, Religion, Hope* (Chicago: University of Chicago Press, 1987).

9. Ibid.

10. Appiah, *Cosmopolitanism.*

11. Dalai Lama, *Ethics for the New Millennium* (New York: Riverhead Books, 1999), 20.

12. Ibid., 22.

13. Hick, "Religious Pluralism and Salvation," *Faith and Philosophy* 5 (1988): 365–377.

14. Allport, *Becoming: Basic Considerations for a Psychology of Personality* (New Haven: Yale University Press, 1955), 50–51.

15. *http://www.chinesefortunecalendar.com/yinyang.htm* Retrieved 3.26.06

16. Voegelin, *Order and History, Volume V: In Search of Order,* Ellis Sandoz, (ed.) (Columbia, MO: University of Missouri Press, 2000), 124.

17. *New Oxford Annotated Bible,* 3rd ed, M.D. Coogan (ed.) (Oxford: Oxford University Press, 2001).

18. Buber, *Good and Evil* (New York: Charles Scribner's Sons, 1952).

19. *http://www.thebigview.com/buddhism/index/html.* Retrieved 3.19.06.

20. Appiah, *Cosmopolitanism,* xv.

21. Bohm, *On Dialogue* (Ojai, CA: David Bohm Seminars, 1990); Isaacs, *Dialogue and the Art of Thinking Together* (New York: Doubleday, 1999); Senge, *The Fifth Discipline: The Art and Practice of the Learning Organization* (New York: Doubleday, 1999).

22. Buber, *I and Thou* (New York: Charles Scribner's Sons, 1970).

23. Ibid., 84–85.

24. Buber, *Between Man and Man* (New York: Macmillan, 1965), 203.

25. Buber, *I and Thou,* 84–85.

26. Stewart and Zediker, "Dialogue's Basic Tension," in John Stewart (ed.), *Bridges Not Walls: A Book about Interpersonal Communication,* 9th ed. (New York, McGraw Hill, 2006).

27. Buber, *Meetings* (LaSalle, IL: Open Court Press, 1973), 26.

28. Gadamer, *Truth and Method* (New York; Crossroads, 1989).

29. Holquist, *Dialogism: Bakhtin and his World* (London: Routledge, 1990).

30. Bohm, *On Dialogue*.

31. *http://www.publicconversations.org* Retrieved 3.26.06.

32. *http://www.publicdialogue.org* Retrieved 3.26.06.

33. Stewart, Zediker and Witteborn, *Together: Communicating Interpersonally, a Social Construction Approach* (Los Angeles: Roxbury, 2005); Stewart, Zediker and Black, "Relationships Among Philosophies of Dialogue," in *Dialogue: Theorizing Difference in Communication Studies,* Anderson, Baxter, Cissna, (eds.) (Thousand Oaks, CA: Sage, 2004).

34. Buber, *Between Man and Man*.

BIBLIOGRAPHY

Allport, Gordon. *Becoming: Basic Considerations for a Psychology of Personality.* New Haven: Yale University Press, 1955. .

Appiah, Kwame Anthony. *Cosmopolitanism: Ethics in a World of Strangers.* New York: W.W. Norton, 2006.

Bohm, David. *On Dialogue.* Ojai, CA: David Bohm Seminars, 1990.

Buber, Martin. *Good and Evil.* New York: Charles Scribner's Sons, 1952.

———. *Between Man and Man.* Trans. R. G. Smith. New York: Macmillan, 1965.

———. *I and Thou.* Trans. Walter Kaufman. New York: Charles Scribner's Sons, 1970.

———. *Meetings.* LaSalle, ILL: Open Court Press, 1973.

Dalai Lama, His Holiness. *Ethics for the New Millennium.* New York: Riverhead Books, 1999.

Gadamer, Hans-Georg. *Truth and Method.* 2nd ed. Trans. J. Weinsheimer & D. G. Marshall. New York: Crossroad, 1989.

Hick, John, "Religious Pluralism and Salvation," *Faith and Philosophy,* 5 (1988), 365–377.

Holquist, Michael. *Dialogism: Bakhtin and his World.* London: Routledge, 1990.

Isaacs, William. *Dialogue and the Art of Thinking Together.* New York: Doubleday, 1999.

Lewis, C. S. *The Abolition of Man.* New York: Macmillan, 1944.

Lyotard, Jean-Francois. *The Postmodern Condition: A Report on Knowledge.* Manchester, IN: Manchester University Press, 1984.

New Oxford Annotated Bible. 3rd ed. Ed. M.D. Coogan. Oxford: Oxford University Press, 2001.

Pearce, Barnett. *Communication and the Human Condition.* Carbondale: Southern Illinois University Press, 1989.

Scharlemann, Robert P. *The Reason of Following: Christology and the Ecstatic.* Chicago: University of Chicago Press, 1991.

Senge, Peter. *The Fifth Discipline: The Art and Practice of the Learning Organization.* New York: Doubleday, 1990.

Stewart, John, Karen. E. Zediker, and Laura Black, "Relationships among Philosophies of Dialogue." *Dialogue: Theorizing Difference in Communication Studies.* Ed. Rob Anderson, Leslie A. Baxter, and Kenneth N. Cissna. Thousand Oaks, CA: Sage, 2004.

Stewart, John, Karen E. Zediker, & Saskia Witteborn. *Together: Communicating Interpersonally, A Social Construction Approach.* 6th ed. Los Angeles: Roxbury, 2005.

Stewart, John & Karen E. Zediker. "Dialogue's Basic Tension." *Bridges Not Walls: A Book about Interpersonal Communication.* Ed. John Stewart. 9th ed. New York: McGraw-Hill, 2006.

Taylor, Mark C. *Erring: A Postmodern A/Theology.* Chicago: University of Chicago Press, 1987.

———. "The End(s) of Theology." *Theology at the End of Modernity.* Ed. Sheila Greeve Davaney. Philadelphia: Trinity Press International, 1991.

Tracy, David. *Plurality and Ambiguity: Hermeneutics, Religion, Hope.* Chicago: University of Chicago Press, 1987.

Voegelin, Eric. *Order and History Volume V: In Search of Order.* Ed. Ellis Sandoz. Columbia, MO: University of Missouri Press, 2000.

http://www.thebigview.com/buddhism/index/html. Retrieved 0.19.06

http://www.chinesefortunecalendar.com/yinyang.htm Retrieved 3.26.06

http://www.publicconversations.org Retrieved 3.26.06

http://www.publicdialogue.org Retrieved 3.26.06

■ ■ ■

Community at the End of the World

PAT J. GEHRKE

"We know, indeed, that it is the end of the world, and there is
nothing illusory (nor 'fin de siecle' nor 'millenarian') about this
knowledge."—Jean-Luc Nancy[1]

Today, in every corner, we hear that the world is ending or, and perhaps more accurately, that it has already come to an end. In the arts, the humanities, and the sciences,
discourses rally to face the end of the world, or to refuse it stubbornly, or to build a
new world. Of course, the planet, life, and humans continue after the end of the
world, but we are today faced with the fact that we no longer belong to a world. As
Jean-Luc Nancy put it, "no longer a *mundus,* a *cosmos,* a composed and complete
order (from) within which one might find a place, a dwelling, and the elements of
an orientation."[2] Whatever is left after the end of the world, it fails today to provide
signification; it recedes from attempts to give it meaning and significance. This is
not to say that life has become unimportant and certainly not that living together is
no longer a serious problem. Quite to the contrary, it means that life and living
together are of the utmost importance, of supreme vitality, for they no longer can
be determined or guided by any order or meaning or purpose that we might once

have found in the world, in philosophy, in ethics, or in community. Instead of the world today we have, Nancy wrote, "a heap, and perhaps a foul one (*un monde immonde*)."[3]

This same sentiment is echoed with various accents and intonations throughout the academy, even while public political discourse profusely and dogmatically refuses the possibility of this end. In the social sciences the world has given way to a cacophony of minutiae that obstinately refuse any overarching organization. In the physical sciences every grand unifying theory becomes either so theoretical and speculative as to delve back into the realm of dubious metaphysics or else is contested and revised and refused by incorrigible phenomena even before it is published. This is not to say that we don't know anything, that we don't have any truths, but quite exactly the opposite. We know far too much, we have an overflowing abundance of truths, and among all this no world can be found. Instead, all this knowledge and all these truths make not a world, but a heap, and perhaps a foul heap at that.

In the wake of all this there is still the sheer fact that we live together. We are living with others. If the fundamental problem for thinking in the early 20th century was being in the world, perhaps best expressed in Martin Heidegger's concern for *Dasein,* today in the early 21st century the question of our time is being together. In Heidegger's terms, then, we find the problem of thinking not to be *Dasein,* but *Mitsein: being-with* (or more literally, *with-being* or being *as with*). What does it mean to be *as with?* How can we be *as with?* While philosophy was obsessed with the question of *being,* the speciality of *being-with* was the provenance of ethics, politics, and rhetoric (the Aristotelean triumvirate). Philosophers and other scholars often located the order and meaning of the *with* in *being,* usually understood as a rational or at least coherent substance that could engender the world with meaning. Thus, the end of the world has also been the end of ethics, the end of politics, and the end of rhetoric. Largely immune to Heidegger's own warning that our obsession with *Sein* would betray us, we still stand in shock at the end of the world. In the retreat of the world as world, in the arrival of the heap, there is also a retreat of politics, ethics, and rhetoric that leaves in its wake the remainder of simply *being as with.*

All of this is not to say, of course, that we are no longer confronted with the political, the ethical, and the rhetorical, any more than we are no longer confronted with the fact that we are living together here and now, even if *we, living, here,* and *now* can no longer form a *world.* Instead, it means simply that we have lost what John Caputo called our "*terra firma.*"[4] Caputo described this disquieting situation as finding himself standing on "an island adrift in a vast sea, so that even if he stands absolutely firm he is in fact constantly in motion. Add to this the thought that the sea is endless, the sky starless, and the island's drift aimless, and you gain some measure of the level of my consternation."[5] Yet, in all this we cannot stop being confronted by the ethical, the political, and the rhetorical. The end of ethics, politics, and rhetoric was simply the end of any determinate meaning, system, or order that might vouchsafe for the ethical, the political, and the rhetorical. Instead, faced with the heap, we ask now how we can be *with* each other. In short, what is the practice of *being as with?* Like Ronald C. Arnett, many today are asking whether something like community is even possible or desirable.[6] One might ask, to put it another way, how one can think about the ethical, the political, or the rhetorical at the end of the world. These are serious questions. They are serious not because of the answers they might provoke but because of the importance of the questions as questions. In these questions is a distress, a destituteness, that might only find voice when the world falls away. Perhaps it is this very distress and destituteness that carries us to the return of the ethical, the commandment of community, and the possibility of communication at the end of the world.

One response to the world's end, and a perfectly reasonable one in many ways, is to seek out some thin thread of theoretical or anthropological commonality upon which one might hang a new world. In many ways this has been the charge of cosmopolitanism for the past three centuries. While cosmopolitanism has been around since the Ancients coined the term (*cosmos* + *polis*), today the principles of cosmopolitanism as both a political enterprise and philosophical system derive largely from Immanuel Kant's ethical writings and his 1784 essay, "Idea for a Universal History with a Cosmopolitan Purpose." While the common thread seems to thin and fray with each passing decade, in the 20th century it was John Rawls and similar neo-Kantians who launched the defense of cosmopolitanism, which resonated with legal and political endeavors ranging from the United States' Civil Rights Act of 1964 to the United Nations' Universal Declaration of Human Rights to Lyndon Johnson's War on Poverty. Yet, there is a significant problem for cosmopolitanism: we no longer have a *cosmos*. Yes, we have a planet (a ball of dirt and gases revolving around a star) and the stars still appear in the sky, but they no longer make a *world*. If there is anything like a *cosmos* left to us today, it lacks any signification that might give it meaning, it cannot offer even the thinnest of threads upon which the world might hang.

While one may object that cosmopolitanism composes a variety of different but interconnected projects (as does Catriona McKinnon[7]) that interconnection has depended upon a universalization of at least some fundamental but substantive principle of justice. As David Held has pointed out, in order to justify such universal principles, cosmopolitanism has most often relied upon some notion of "impartialist reasoning," whether that be the autonomous reason of Kant's ethics or Rawls's veil of ignorance and the original position.[8] The end of the world, however, rips the rug from beneath any such appeal to impartial universals. If we can find anything that is, in any sense, left to the status of universal today, it is an anthropological commonality that can be traced historically to determine its moment of emergence and the relations of power that accompanied its establishment and transformation. Thus, in place of the kind of impartial or grand universals promised in Kant and Rawls we are left today with partial universals: perhaps manifestations of globalisation, colonialisms, or regimes of power/knowledge that excise all exceptions to produce anthropological uniformities and then celebrate them as universal principles. These are partial not in that they are incomplete or fragmented (which they may or may not be) but because they are interested, they are invested in certain relations and plays of power or relations of domination.

This critique has devastated cosmopolitanism in the past decades, thinned it into an ephemeral specter of a philosophy, but as it faded the question of community came to the fore. After all, was not cosmopolitanism the dream of a global community? Was it not the articulation of the possibility of the community of all people? Of community *par excellence?* In one very important way the answer must be yes: Cosmopolitanism was the sincere and complete articulation of the dream of community grounded in the *in-common,* the shared. As such, it sought to be the final articulation of the world that would allow the world to manifest as embodied cosmology. But, like all such notions of community, it was predicated upon a significant violence. As Alphonso Lingis wrote, "The community that produces something in common, that establishes truth and that now establishes a technological universe of simulacra, excludes the savages, the mystics, the psychotics—excludes their utterances and their bodies. It excludes them in its own space: it tortures."[9] This is not the exclusion that forces one to leave the city, that banishes one to be outside the space of the community. Much worse, "it excludes them in its own space"; it banishes those it excludes but retains them within its space, in a state of captive and perpetual banishment. It tortures.

And so we come to the problem of community at the end of the world. There is no denying that we are still living with each other—we must live with each other. We are *Mitsein: being as with,* but we have no *in-common* with which we might make sense of either *being or with.* Or, if there is any *in-common* it is already partial: suspect, interested, embroiled in history and relations of power, refusing to allow it to become the grounds for any answer. We are left with nothing less (nor more) than the mere existence of being-with. Put succinctly: *the sheer fact that we are "with" is the (and the only) determinate fact of community.*

In this space one might hope for the production of some negotiated or intersubjective ground through an idealized or impartial event of communication. Yet, the critique of the in-common has made not only the impartial suspect but also placed into question the status of communication. This includes not only the notion of communication as sharing but also the status of language as shared and the possibility of the inter-subjective. It would take a particularly idealized and perhaps even naïve view of communication to sustain a faith in speech or writing as the pathway to uncovering a pregiven in-common substance or the balanced procedure for establishing mutually beneficial agreements and intersubjective truths. The critiques of language and communication as systems of power and as historically situated institutions have not only been well documented by the likes of Jacques Derrida and Michel Foucault but also by more traditional linguists such as James Milroy and Lesley Milroy and scholars of lexicography like Ronald Wells.[10] Even modes of grammar, standardization of spelling and pronunciation, and the practice of definition have been traced to class conflict, racial discrimination, gender biases, colonialisms, and innumerable other partialities.

Given this situation, being placed here at the end of the world, in nothing more than the sheer fact of *being as with,* what is left for the thinking of community and communication? What can we say of community or communication at the end of the world? One temptation may be to transpose the question of being onto the question of community. If the question is no longer what is the essence or meaning of being, perhaps it is instead what is the essence or meaning of community. In such a transposition, however, the question returns to a question of being, subordinating the issue of community to a status or condition of being. It returns us to the ontological attention to being and away from the phenomenological attention to *with.* Indeed, in the move from *Dasein* to *Mitsein* the focus must shift not only from *Das* to *Mit* but also from *Sein* to *Mit.* The impetus here is not to push our thinking toward an ontology of community, but to the sheer fact of *with;* the sheer fact of community. *Mitsein* is the subordination of all questions of *sein* to the sheer law of community; it is not a being who is with other beings (or not simply this) but is being *as with.* This is not a community of laws, but the mere law that there is no being other than, outside of, or beyond the sheer fact of *with.* Put this way the *with* is not a precondition of being and not the ground of being, but is the totality of the fact of being. As Nancy put it, "The question should be the community of being and not the being of community. Or, if you prefer: the community of existence and not the essence of community."[11] We turn, then, to the sheer fact of community, on face, and not to any meaning, structure, or form that might be given to community or communities. Of course, this is much closer to what Heidegger himself had proposed in the notion of *Mitsein* than what became of that term as it circulated throughout the humanities.

Compearance is the term that Nancy and others use to describe this simple and sheer notion of *being as with.* At its simplest *to compear* is simply to appear, usually before someone else, such as a judge or magistrate. This is not far afield from the sheerest notion of community. "To appear before" articulates the awesome simplicity of *being as with,* the sheer fact that one does not appear to oneself or alone, one does not appear and then come into community, but that appearance is always *appearance-to* or *appearance-with,* compearance. It is at this point that we can perhaps finally do away with all appeal to *being*. In compearance we find a clarity that can circumvent the confusion of *Mitsein* and *being-with*. If we are too easily diverted by the recurrence of the themes of being—our obsession with *Sein*—then perhaps we are best served by a term that has the least appeal to *being* possible within the confines of our partial language. In compearance is the simple fact of appearing before, appearing with, that does not require any reason or purpose or substance be given to that appearance. In fact, compearance does not require even any connection, purpose, or sharing. Nancy wrote, "Compearance is of a more originary order than that of bond."[12] It is, indeed, prerequisite to any bond or substance or relationship that might emerge between whatever singular humans might compear. There is the sheer fact of compearance, this simplest event, and all meaning, all interpretation, and all communication is only possible in its wake. Through language we make sense of— give sense to—compearances, but such a "making sense" must also retreat from the sense of compearance as such.

In this shift to a discourse of compearance of singularities we disperse the unity of being, finally divesting ourselves of the inheritance of *Sein,* whether *Dasein* or *Mitsein.* Beings may instead be simply (and not-so-simply) singular events of compearance. Singularities are the points of compearance, the simple "taking-place" as Giorgio Agamben wrote.[13] For Nancy, singularities "designate precisely that which, each time, forms a point of exposure, traces an intersection of limits on which there is exposure."[14] To place it in more Foucauldian terms, a singularity is the interplay of forces, relations, discourses, and practices that form a point of articulation at a given moment—a point that we might call a person, a subject, an individual, you, or I. As such, one cannot coherently speak of a being that comes into community with other beings but instead speaks of an appearing-to, a compearance, and every compearance is singular, interested, scattered, historical, and conditioned, not as a prerequisite of its existence but as its very existence, *qua existent.*

Singularity, thus, is the "exposure itself, punctual actuality" of compearance, not any kind of identity or identification.[15] In its punctual actuality, singularity testifies to its finitude, its temporality, the fact that it is just this compearance here and now. Such an exposure is the most fundamental, most important, and perhaps most elusive thought of communication. In every communication, in whatever form or media or mode, in the recurrence of the inevitable event of communication, there is the punctuating and recurring announcement of the compearance of singularities. What is unleashed in communication, wrote Nancy, "is the *passion* of singularity as such… of sharing its singularity."[16] This sharing is not a sharing of any substance, bond, blood, commitment, or commonality; at least not beyond the simple fact that all appearance is compearance, that singularities are dependent upon the continual compearance of/with other singularities for their own possibility. Thus, communication is not *first* the communication of any quality or characteristic or idea, but *first and most vitally* it is "a relation that communicates no sense other than the relation itself."[17] Put perhaps more simply: the first and most vital fact of communication is the communication of compearance and singularity without giving any shape, meaning, or substance to compearance or to singularity beyond the simple, sheer fact of compearing singularity.

Before (and within and through) all our thoughts and attempts at communication as sharing or bridging or offering or exposure of thoughts or meanings or subjectivities there is always (and also) this communication of singularities compearing. It is thus, Nancy explains, that "singular beings are given—without a bond *and* without communion, equally distant from any notion of connection or joining from the outside and from any notion of a common and fusional interiority. Communication is the constitutive fact of an exposition to the outside that defines singularity."[18] Of course, this does not mean that I don't say words, have sentences, full of weight or levity, but that the first question of ethics and community is not found in these words or in anything I say, but in a far more originary communication that thrusts singularities into compearance. If we have been attentive to communication theory and to the importance of communicating and listening, we have done so at the expense of listening to this *arche*-communication. If we have been concerned with authentic dialogue and effective techniques of discussion, it has been at the expense of the dialogue of compearing singularities. At the end of the world we need another form of listening, not because all of these other theories and principles have been wrong or misguided, but because they have made us look away from the sheerest truth of community at the end of the world. We have heard what compearing singularities are saying but been deaf to the saying of compearing singularity as such. Communication at the end of the world is the listening to/for this incommunicable community of singularity.[19] What we need here, at the end of the world, is an art of such listening/communicating, an art of communication that can give due attention to the compearance of singularities as the *arche*-articulation of community and the very possibility of ethics.

The term *art* here may be misleading, but let me be clear that in its selection I wish to distinguish what is needed from any kind of program, method, or system that might serve to regiment means or modes of interaction and communication. An art cannot vouchsafe our passage, it does not ensure results, it cannot command an end, and it is decidedly *un*scientific. These qualities are not only necessary for the possibility of listening to compearing singularities but may themselves be expressions of that art of listening. In Ancient terms we might call an art a *techne*,[20] but to do so we would have to unshackle *techne* from its contemporary inheritance of techniques and technologies that left only the merest residue of judgment and *praxis* and amplified instead predictability and productivity. Rather, the art of communication at the end of the world must be without sovereignty or domain. As Nancy put it, what we need is a *techne* that can "resemble a *praxis* more than a *poiesis*. It transforms its agent—itself and the technician—more than it fashions a product."[21] There is no doubt that much consideration and thought must inform such an art, as must be the case for every art, but it is not a theorization in the sense of *theoria;* it does not offer a synoptic or panoptic view of its object: but gives us instead a fragmentary and fractal vision that opens up tactics that can enable a concerted effort to listen to the compearance of singularities first, before and always while (but never instead of) listening to what is said.

The critical move for the ethics and politics of communication at the end of the world is to develop this attitude of listening, this art that would strive to maintain the question of ethics and the question of politics *as questions.* It is striving to practice the ethics of the demand for an ethics, what we can also call the ethico-political.[22] The maintenance of the question as question is an attempt to guard the importance of the question from all those attempts to answer it, those attempts to give it law, closure, or dogma that would make the question recede and be forgotten under the signs of the juridical or the moral. As Nancy put it, "the obligation is not to unravel an infinite number of successive questions" but instead, "the obligation is more simply, more modestly, one of maintaining [*garder*] the question as question."[23] Alternatively, one could articulate this "question" as a call, as Jacques Derrida and Emmanuel Levinas did. In one of his conversations with Nancy, Derrida argued that the accent of the call differs somewhat from that of question, as it implies an obligation and responsibility of which one can never be acquitted.[24]

In both the case of Nancy's *question* and Derrida's (and Levinas's) *call,* one of the key elements is the irrevocable, that of which one cannot be acquitted or declined. In stark distinction from liberalism and humanism the call or question asks not for the answer but for an engaged and incessant response. The responsibility is to guard the question as question, listen to the call, and respond so as to keep the question and the call open. The greatest offense to the question (or call) of the ethico-political would be to respond so as to foreclose the return of the question or predetermine future responses. Instead, an ethico-political *techne* is an art of communication as "enjoyment and suffering rather than completion and verification."[25] To practice such requires not only a certain modesty in regards to the approach of the call, the event of the question, but also an acceptance of one's inevitable vulnerability and weakness. Here Nancy uses the term "distress;" Derrida preferred the word "destitute," and we can find a connection to what Maurice Blancot termed "disaster."[26] This is the experience of not knowing what to do, of really being faced with the question as a question, and being stuck there, having been called out of oneself, interrupted, unable at that moment to apply an archetype, schema, or answer. Instead one is called into response, to face the radical question of ethics and politics, in a space in which the response can have no model, the question can have no answer, except perhaps the art of guarding the openness to this sheer compearance, which itself is neither a model nor an answer. This is an art of guarding the question, of maintaining the call, holding on to this distress and destituteness as the communication of the community of sheer compearance. Here, if there can be anything like *being* it is not a thing, *a being,* but a practice, an art of compearance, a *being-with* which is not a being with other beings but a "with-ness," the mere fact that all appearing is compearing.

Of course all of this still leaves one with the inescapable and impossible question, "What is to be done?" One is confronted by the urgency of the problems before us every day, regardless of one's political or philosophical inclinations: the recurrence of State-sponsored violence, the starvation of millions of people, the poisoning of the planet, the despair and ennui of the lives of so many, the perpetual looming promise of nuclear, chemical, or biological catastrophe, the unyielding brutality of poverty, the viciousness of mundane daily life, and the list goes on until one is all-but-suffocated beneath this foul heap. Surely, something must be done. Of this there can be no doubt. The great danger, and this may have been the ultimate failure of cosmopolitanism, is that asking "What is to be done?" is most commonly to ask, as Nancy noted, "'how to act' in order to achieve an already given goal. 'Transforming the world' then means: realising an already given interpretation of the world, and realising a hope."[27] Under this model we find ourselves always stuck in the generation of and commitment to speculative and counterfactual ideals. The *noumena* of community, politics, justice, ethics, and communication are placed prior to and govern over the phenomenal, even before the phenomena occur. We are called to make answers in advance or at least to produce a formula or schema that can readily provide us these answers. We are given hypothetical tests and calculations that are to be our yardsticks. We gain models and systems of response, standardized techniques of communication, ethical credos, universal principles of rights and duties, but in each such move we turn further and further away from this first phenomenal fact of community and the distress of its interruption of all our ready systems of response. To paraphrase Nietzsche, we adopt a certain nihilism in which we turn ourselves away from our lived experience—the facticity of the sheer compearance of community as phenomena—and turn instead to the Ideal, to this community of "perfected" relations between people. This is the ultimate nihilism, a saying "no" to all of this life to dwell instead in that which is beyond or other to life. It defiles this life, staining it with sin at its very origin, defining it as fallen from grace, yet simultaneously placing us under the rule and conscription of a perfect god. It tortures.

Yet, something must be done. We cannot deny the importance, the very inescapability of the "What is to be done?" The move cannot be to turn away from this question but instead to understand that in the community at the end of the world we must find another way to ask it. "What is to be done?" must be asked, but in the communication of community as sheer compearance the question cannot carry with it the presumption of that "already given goal." Instead, it must be asked again with no goal at all, except, perhaps, an attentiveness to compearance. This is the first and most vital political step to be taken today: to ask "What is to be done?" without presumption of an ideal, a goal, an interpretation of the world that the doing ought to achieve. That very question itself is the opening space for the emergence of a politics of democracy, a democratic politics, a democracy that is not a totem or artifice, democracy that is not a State or a system, a democracy that has no need of universal rights or common principles of humanity. This must be the most basic and perhaps most radical democracy: a democracy that can be open to everything and everyone, a democratic democracy, a radical democracy.

At the end of the world perhaps no project is more important or more precarious than the development of democracy. In the retreat of sense and signification we are left without any sense of meaning, purpose, or objective (which is not to say with nonsense, which itself can be a type of sense).[28] We are adrift like Caputo without so much as the stars in the sky to guide us. So, what then can democracy mean? We must first separate democracy from all those common and contemporary uses of it that would equate it with the organization of a State and a Market. As democracy is conflated with the neoliberal and neoconservative dreams of "market democracy" it becomes a system of governmentality and economy. It is this problem of contemporary "democracy" that will, as Nancy put it, "destroy 'democracy' if 'democracy' persists in tolerating it."[29] The end of the world threatens that in the retreat of sense and signification the only thing left for market democracy will be its naked brutality as a part of expanding global markets, a sort of spectral God-term that has no substance except its own righteous indignation at the bodies and blood that would stand in the way of its expansion. In this kind of "democracy" there is no difference between democracy and totalitarianism: neither can permit or sustain that which would oppose it. Indeed, nothing could be more undemocratic than the democracy that demands your allegiance, your loyalty, your belief in it or its ideals.

Instead, if we are to engage in a process of democratic politics it must shift its attention away from the State as the site of politics or the guarantor of democracy. We must take up democracy as an event of living. We must take up democracy as an art of living. We must work toward a politics of communication, a politics of the compearance, a politics of a community that is "without father or mother, anterior rather than posterior to all law and common substance."[30] What could such a politics of communication look like? How can one think or speak in a tone, an accent, an inclination that would guard the question or call of ethics and politics, that would pay attention to this anterior law of democracy that has no common substance? First, it must be a politics of communication that is "taken in the opposite sense of all our communicative ideologies."[31] It must find a movement that does not depend on the shared, the in-common, the making-common, or the intersubjective that for so long have (and continue to have) an overbearing influence on our thinking of communication. It resides first in communication as the event of compearance, as the announcement (and incessant invocation) of the sheer community made of nothing more than the fact that appearing is always appearing *with* or appearing *before* an Other—a specific other before me.[32] It must be a communication that always remains open, guards its own openness and vulnerability against all those impulses that would validate or invalidate the specific movements of conversations that take place within it. As such, a truly democratic communication space will be without any essential definition. As Charles Scott wrote, "It verifies neither the play of power that dominates within it for a time nor the insurrections that interrupt the effectiveness of these powers."[33] Instead, it is a communication that has no first principles at all, no guiding moral or ethical credo or law, no political objective or goal, except to maintain its openness and recurrence, to be on the guard, on watch, for all those moves that would attempt to control communication by subordinating it to a law.[34]

This politics of democratic communication shares with Ron Arnett and Pat Arneson's articulation of dialogic civility a responsiveness "to the demands of the historical moment."[35] In the historical moment it needs no grand theory or ideal principle upon which to base action but finds its tactics and articulation in each moment. As Scott said of Foucault's politics, it "refuses an overarching, theoretical justification and rests its case on specific, highly focused problems of power within circumstances that call for action and that can change and lose both necessity and urgency."[36] In this way, the art of compearance is always manifest in a spatio-temporal locality while bounded to infinite space and time. To put it another way, all compearance always occurs on a finite plane of interaction, but the boundaries of that plane's geography and chronology move infinitely as we approach or recede from them, like the horizon. In short, we exist in localities and can only act in the space of those localities, but there are no definite borders or contours to these localities.

Thus we may come to something like a contingent provincialism or an uncommitted localism. The importance of the contingent and the uncommitted should not be underestimated. In the art of compearance all relations are always in process, always moving, in that every moment is yet another appearance-to and appearance-with that again makes possible the very idea that I might speak or act or respond in any way. Thus any province or locale cannot be determinate or a site of commitment in itself but is a pragmatic yet indeterminate experience of space (both geographic and virtual) as well as time that opens the locality's borders to all forms of immigration and emigration, joyfully risking not only the mutation but the very dissolution or reconstitution of that space and time. The provincialists' insistence upon a defined province or a commitment to the local smothers compearance under the instantiation of substance and meaning so that the function of the *with* can only be to realize the pregiven purpose, model, or meaning of that pre-given community. Contrarily, in the suspension of determination and the withdrawl from commitment one leaves open spaces for a democratic art of compearance that grounds itself in nothing more nor less than the simple fact that all appearance is compearance, that before every bond, purpose, commitment, sharing, agreement, or fraternity there is the simple and sheer *with*.

The thinness, the insubstantiality, of this *with* may yet still be enough to hold us to one another. Rightly its irrevocable call is of an order more awesome and compelling than every purpose or meaning that has ever been given to the world. Could this by itself be enough to meet the standard set by Arnett for "an action or idea that pulls people together, reminding them of their collective existence?"[37] Rather than an institutional ideal such as a democratic republic or an ideological commitment such as liberalism, perhaps we can accustom ourselves to merely compearance and cultivate a practice of democratic living that can be engaged, but open. The first meaning of democracy is thus to practice democracy, to engage democratically, to leave everything open for renegotiation. If one practices a democratic art of compearance (and it seems that any art of compearance would have to be democratic or else risk losing all sight of compearance) then there is no issue, no status, no law that cannot itself be open for revision.

The very right of citizenship itself must be unhinged from the institution or even the geography and borders of a state. In ancient Athens there was no penalty more severe, more awful, than to be stripped of citizenship. As Socrates articulated in the Crito and Levinas explained in *Otherwise Than Being*, it was a fate worse than death. While non-citizens may be expelled from a city or state, they can also be imprisoned within the very institutions that deny them citizenship, enslaved either literally by law or figuratively by poverty, enclosed within the economy and the legal system, retained within the space of the State, while being denied any legitimate existence in any of these spaces. While market democracies must protect the rights of citizenship to ensure stability in markets (which take priority over democracy in these governments, or perhaps more accurately become the very meaning of democracy), a democratic art of compearance cannot excise the Other as non-citizen but takes all who traverse a space to be potential citizens of that space.

In the democratic art of compearance citizenship is not a legal right granted or taken away by a state, but a set of practices and a mode of engagement with a locale. As Nancy put it, "Citizenship is one or more roles, one or more procedures, a way of carrying oneself, a gait."[38] There is no foundation to citizenship, no meaning to it, except as given by this particular locale at a particular moment. The citizen is the one who "occupies and traverses this space, the one who is defined by it, by the sharing of its exteriority," and thus as space and time move or as one moves with space and time the complex arrangement of rights and obligations entwined with citizenship are refigured and renegotiated.[39] Understood thus, the undocumented worker is a citizen of this space and time, engaged and approachable, invested and interested, traversing this space and invited to participate in the democratic art of compearance. The very constitution of this locale and what it may call upon its citizens to do or what it might enable them to accomplish are thus as open to all who traverse it as to any other if we can step back from our insistence to give this locale a determinate meaning or purpose, if we can accept the necessity of being committed to being uncommitted.

Cosmopolitans have often objected that common substance or at least a common commitment is necessary for collective problem solving. Indeed, even committed provincialists have made such claims, differing only on the scope of the commonality in question. The cosmopolitans will concede, as Held put it, that one does not need to give up local concerns such as affiliations to family and countrymen but insist that we "must acknowledge these as morally contingent" and that our most important duties are to "humanity as a whole."[40] The tension and difficulty given by both views lie largely in their assignation of some determinate boundary that would delimit the geography as local or global. In cartographic terms, provincialists are stuck with the decidedly arbitrary choice of assigning borders to localities: shall we say that river over there is the limit, or that row of trees, or a zip code line, or a school district division, or the division of representation in the lower body of a congress or parliament, or a county line, or a city limit, or the edge of a cluster of ethnically similar families and businesses, or at the site of a linguistic shift, or where the mountains impede my vision? Alternatively, cosmopolitans are confronted with the need to give the world meaning so that one can actually bring the cosmos to bear upon decision and action. In the end, both camps tend to concede a great deal to the other with provincialists agreeing that one must take broad concerns of the greater world into account, even if only for one's own long-term benefit, while cosmopolitans concede that we reside in and most practically act at the local level based upon local knowledge. The battle then resides on the matter of where one ought to place greater weight when conflict between the local and the global emerges.

The problem, of course, is that all these things are far too fluid and open to new configurations at every moment. What counts as the space being traversed may not only be geographic but also lie on a plane of interests or concerns that have nothing to do with geography. Likewise, whatever might be left to be said of this heap we have instead of a world, there is no doubt that all its practices and operations can change radically and in relatively brief time. If there is to be anything like community or ethics at the end of the world, it cannot hold fast to the commitments and beliefs that are grounded in determinate localities, substantive being, or any meaning to the cosmos. Instead, perhaps we can settle into the disquieting and awesome call (or question, if you prefer) of community and ethics at the end of the world. It is a call and a question that has the primary operation of forestalling any answer. In fact, to provide an answer is to fail to answer to the call. The call is to call us out of ourselves, out of our cosmologies and defined localities, to experience the distress that must be awakened if we are to attempt something like a democratic art of compearance. Thus, perhaps, compearance can offer us a democratic art of living that needs no model, no rules, and no meaning, except that it must always be taken up again and again, in every moment. The distinction between local and global and the span of localities or the scope of citizenship likewise become fluid elements of practices that can shift suddenly as one moves from an interaction or event to another. It leaves us open to beliefs and ideas and events as they confront us and makes all outcomes negotiable.

Foucault once said he believed in everything. This can only be a sensible statement if we can separate belief from commitment. What I think Foucault was hinting toward is that it is not the belief in things that causes so much trouble but the commitment to those beliefs. We must believe in the possibility of everything but retract from commitment to any particular thing. If one can believe without commitment, then one can be open to all belief, open to a democratic exchange and transformation of belief.

There is a great skepticism about this kind of social and political practice. A democratic art of compearance is met from both the liberal and conservative with an incredulity at its disavowal of commitment and a serious pessimism about its hope for a better future. In no small part this may be because traditional political and rhetorical theory has strongly wedded commitment and belief. However, part of this has to do with the project of Western political philosophy since the Classical period: to find an institutional arrangement that can best ensure the most ideal conditions of living at least for its own citizens if not for humanity more broadly. Indeed, even ethical theory has largely sought out ideal institutional configurations or else the replication of the institutional and bureaucratic system in the individual through moral codes. In the formulation of laws, rules, and procedures for ethical life, the *techne* of *ethos* was reduced to the technical apparatus of ethical systems. Of course, it is certainly true that one can produce more stable and more predictable outcomes with greater reliance upon institutional norms and codified systems, but these kinds of ethical and political operations must fundamentally avoid the question and call of ethics. By their very nature such systems must be determinate, must not be open to individual events of compearance, and most certainly cannot be practiced as a democratic art of living. Instead they insist upon the stability and regularity that might ensure some minimally safe passage, some guaranteed acceptable outcome, even if the cost of it is the very idea of an ethico-political art.

Interestingly, what is also lost in these systems of ethics and politics is any need for hope. Certainly there is need for commitment and faith: commitment to the political system and faith that it will produce its promised outcomes. Such is the very definition of ideology. But in cases where one has commitment and faith, what need does one have of hope? If one's religious or philosophical or political commitments include a faith in the righteousness and triumph of those commitments, then hope can be an expression of the wavering of faith. Hope is what comes when we can't be sure, when we can't trust it to be ensured, when we can't have faith. Hope is what one can have without any expectation of an outcome. As McKinnon put it, pessimism and hope are consistent: "hope can be retained even in the bleakest of circumstances."[41] Arnett and Arneson even wed hope with cynicism to find a "hope within limits."[42] Faith, however, tells us it has to all make sense somehow. Faith dictates that our religious, philosophical, or political commitments must, somehow, eventually, produce the right result or an outcome that fits in the grand scheme of the world. In this way, hope's greatest threat lies not from despair, for despair is the state in which hope is most needed. Instead, the greatest threat to the possibility of hope is from faith, for where one can have faith, one has no need for hope. The democratic art of compearance has no need for faith, just as it has no need for commitment. Instead, it can believe in everything and hold out hope even in moments of madness. As an art, it opens its practitioners up to a transformation and leaves undecided what the outcome of that transformation must be, but one can always be hopeful, even if one has no reason or cause for hope.

There is no doubt we have much need for hope today. There is a great deal to do in this world. There is a great deal to be done and it seems the same problems reemerge decade after decade. However, we can no longer believe that commitment and faith to project or ideal can guide us out of this foul heap. Indeed, the best perhaps that we can do is to fashion an art of living that itself practices the ethico-political relation of compearance that places all of us in obligation to one another, an obligation that is before even the thinking of cosmos or province. It is not that a democratic art of compearance promises us a better future, though I do hold out hope that the future will be better than today. What the democratic art of compearance might offer is a way of engaging today that enacts an ethical *praxis* that can open us to the fact of our present condition. Nancy articulated this well when he wrote, "What will become of our world is something we cannot know, and we can no longer believe in being able to predict or command it. But we can act is such a way that this world is a world able to open itself up to its own uncertainty as such."[43] That is the task of a democratic art of compearance. To be open and hopeful without any determinate commitment or faith is to guard the question and the call so that compearance may recur and democracy can become a mode of living rather than a structure or institution. It is a mad hope, unreasoned and unfettered, that knows full well that hope itself ensures nothing except that there is always a reason to do something. Thus, hope always pushes us to reengage, and because hope needs no specific commitment and is unshackled from any faith, it can emerge each time open to the radical possibility of democratic living. I can think of no other project more vital at this juncture in history than to guard democracy and hope from the expanding forces of markets and faith.

NOTES

1. Jean-Luc Nancy, *The Sense of the World,* Minneapolis: University of Minnesota Press, 1998, p. 4. Italics in original.

2. Nancy, *Sense,* 4. Italics in original.

3. Jean-Luc Nancy, "Of Being-in-Common," *Community at Loose Ends,* Miami Theory Collective (Eds.), Minneapolis: University of Minnesota Press, 1991, p. 5. Italics in original.

4. John D. Caputo, *Against Ethics: Contributions to a Poetics of Obligation with Constant Reference to Deconstruction,* Bloomington: Indiana University Press, 1993, p. 3.

5. Ibid.

6. Ronald C. Arnett, "Communication and Community in an Age of Diversity," Communication Ethics in an Age of Diversity, Josina M. Makau and Ronald C. Arnett (eds.), Urbana: University of Illinois Press, 1997. 31.

7. Catriona McKinnon, "Cosmopolitan Hope," *The Political Philosophy of Cosmopolitanism,* Gillian Brock and Harry Brighouse (Eds.), Cambridge: Cambridge University Press, 2005, p. 234.

8 David Held, "Principles of Cosmopolitan Order," in *The Political Philosophy of Cosmopolitanism,* Gillian Brock and Harry Brighouse (Eds.), Cambridge: Cambridge University Press, 2005. pp. 20–23.

9. Alphonso Lingis, *The Community of Those Who Have Nothing in Common,* Bloomington: Indiana University Press, 1994, p. 13.

10. James Milroy & Lesley Milroy, *Authority in Language: Investigating Standard English,* New York: Routledge, 2005, and Ronald A. Wells, *Dictionaries and the Authoritarian Traditions: A Study in English Usage and Lexicography,* Hague: Walter De Gruyter Inc., 1973.

11. Nancy, "Of Being," 1.

12. Jean-Luc Nancy, *The Inoperative Community,* Minneapolis: University of Minnesota Press, 1991, p. 29.

13. Giorgio Agamben, *The Coming Community,* Minneapolis: University of Minnesota Press, 1993, p. 19.

14. Nancy, "Of Being." 7

15. Nancy, "Of Being," 7.

16. Nancy, *Inoperative,* 32.

17. Nancy, *Sense,* 117.

18. Nancy, *Inoperative,* 29.

19. Nancy, *Inoperative,* 76.

20. While Nancy and many other European writers choose the transliteration *tekne,* I have here chosen to use *techne,* the more commonly chosen transliteration among writers working in English. One should not take this difference in transliteration as a sign of anything more than adaptation to regional convention.

21. Nancy, *Sense,* 101.

22. Jean-Luc Nancy, "The Free Voice of Man," *Retreating the Political,* Phillipe Lacoue-Labarthe and Jean-Luc Nancy, Simon Sparks (Ed.), New York: Routledge, 1997, p. 34.

23. Nancy, "Free Voice," 39.

24. Jacques Derrida, "Debate," *Retreating the Political,* Phillipe Lacoue-Labarthe and Jean-Luc Nancy, Simon Sparks (Ed.), New York: Routledge, 1997, pp. 53–54.

25. Nancy, *Sense,* 139.

26. Nancy, "Free Voice," 32; Derrida, "Debate," 53; Maurice Blanchot, *The Writing of Disaster,* Lincoln: University of Nebraska Press, 1995.

27. Jean-Luc Nancy, "What Is To Be Done?" *Retreating the Political,* Phillipe Lacoue-Labarthe and Jean-Luc Nancy, Simon Sparks (Ed.), New York: Routledge, 1997, p. 157.

28. Lewis Carroll's writings make a wonderful example of the particular type of sense represented by nonsense. Carroll's background in mathematics (under his given name, Charles Lutwidge Dodson, he published *A Syllabus of Plane Algebraical Geometry* in 1860) and in particular his appreciation for abstract mathematics produced decidedly ordered nonsense. It was nonsense, certainly, but it very much did have a sense to its operation at every moment.

29. Nancy, *Inoperative,* XXVII.

20. Nancy, *Sense,* 115.

31. Nancy, *Sense,* 114.

32. The capitalized Other is used to signify a specific other, like another singularity or the other person, whereas the lowercase other is used to signify the more generic. This distinction is common among translators of contemporary French work and reflects a distinction in the French between two very similar terms (autrui and autre). For example, see Alphonso Lingis's translator's preface and footnotes in Emmanuel Levinas, *Otherwise Than Being or Beyond Essence,* Boston, MA: Kluwer Academic Publishers, 1991.

33. Charles E. Scott, *On the Advantages and Disadvantages of Ethics and Politics,* Bloomington: Indiana University Press, 1996, p. 184.

34. Ibid.

35. Ronald C. Arnett and Pat Arneson, *Dialogic Civility in a Cynical Age: Community, Hope, and Interpersonal Relationships,* Albany: State University of New York Press, 1999, p. 299.

36. Scott, *On the Advantages,* 188.

37. Arnett, "Communication and Community," 39.

38. Nancy, *Sense,* 104.

39. Nancy, *Sense,* 104.

40. Held, 10–11.

41. McKinnon, 240.

42. Arnett and Arneson, 25–26.

43. Nancy, *Sense,* 101.

BIBLIOGRAPHY

Agamben, Giorgio. *The Coming Community,* Minneapolis: University of Minnesota Press, 1993.

Arnett, Ronald C. "Communication and Community in an Age of Diversity," *Communication Ethics in an Age of Diversity,* Eds. Josina M. Makau and Ronald C. Arnett, Urbana: University of Illinois Press, 1997.

Arnett, Ronald C. and Pat Arneson. *Dialogic Civility in a Cynical Age: Community, Hope, and Interpersonal Relationships,* Albany: State University of New York Press, 1999.

Blanchot, Maurice. *The Writing of Disaster,* Lincoln: University of Nebraska Press, 1995.

Caputo, John D. *Against Ethics: Contributions to a Poetics of Obligation with Constant Reference to Deconstruction,* Bloomington: Indiana University Press, 1993.

Derrida, Jacques. "Debate," *Retreating the Political,* Phillipe Lacoue-Labarthe and Jean-Luc Nancy, Simon Sparks (Ed.), New York: Routledge, 1997.

Held, David. "Principles of Cosmopolitan Order," *The Political Philosophy of Cosmopolitanism,* Eds. Gillian Brock and Harry Brighouse. Cambridge: Cabmridge University Press, 2005.

Levinas, Emmanuel. *Otherwise Than Being or Beyond Essence,* Tr. Alphonso Lingis. Boston: Kluwer Academic Publishers, 1991.

Lingis, Alphonso. *The Community of Those Who Have Nothing in Common,* Bloomington: Indiana University Press, 1994.

McKinnon, Catriona. "Cosmopolitan Hope," *The Political Philosophy of Cosmopolitanism,* Eds. Gillian Brock and Harry Brighouse. Cambridge: Cambridge University Press, 2005.

Milroy, James, and Lesley Milroy. *Authority in Language: Investigating Standard English,* New York: Routledge, 2005.

Nancy, Jean-Luc. "Of Being-in-Common," *Community at Loose Ends,* Eds. Miami Theory Collective. Minneapolis: University of Minnesota Press, 1991.

———. *The Inoperative Community,* Minneapolis: University of Minnesota Press, 1991.

———. "The Free Voice of Man," *Retreating the Political,* Phillipe Lacoue-Labarthe and Jean-Luc Nancy, Simon Sparks (Ed.), New York: Routledge, 1997.

———. "What is to be Done?" *Retreating the Political,* Phillipe Lacoue-Labarthe and Jean-Luc Nancy, Simon Sparks (Ed.), New York: Routledge, 1997.

———. *The Sense of the World,* Minneapolis: University of Minnesota Press, 1998.

Scott, Charles E. *On the Advantages and Disadvantages of Ethics and Politics,* Bloomington: Indiana University Press, 1996.

Wells, Ronald A. *Dictionaries and the Authoritarian Traditions: A Study in English Usage and Lexicography,* The Hague: Walter De Gruyter Inc, 1973.

A Dialogic Ethic in the Public Rhetoric of Angelina Grimké

PAT ARNESON

The years 1828–1928 have been called the "Golden Age of American Oratory." During this time, people witnessed great public debates on a variety of topics. Although freedom of speech was clearly written into the Bill of Rights to the Constitution of the United States, some people were not permitted to speak—and some truths could not be spoken. Women were publicly and privately disciplined for speaking out, yet hundreds regularly took the platform to assert their ideas related to anti-slavery, temperance, and labor movements. One of those speakers was Angelina Grimké.

This chapter considers how a dialogic ethic might function in public rhetoric. My understanding of a dialogic ethic in public rhetoric is grounded in Hans-Georg Gadamer's[1] philosophical hermeneutics and Krista Ratcliffe's[2] rhetorical listening. Gadamer's ontological understanding allows a shared communicative "place" where interpretation occurs. Ratcliffe offers rhetorical listening as a trope for interpretive invention that "may provide grounds for revising identifications, uneven power dynamics, and ignorance."[3] Angelina Grimké's public rhetoric is considered in the light of a dialogic ethic.

A DIALOGIC ETHIC

This section draws upon hermeneutics and rhetorical listening to ground a dialogic ethic for public rhetoric. Central to this ethic is the dialogic character of understanding and the possibility of interpretive invention through rhetorical listening. A dialogic ethic in the public sphere also takes into account a speaker's rhetorical disposition and the centrality of content in the rhetorical process.

THE DIALOGIC CHARACTER OF UNDERSTANDING

The philosophical inquiry of hermeneutics has not traditionally emphasized the question of the ethical life. David P. Haney recalled that when Jacques Derrida accused Hans-Georg Gadamer of depending on a Kantian concept of "good will" in his hermeneutics, Gadamer replied that "hermeneutic understanding is ethically neutral. It has 'nothing to do with ethics' because '[e]ven immoral beings try to understand one another.'"[4] Yet Gadamer's hermeneutics contributes to thinking about the realm of the ethical by offering an "ontology of understanding as a developmental foundation for...ethics."[5] And, as Haney suggests, "even evildoers must listen to each other generously if they are to work together."[6]

Hans-Georg Gadamer's philosophical hermeneutics emphasizes the significance of historical context, lived-experience, and language for interpretive understanding. Hermeneutical reflection, as a form of critical questioning and dialogue between different horizons or world views, makes judgment possible. For Gadamer, prejudice represents not only the link with our tradition but also the original source of all our judgments. While we can never fully escape our prejudices, this does not mean that we cannot encounter them critically. "The important thing is to be aware of one's own bias, so that the text can present itself in all its otherness and thus assert its own truth against one's own fore-meanings."[7] The ground for understanding prejudice lies within people's historical being and our union with tradition.[8] Living traditions are sites of ongoing debates, internal revisions, and critical turns. Gadamer acknowledges that the hermeneutic approach toward tradition is historically oriented. One cannot simply absorb tradition but one has to enter a reasonable dialogue with tradition to interpret the content it holds.

A common situation of communication—which is permanently in flux—is found in understanding. The hermeneutic circle of interpretation is determined by the continual mutual influence of part and whole: "the whole, in terms of which the part is to be understood, is not given before the part.... Fundamentally, understanding is always a movement in this kind of circle."[9] As one interprets a text, one must not fix a meaning; openness to particularities of meaning gives a newness to the whole *and* the unfolding of the whole presents us with new understandings. Hans-Georg Gadamer's concern is not with arguing about a specific interpretation: "It is not the art of arguing (which can make a strong case out of the weak one) but the art of thinking (which can strengthen objections by referring to the subject matter)."[10] To gain a sense of the matter at hand, the interpreter must sustain an openness, asking questions to reveal fluid possibilities that inform one's interpretations and guide social action.

Michael McGee explains that *phronesis* is "a kind of knowledge in Aristotle's architectonic usually translated as 'practical wisdom' or 'practical knowledge.'"[11] "In Greece, the impulse of practical philosophy developed into the vision of the *phronimos,* a person imbued with practical wisdom who is able to bridge the life of the mind and the life of the polis."[12] *Phronimos* emphasizes that "[m]orality is anchored in, and authorized by, one's interpretation of the tradition (and one's simultaneous application of such *phronesis* to his or her own circumstances)."[13] *Phronesis* has no particular end; rather *phronesis* concerns itself with right living in general and is characterized by practical reasoning, knowledge, and wisdom. *Phronesis* establishes a link between ethics and rhetoric in which rhetoric is more than simply a discursive application of power. For Hans-Georg Gadamer, *phronesis* is "right" action within a particular situation.

Hans-Georg Gadamer noted in "The Ideal of Practical Philosophy" that ethics is concerned with the seamless application in concrete situations of the "factuality...of the convictions, values, and habits that we all share."[14] This implies the creation of a common interpretive situation for understanding. Hermeneutic interpretation of values returns "practical philosophy to its ancient privilege of not merely recognizing the good, but demanding it as well."[15] The philosophical issues contained within ethics arise when a "person acting must view the concrete situation in light of what is being asked of him [her] in general."[16] Understanding is dialogic in nature and grounds *phronesis*. Putting one's thinking to "right" use is enabled by rhetorically listening to the other.

RHETORICAL LISTENING

Krista Ratcliffe explains that *rhetorical listening,* as "a stance of openness that a person may choose to assume in relation to any person, text, or culture,...may be employed in many different contexts for many different put purposes."[17] She offers rhetorical listening as "a trope for interpretive invention."[18] By using the term *interpretive invention,* Ratcliffe intends "the necessary intersections between *interpretation,* which is the dominant term for making meaning in philosophical hermeneutics, and *invention,* which is the dominant term for making meaning in rhetorical studies."[19]

Krista Ratcliffe notes that traditional rhetorical theories subordinate listening to privilege the tropes of speaking, writing, and reading. Defining *rhetorical listening* as a trope "emphasizes the discursive nature of rhetorical listening…[and] plays with the etymology of the term *trope* as 'a turning.'… [R]hetorical listening turns hearing (a reception process) into invention (a production process),…inviting rhetorical listening into the time-honored tradition of rhetorical invention."[20] Rhetorical listening enables one to hear discursive intersections of cultural categories and cultural positions, especially the discursive intersections of gender and race/ethnicity. Rhetorical listening exposes the blinders that privilege provides to privileged people by providing "a means of questioning the logos" at play with/in texts.[21]

Krista Ratcliffe explains that *logos* is generally understood as a system of discourse within which a culture reasons and derives its truth. She draws upon the work of Martin Heidegger, who explores "the relationship between the Greek noun *logos* and its verb form *legein.*" *Legein* "in its fullest sense means both 'saying' and 'laying.'… '[L]aying' entails laying others' ideas in front of us in order to let these ideas lie before us. This laying-to-let-lie-before-us functions as a preservation of others' ideas…and, hence, as a site for listening."[22] Because we have inherited a tradition that divides *logos* in this way, our culture has privileged "saying" and has displaced "laying" (listening). Ratcliffe suggests that rhetorical listening may precede conscious identifications which, Kenneth Burke further argues, must precede persuasion. Such conscious identifications "may provide grounds for revising identifications troubled by history, uneven power dynamics, and ignorance."[23]

Rhetorical listening is advanced as a feminist literacy, "in which awareness of gender is complicated by other cultural categories, such as 'race' (including whiteness). The purpose of such literacy…is to facilitate cross-cultural dialogues."[24] Cross-cultural dialogues include the expression of narrative and counter-narrative within a given culture and acknowledge speaker-listeners and listener-speakers in oral discourse. I use the terms "speaker-listener" and "listener-speaker" to highlight the tropes of listening and speaking as both synchronic and diachronic in the rhetorical process.

Rhetorical listening occurs when a listener (listener-speaker) invokes one's capacity and one's willingness toward four moves. First, rhetorical listening promotes "an *understanding* of self and other that informs our culture's politics and ethics."[25] "[U]nderstanding means listening to discourses not *for* intent but *with* intent—with the intent to understand not just the claims but the rhetorical negotiations of understanding as well."[26]

> Standing under our own discourses means identifying the various discourses embodied within each of us and then listening to hear and imagine how these discourses might affect not only ourselves but others…. [This] echoes Hans-Georg Gadamer's belief that 'the primacy of hearing is the basis of the hermeneutical phenomenon'…: That is, we speak because someone is listening.[27]

"Standing under" is not intended to reflect foundational meanings, rather to imply "a place, a location, a standpoint for listening."[28]

Second, rhetorical listening proceeds "from within a *responsibility* logic, not from within a defensive guilt/blame one."[29] Krista Ratcliffe modifies "responsibility"[30] to read "accountability"[31] in her later work, noting "we are indeed all members of the same village, and…all people necessarily have a stake in each other's quality of life."[32]

Third, rhetorical listening locates "identification in the discursive spaces of both *commonalities* and *differences*."[33] When practicing rhetorical listening, we are invited to consciously locate our identifications in places of commonalities and differences. This double focus juxtaposes traditional and postmodern rhetorical concepts of identification.

Fourth, rhetorical listening accentuates "commonalities and differences not only in *claims* but in *cultural logics* within which those claims function."[34] A claim asserts a person's thinking; a cultural logic is a belief system or shared way of reasoning within which a claim may function. Krista Ratcliffe asserts that arguments and analyses of arguments rarely focus on the cultural logics that ground such claims. Rhetorical listening invites listeners to acknowledge both claims and cultural logics. Listeners may still disagree with each other's claims, but they become aware that the other is not simply "wrong" but instead is functioning from within a different system of logic. A person learns when one listens to the claims in other people's stories and when one listens to the competing cultural logics that stories reveal.

These four moves center rhetorical listening with the ongoing intent to understand discourses. Krista Ratcliffe notes that rhetorical listening opens people up to "being challenged, convicted, and hurt by the truth." She asserts that if questions make a listener uncomfortable, this discomfort "signifies already existing troubled identifications, and it underscores the need for standing under the discourses of ourselves and others—and listening."[35] The public sphere is one place to address differences in cultural logic.

RHETORIC IN THE PUBLIC SPHERE

The public sphere is generally associated with discussions about democracy. In this respect, the public sphere is a resource for promoting discussions of civil society and public life. During the antebellum era, speakers embodying different perspectives spoke regularly in public to address societal issues. Opinions expressed within communities include both shared and differing values. Issues that divide communities are grounded in those differing values.

Traditional theories of rhetoric celebrate commonality as the place of identification that leads to persuasion. The rhetorician is thus confronted with a difficulty: "how to make common minds that are distinct and unique. For such 'making common' is precisely what the activities of communication, literally conceived, intend."[36] The 'rhetorical,' which may be present in all discourse, refers to those dimensions of discourse that function to induce judgment or provoke a decision.

Stanley Deetz notes that rhetoric happens in the attempt to subvert the dominant opinion. While "the study of rhetoric has focused on the invention of messages for the sake of gaining adherence to the speaker's point of view…the rhetorical dimension of interaction, private or public, is the politics of the interaction."[37] Rhetoric poses questions to create discussion where there appears to be no need for discussion: "[t]o be rhetorical is to present the message in such a way as to maximize the possibility of participation in the interaction."[38]

Christopher L. Johnstone notes that rhetoric "generates opportunities for humane knowing because it invites participants to examine the very ground of their being."[39] He suggests a dialogic orientation seems most productive in this regard. "Two salient points emerge from such a conclusion. First, humane rhetoric is not to be construed on the model of the 'one-time public speech,' but rather as a qualitative dimension of ongoing, ordinary contact between people."[40] I suggest that ongoing contact between people in the public sphere could be present as sustained societal discourse about a given topic, rather than limiting humane rhetoric to individuals in conversation. This would expand a dialogic orientation to rhetoric to include an ongoing societal conversation about a topic of concern to citizens. Second, "such contact must be undertaken in what Richard Johannesen has described as 'a spirit of dialogue'" which may be characterized by qualities including mutuality, open-heartedness, directness, honesty, spontaneity, and so forth.[41] I suggest that a speaker-listener could approach rhetorical engagement with qualities of humane rhetoric, using rhetorical listening to understand the rhetorical situation; such a stand need not be reciprocated by audience members (listener-speakers) for the speaker to "stand under" this logic of a dialogic ethic.

On the basis of Hans-Gadamer's work and drawing upon Karl-Otto Apel and Richard Rorty, Stanley Deetz identified

> an ethical principle based on the very conditions for communicative understanding.… Every communicative act should have as its ethical condition the attempt to keep the conversation—the open development of experience—going.… That is, the communicative act should be responsive to the subject matter of the conversation and at the same time help establish the conditions for future unrestrained formation of experience.[42]

Listening to a rhetor may call into question one's central ways of life. Hans-Georg Gadamer points to the subject matter as a guide to the formation of the individual and expression. Stanley Deetz notes that while most communication studies scholars "consider what each person has to say about the subject matter, Gadamer focuses on what the subject matter 'says' to each" person. [43]

Christopher L. Johnstone recalled Karl Wallace's study of the substance of "good reasons" in rhetoric: "the substance of rhetorical proof has to do with values and value-judgments, i.e., with what is held to be good."[44] The logic which grounds good reasons may vary from culture to culture. Michael McGee explains that "the substance of moral reasoning is an interpretation of traditional beliefs and commitments applied to concrete problems in the present…the *phronesis* gained from hermeneutical reflection has nothing to do with domination, but rather with willing subordination."[45] One can use issues to frame and set a public agenda. For people who do not directly participate in a rhetorical debate "each point of clash becomes a problem to solve, and all issues together constitute an agenda for thinking…about the possibilities of *phronesis*."[46] McGee cites Hans-Georg Gadamer: "Hermeneutics in the sphere of literary criticism and the historical sciences is not 'knowledge as domination,' that is appropriate as a 'taking possession of,' but rather a subordination to the text's claim to dominate our minds."[47] Rhetorical listeners are challenged to understand what they are doing in a new way. Old categories will no longer work for them. The context of the conversation is transformed "precisely because it is philosophical, comparative, dialogic, and critical."[48]

I propose that a dialogic ethic in public rhetoric, in short, be grounded in three aspects of interpretive understanding. This first includes an awareness of the significance of historical context, which requires engaging a living tradition and promoting an understanding of self and other to inform culture's politics and ethics. This embraces rhetorical listening as it is related to a responsibility logic that recognizes all people have a stake in the quality of one another's life. Second, a dialogic ethic for public rhetoric includes an awareness of the significance of lived-experience, hermeneutical reflection, critical questioning, and dialogue between different horizons and world views. Rhetoric will reflect thinking about the subject matter, not arguing a person down. This includes rhetorical listening for identification of commonalities and differences in rhetoric and addresses claims in the argument and cultural logics in which the claims function. Third, an awareness of language is necessary, establishing a relationship between ethics and rhetoric, and advocating phronesis—"right" action in a particular situation. The speaker-listener poses a question with a rhetorical disposition that invites discussion about the content under examination.

ANGELINA GRIMKÉ'S ABOLITIONIST RHETORIC

Angelina Grimké was a public advocate of moral reform who lived from 1805–1879. During her lifetime, Grimké witnessed active slavery in the South, the Civil War, the signing of the Emancipation Proclamation, Juneteenth (June 19th, 1865, which marks the end of slavery in the United States), and the period of Reconstruction. Grimké's journal reveals that her youth was marked by a growing consciousness of the inhumanity and immorality of slavery. This awareness prompted her to question and resist this social practice.

Angelina Grimké joined the Philadelphia Female Anti-Slavery Society in the spring of 1835. On August 22, 1835, William Lloyd Garrison, editor of the *Liberator,* published his "Appeal to our Fellow Citizens" to end slavery. Grimké gave her private thoughts public expression in a response to Garrison's "Appeal" when on August 30, 1835 she wrote a letter to him in which she stated: "The ground upon which you stand is holy ground: never—never surrender it. If you surrender it, the hope of the slave is extinguished.... This is a cause worth dying for. I say so, from what I have seen, and heard, and known, in a land of slavery."[49] Her letter was published in the *Liberator* on September 19, 1835 under the title "Slavery and the Boston Riot." Gerda Lerner noted that "[w]ithout any direct action on her part, she [Grimké] was placed before the public as an active abolitionist."[50]

Suzanne M. Daughton explained that even if Angelina Grimké had wanted to, neither she nor any woman "could have fulfilled the expectations of 19th century traditional, male, mainstream public address which sought to build and preserve public consensus."[51] There was little hope that Grimké could even approach the traditional objectives of rhetoric: "to dispel prejudice, adapt her message to her audience, and unite her listeners in support of her cause."[52] Grimké rhetorically invented an approach to compel change (particularly in her female listener-speakers) by expressing a counter-narrative in a way that could open possibilities for a new understanding of democracy.

A DIALOGIC ETHIC IN GRIMKÉ'S PUBLIC RHETORIC

Angelina Grimké was an active public speaker for the abolition of slavery. In addition to the Weld Manuscripts Collection at the William C. Clements Library at the University of Michigan, several sources document her public rhetoric.[53] The analysis that follows draws upon various speeches and letters to reveal a dialogic ethic in Grimké's public rhetoric. These aspects of interpretive understanding—enabled by inventional rhetoric—overlap, co-inform, and extend/intend one another.

1. *Understanding a Tradition of Politics and Ethics.* This aspect of a dialogic ethic for public rhetoric includes an awareness of the significance of historical context, engaging a living tradition, promoting an understanding of self and other to inform a culture's politics and ethics, rhetorical listening related to a responsibility logic, and the recognition that all people have a stake in the quality of one another's life.

Angelina Grimké was certainly aware of the significance (signify-ance) of the historical context, which greatly affected her abolitionist rhetoric. In the early 19th century both social and intellectual life centered on public presentations. The American Anti-Slavery Society spread the anti-slavery message by sending speakers or "agents" such as Grimké into communities to address citizens and to organize anti-slavery societies. Antislavery organizers in the West and Northeast were regularly heckled, attacked, stoned, and beaten. Segregationists made every effort to deny abolitionists a hearing, frighten their audiences away, and keep free black people from attending their meetings. The press frequently prepared the ground for violence with distortions of abolitionist views and outright lies.[54] The violence of that time was understood by Grimké and naturally incorporated into her rhetoric.

Angelina Grimké sought to understand her standpoint and others' standpoint in discussions about the political and ethical dimensions of slavery. Grimké's diary records a woman of character "whose lineaments grew from the give and take of conflict, debate, and moral argument.... [B]y confronting her supporters and embracing her critics, Angelina put herself on the line by putting others on the line."[55] In her letter published in the *Liberator* and her presentations as an agent of the American Anti-Slavery Society, Grimké was able to open up "the possibility of change by placing ideas, people, and events into broader contexts of meaning, to exhibit the need for community and the very process through which it might come about...: 'It is because I feel a deep and tender interest in your present and eternal welfare,' Grimké began, 'that I am willing thus publicly to address you.'"[56]

At the ground of her reasoning was "a view of human rights that carried with it imperatives of duty and collective action, but beneath even that level of analysis, she found and gave public expression to principles that remained unshaken for the rest of her life—that human rights knew no boundaries, no sex, no domain."[57] These principles, documented in her diaries and gained from years of personal reflection, illustrate her dialogic ethic.[58]

2. *Critical Questioning and Dialogue about the Subject Matter.*[59] This aspect of a dialogic ethic for public rhetoric includes an awareness of the significance of lived-experience, hermeneutical reflection, critical questioning, and dialogue between different horizons and world views. The rhetoric reflects an emphasis on content by revealing thinking about the subject matter, not arguing a person into submission. Rhetorical listening enables a speaker-listener to identify commonalities and differences in rhetoric as well as address claims in the argument and cultural logics in which the claims function.

Angelina Grimké's rhetorical preparation exhibits hermeneutic reflection and critical questioning. Stephen Browne notes that Grimké's rhetoric is critical "to the extent that it defines what is at stake in the given encounter. The root meaning of critical (*kritikos*) [is] the feminine 'ability to discern.'" Grimké's public rhetoric includes "an overriding concern with distinguishing properly the relationships that bind and destroy human community…. To stage an encounter and enter into it critically is in this regard to discern what goes with what, who with whom." Critical questioning reshapes one's commitments "by submitting conventional boundaries to an unforgiving scrutiny."[60] The rhetorical function reconstitutes the conditions of and for public action.

In the symbolic interplay of speaker, subject, and audience, Grimké constructed a model of interpretation enabling her to "reread the text of the world."[61] This reading of the text of society dramatizes the transformation of the referent that is possible.

> In July 1837, the [Grimké] sisters were ready to lecture at Amesbury when they were handed a letter, stating that two Southern gentlemen wish to give *their* views. After reading the letter to the audience, Sarah [Grimké] asked the two men to proceed…. The Grimkés responded; after an hour's discussion Angelina gave her scheduled lecture. The two men then requested another 'free discussion.' The 'debate,' as it soon came to be called, was fixed for the 19th of July. About 1000 persons attended this unheard-of spectacle, which was carried over to a second day.[62]

This "debate" was an exchange grounded in different cultural logics. Grimké spoke using claims within a different cultural logic than that assumed by male speakers. "[I]nstead of trying to approximate the traditional (male) model of rhetorical practice [in her Pennsylvania Hall address], Grimké renounced it resounding through a combination of rhetorical techniques that capitalized on her experiences as a woman."[63] Grimké retained the traditional view of a woman "by using Biblical quotations and religious tone throughout her speech. In addition, she used personal narratives as a form of proof…. This technique facilitates an autonomous and supportive community of woman who view their own personal experiences as political."[64] Sharing her experiences in a slaveholding society, Grimké used her rhetoric to reshape an understanding of community and help people imagine a new way of uniting as a society.

When assessing dominant claims structured within the cultural logic of the time, "one fact remained clear to her [Grimké]: slavery by its very nature, by the false order it imposed and its mimicry of familial and social relationships, could not but result in violence in one form or another."[65] The substance of Grimké's rhetorical efforts reveal her engagement of a dialogic ethic in the form of rhetorical understanding inspired to move the tradition-bound narrative that people held. She sought to shift it toward recognition of human equality—black and white, male and female. "[S]he developed and used the resources of argument and public debate to create [new] relationships among ideas, values, and people."[66]

> Grimké understood not only that change required violence, but that desirable change required the ability to read violence in optimal ways. Violence disorders, and in disorder-

ing it calls into question the structures of commitment through which communities define themselves. This disordering becomes rhetorically significant when it destabilizes the interpretive communities for which the abolitionist message was constructed. The opportunity that violence affords for the reordering and reconstitution of community is met by offering up a new vocabulary, a symbolic means to transform events and ideas into a new rationale for human relations and collective action.[67]

Grimké's critical (discerning) questions enabled her to assess claims by examining the cultural logic in which those claims functioned. This stance grounded her dialogic ethic of public rhetoric.

3. Phronesis in the Relationship of Ethics and Rhetoric. This aspect of interpretive understanding includes advocating *phronesis* in an awareness of language by establishing a relationship between ethics and rhetoric. The speaker-listener poses a question with a rhetorical disposition that invites discussion about the content under examination to advocate "right" action.

Angelina Grimké's language transported her perspective on "right" action. "Grimké's stock in trade was, like most but not all of the abolitionists, language. She, like her colleagues in the business of moral reform, had little else to go on but the commitment and community that language could bring about. When she sought to achieve certain ends, she did so critically: she developed and used the resources of argument and public debate to create relationships among ideas, values, and people."[68] Relying on "rational and systematic" reasoning, Grimké created a new "language of reform"—a "counterdiscourse"—focused on the traditional concept of duty.[69] Transforming the ideals of femininity, she employed duty as a "moral imperative" for both men and women and as a "rationale for public action."[70]

Stephen H. Browne identified binary relations used in Grimké's speeches that illustrate how unstable the meaning structures framing one's moral order are made to be: "speaker-audience; curiosity-sympathy; outside-inside; slavery-freedom; North-South; silence-speech; duty-dereliction; remembering-forgetting; blindness-insight; violence-quiescence."[71] These and others "fall into each other…the effect of which is to first destroy and then reconstruct the structure of convictions that is Grimké's subject."[72]

Angelina Grimké problematized the rhetorical event by disrupting the speaker-audience relationship. She would announce that there was not a problem with the "audience" but with people who *think* they comprise an audience simply because they have gathered together. Her speeches reveal that she called into question why people were collectively assembled—was it "curiosity merely…or a deep sympathy with the perishing slave, that has brought this large audience together?"[73] This pattern of disrupting unreflective meanings imposed a disjunction of taken-for-granted assumptions and presented listeners with a choice. Grimké guided rhetorical listeners toward *phronesis* in her rhetoric.

CLOSING

Hans-Georg Gadamer's ontology of understanding and Krista Ratcliffe's rhetorical listening create a space for interactants to consider their interpretations of a social situation in light of "right" action. Angelina Grimké's construction of rhetorical arguments reveals various aspects of a dialogic ethic for public rhetoric. As a rhetorical listener, Grimké proceeded to first dismantle and then reassemble for rhetorical listeners in her audience the communal convictions regarding the abolition of slavery. In so doing, her rhetorical efforts contributed to transforming the culture of the United States of America.

NOTES

1. Gadamer, *Philosophical Hermeneutics* (Berkeley: University of California Press, 1976); Gadamer, *Truth and Method* (New York: Continuum, 1960/1999).

2. Ratcliffe, "Rhetorical Listening: A Trope for Interpretive Invention and a 'Code of Cross-Cultural Conduct.'" *College Composition and Communication* 51 (1999):195–224; Ratcliffe, *Rhetorical Listening: Identification, Gender, Whiteness* (Carbondale: Southern Illinois University Press, 2005).

3. Ratcliffe, *Rhetorical Listening*, 19.

4. Haney, *The Challenge of Coleridge: Ethics and Interpretation in Romanticism and Modern Philosophy*, (University Park: Pennsylvania University Press, 2001), 13.

5. Deetz, "Reclaiming the Subject Matter as a Guide to Understanding: Effectiveness and Ethics in Interpersonal Interaction." *Communication Quarterly* 38 (1990): 226.

6. Haney, *Challenge of Coleridge*, 7.

7. Gadamer, *Truth and Method*, 269.

8. Dobrosavljev, "Gadamer's Hermeneutics as Practical Philosophy." *FACTA UNIVERSITATIS. Series: Philosophy, Sociology and Psychology* 2 (2002): 605–618.

9. Gadamer, *Truth and Method*, 190.

10. Ibid., 367.

11. McGee, "Phronesis in the Gadamer versus Habermas Debates." *Judgment Calls: Rhetoric, Politics and Indeterminacy* (Boulder, CO: Westview Press, 1998), 13.

12. Ibid., 20.

13. Ibid., 28.

14. Gadamer, "Ideal of Practical Philosophy," 58.

15. Gadamer, "The Ethics of Value and Practical Philosophy," *Hermeneutics, Religion and Ethics*, (New Haven, CT: Yale University Press, 1999), 116.

16. Gadamer, *Truth and Method*, 316.

17. Ratcliffe, *Rhetorical Listening*, xiii.

18. Ratcliffe, "Rhetorical Listening," 195.

19. Ibid., 222 n.1.

20. Ibid., 195.

21. Ibid., 196.

22. Ratcliffe, *Rhetorical Listening*, 23–24.

23. Ibid., 19.

24. Ratcliffe, "Rhetorical Listening," 195.

25. Ibid., 204.

26. Ratcliffe, *Rhetorical Listening*, 28.

27. Ibid.

28. Ratcliffe, "Rhetorical Listening," 221.

29. Ibid., 204.

30. Ibid.

31. Ratcliffe, *Rhetorical Listening*, 31.

32. Ibid., 31–32.

33. Ratcliffe, "Rhetorical Listening," 204.

34. Ibid.

35. Ratcliffe, *Rhetorical Listening*, 34.

36. Johnstone, 184.

37. Deetz, "Reclaiming the Subject Matter," 239.

38. Ibid., 239–240.

39. Johnstone, "Ethics, Wisdom, and the Mission of Contemporary Rhetoric: The Realization of the Human Being," *Central States Speech Journal* 32 (1981): 185.

40. Ibid., 186.

41. Ibid.

42. Deetz, "Reclaiming the Subject Matter," 232.

43. Ibid., 231.

44. Johnstone, "Ethics, Wisdom, and the Mission," 187.

45. McGee, "Phronesis," 38–39.

46. Ibid., 38.

47. Ibid., 39.

48. Pearce and Littlejohn, *Moral Conflict: When Social Worlds Collide* (Thousand Oaks: Sage, 1997), 215.

49. Gold, "The Grimké Sisters and the Emergence of the Women's Rights Movement." *Southern States Speech Journal* 40 (1981): 344.

50. Lerner, *The Grimké Sisters from South Carolina: Pioneers for Women's Rights and Abolition* (New York: Schocken Books, 1971), 127.

51. Daughton, "The Fine Texture of Enactment: Iconicity as Empowerment in Angelina Grimké's Pennsylvania Hall Address." *Women's Studies in Communication* 18 (1995): 19.

52. Ibid., 20.

53. Barnes and Dumond, *Letters of Theodore Dwight Weld, Angelina Grimké and Sarah Grimké, 1822–1844* (Gloucester, MA: P. Smith, 1965); Ceplair, *The Public Years of Sarah and Angelina Grimké: Selected Writings, 1835–1839* (New York: Columbia University Press, 1989); Wilbanks, *Walking by Faith: The Diary of Angelina Grimké, 1828–1835* (Columbia: University of South Carolina Press, 2003).

54. Gold, "The Grimké Sisters"; Lerner, *The Grimké Sisters.*

55. Browne, *Angelina Grimké: Rhetoric, Identity and the Radical Imagination* (East Lansing: Michigan State University Press, 1999), 34.

56. Ibid., 67.

57. Ibid., 110.

58. Wilbanks, *Walking by Faith;* see also Barnes and Dumond, *Letters;* Lerner, *The Grimké Sisters.*

59. A dialogic ethic directs attention to rhetorical *content.* This is against the psychological emphasis toward the rhetor's ego that some scholars have taken toward protest rhetoric (see, for example, Gregg, "The Ego-Function of the Rhetoric of Protest." *Philosophy and Rhetoric* 3 (1971): 71–91), and even some interpretations of Angelina Grimké's public rhetoric (see, for example, Gold, "The Grimké Sisters").

60. Browne, *Angelina Grimké,* 38.

61. Browne, "Encountering Angelina Grimké: Violence, Identity, and the Creation of Radical Community," *Quarterly Journal of Speech* 82 (1996): 61.

62. Gold, "The Grimké Sisters," 353.

63. Daughton, "The Fine Texture," 20.

64. Ibid.

65. Browne, "Encountering Angelina Grimké," 57.

66. Browne, *Angelina Grimké,* 37.

67. Browne, "Encountering Angelina Grimké," 56.

68. Browne, *Angelina Grimké,* 37.

69. Ibid., 97, 101.

70. Ibid., 99.

71. Ibid., 37.

72. Ibid., 160.

73. Ibid., 153.

BIBLIOGRAPHY

Barnes, Gilbert H. and Dwight L. Dumond, eds. *Letters of Theodore Dwight Weld, Angelina Grimké and Sarah Grimké, 1822–1844* (Vols. I and II). 1934. Gloucester, MA: P. Smith, 1965.

Browne, Stephen H. "Encountering Angelina Grimké: Violence, Identity, and the Creation of Radical Community." *Quarterly Journal of Speech 82* (1996): 55–73.

Browne, Stephen H. *Angelina Grimké: Rhetoric, Identity and the Radical Imagination.* East Lansing: Michigan State University Press, 1999.

Ceplair, Larry, ed. *The Public Years of Sarah and Angelina Grimké: Selected Writings, 1835–1839.* New York: Columbia University Press, 1989.

Daughton, Suzanne M. "The Fine Texture of Enactment: Iconicity as Empowerment in Angelina Grimké's Pennsylvania Hall Address. *Women's Studies in Communication 18* (1995): 19–43.

Deetz, Stanley. "Reclaiming the Subject Matter as a Guide to Mutual Understanding: Effectiveness and Ethics in Interpersonal Interaction." *Communication Quarterly 38* (1990): 226–243.

Dobrosavljev, Duška. "Gadamer's Hermeneutics as Practical Philosophy." *FACTA UNIVERSITATIS. Series: Philosophy, Sociology and Psychology 2* (2002): 605–618.

Gadamer, Hans-Georg. "The Ethics of Value and Practical Philosophy." *Hermeneutics, Religion, and Ethics.* Trans. Joel Weinsheimer. New Haven, CT: Yale University Press, 1999. 103–118.

Gadamer, Hans-Georg. "The Ideal of Practical Philosophy." *Praise of Theory: Speeches and Essays* (Trans. Chris Dawson). New Haven, CT: Yale University Press, 1998. 50–61.

Gadamer, Hans-Georg. *Philosophical Hermeneutics.* Berkeley: University of California Press, 1976.

Gadamer, Hans-Georg. *Truth and Method* (2nd rev. ed.). 1960. New York: Continuum, 1999.

Gold, Ellen Reid. "The Grimké Sisters and the Emergence of the Woman's Rights Movement." *Southern Speech Communication Journal 46* (1981): 341–360.

Gregg, Richard B. "The Ego-Function of the Rhetoric of Protest." *Philosophy and Rhetoric 3* (1971): 71–91.

Haney, David P. *The Challenge of Coleridge: Ethics and Interpretation in Romanticism and Modern Philosophy.* University Park: Pennsylvania University Press, 2001.

Johnstone, Christopher Lyle. "Ethics, Wisdom, and the Mission of Contemporary Rhetoric: The Realization of Human Being. *Central States Speech Journal 32* (1981): 177–188.

Lerner, Gerda. *The Grimké Sisters from South Carolina: Pioneers for Woman's Rights and Abolition.* 1967. New York: Schocken Books, 1971.

McGee, Michael Calvin. "Phronesis in the Gadamer Versus Habermas Debates." In John M. Sloop and James P. McDaniel, eds. *Judgment Calls: Rhetoric, Politics, and Indeterminacy.* Boulder, CO: Westview Press, 1998. 13–41.

Pearce, W. Barnett and Stephen W. Littlejohn. *Moral Conflict: When Social Worlds Collide.* Thousand Oaks: Sage 1997.

Ratcliffe, Krista. *Rhetorical Listening: Identification, Gender, Whiteness.* Carbondale: Southern Illinois University Press, 2005.

Ratcliffe, Krista. "Rhetorical Listening: A Trope for Interpretive Invention and a "Code of Cross-Cultural Conduct." *College Composition and Communication 51* (1999): 195–224.

Wilbanks, C., ed. *Walking by Faith: The Diary of Angelina Grimké, 1828–1835.* Columbia: University of South Carolina Press, 2003.

Eros, Logos and Sophia in Plato

Philosophic Conversation, Spiritual Lovemaking, and Dialogic Ethics

CHRISTOPHER LYLE JOHNSTONE

> *Who is my father in this world, in this house,*
> *At the spirit's base?*
> *My father's father, his father's father, his—*
> *Shadows like winds go back to a parent before thought,*
> *Before speech, at the head of the past....*
> *—Wallace Stevens*

> *The longing not to die, the hunger for personal immortality,*
> *the effort by which we strive to persevere in our own being,*
> *this is the emotional basis for all knowledge and the intimate*
> *point of departure for all human philosophy.*
> *—Miguel de Unamuno*

When I was asked to contribute to this volume, I was invited to "engage the title theme"–focusing as it does on dialogue, ethics, cosmopolitanism, and provinciality– "from the bias of [my] own work." In what follows, I seek to honor this invitation. To my thinking, the apparent dichotomy between "cosmopolitanism" and "provinciality" reflects the distinction between "universalism" and "relativism" in matters of epistemology and morality. Moreover, both pairs echo the ancient contrast between *physis* (nature, understood as an abstract conception of the cosmic force that underlies all physical and mental processes) and *nomos* (custom, law or convention, rooted in local beliefs and practices). Moral philosophers in the West since the time of Socrates and the Sophists have grappled with the problem of universalism/globalism vs. relativism/provinciality, of *physis* vs. *nomos*, in seeking to identify the legitimizing grounds of moral choice and moral action. To what extent can any set of moral and ethical beliefs, principles, or values be universalized, and to what extent must they be limited by the particulars of local cultural and social conditions?

This essay argues for a vision of dialogue and of dialogic ethics that is inflected by Plato's thinking about love, speech, and wisdom and that provides for the simultaneous adherence to both horns of this apparent dilemma. Specifically, Plato's treatment of these three ideas in the *Phaedrus* and *Symposium* suggests that, while there are universal/global forms of knowledge to which all humans have access and by which they are thereby united, one must be attentive to the uniquely situated character of the other in seeking through dialogue to realize this knowledge in oneself and in the other. The organizing metaphor for this treatment is *eros*, the impulse toward procreation in and through beauty. From Plato's employment of this metaphor we can derive a set of moral ideas that might guide the conduct of conversation.

What is supposed to happen when two people talk to each other? Does it even make sense to ask this question? Perhaps nothing is "supposed" to happen when we engage in conversation, in relating, in dialogue. Perhaps it does not matter what happens. On this view, there would be no such thing as "good" or "bad," "right" or "wrong," in communication between people: no set of ends we should pursue, no obligations or responsibilities to fulfill. In short, maybe there is no such thing as "ethics" in human communication. If this is so, then this will be a very short chapter and, indeed, a very short book.

On the other hand, perhaps it *does* matter what takes place when we engage each other in conversation–in friendship, in marriage, in the family, in the classroom, in the workplace, on the streets, at the café, at international conferences, in meetings. Perhaps such conversations have the capability of producing profoundly important effects on thinking, action, the quality of our lives, the significance we find in our experience, our happiness. This view, of course, is the starting point for any discussion of "ethics" in communication; for if the quality of our converse is a factor in the quality of our lives, then how we talk and listen to one another certainly "matters" on a personal level. If this is so, then it makes sense to consider what is "good" and "bad" in communication, about the intrinsic qualities and extrinsic consequences that affect us personally in good and bad ways. And so, it makes sense to ask about our obligations and responsibilities when we interact with other human beings.

There are many ways to think about these matters and many approaches to answering the kinds of practical, ethical questions we encounter in our communicative lives. Some who have thought and written about them maintain that our most fundamental obligation is to treat the other with love[1] or *con amore.*[2] Others have proposed, along similar lines, an "ethic of care."[3] One scholar has recently argued that our most basic duty lies in the act of acknowledgment.[4] In other cases, various sets of general ethical principles or moral guidelines have been proposed for application in particular communicative contexts for determining where the responsible course of conduct lies,[5] while some reject altogether the very concept of "general ethical principles," arguing instead for an idea of responsibility rooted in freedom and in responsiveness to the Other in her/his own uniqueness and particularity.[6]

I have found much in these various viewpoints that is interesting and useful, and I do not propose to argue against any of them. Rather, I intend to pursue an approach suggested by some terms in the title of this volume–"dialogue," "cosmopolitanism," "provincialism"–and by my personal interest in the idea of *wisdom.* I am concerned with how our intercourse with one another can make us wiser people and so contribute to our ability to live meaningful, fulfilling lives. If there is such a thing as wisdom, and if human beings are in some measure capable of attaining it, then one way of thinking about the question of my obligations when I encounter another in dialogue would be to consider how I might engage the other so as to move us both closer to it. I have considered this issue previously,[7] and I am using one element of that discussion as a starting point here. In the earlier essay, I explored the ethical implications of our species-designation, *Homo sapiens,* understood as "the human that knows" or "the wise human" (as distinct from "the upright-walking human," *Homo erectus,* or "the able human" or "handy man," *Homo habilis*): "A humanistic ethic that embraces [this conception] of human nature will commit its adherents to the pursuit of wisdom, for in this pursuit lies the fulfillment of human being."[8] In the remainder of that paragraph I offered a brief sketch of the conception of wisdom that informed my thinking at that time. "Human wisdom," I wrote, "involves a kind of knowing, as is indicated by the significance of *sapience.* Wisdom is both a grasping of 'the way things are'–of the patterns and regularities in human experience and of how these fit into the *kosmos*–and an appreciation of the truths thus grasped.... It is generated by apprehensions of the truths of human nature, by one's realization or understanding of how humanness 'fits into' the nature of things."[9]

Beginning, then, with the idea that there is some fundamental "nature" (*physis*) or common "substance" in virtue of which an organism can be described as "human,"[10] we might ask whether there are things that can be "known" by all humans, by virtue of their being human. Are there "truths of human nature" to which we have access, and the knowledge of which constitutes a kind of "human wisdom?" If so, in what do they consist, and how can we know them? Finally, how can the *technai* or "arts" of conversation be employed so as to contribute the process of knowing?

The answers to these questions advanced here are rooted in the thinking of Plato, though they are not wholly "Platonist." The first Western thinker to elucidate what we might call an "art of epistemic conversation," Plato's dialogues manifest principles and techniques for philosophically productive encounters with other people. Particularly in his two principal dialogues on love, the *Phaedrus* and the *Symposium,* Plato presents visions of wisdom and its attainment that can enrich our own thinking about these matters. In what follows, I draw on Plato's conception of wisdom and on his prescriptions for its acquisition primarily as these are depicted in the two dialogues, focusing particularly on the role of "erotic" conversation in the process of coming to wisdom.

One need not accept Plato's metaphysics in order to use his thought and to recognize that there are things that all human beings–irrespective of geographic location, historical era, culture, gender, ethnicity, and ideology–have in common. We are all born; we all die. We live our lives, to a greater or lesser extent, in the company of others. We are cared for while young by more mature members of our family or social group. We all seek the company of others, yet we all strive for some degree of independence from them. We seek to realize our personal aspirations. We all react to pleasure and pain. We all respond to the aesthetic in our experience–to encounters with the beautiful and the ugly. We all respond to the feeling of having been treated badly by others. We all must deal with the fact that there are forces at work in our lives that are beyond our control. We all experience change, growth and decay, transformation. These are sources of similarity, of commonality, of universality among people across the globe and throughout human history. When Plato writes about abstract, universal Forms or Ideas that constitute the true essences of such experienced qualities as "justice," "beauty," "pleasure," "goodness," the "sacred," or "love," we might construe such terms as identifying general categories of experience to which all humans are subject. Every person, in every place, in every age, has encountered these qualities. They are, indeed, universals of human experience.[11]

There is, for Plato, another dimension of our humanity that unifies us still more fundamentally. Insofar as we are alive, we are possessed of (and by) *psyché,* the immaterial and immortal soul or life-force that animates the body (*soma*). It is *psyché* that distinguishes the living person from the corpse, and it is our possession of and by *psyché* that unites us in the most primal way, both with each other and with all existence. If there are natural and/or moral "truths" or "realities" to which the soul has access, then, individuals have in common an ability to apprehend these. If there is a "way of things"–a Tao, a "*gnômên* (plan) by which all is steered through all" (Heraclitus, DK 41), a *physin apeiron* (unbounded nature) from which all things come and into which they return (Anaximander, DK 12 A9)–and if, as Plato maintains in the *Phaedrus,* it is *Psyché* that "has the care of all that is inanimate and traverses the whole universe...and controls the whole world,"[12] then delving deep within one's own soul will lead one ultimately to "the source and principle" of the cosmic order.[13] It is in this spirit, I think, that Heraclitus, writing perhaps a century before Plato took up his own philosophical enterprise, asserted that the soul possesses a *logos* (principle) so deep that one cannot find its limits "even if you travel over every way" (DK 45), and that "all things come to pass in accordance with this *logos*" (DK 1). Since wisdom, for Heraclitus, lies in understanding that "all things are one" (DK50), then we can gain wisdom by searching into our own souls for the universal tune that orders the cosmic dance.

A brief comment on my metaphor here: Recently, I was watching the program *Nova* on PBS, and the program focused on astrophysics, Albert Einstein's contributions to this field, and the quest for a "theory of everything." The central idea emerging from the program was that there is a single directive force at work in the cosmos, and that eventually the ideas of gravity, electro-magnetism, and the strong and weak nuclear forces will be understood in terms of this underlying force, of which they are manifestations or dimensions. The dominant theory in this quest at the moment is "string theory," wherein everything that exists is understood as being constituted by combinations of "strings" of buzzing, vibrating, humming energy, each string (or type of string) pulsating at its own frequency. The universe is comprised of infinite such vibrating strings. This notion led me to wonder if the totality of these vibrations is akin to what the Ancients understood as the "music of the spheres," the *harmonia* whereby all things fit together. This cosmic chord–or is it a symphony?–is detectable by the individual person because our own souls are but particular resoundings of that chord, and at bottom we are attuned to it. If we can learn to hear our own "tuning," our own "chord," then we can apprehend at least that particular sounding of the cosmic music.

This is essentially the idea toward which I find Plato pointing in the two dialogues examined here; for, as he indicates in the *Phaedrus*,[14] "the mind itself has a kind of divining power." On this view, what we all have in common most fundamentally is the unity of our individual souls with the cosmic Soul, and thus with the directive impulse in all existence. Because the person is an embodiment of Nature, one can find Nature in one's deepest self. This is yet another form of universality–of global identity–among all humans. We are One in embodying the constituting, guiding principle of the cosmos.

A "PLATONIC" CONCEPTION OF WISDOM

The attainment of wisdom or sophia is a topic in many of Plato's dialogues. It is described as the most beautiful of all things in the Greater Hippias,[15] while in the

Phaedrus it is characterized as a "condition of the soul" in which one experiences a kind of communion with "the realm of the absolute, constant and invariable, through contact with beings of similar nature."[16] In the Laws, wisdom is a state of "concord" and "consonance" of the soul with what "judgment pronounces to be noble or good."[17] *The Republic,* in the Allegory of the Cave, depicts a process of painful struggle by which an individual can attain knowledge of the true nature of things, thus acquiring genuine wisdom.[18] In the *Phaedrus*, wisdom is described in terms of understanding those universal, unchanging truths that the human soul apprehended before birth and that remain imprinted there, though they are forgotten.

Let us look more closely at Plato's treatment of wisdom in the *Phaedrus*. The pretext of this treatment centers on three speeches designed to consider the question of whether it is more advantageous to affiliate with the non-lover rather than with the lover. The first of these speeches was ostensibly written by the orator Lysias, and it argues that the non-lover is to be preferred over the lover because the former will not be driven by erotic attraction to the beloved to manipulate and exploit him merely for physical gratification. Socrates, finding the speech to be technically deficient, gives his own version of this argument so that the speech displays the organic structure, clear definitions, and sound reasoning that were lacking in Lysias' effort. However, since love (*eros*) is a god, he must be honored rather than rejected. Hence, in order to atone "for some offense to heaven,"[19] Socrates creates yet another speech in which the true character of love is explained, and its connection to wisdom is portrayed in the form of a myth about the nature of the soul.[20]

It is the nature of the soul, like a wing, to rise up "to the region where the gods dwell, and more than any other bodily part it shares in the divine nature, which is fair, wise, and good, and possessed of all other such excellences."[21] Before it is joined to a body, the individual soul traverses the heavens with the souls of the gods, following them as they "pass to and fro, each doing his own work."[22] Thus does the soul grasp absolute Reality, for "It is there that true being dwells, without color or shape, that cannot be touched; reason alone, the soul's pilot, can behold it, and all true knowledge is knowledge thereof…. Wherefore when at last she has beheld being she is well content, and contemplating truth she is nourished and prospers, until the heaven's revolution brings her back full circle."[23] As the soul is borne through its revolutions around the realm of Being, it "discerns justice, its very self, and likewise temperance, and knowledge…, the veritable knowledge of being that veritably is."[24] Thus, before it enters a physical body, the soul has seen the Forms–the Essences–of such moral qualities as Justice and Moderation, and of the other eternal verities that underlie our experience of the world; for "every human soul has, by reason of her nature, had contemplation of true being…."[25]

As I suggested earlier, we are not obliged to accept Plato's metaphysics in order to make use of his insight. What Plato tells us here is that the universe "makes sense" intellectually, that it coheres and exhibits a rational order. Like some of his presocratic predecessors, and like some contemporary cosmologists and physicists who succeeded him, Plato invites us to understand that the universe is governed by laws and that these can be grasped by the human intellect.[26] Since the human soul–and particularly the thinking, reasoning, speculative part of the soul that "pilots" it–is continuous with the rational *Psychê* that orders the cosmos, humans can grasp the ordering principle of the universe because it is, in the end, the ordering principle of their own souls. We can glimpse the "divine" (unchanging, timeless, deathless) principle of the cosmos because our souls, in their deepest nature, are also divine. We are One with the cosmic Soul.[27] What Plato ends up showing us is how, in the context of a particular sort of relationship, we can use our talk to open ourselves and each other to that nature, to that Soul.

BEAUTY, EROS, AND CONVERSATION: THE ASCENT TO WISDOM

Plato's account of wisdom in the *Phaedrus* proceeds to describe how the soul, when it is joined with flesh, is pulled down from the heavenly realm by certain unruly passions and becomes "burdened with a load of forgetfulness."[28] It thereby loses sight of the divine vision it once had. Knowledge of the true natures of things, acquired before birth, falls into the depths of the soul as dreams fade upon awakening. Wisdom, then, involves a kind of "deep remembering," a recollection of the time before time when our souls beheld the unchanging truths of the cosmos. The idea that true wisdom involves the recovery or remembrance (the Greek term is *anamnêsis*, literally "un-forgetting") of truths hidden deep within the soul is a principal doctrine in Plato's mature dialogues (e.g., *Meno* 81c ff., 98a; *Phaedo* 72e, 75, 92), including the *Phaedrus* and the *Symposium*.

In the *Phaedrus*, as the myth unfolds, the soul is likened[29] to a union among a charioteer (Reason) and two winged horses, one representing the noble passions (such as the love of honor, temperance, and decency), the other symbolizing such base appetites as wantonness, avarice, and gluttony.[30] The tendency of the former is to pull the soul upward toward the heavens, where it may again dwell in the divine realm. However, in many cases the chariot is held down by the lure of physical pleasure and the yearning for sensual gratification. When such souls are led to "deeds of unrighteousness,…they [forget] the holy objects of their vision" because their intellectual perception has been dimmed.[31] Encountering embodiments of justice or temperance in their earthly experience, their "dull organs" of sense are unable to "behold what is imaged…." However, "with beauty it is otherwise." The apprehen-

sion of beauty in the face or body of another awakens in the soul a shadowed recollection of "beauty in all its brightness" seen in the time before birth, when

> we beheld with our eyes that blessed vision…[and were] initiated into that mystery which
> is rightly accounted blessed beyond all others; whole and unblemished were we that did
> celebrate it, untouched by the evils that awaited us in days to come; whole and unblemished
> likewise, free from all alloy, steadfast and blissful were the spectacles on which we gazed
> in the moment of final revelation; pure was the light that shone around us, and pure were
> we, without taint of that prison house which now we are encompassed withal, and call a
> body, fast bound therein as an oyster in its shell.[32]

The apprehension of physical beauty in another stirs the soul, and it yearns for
a sort of reunion with what it once possessed–the vision of perfect, divine beauty.
For a soul whose initiation into the mystery of beauty is long past, or who been
corrupted by corporeal existence, the perception of another's beauty engenders
impulses toward physical procreation: "he looks upon [the beauty of the other] with
no reverence, and surrendering to pleasure he essays to go after the fashion of a four-
footed beast, and to beget offspring of the flesh,…consorting with wantonness…."[33]
However, "when one who is fresh from the mystery, and saw much of the vision,
beholds a godlike face or bodily form that truly expresses beauty,"[34] the noble passions lead the soul to regard the other with "reverence as at the sight of a god"[35] and
to ascend toward the divine realm of pure beauty.

The conflict between the base and noble passions is a fundamental moral tension
in Plato's conception of the soul and in his vision of the path to wisdom. The
charioteer–the reasoning power that steers the soul–must struggle with these contending forces. The ignoble soul is the one in whom the base passions–"hot-blooded,
consorting with wantonness and vainglory"[36]—overpower both Reason and the
noble impulses, leading one to pursue physical union with the object of one's desire.
In contrast, when these passions have been "bridled" and broken, they become
obedient to the commands of Reason and are made to work in harmony with the
virtuous impulses.[37] In this case, the soul seeks not physical but spiritual union with
the other; for, beholding the other's beauty with "reverence and awe," the soul is
reminded of what it grasped before birth–the divine realm of cosmic truth. Significantly,
in the beauty of the other one beholds one's own beauty, for the beloved "is as it were
a mirror in which he beholds himself."[38] When we perceive our deepest selves in the
other, we are, in fact, glimpsing the Self we have in common. In this moment of
Self-recognition, this flash of vision into the deepest core of our beings, we come to
true wisdom, to a reminder of the knowledge that resides in our Soul. "And so," Plato
concludes, "if the victory be won by the higher elements of mind guiding them into
the ordered rule of the philosophical life, their days on earth will be blessed with
happiness and concord, for the power of evil in the soul has been subjugated, and
the power of goodness liberated; they have won self-mastery and inward peace."[39]

The attainment of genuine wisdom, which consists in one's recollection of the essential truths of the cosmos, requires that the erotic impulses released in the soul by an encounter with another's beauty be channeled from the desire for physical union to some form of corresponding spiritual intercourse. The central ideas in this account are developed more fully in the *Symposium,* where the central role of *eros* is linked with the process of conversation. Particularly in the image of erotic love, the organizing metaphor of this dialogue, Plato directs our attention to those features of conversation that render it capable of leading two souls–two *psychai*–to the sorts of insights that comprise genuine wisdom. As we consider this dialogue in some detail, I seek to identify elements in his account of *eros* that can enhance our understanding of how Plato viewed the philosophical potency of conversation.

As readers familiar with this dialogue will recall, the *Symposium* takes the form of a series of speeches presented at a dinner party among Socrates and several of his friends and acquaintances. The occasion, ostensibly reported some years after the fact, is a dinner given for his friends by the tragic poet Agathon when he won the prize for outstanding drama with his first tragedy in 416 B.C.E. Following the meal, the diners decide that, instead of the normal after-dinner entertainment by flute-girls, the company would amuse itself with talk, and that this should take the form of a speech by each participant in praise of love (*eros*). The participants speak in their seating order, starting with Phaedrus, so that Socrates is the last to speak. Though the view of each speaker is ultimately rejected by Socrates when he renders his own account, each contributes some element to the vision he eventually integrates into the comprehensive view he articulates, and that is presumably embraced by Plato. As I briefly recount the conception of love provided by each speaker, I identify elements in each that are retained or reconfigured by Socrates in his own account. By illuminating the metaphorical force of these elements we can discern Plato's view that "erotic" conversation is a method by which wisdom is acquired, and we can identify characteristics of dialogue that are essential to its philosophical efficacy.

Plato's conception of *eros* is constructed progressively throughout the dialogue, as each speaker contributes his own brushstroke to the portrait that emerges finally in the speech of Socrates. The first two speakers, Phaedrus and Pausanius, confine themselves to a treatment of erotic love in its most obvious sense. Phaedrus begins his account by noting that *Eros* is a "great god, wonderful alike to mankind and to the gods"[40] and that there is widespread agreement about its extreme antiquity.[41] He goes on to describe the virtues of the lover–his/her nobility, courage, and willingness to sacrifice on behalf of the beloved. Phaedrus concludes by remarking that "Love is the oldest and most glorious of the gods, the great giver of all goodness and happiness (*aretês kai eudaimonias*) to men, alike to the living and the dead."[42]

Two points in this speech recur throughout the discussion of *eros* and find their way into Plato's ultimate vision: Love's divinity and its (his) beneficence toward humankind. The latter idea is a constant in the speeches that precede Socrates' address, and it is a central feature of the conception of love he articulates. *Eros* is a positive force in human life; it improves rather than weakens the human condition. The former feature—Love's divinity—undergoes some modification by the time Socrates considers it. Nonetheless, *eros* retains its association with the divine (*theos*), and this connection is central to its characterization. It is true that, in Plato's time, common belief and practice reflected the conviction that divine forces affected the course of human and cosmic events, but Plato's conception of divinity had evolved considerably from what lay behind the tales of Homer and Hesiod. Without tracing in detail the transition from mythopoesis to philosophy, suffice it to say that the notion of *theos* as it was represented in philosophical writing of the fourth century B.C.E. had developed far beyond the Homeric conception of anthropomorphic Olympians, to a more abstract, positivistic idea.[43] This idea included the general attributes of the gods without particularizing and personalizing these attributes. In Plato's lifetime, the philosophical idea of divinity emphasized the qualities of immortality or timelessness, omnipresence, and omnipotence but did not include the personalities and motivations associated with the Homeric gods. Thus, when Plato identifies *Eros* as a *theos,* he may be taken to intend that it is a universal, pervasive force in the world, and that it affects all people in one way or another. This idea is carried forward in the remaining speeches.

Pausanias, though hardly more profound than Phaedrus, is a good deal more subtle, and he introduces a distinction between a nobler and a baser kind of love that prepares the way for Socrates. Pausanias identifies Love with Aphrodite, and he distinguishes between two incarnations of the goddess[44]: "One, the elder, sprung from no mother's womb but from Heaven (*Ouranos*), whence we call her Heavenly, while the younger, daughter of Zeus and Dione, we call Popular (*Pandemos*)." Pausanias concludes, following this, that there are two kinds of love, one "heavenly" and divine and the other "earthly" and human. He goes on to explain that the latter "governs the passions of the vulgar" (*oi phauloi,* the mean, petty, or base folk); for "first, they are as much attracted by women as by boys; next, whoever they may love, their desires are of the body rather than of the soul; and, finally, they make a point of courting the shallowest people they can find, looking forward to the mere act of fruition and careless whether it be a worthy or unworthy consummation."[45] Heavenly Love, on the other hand, "springs from a goddess whose attributes have nothing of the female, but are altogether male," and is "innocent of any hint of lewdness." Those who are inspired by this kind of Love "turn…to the male, preferring the more vigorous and intellectual bent."[46]

If we can see past the conspicuous misogyny at work in Pausanias' view of human relationships, there are two points to be taken from his speech that later find their way into Socrates' account of the matter, and that are keys to understanding Plato's conception of "heavenly *eros*" as the impetus toward wisdom. First is the distinction between physical and spiritual love (though these are not mutually exclusive for Pausanias), which points to two distinct paths along which one may be led by the force of erotic desire. Those in whom physical desire is strongest (think of the unruly horse) are led by it to purely physical gratification (whether with a member of the same or the opposite sex), while those in whom spiritual desire is powerful seek intellectual rather than bodily couplings and satisfactions. A second point occurs later in the speech, after Pausanias further contrasts the base and noble lover and examines the attitude of various states and forms of government toward homosexuality. He considers the question of whether it is possible to submit to any form of servitude to one's beloved "without offending our ideas of decency." He concludes that, "just as the lover's willing and complete subjection to his beloved is neither abject nor culpable, so there is one other form of voluntary submission that shall be blameless–a submission which is made for the sake of virtue (*aretê*)…[and] increase of wisdom (*sophia*)…."[47] The noble lover, then, may yield without shame to the beloved in the pursuit of intellectual excellence and divine knowledge. This linkage of Heavenly *Eros* with the pursuit of virtue and wisdom, and the idea of yielding to the beloved in this pursuit, become for Plato defining features of the best sort of erotic relationship between two people. As we shall see, it will be taken up again by Socrates.

Pausanias should be succeeded by Aristophanes, but the latter suffers from a hiccup and, after prescribing for this, Eryximachus takes Aristophanes' turn. Though much of Eryximachus' speech is unremarkable and rather pedestrian, it has its contribution to make to the emerging portrait. Love, he says, "besides attracting the souls of men to human beauty,…has many other objects and many other subjects, and…his influence may be traced both in the brute and the vegetable creations, and I think I may say in every form of existence–so great, so wonderful, and so all-embracing is the power of Love in every activity, whether sacred or profane."[48] The treatment of love as a cosmic principle at work in the whole of existence, though pushed by Eryximachus to the threshold of absurdity, marks a significant transition from the narrow sense of physical desire expressed by Phaedrus, and to that extent it prepares for the ascent from physical to intellectual love foreshadowed by Pausanias and developed fully by Socrates.

This idea of *Eros* as a cosmic force, timeless and universal, permeating human experience as a kind of profound yearning or desire, is deepened by Aristophanes. Using as his vehicle a fantastic myth about the first human beings and their rebellion against the gods, Aristophanes portrays love as a longing for the restoration of a lost state of unity with another person, and he describes happiness as the result of this restoration. Speaking of "the whole human race, women no less than men," he says that happiness "is to be found in the consummation of our love, and in the healing of our dissevered nature by finding each his proper mate."[49] Though the tale he tells describes this longing in physical terms–as the desire for reunification with one's bodily "missing half"–the imagery suggests that love is experienced as an excruciatingly intense yearning for restoration to a primordial condition of unity, for a return to one's original nature. On the level of physical love, this yearning is a desire for bodily consubstantiality: Aristophanes speaks of being "fused" (*syntêxai*) and "welded" (*symphysêsai*) into "the closest possible union."[50] This yearning, however, can also be understood on a spiritual level as a longing for the fusion of soul with soul, as a hunger for a psychic union in which one's personal identity is either expanded to include the other, or is lost altogether in a new consciousness of Selfhood.[51] This, in any case, is the direction in which Socrates ultimately takes the imagery introduced by Aristophanes.

An interlude of some length follows, after which Agathon tenders his own panegyric to *Eros*. Though it is somewhat empty and precious compared to Aristophanes' effort, Agathon's account also makes its contribution to the evolving conception of Love. Through a consideration of the youth and delicacy of Love, Agathon demonstrates the beauty and goodness of the god. Indeed, he is the most beautiful and best of the gods,[52] and it is he who governs us in both drinking and speaking.[53] While Agathon is prone to exaggeration and ornamentation, he nonetheless introduces ideas that emerge as central in Socrates' account. Here, for the first time, we are invited to observe the linkage of *Eros* with both beauty and goodness and to see him as manifesting his power in speech itself.

We turn now to the discourse of Socrates, which represents the fullest expression of Plato's conception of *Eros* and its role in the quest for wisdom. The discussion between Agathon and Socrates that follows the former's speech allows for a dialectical exchange establishing certain preliminary conclusions.[54] The positions are, first, that Love is a relative name like Father or Mother, in that it implies the existence of an object loved; second, that Love desires its object; third, that desire is not felt for what is already possessed; and fourth, that since the object of Love, on Agathon's own showing, is beauty, Love cannot be beautiful. Nor, by the same reasoning, can it be good. The point is thus settled that Love is the consciousness of a desire for a good not yet acquired or possessed. A hint of this has already been given in Aristophanes' fantasy, but it is now established on rational grounds as a foundation for the exposition of Plato's own view.

Against the backdrop constructed by the other speakers, Socrates develops a view of *Eros* that includes–albeit in modified forms–some of their ideas, and that has important ethical implications for the practice of conversation. *Eros* retains its linkage with the divine, the beautiful and the good, the improvement of humankind, wisdom and virtue, intense yearning for a sort of communion with another and for restoration of a lost unity, and our noble and base natures. In the final analysis, he offers a conception of *Eros* in which conversation between two people is the form taken by spiritual procreation. Wisdom and virtue–the progeny of such a union–reside in the recovery of knowledge acquired when the soul was in its primordial state but has lost. What is particularly interesting to me is what we can infer about the character of such conversation by illuminating the sexual metaphor that Socrates employs to describe it.

Using the narrative device of a secondhand account provided by "a Mantinean woman, called Diotima,"[55] Socrates explains that *Eros,* while not divine himself, bridges the gap between the divine and the human worlds. He is a "very powerful spirit (*daimôn megas*), and spirits…are halfway between god and man."[56] *Eros,* then, is one of many messengers or envoys "that ply between heaven and earth, flying upward with our worship and our prayers, and descending with the heavenly answers and commandments, and since they are between the two estates they weld both sides together and merge them into one great whole…. It is only through the mediation of the spirit world that man can have any intercourse, whether waking or sleeping, with the gods."[57] Though he is not divine himself, *Eros* nonetheless gives humans access to the divine realm–that is, to the realm of the timeless, universal, absolute truths of the cosmos. As an intermediate being (and, therefore, being an intermediary), he provides a means by which humans can come to understand divine things, including Wisdom (*sophia*), Beauty (*to kalon*), the Good (*to agathos*), and Resourcefulness (*euporia*).[58]

Diotima, in what may have been a prophetic allusion to Aristophanes' speech, observes that "it has been suggested…that lovers are people who are looking for their other halves."[59] While not especially taken with the image, she nonetheless accepts it as long as the "missing half" is understood as "the good and nothing but the good."[60] It is at this point that Plato, through Diotima's words, introduces the final, decisive element into the conception of Love he is advancing. All of the previously considered elements–the connections with the divine, with beauty and the good, with wisdom and virtue, with the longing or yearning for what one lacks, with the physical and spiritual expressions of this yearning–come together in her extended exposition of the sexual metaphor: Love as the procreative impulse.

The "work" or "function" (*ergon*) of love, Diotima says, "is begetting in beauty both bodily and spiritually…. All humans are pregnant…both in body and in soul; on reaching a certain age our nature urges us to procreation, never in ugliness but only in beauty…. It is a divine affair, this engendering and bringing to birth, an immortal element in the creature that is mortal…because this is something ever-existent and immortal in our mortal life."[61] A little later, Diotima distinguishes, as Pausanias had, between "those whose procreative impulse is physical" and those whose creative desire is "of the soul"[62]—a key dichotomy in understanding Plato's view of the quest for wisdom. In both cases, Diotima tells Socrates, the longing for immortality–and thus for participation in the divine–is the motive force at work. Men whose impulse is physical, she says, "turn to women as the object of their love, and raise a family, in the blessed hope that by doing so they will keep their memory green 'through time and through eternity.' But those whose procreancy is of the spirit rather than of the flesh...conceive and bear the things of the spirit. And what are they? you ask. Wisdom (*phronêsis*) and all the other virtues."[63]

For Plato, then, the ideal love–the heavenly *Eros*–is a yearning in the human soul for a procreative fusion with another soul, a union to be undertaken and carried out in beauty and to issue in the apprehension by both of absolute Beauty, Justice, Virtue, and all the other divine Essences that are mirrored in the particulars of human experience. Particularly important here, turning again to the imagery of "begetting" and pregnancy, is that these apprehensions or insights already dwell, if only embryonically, within the individual soul. We are, each of us, already pregnant with the seeds of wisdom, and it is the act of loving in and through beauty that brings these seeds or embryos to full term, so that they can be brought forth in speech as our spiritual offspring. Moreover, the form of action through which gestation is achieved is also *talk*. Through their conversation with one another, two lovers can co-create, in one another and within themselves, opportunities for the insights and understandings that constitute the highest form of knowledge humans can attain.

The "ascent passage" of Diotima's speech[64] supports and illuminates this interpretation of Plato's views. Without detailing this well known section of the dialogue,[65] it can readily be seen that it traces the movement of the spiritual lover from the first encounter with physical beauty in another individual, "so that his passion may give life to noble discourse (*logos kalos*),"[66] through a realization that all physical beauty is one and the same no matter in whom it is perceived, to an acknowledgment that "the beauties of the body are as nothing to the beauties of the soul, so that wherever he meets with spiritual loveliness, even in the husk of an unlovely body, he will find it beautiful enough to fall in love with and to cherish–and beautiful enough to quicken in his heart a longing for such discourse as tends toward the building of a noble nature."[67] It is precisely such discourse that delivers the two lovers of those "soul-children" with which they have been pregnant. As Guthrie observes, "a man pregnant in *his own* soul, when he converses with a fair youth, brings forth what he has long been pregnant with, and the two cherish it together."[68] If we are always already pregnant, then both lover and beloved will bring forth their insights and "cherish [them] together."

From the apprehension of spiritual beauty, the lover proceeds to contemplate the "beauty of laws and institutions," thence to the several branches of knowledge (*epistêmai*), and thence to the final epiphany,[69] the moment of deepest insight, when there bursts upon him that wondrous vision which is the very soul of the beauty he has toiled so long for. It is an everlasting loveliness which neither comes nor goes, which neither flowers nor fades, for such beauty is the same on every hand, the same then as now, here as there, this way as that way, the same to every worshiper as it is to every other. Nor will his vision of the beautiful take the form of a face, or of hands, or of anything that is of the flesh. It will be neither words, nor knowledge, nor a something that exists in something else, such as a living creature, or the earth, or the heavens, or anything that is–but subsisting of itself and by itself in an eternal oneness, while every lovely thing partakes of it in such sort that, however much the parts may wax and wane, it will be neither more nor less, but still the same inviolable whole.[70]

This vision, the woman from Mantinea concludes, reveals the kind of life that is "ever worth the living"–the contemplation of "the very soul of beauty."[71]

TOWARD AN ETHICS FOR SPIRITUAL/EROTIC DIALOGUE

So, what might we take from Plato's account here that illuminates the process of remembrance by which true wisdom is acquired? Clearly, the role of Beauty–of the aesthetic experience–is central. What happens when we encounter beauty–in a face, a figure, a piece of music, a landscape, a sunset, a thought or idea, a mind? We yield to it; we open ourselves up to it, and it fills us with wonder and awe. It also awakens a deep longing to be taken into it, to be possessed by it, to become one with it. We want to lose ourselves in the face, the music, the sunset, the thought, and to dwell in that place where there is only the Beautiful. When the beauty we encounter is in another's face or body or soul, we are willing to yield ourselves to it, and we want to become one with it. The erotic is our response to the beautiful, whatever form it takes.

A second important idea here, of course, is that when two people respond to the beauty in each other, the willingness to yield and the longing for communion create opportunities for insight and deep remembering. The experience of wonder– *thauma*–opens a portal through which we may glimpse the eternal. If the truths of the cosmos are imprinted on the souls of all humans before birth, then when two lovers engage in "spiritual intercourse," as they ascend toward the "wondrous vision" of the very essence of Beauty and the Good, they are also descending toward the depths of their own souls. Indeed, in the end, ascent and descent arrive at the same place: the cosmic *Psyche* that is the life-force of the universe. I cannot help but be reminded here of Heraclitus' saying that "the way up and down is one and the same" (DK 60), and of a particular translation of the first verse in Lao Tzu's *Tao Te Ching*:

Existence is beyond the power of words to define. Terms may be used, but are none of them absolute. In the beginning of heaven and earth there were no words. Words came out of the womb of matter; and whether a man dispassionately sees to the core of life or passionately sees the surface, the core and the surface are essentially the same, words making them seem different only to express appearance. If name be needed, wonder names them both: From wonder into wonder existence opens.[72]

To be brought to a state of wonder by an encounter with beauty is to be opened to the highest/deepest truths of the universe.

Another key point is that the divine vision comes not gradually, through an accumulation of individual facts, but as an instantaneous seeing into the very heart of being. As Plato describes it in the *Seventh Letter,* "like a blaze kindled by a leaping spark, it is generated in the soul and at once becomes self-sustaining."[73] As two interlocutors are drawn ever deeper into their own souls through the process of opening themselves to one another, they come ever closer to the divine reality at the center of their beings. The flash of insight, the moment of epiphany, occurs when the mind seizes and is seized by an understanding of the world that suddenly orders experience in a new and more complete manner. One makes a shift in perspective, and the new prospect brings together formerly disparate aspects of experience in a way that discloses an underlying unity, a perception that "all things are one." In that moment, the cosmos makes sense in a new and wonderful way, and one feels a unity both with the beloved and with all that is.

What, then, is the form of the "spiritual intercourse" through which the spark of insight is kindled? Significantly, each stage of this ascent/descent involves the use of "beautiful speech," "words that will tend to the betterment of the young," and "the most fruitful discourse." It is *talk,* conversation, through which the procreative quest for wisdom takes place. Indeed, later in the evening, when he arrives drunk and loquacious, Alkibiades describes Socrates' unique personality and his erotic effect on others (most notably on Alkibiades himself) in terms of his *logoi*–his "talk," "arguments," and "speeches."[74] What is the character of this talk? Clearly, it is *erotic,* and the centrality of the sexual metaphor invites us to see in philosophical conversation a form of *eros* and to examine its nature. Hints about this nature can be gleaned from what Plato has said here, and from what he said about the true lover in the *Phaedrus,* but it is the image of spiritual "love-making" that I find particularly suggestive. In order to illuminate the implications of this metaphor, we must to some extent go beyond Plato's explicit guidance, as we shall see. [75]

If the truths to be remembered and grasped are universal, the erotic process by which they are apprehended is particular and personal: it centers on the uniqueness of the souls who seek fusion with one another through dialogue. We may infer this, perhaps, from Plato's account of a "true art" of rhetoric toward the end of the *Phaedrus.* If a speaker is to employ the persuasive power of speech responsibly, Plato has Socrates tell us, in addition to knowing "the truth about the subject that you speak or write about,…you must have a corresponding discernment of the nature of the soul, discover the type of speech appropriate to each nature, and order and arrange your discourse accordingly, addressing a variegated soul in a variegated style that ranges over the whole gamut of tones, and a simple soul in a simple style."[76] Though not specifically describing the nature of philosophical conversation here, Plato suggests that, if another's soul is to be led by speech to the truth that lies within it, one's language must be suited to the other's unique soul. The art of erotic conversation must be attentive to the psychological and existential particularities of the interlocutors. One must engage the other in terms of her/his own *êthos,* her/his "customary dwelling place."[77] In this respect, philosophical conversation is always situated, embodied, local, immediate, particular. However, because each individual soul is ultimately a manifestation of the single cosmic Soul, the truths to be found within the individual are finally universal and unvarying. Here, I believe, is where Plato's conception permits us to avoid the "universalism vs. relativism" dilemma I mentioned at the outset. In the first instance, spiritual love-making requires an acute sensitivity and responsiveness to the particularity and uniqueness of the Other even as it carries us toward the realm of the universal.

What remains, then, is to consider the qualities of spiritual intercourse that can make the universal accessible to the individual. In such qualities we can discern prescriptions for philosophically productive conversation–ethical guidelines for "fruitful discourse." What is "love" in conversation? It might be helpful to approach this question by considering three constituting dimensions of dyadic intercourse: the spirit in which it is undertaken, the content of conversation, and the language used in its practice. First, then, when Plato holds that wisdom consists in knowing the cosmic truths imprinted on the soul before birth, and thus that it comes from "knowing thyself," we must grasp the mind-set or attitude that permits one to take advantage of the opportunities for self-knowledge afforded by erotic dialogue. What is the "spirit" of spiritual love-making? Putting the matter another way, what is the "erotic consciousness" that must inform our relating if we are to be led to the most profound insights into the truths of our own beings?[78]

The lover of wisdom is characterized first and foremost by a willingness to submit to Beauty, a readiness to yield the self to the experience of fusion and transcendence, an openness to the journey on which *eros* sends us. Martha Nussbaum writes that "knowledge of love is not a state or function of the solitary person at all, but a complex way of being, feeling, and interacting with another person. To know one's own love is to trust it, to allow oneself to be exposed. It is, above all, to trust the other person…."[79] Perhaps more appropriately in the context of Plato's conception, it is to trust one's self to What Is and to the divinity and goodness of Beauty. When Plato writes of love that it involves a willingness to submit, yield, or surrender to the inspiration of Beauty, he implies that it involves a readiness to be vulnerable, to risk oneself in the enterprise of loving. Henry Johnstone, Jr., in proposing some ethical principles for practicing "rhetoric *con amore* [with love]" describes the "duty of Openness" as a willingness to *listen* to the other, and so as a willingness to be affected by the other.[80]

A corollary to the idea of *openness to the other* is *openness with the other,* willingness to share one's own soul with the other. If *eros* manifests itself as a longing for fusion with another soul, then one must both be open to the other's soul and be ready to reveal one's own deepest insights and sentiments in the course of conversation. Fromm writes that, "In the most general way, the active character of love can be described by stating that love is primarily a *giving,* not receiving."[81] What does one person give to another? According to Fromm,

> He gives of himself, of the most precious he has, he gives of his life. This does not necessarily mean that he sacrifices his life for the other–but that he gives him of that which is alive in him; he gives him of his joy, of his interest, of his understanding, of his knowledge, of his humor, of his sadness–all expressions and manifestations of that which is alive in him.... He does not give in order to receive; giving is in itself exquisite joy. But in giving he cannot help bringing something to life in the other person, and this which is brought to life reflects back to him; in truly giving, he cannot help receiving that which is given back to him.[82]

Thus is *eros* projective as well as receptive. Just as the erotic attitude involves a willingness to allow the other's spiritual beauty into oneself and to be kindled by it, so does it include the impulse to reach out to the other, to touch and caress her/him, to disclose oneself to him/her. Moreover, the impulse to give oneself to the other, to reach out to and touch the other, is to be understood not as an effort to "impress" the other, nor to guide or direct her/him toward some self-conceived "truth." Rather, it is a willingness to extend oneself toward the other, to put oneself out for the sake of the other, and to be guided by the other's movement toward her/his own sense of What Is. "The caressing hand," Bauman writes, "characteristically, remains open, never tightening into a grip, never 'getting hold of'; it touches without pressing, it moves obeying the shape of the caressed body...."[83] Thus, even in reaching toward the other, in extending one's self into the psychic space of the other, one is simultaneously expressing oneself authentically and adjusting or adapting oneself to the other.

Related to both conceptions of openness is the idea of *responsibility*–that is, willingness to be *for the other* rather than for oneself. Bauman, in discussing Levinas' conception of moral responsibility, observes that

> Morality is a *transcendence* of being; morality is, more precisely, the *chance* of such transcendence.... Morality has no 'ground,' no 'foundation.'...It is born and dies in the act of transcendence.... Confronting the Other not as a person (*persona:* the mask worn to

signify the role played, that role having been first described and prescribed in the scenario), but as the *face*, is already the act of transcendence…. I am fully and truly *for* the Other, since it is I who give her the right to command, make the weak strong, make the silence speak, make the non-being into being through offering it the right to command me. 'I am for the other' means I give myself to the Other as hostage. I take responsibility for the Other.[84]

This attitude of responsibility is essentially a commitment to the spiritual well-being of the other, and a willingness to subordinate oneself to her/him in the ascent/descent toward wisdom. In the *Theaetetus*, Plato has Socrates describe himself as *maieutikos*, skilled in the art of midwifery, by which art he assists others in giving birth to the wisdom with which they are pregnant.[85] Fromm observes that "love implies *care*…. *Love is the active concern for the life and the growth of that which we love*. Where this active concern is lacking, there is no love."[86] So it may be with the spiritual lover in all cases: truly to love the other is to devote oneself to bringing *the other's* soul-children to full term and to assist in "delivering" them in moments of profound insight. One embarks on the path of spiritual *eros,* accordingly, not for the sake of one's own ascent toward wisdom, but for the sake of the other's. Love is a fundamentally selfless act. Moreover, it is not *my own* understanding of What Is that I help the other grasp; rather, I must commit myself to helping the other discover *within her/himself* the fundamental realities of the cosmos.

Additional features of an "erotic consciousness" can be derived from the imagery of the erotic encounter. True "love-making" (in contrast to mere sexual union) involves what Fromm terms *concentration*.

To be concentrated in relation to others means primarily to be able to listen….

> To be concentrated means to live fully in the present, in the here and now, and not to think of the next thing to be done, while I am doing something right now. Needless to say, that concentration must be practiced most of all by people who love each other. They must learn to be close to each other without running away in the many ways in which this is customarily done.[87]

Concentration, in the context of loving dialogue, means being present for the other, sensitive to her/his situatedness and feelings, responsive to his/her immediate needs in the ascent/descent toward Truth. In a similar vein, Fromm also notes that "the main condition for the achievement of love is the *overcoming* of one's *narcissism*… in which one experiences as real only that which exists within oneself…."[88] This is akin to the quality of selflessness considered above in connection with responsibility, and it invokes the idea of *respect*, "the ability to see a person as he is, to be aware of his unique individuality."[89] It means being able to "transcend the concern for myself and see the person in his own terms."[90] Finally, the genuine lover is *patient*. Patience is a willingness to let the other proceed toward wisdom at her/his own pace, in her/

his own way. By being patient, the lover gives time and thereby enables the other to find the Self in her/his own time.[91]

As important as the spirit of erotic dialogue is the content. What should we talk about, if we would have our talk carry us toward the most profound truths humans can grasp? Two ideas are central here. One is that philosophical conversation must concentrate on the general ideas that manifest themselves in the particulars of daily experience in life. Plato's dialogues are full of examples, as we find Socrates conversing with this or that person about the nature of such concepts as Justice (*Gorgias, Republic*), Friendship (*Lysis*), Love (*Phaedrus, Symposium*), Piety (*Euthyphro*), Beauty (*Hippias Major*), Virtue (*Protagoras, Republic*), the Good (*Theaetetus, Republic, Philebus*), and Evil (*Crito*). Conversations often present opportunities for examining such ideas, so that we may, as Thoreau might put it, talk about "not the Times,… [but] the Eternities."[92] I observed a conversation one time that began in the most ordinary fashion: two people were talking about their backgrounds, getting acquainted with one another, discussing family and upbringing and jobs, when one asked the other, "Are you religious?" "It depends," came the answer, "what you mean by 'religious.'" "Do you believe in God?" asked the first. "It depends on what you mean by 'God.'" And thence proceeded a conversation between the two about each of their senses of what "God" means, what "God" is (and is not), and what they believed about these matters. Neither, I daresay, sought to convince the other of anything; rather, these two people engaged in a mutual exploration of an important idea, and they were perhaps led by it to deeper understandings of their own, most fundamental convictions about that idea.

The second key idea concerning the content of our spiritual intercourse is that it must be *authentic, honest, truthful.* Plato has Socrates express frustration whenever he encounters an interlocutor who seems not to be answering his questions genuinely. For example, in the *Gorgias,* Socrates chides his interlocutor, Callicles, for failing to answer questions honestly as they investigate the natures of good and evil, pleasure and pain. "Give me no haphazard answers contrary to your opinion," says Socrates,[93] because in order "to know what is true and what is false in the subject under discussion,"[94] partners in philosophical inquiry must speak their authentic minds. When I engage and am engaged by another in meaningful conversation about the most important matters, I am obliged to share my own true thoughts, uncertainties, insights, puzzlements. Love is not a game—we don't play with words and ideas when we encounter another in a spirit of *eros.* Rather, love demands that we "bare our souls" to one another, that we become naked and vulnerable, that we share our deepest senses of the things we talk about.

What, now, of the forms of erotic talk? What uses of language do most to create opportunities for the most profound insights of which we are capable? Again, two features suggest themselves from Plato's portrayals of philosophical conversation.

One emphasizes the centrality of *questions*. In order to assist the other in the delivery of whatever deep insights might be gestating within him/herself, I must continually invite him/her to go beyond/deeper than where s/he is at the present moment. What *do* you mean by "God?" What *do* you think "beauty" is? And as you explore your own thinking and feeling about these matters, as you work to articulate this or that sense of the idea under consideration, I must continue to ask questions, to probe, to penetrate into the deeper layers of your *psyché*, to create openings for you to go more deeply still. The Platonic/Socratic *eros* is largely an art of asking the right question at the right time as conversation unfolds, even as I submit to the questioning of the other. And as we reciprocate our questioning and our disclosures, the conversation leads us ever deeper into ourselves and each other until, perhaps, we recognize ourselves in one another, we encounter some fundamental truth to which we both have been led, and we confirm our shared insight even as we grasp that "existence is beyond the power of words to describe," and we linger in the satisfied silence of our personal/common understanding.

The other principal feature emphasizes the role of analogical or metaphorical expression. Again drawing on Plato's Socrates as the exemplar of erotic dialogue, we can see that a recurring element in his talk is his employment of analogies as a way of stimulating deep thinking about abstract concepts. Certainly the vivid analogies in the *Phaedrus* (where the soul is characterized as being like a charioteer and two horses of opposing impulses and desires) and the *Symposium* (particularly Aristophanes' colorful account of why *Eros* is a longing for physical (re)union with one's severed other half) are instrumental in allowing participants (and perhaps readers) to envision the true natures of the subjects under consideration. Most conspicuously, the analogy between physical and spiritual procreation creates important opportunities for understanding how conversation can yield profound insight into the nature of things. Metaphorical thinking, supplemented by analytical modes, seems to be fundamental to the generation of insight. In his study of Giovanni Batistta Vico's thought, for example, Verene observes that "The metaphor…is the very basis of thought. Whenever the mind is deadlocked or fatigued with old forms of thought, it can find a new starting point, a revival, only by the power of the metaphor."[95] The metaphor liberates the mind from literal and analytical ways of thinking about the world and creates an opportunity for the shift in perspective that induces insight. The metaphorical vision creates an opening in experience, a portal on the unities underlying the flow of events, an aperture through which the first principles of nature can be glimpsed again by the soul.

CONCLUSION

In his description of "the practice of love," Fromm maintains that "…the art of lov-ing requires the practice of faith."[96] I believe that the quasi-Platonist understanding of philosophical conversation advanced here requires just such a practice. It is an act of faith, after all, to believe that the cosmos makes sense, that it is governed by laws or principles that are universal in their application, coherent, self-consistent, stable, enduring. It is an act of faith to believe that the human mind is capable of grasping those principles, and that they are embedded in our very souls. It is an act of faith to believe that my loving another will awaken a loving response in him/her, and that together we can penetrate to the cosmic truths that are hidden in the depths of our souls. So, too, in its way, is this chapter an act of faith, inasmuch as I offer it in the hope that it will be considered on its own terms, and that the reader will consider it with the same openness and generosity of spirit that I described above. My wish, at any rate, is that my effort at reaching out to you—with all of the authenticity, truth-fulness, and honesty I can muster—will provide meaningful opportunities for you to look deeply into yourself and see whether there are ways in which Plato's vision holds true for you.

One source of resistance to the account provided here might be the enduring impression so many of us have that, in Plato's scheme, the relationship between lover and beloved is unbalanced and presumptuous. Plato is often viewed as portraying a conception of philosophical conversation in which a person who already possesses wisdom (the lover) leads another (the beloved) to those "truths" and "realities" the lover has grasped even before the encounter begins.[97] This is not my understanding of Plato's theory of love, as the foregoing should make clear. Rather, in the spirit of humility and receptivity I have attributed to the Socrates of Plato's dialogues, the interpretation offered here is predicated on the assumption that, even if the lover has glimpsed for her/himself some of the universal truths that dwell in the depths of her/his soul, they cannot be "implanted" in the soul of the other. I cannot impregnate my beloved with my own wisdom. Rather, I love the other in order to assist her/him in giving birth to her/his *own* insights, her/his *own* incarnations of the truths that dwell within us all. As we talk and listen to one another, we lead each other and ourselves to the threshold of the inexpressible, to the core of existence. It is up to each of us to be enlightened in our own way by this, and thereby to behold the one Truth to which our different paths have led us.

Finally, we must acknowledge in the entire enterprise the centrality of beauty. There is something about the aesthetic experience—the encounter with what awakens in us feelings of awe, wonder, and worshipfulness—that enables us to transcend our individuality, our situatedness, our provinciality, and to experience our unity with the essence of the cosmos. The structure and movement of the heavens, the operation of nature in the evolution and transformation of life, the workings of human nature in our fleeting moments with one another–these *are* beauty in the unfolding of our lives. To the extent that we can open ourselves to them, particularly in the company of those whom we love, we can see into the deepest mysteries of our beings. This, too, is an act of faith.[98]

NOTES

1. Fletcher, *Situation Ethics: The New Morality* (Philadelphia: Westminster Press, 1966); Fletcher, *Moral Responsibility: Situation Ethics at Work* (Philadelphia: Westminster Press, 1967); Brockriede, "Arguers as Lovers," *Philosophy and Rhetoric* 5 (1972): 1–11; Caputo, *Against Ethics: Contributions of a Poetics of Obligation with Constant Reference to Deconstruction* (Bloomington, IN: Indiana University Press, 1993).

2. Johnstone, Jr., "Towards an Ethic of Rhetoric," *Communication* 6 (1981): 305–314.

3. Gilligan, *In a Different Voice: Psychological Theory and Women's Development* (Cambridge, MA: Harvard University Press, 1982).

4. Hyde, *The Life-Giving Gift of Acknowledgment: A Philosophical and Rhetorical Inquiry* (West Lafayette, IN: Indiana University Press, 2006).

5. Eubanks, "Reflections on the Moral Dimension of Communication," *The Southern Speech Communication Journal* 45 (1980): 297–312; Johnstone, "Reagan, Rhetoric, and the Public Philosophy: Ethics and Politics in the 1984 Campaign," *Southern Communication Journal* 60 (1995): 93–108; Johnstone, "Evolution, Speech, and Morality: Toward a Rhetoric of Survival," *Dialogue and Universalism* 5 (1995): 85–104.

6. Levinas, *Ethics and Infinity: Conversations with Phillippe Nemo* (Pittsburgh: Duquesne University Press, 1985): Bauman, *Postmodern Ethics* (Cambridge, MA: Blackwell, 1993).

7. Johnstone, "Ethics, Wisdom, and the Mission of Contemporary Rhetoric: The Realization of the Human Being," *Central States Speech Journal* 32 (1981): 177–188.

8. Ibid., 180.

9. Ibid., 180.

10. As is no doubt clear, this "universalist" and "essentialist" way of thinking about the human being emphasizes *similitude* rather than *difference*. It dwells on what we have in common, instead of what individuates us. In this respect, it is at odds with much "postmodernist" thought concerning ontology and ethics. See, for example, Bauman (1993) and Caputo (1993).

11. Nussbaum, "Human Function and Social Justice: In Defense of Aristotelian Essentialism," *Political Theory* 20 (1992): 202–246.

12. Plato, *Phaedrus,* R. Hackforth (trans.) in Edith Hamilton and Huntington Cairns (eds.), *The Selected Dialogues of Plato* (New York: Pantheon Books, 1961), 246b-c.

13. Ibid., 245c. (Unless otherwise noted, all quotations from the *Phaedrus* are from Hackforth's translation.)

14. Ibid., 242c.

15. Plato, *Greater Hippas,* in Edith Hamilton and Huntington Cairns (eds.), *The Selected Dialogues of Plato,* (New York, Pantheon Books, 1961), 296a.

16. Plato, *Phaedo,* in Edith Hamilton and Huntington Cairns (eds.), *The Selected Dialogues of Plato* (New York: Pantheon Books, 1961), 79d.

17. Plato, *Laws,* in Edith Hamilton and Huntington Cairns (eds.) *The Selected Dialogues of Plato* (New York: Pantheon Books, 1961), III.689a-d.

18. Plato, *Republic,* in Edith Hamilton and Huntington Cairns (eds.), *The Selected Dialogues of Plato* (New York: Pantheon Books, 1961), 514a-516c.

19. Plato, *Phaedrus,* 242c.

20. In justifying his need to recant his own "irreverent" speech on love, Socrates tells Phaedrus, "If love is, as he is indeed, a god or a divine being, he cannot be an evil thing; yet this pair of speeches treated him as evil. That then was their offense toward Love, to which was added the most exquisite folly of parading their pernicious rubbish as though it were good sense because it might deceive a few miserable people and win their applause.... Suppose we were being listened to by a man of generous and humane character, who loved or had once loved another such as himself. Suppose he heard us saying that for some trifling cause lovers conceive bitter hatred and a spirit of malice and injury toward their loved ones. Wouldn't he be sure to think that we had been brought up among the scum of the people and had never seen a case of noble love? Wouldn't he utterly refuse to accept our vilification of Love?.... Then out of respect for him, and in awe of Love himself, I should like to wash the bitter taste out of my mouth with a draught of wholesome discourse . . ." (242e-243d).

21. Ibid., 246d-e.

22. Ibid., 247a.

23. Ibid., 247c-d.

24. Ibid., 247d-e.

25. Ibid., 249e. Also see *Phaedo* (75c-d): "Then if we obtained it before our birth, and possessed it when we were born, we had knowledge, both before and at the moment of birth, not only of equality and relative magnitudes, but of all absolute standards. Our present argument applies no more to equality than it does to absolute beauty, goodness, uprightness, holiness.... So we must have obtained knowledge of all these characteristics before our birth." Similarly in the *Meno* (81c-d): "Thus the soul, since it is immortal and has been born many times, and has seen all things both here and in the other world, has learned everything that is. So we need not be surprised if it can recall the knowledge of virtue or anything else which...it once possessed. All nature is akin, and the soul has learned everything...."

26. By "presocratic" I have in mind such thinkers as Anaximander, Heraclitus, and Pythagoras. Useful accounts of their views are to be found in Guthrie (1962), Kirk, Raven, and Schofield (1983), and Kahn (1979, 1994). Such modern thinkers as Albert Einstein, Stephen Hawking, and Carl Sagan, among others, have advanced the idea that cosmic processes are governed by laws of energy, matter, and motion.

27. This interpretation of Plato's thinking emphasizes its quasi-mystical elements, which resonate with some modern accounts of the experience of union with "what is." For example, philosopher Alan Watts (1967) writes, "This mysterious something has been called God, the Absolute, Nature, Substance, Energy, Space, Ether, Mind, Being, the Void, the Infinite–names and ideas which shift in popularity and respectability with the winds of intellectual fashion, of considering the universe intelligent or stupid, superhuman or subhuman, specific or vague. All of them might be dismissed as nonsense-noises if the notion of an underlying Ground of Being were no more than a product of intellectual speculation. But these names are often used to designate the content of a vivid and almost sensorily concrete experience–the 'unitive' experience of the mystic, which, with secondary variations, is found in almost all cultures at all times" (133). Watts ends up referring to the indefinable, indwelling, all-encompassing "reality" of the cosmos as "IT," portraying this idea in the words of James Broughton: "*This it It and I am It and You are It and so is That and He is It and She is It and It is It and That is That*" (James Broughton, *The Bard and the Harper*, recorded by James Broughton and Joel Andrews. LP–1013, produced by Musical Engineering Associates, Sausalito, CA, 1965. Cited in Watts, p. 145, note 4). Also see William James (1929), whose account of "cosmic consciousness" (pp. 389–91) echoes something of Plato's mystical vision.

28. Plato, *Phaedrus*, 248c.

29. Ibid., 246a-b, 253c-e.

30. In the *Republic* (IV.439d-441a), Plato provides a similar account of the soul's elements, dividing it into Reason (which deliberates and "reckons" about action), the "Spirited" or passionate part (*thymos*, in virtue of which we feel anger and other strong emotions), and the Appetites (associated with love, hunger, thirst, and "the flutter and titillation of other desires").

31. Plato, *Phaedrus*, 250a.

32. Ibid., 250b-c.

33. Ibid., 250e.

34. Ibid., 251a.

35. Ibid.

36. Ibid, 253e.

37. Plato's colorful description of this process (254e) is worth reviewing: "The driver,...like a racer recoiling from the starting rope, jerks back the bit in the mouth of the wanton horse with an even stronger pull, bespatters his railing tongue and his jaws with blood, and forcing him down on legs and haunches delivers him over to anguish. And so it happens time and again, until the evil steed casts off his wantonness; humbled in the end, he obeys the counsel of his driver, and when he sees the fair beloved is like to die of fear. Wherefore at long last the soul of the lover follows after the beloved with reverence and awe."

38. Plato, *Phaedrus*, 255d.

39. Ibid., 256a-b.

40. "*megas theos...thaumastos en anthrôpois te kai theois*," Plato, *Symposium*, Michael Joyce (trans.), in Edith Hamilton and Huntington Cairns (eds.), *The Selected Dialogues of Plato* (New York: Pantheon Books, 1961), 178a.

41. Unless otherwise noted, quotations of the *Symposium* are from Joyce's translation.

42. Plato, *Symposium*, 180b.

43. On the transition from a mythic to a philosophical conception of the divine, see Guthrie (1953, 1962; Vernant 1982, 1983). In his *History* (1962), Guthrie comments, "with the Greeks we stand at the beginning of rational thought in Europe. It follows that we shall not only be concerned with reasoned explanation of scientific observation, but shall be watching the emergence of these activities from the mists of a pre-scientific age. This emergence is not sudden, but slow and gradual…. I shall not…assert that at one bound the line was crossed between pre-rational, mythical or anthropomorphic conceptions and a purely rational and scientific outlook. No such clearly-marked line existed, or exists today" (p. 1).

44. Plato, *Symposium*, 180d.

45. Ibid., 181b.

46. Ibid., 181c.

47. Ibid., 184c.

48. Ibid., 186a-b.

49. Ibid., 193c.

50. Ibid., 192d-e. The Greek verbs are instructive in this passage. *Syntêxai* derives from *syntêkô*, "to fuse into a single mass," "to weld together." *Symphysêsai* declines from *symphysis*, which denotes a "natural (*physis*) growing together" and a "continuity of substance." Both suggest a complete fusion of two things into a single entity, and the latter connotes an organic unity. This yearning for physical unity or "growing together" is the essence of erotic desire.

51. See Levy (1979). Psychologist Erich Fromm (1956), in his own account of the nature of love, writes that "the deepest need of man…is the need to overcome his separateness, to leave the prison of his aloneness. The *absolute* failure to achieve this aim means insanity…. Man–of all ages and cultures–is confronted with the solution of one and the same question: the question of how to overcome separateness, how to achieve union, how to transcend one's own individual life and find at-onement" (p. 9). Similarly, a bit later he remarks that "The full answer [to the problem of separateness] lies in the achievement of interpersonal union, of fusion with another person, in *love*. This desire for interpersonal fusion is the most powerful striving in man, it is the most fundamental passion, it is the force which keeps the human race together, the clan, the family, society" (p. 18). Also see his discussion of *erotic love*, pp. 52–57.

52. Plato, *Symposium*, 195a-197d.

53. Ibid., 197e.

54. Ibid., 199c-201c.

55. Ibid., 201d.

56. Ibid.

57. Ibid., 202e-203a. In his translation of the *Symposium* for the Loeb edition, Lamb (Plato, 1925) notes that "*Daimones* and *to daimonion* represent the mysterious agencies and influences by which the gods communicate with mortals" (p. 179). Murray (1925, p. 175) holds that the term means the same thing as "Angel," from *angelos*, a "messenger" (especially from god).

Burkert's (1985) discussion of the term and its role in Greek religion is particularly helpful (pp. 179–81).

58. Ibid., 204b-e.

59. Ibid., 205e.

60. Ibid., 206a.

61. Ibid., 206c-207a, my translation. The Greek terms are important here. "Begetting" is a translation of *tokos,* "a bringing forth, childbirth, procreation." It is the organic, natural process of "engendering" (*gennêsis,* at 206c) or producing offspring, consistent with the use of *kuousi* (from *kuopsore,* to be with young, to be pregnant) to describe the creative impulse in the human soul. All of these words and ideas express the process of acquiring wisdom as natural, organic, and even as mammalian.

62. Ibid., 208e-209a.

63. Ibid., 209a-b.

64. Ibid., 210a-211c.

65. Useful accounts of the "ascent passage" are to be found in Cornford, 1967, pp. 76–78; and in Guthrie, 1986, pp. 387–95.

66. Plato, *Symposium,* 210a.

67. Ibid, 210b-c.

68. Guthrie, *Myth and Reason* (London: The London School of Economics and Political Science, 1953), 390.

69. The term *epiphany* comes from the Greek *epiphaneia,* meaning an "appearance, a coming into light or view" (as with the sun at dawn) or "a sudden appearance" (as with an enemy during war). In *koinê* Greek, it refers to the coming of Christ. According to Natanson (1968), it denotes "a momentous and instantaneous manifestation of reality;…a sudden breaking into experience with arterial force, revealing 'that which is' with utter truth and candor" (p. 135). This latter is the sense in which I use the term here.

70. *Symp.* 210e-211b. The phrase "wondrous vision which is the very soul of beauty" is Joyce's translation of *katopsetai ti thaumaston tên physin kalon.* The first of these terms is the future tense of *kathoraô,* a verb meaning "have deep insight, keen vision." *Thaumaston,* "wonderful" or "marvelous," comes from *thaumazô,* "wonder or marvel at, to worship." What is indicated here is that, in the moment of aesthetic rapture, one's soul is in a state of wonder and worshipfulness, and that in this state it can "see" into the very nature of Beauty.

71. Plato, *Symposium,* 211d.

72. Lao Tzu, *The Way of Life* (New York: Capricorn Books, 1944), 25.

73. Plato, *Seventh Letter,* L. A. Post (trans.), in Edith Hamilton and Huntington Cairns, eds., *The Selected Dialogues of Plato* (New York: Pantheon Books, 1961), 341d. Using a similar metaphor, Thoreau (1965) wrote that "knowledge does not come to us by details, but in flashes of light from heaven" (p. 727).

74. Plato, *Seventh Letter,* 221d-222a.

75. I have found particularly helpful the thinking of Erich Fromm (1956), whose conception of *erotic love* is clearly inspired by Plato's. In his account of "the theory of love," Fromm describes the nature of "erotic love" as "the craving for complete fusion, for union with another person" (pp. 52–53). A little later, Fromm's account parallels my own interpretation of Plato's view of *eros* and the deepest nature of *psychê:* "Erotic love is exclusive, but it loves in the other person all of mankind, all that is alive. It is exclusive only in the sense that I can fuse myself fully and intensely with one person only…. Erotic love…has one premise. That I love from the essence of my being–and experience the other person in the essence of his or her being. In essence, all human beings are identical. We are all part of One; we are One" (pp. 54–55). I shall draw on Fromm's account of "the practice of love" (p. 107ff.) in describing the qualities of truly loving dialogue.

76. Plato, *Phaedrus,* 277b-c.

77. Liddell and Scott, *A Greek-English Lexicon* (Oxford: The Clarendon Press, 1996).

78. Fromm (1956) writes that "Love is not primarily a relationship to a specific person; it is an *attitude,* an *orientation* of *character* which determines the relatedness of a person to the world as a whole, not toward one 'object' of love" (p. 46).

79. Nussbaum, *Love's Knowledge: Essays on Philosophy and Literature* (New York and Oxford: Oxford University Press, 1990), 274.

80. Johnstone, Jr., "Toward an Ethics of Rhetoric," 310. Lao Tzu (1944) casts this idea in gendered terms to emphasize the quality of *receptiveness:* "Can you hold the door of your tent wide to the firmament?…Can you, mating with heaven, serve as the female part? Can your learned head take leaven from the wisdom of your heart? If you can bear issue and nourish its growing, if you can guide without claim or strife, if you can stay in the lead of men without their knowing, you are at the core of life" (p. 30). Look carefully at the sexual metaphor here: "Can you, mating with heaven, serve as the female part?" Can you receive the gifts of the cosmos, taking them into yourself? Can you surrender yourself, yield yourself, to the flashes of light, so that within your soul might be kindled the sparks of knowledge that will grow, with proper care, into the vision that is wisdom? Also see Brockriede (1972), pp. 5–8.

81. Fromm, *The Art of Loving* (New York: Harper & Brothers, 1956), 22.

82. Ibid., 24–25.

83. Bauman, *Postmodern Ethics,* 92. In elaborating this idea, Bauman writes that "the caress is the gesture of one body reaching towards the other; already, from the start, in its inner 'structure,' an act of *invasion,* let it be just tentative and exploratory" (p. 93).

84. Ibid., 72–74.

85. Plato, *Theaetetus,* in Edith Hamilton and Huntington Cairns (eds.), *The Selected Dialogues of Plato* (New York: Pantheon Books, 1961), 150b-d. The historical Socrates, of course, is famous for his disclaimer of any wisdom of his own. "I am so far like the midwife that I cannot myself give birth to wisdom, and…though I question others, I can myself bring nothing to light because there is no wisdom in me…. Those who frequent my company at first appear, some of them, quite unintelligent, but, as we go further with our discussions, all who are favored by heaven make progress at a rate that seems surprising to others as well as to themselves, although it is clear that they have never learned anything from me. The many admirable truths they bring to

birth have been discovered by themselves from within. But the delivery is heaven's work and mine" (*Thea.* 150c-d).

86. Fromm, *The Art of Loving*, 26. In his account of *responsibility* as an element of love, Fromm comments that "responsibility, in its true sense, is an entirely voluntary act; it is my response to the needs, expressed and unexpressed, of another human being. To be 'responsible' means to be able and ready to 'respond'" (pp. 27–28). Also see Mayeroff (1971), especially pp. 3–8, 30–34; and Niebuhr (1963), especially pp. 47–68.

87. Fromm, *The Art of Loving*, 114.

88. Ibid., 118.

89. Ibid., 28.

90. Ibid., 29.

91. Mayeroff (1971) remarks that "Patience is not waiting passively for something to happen, but is a kind of participation with the other in which we give fully of ourselves" (p. 12).

92. Thoreau, "Life Without Principle," in *Walden and Other Writings of Henry David Thoreau*, (New York: Random House, 1965), 727.

93. Plato, *Gorgias*, in Edith Hamilton and Huntington Cairns (eds.), *The Selected Dialogues of Plato*, (New York, Pantheon Books, 1961), 500b.

94. Plato, *Gorgias*, 505e.

95. Verene, *Vico's Science of the Imagination* (Ithaca: Cornell University Press, 1981), 117.

96. Fromm, *The Art of Loving*, 121.

97. E.G., Scott, "On Viewing Rhetoric as Epistemic," *Central States Speech Journal* 18 (1967): 9–17.

98. Earlier versions of this chapter were presented at the National Communication Association Convention in Chicago, Illinois, in April 1994; and at the Biennial Conference on Communication Ethics, held at Duquesne University in Pittsburgh, Pennsylvania, in June 2006. I also wish to acknowledge the assistance I received in revising this paper from my friends Walt Fisher and Bill Rawlins.

BIBLIOGRAPHY

Bauman, Zygmunt. *Postmodern Ethics*. Cambridge, MA: Blackwell, 1993.

Brockriede, Wayne. "Arguers as Lovers." *Philosophy and Rhetoric* 5 (1972): 1–11.

Burkert, Walter. *Greek Religion*. Cambridge, MA: Harvard University Press, 1985.

Caputo, John D. *Against Ethics: Contributions to a Poetics of Obligation with Constant Reference to Deconstruction*. Bloomington, IN: Indiana University Press, 1993.

Cornford, Francis M. "The Doctrine of Eros Is Plato's *Symposium*," in Cornford, *The Unwritten Philosophy*. Cambridge: Cambridge University Press 1967, pp. 68–80.

Eubanks, Ralph T. "Reflections on the Moral Dimension of Communication." *The Southern Speech Communication Journal* 45 (1980): 297–312.

Fletcher, Joseph. *Situation Ethics: The New Morality.* Philadelphia: Westminster Press, 1966.

———. *Moral Responsibility: Situation Ethics at Work.* Philadelphia: Westminster Press, 1967.

Fromm, Erich. *The Art of Loving.* New York: Harper & Brothers, 1956.

Gilligan, Carol. *In a Different Voice: Psychological Theory and Women's Development.* Cambridge, MA: Harvard University Press, 1982.

Guthrie, W. K. C. *Myth and Reason.* London: The London School of Economics and Political Science, 1953.

———. *A History of Greek Philosophy,* Vol. 1. Cambridge: Cambridge University Press, 1962.

———. *A History of Greek Philosophy,* Vol. 4. Cambridge: Cambridge University Press, 1986.

Hyde, Michael J. *The Life-Giving Gift of Acknowledgment: A Philosophical and Rhetorical Inquiry.* West Lafayette, IN: Purdue University Press, 2006.

James, William. *The Varieties of Religious Experience.* New York: The Modern Library, 1929.

Johnstone, Christopher Lyle. "Ethics, Wisdom, and the Mission of Contemporary Rhetoric: The Realization of Human Being." *Central States Speech Journal* 32 (1981): 177–88.

———. "Reagan, Rhetoric, and the Public Philosophy: Ethics and Politics in the 1984 Campaign." *Southern Communication Journal* 60 (1995): 93–108.

———. "Evolution, Speech, and Morality: Toward a Rhetoric of Survival." *Dialogue and Universalism* 5 (1995): 85–104.

Johnstone, Henry W., Jr. "Toward an Ethics of Rhetoric." *Communication* 6 (1981): 305–14.

Kahn, Charles H. *The Art and Thought of Heraclitus.* Cambridge: Cambridge University Press, 1979.

———. *Anaximander and the Origins of Greek Cosmology.* Indianapolis: Hackett Publishing Co, 1994.

Kirk, G. S., J. E. Raven, and M. Schofield. *The Presocratic Philosophers,* 2nd edition. Cambridge: Cambridge University Press, 1983.

Lao Tzu. *The Way of Life.* Trans. Witter Bynner. New York: Capricorn Books, 1944.

Levinas, Emmanuel. *Ethics and Infinity: Conversations with Phillippe Nemo,* trans. Richard A. Cohen. Pittsburgh: Duquesne University Press, 1985.

Levy, Donald. "The Definition of Love in Plato's *Symposium.*" *Journal of the History of Ideas* 40 (1979): 285–91.

Liddell, H. G. and R. Scott. *A Greek-English Lexicon,* 9th ed (revised). Oxford: The Clarendon Press, 1996.

Mayeroff, Milton. *On Caring.* New York: Harper and Row, 1971.

Murray, Gilbert. *Five Stages of Greek Religion.* New York: Columbia University Press, 1925.

Natanson, Maurice. *Literature, Philosophy and the Social Sciences: Essays in Existentialism and Phenomenology.* The Hague: Martinus Nijhoff, 1968.

Niebuhr, H. Richard. *The Responsible Self.* New York: Harper and Row, 1963.

Nussbaum, Martha C. *Love's Knowledge: Essays on Philosophy and Literature.* New York and Oxford: Oxford University Press, 1990.

————. "Human Functioning and Social Justice: In Defense of Aristotelian Essentialism." *Political Theory* 20 (1992): 202–246.

Plato. *Phaedrus*. Trans. R. Hackforth, in Edith Hamilton and Huntington Cairns, eds., *The Selected Dialogues of Plato*. New York: Pantheon Books, 1961. pp. 475–525.

————. *Symposium*. Trans. Michael Joyce, in Edith Hamilton and Huntington Cairns, eds., *The elected Dialogues of Plato*. New York: Pantheon Books, 1961. pp. 526–74.

————. *Symposium*. Trans. W. R. M. Lamb. Cambridge, MA: Harvard University Press, 1983.

————. *Phaedo*. Trans. Hugh Tredennick, in Edith Hamilton and Huntington Cairns, eds., *The Selected Dialogues of Plato*. New York: Pantheon Books, 1961. pp. 40–98.

————. *Seventh Letter*. Trans. L. A. Post, in Edith Hamilton and Huntington Cairns, eds., *The Selected Dialogues of Plato*. New York: Pantheon Books, 1961. pp. 1574–98.

————. *Meno*. Trans. W. K. C. Guthrie, in Edith Hamilton and Huntington Cairns, eds., *The Selected Dialogues of Plato*. New York: Pantheon Books, 1961. pp. 353–84.

Scott, Robert L. "On Viewing Rhetoric as Epistemic." *Central States Speech Journal* 18 (1967): 9–17.

Thoreau, Henry David. "Life Without Principle," in *Walden and Other Writings of Henry David Thoreau*. New York: Random House, 1965. pp. 711–32.

Verene, Donald Phillip. *Vico's Science of the Imagination*. Ithaca: Cornell University Press, 1981.

Vernant, J.-P. *The Origins of Greek Thought*. Ithaca: Cornell University Press, 1982.

————. *Myth and Thought Among the Greeks*. London: Routledge and Kegan Paul, Ltd, 1983.

Watts, Alan. *The Book: On the Taboo Against Knowing Who You Are*. Toronto: Collier Books, 1967.

Scripting Jewishness Within the Satire *The Hebrew Hammer*

RONALD L. JACKSON II AND JAMIE MOSHIN

Heralded as an homage to the 1970s blaxploitation movie era, the critically acclaimed Sundance film festival picture-turned-Comedy Central flick *The Hebrew Hammer* begins on a solemn but familiar note. The film proper opens on little Mordechai Jefferson Carver, an 8- or 9-year-old Jewish elementary school student, walking to his Catholic school as the song "Dreidel Dreidel Dreidel" is piped from on high. He clutches his Sandy Koufax lunchbox as his classmates attack him with popular Jewish stereotypes—"Jews have big noses, eat bagels and love money." The camera then cuts to a scene where his White female teacher, in the spirit of cultural tolerance during Christmas time, tells the racially homogenous class of all White students that they should honor Mordechai's holiday, Chanukka, "even though his people have bizarre naming rituals and customs and are cheap." The narrative continues with Mordechai on his way home from school, passing shops advertising that Jews/Kikes are not welcome when suddenly Mordechai has his dreidel smashed by Santa Claus. This is the way we are introduced to the title character, the Hebrew Hammer, a name derived from that of Judah Macabee, the hero in the actual story of Hanukkah whose name means Judah the Hammer.

This action comedy movie, developed in the tradition of the Blaxploitation film genre, attempts to do many things rhetorically and also holds several promises that will be deconstructed in this essay: (1) to develop the first Jewish superhero (to appear on film) that will lead the Jewish Justice League out of a cultural quagmire;(2) to present to the viewing audience the first Jewsploitation film while giving homage to Blaxploitation;(3) to demonstrate how the persecutory experiences of Jews and Blacks in the United States are similar; and (4) to educate audiences about Jewish stereotypes as well as Jewish identities.

In some ways Jewish director Jonathan Kesselman's film is successful; and in many other ways it is also problematic. Despite the official movie website's misguiding claim that the protagonist is sexy and strong, if the point of the movie is to embody an action hero that defies Hollywood's portrayal of stereotypical Jewish characters as weak and aloof, then the movie may be considered successful. Through its satiric commentaries, there is something both salvatory and restorative about the generally positive image of Jews portrayed in the film. Yet, its problems lie in its use of Jewish humor to capture an unwitting audience, its use of satire to make a statement about Jewish identities, and its adoption of a Blaxploitation formula to both tell a primarily Jewish story and to liken Jewish and Black subjugation.

Within this essay we will present a plot synopsis, a discussion of humor rituals, an explanation of satire, and then a critical analysis of Blaxploitation and Jewsploitation, all as a means for exploring the achievements and problems of this film.

SYNOPSIS OF *THE HEBREW HAMMER*

With the film slogan, "Part Man. Part Street. Part Kosher," *The Hebrew Hammer* is introduced to viewers as the first "Jewsploitation" film. Kesselman wants his viewers to know immediately that he is borrowing from the Blaxploitation genre. In this movie which began as Kesselman's second semester short film while studying at USC film school, he offers winks to *Shaft* and *Sweet Sweetback's Baadasssss Song* via a song/credit montage that follows *Shaft* to the letter along with styling reminiscent of *Sweet Sweetback's Baadasssss Song's* trademark pimp characters. *The Hebrew Hammer's* theme song echoes *Shaft*, but with distinctly Jewish overtones. The song's lines, spoken by an Isaac Hayes sounding voice, are "Who's the certified, circumcised dick that's a sex machine to all the chicks? Hammer! (Background response) Amen. He's just trying to do some good helpin' brothas in the hood. Hammer! (Background response) Right on!" Additional lines include: "He's a bad mutha—*sheket bavakashah*," and, most disturbingly, "Who's the kike who will help all gentiles?" As we hear the derivative theme song, the credits flash across the screen, all in Hebrew-esque letters.

As described earlier the opening scene shows Mordechai as a little kid in a classroom and thereafter walking home from school. Subsequently, the film jumps to the present-day, Orthodox Mordechai (Adam Goldberg), who is resplendent in a Jewified pimp-like blaxploitation outfit: he wears a black leather trench coat, a black cowboy hat with an extremely long feather, a tallis, a yarmulke (when the situation calls for it), and a chai necklace. We join him as he patrols the streets of Brooklyn (or "the hood"), greeting fellow Jews in Hebrew or Yiddish, rescuing the yarmulkes of tormented boys, and the like.

The audience is then transported to the North Pole, where we are in time to witness a board meeting chaired by the current Santa Claus. We learn that "Santa" is a position passed down from generation to generation and that the present incarnation is a forward-thinker; he believes in unity between Christians, Jews and African Americans and pushed for the adoption of the term "Happy Holidays." His son Damien (Andy Dick), however, does not share his father's views. His vision for the world is the destruction of Hanukkah, and the first step on this path is the assassination of his father.

After the murder, the Jewish Justice League (JJL), comprised of the influential heads of such forces as the World Wide Jewish Media Conspiracy, the Anti-Denigration League, and the Coalition of Jewish Athletes (which has no representative), meets to discuss how best to deal with this new menace to Jewishness. The Head of the JJL, Bloomenbergensteinthal (Peter Coyote) is desperate to find an agent who will confront Damien and deliver the people of Israel. As the representatives consume bagels and throw out names of various weak, scholarly Jews who might defend Hanukkah, Esther Bloomenbergensteinthal (Judy Greer), the daughter of the Head, suggests that Mordechai Jefferson Carver—The Hebrew Hammer—be selected as their hero. The JJL initially balks, due to previous catastrophic run-ins with this loose cannon, but then concedes.

In an attempt to convince the Hebrew Hammer—a circumcised private dick (i.e., detective)—to take the case, Esther accompanies him to his mother's for Sabbath dinner. Mrs. Carver (Nora Dunn) is a squealing, Yiddish-speaking, force-feeding, guilt-provoking, "typical" Jewish mother. Concerned that she is not going to be able to persuade the Hammer, Esther turns to Mordechai's mother for help. Mrs. Carver proposes a deal: "I'll help you with Hanukkah if you give him a little blowjob here and there." She then unleashes the Jewish mother arsenal upon her son, nagging and guilting him until he finally relents. Esther then accompanies the Hammer to the headquarters of the JJL, where he must pass through a battery of tests to prove that he is indeed a Jew: Carver must state his full Hebrew name, name six dishes on the Passover Seder plate, demonstrate musical aptitude, display his circumcised member, and show his capacity for whining. Subsequently, the Hammer meets with Bloomenbergensteinthal, who convinces Carver that "the fate of Hanukkah rests on your shoulders," to which Carver, the anxious Jew, replies, "that's a lot of pressure for one Jew; I'm schvitzing as it is."

To garner support for his mission, the Hebrew Hammer pays a visit to the Kwanzaa Liberation Front (KLF). There he rendezvous with his compatriate Mohammed Ali Paula Abdul Rahim (Mario Van Peebles), who is the leader of the beat-boxing, gun-toting, marijuana-smoking misfits who decry the encroachment of the White man. Mordechai greets him with "My main man nigger Rahim," to which Rahim replies, "My main man kike." Rahim warns Carver that the word on the street is that "Santa gonna fuck Hanukkah's shit up." Based on bad information from an insider that Damien has placed within the KLF, the Hebrew Hammer attempts a sneak attack on the evil Santa, only to find himself at "Duke's Nazi Bar," with wall advertisements of a Gestapo pool party and "Old Adolf Ale." After withstanding a volley of insults and threats, the Hammer shoots up the bar and everyone in it. On his way out of the joint, Carver runs into Melvin van Peebles (director/writer/star of *Sweet Sweetback's Baadasssss Song*) in a cameo reprise of his role of Sweetback, who informs his Jewish follower that he is "taking a page out of Sweetback's book."

In the meantime, Damien Claus, with the help of his helper, Tiny Tim (Sean Whalen) is putting his plan into motion. To the sounds of R&B singer Curtis Mayfield's "Pusherman," Tiny Tim floods the streets with free copies of *It's a Wonderful Life*. As little Jewish kids are exposed to Jimmy Stewart's good cheer, they begin throwing their Jewishness by the wayside. To get to Damien, Carver and Esther dress up like a gentile couple, replete with blonde wigs, Jesus hats, and the like. These "gentiles" speak like 1950's-era TV sitcom characters and carry an American flag to display their overt patriotism. They meet up with Damien in the mall, where he is telling little Christian fans that Jews sacrifice gentile children. The children turn on the Jews, chasing them through the store, whereupon they are saved by Harriet Tubbleman and her Underground Jewish Railroad, which is literally an underground rollercoaster car. Kesselman unmistakenly presents this character as a send-up to Black freedom-fighter and "conductor of the underground railroad" Harriet Tubman who is otherwise known as "Black Moses."

Carver and Esther finally have sex, spicing up their intercourse with a dialogue about how they will raise their children. In the moments after coitus, Esther makes the mistake of telling Carver that she likes his mother. He becomes completely neurotic, telling her that "my mother's my pimp and she's whoring her bitch son out." Esther's father, a member of the JJL, then calls to tell the Hebrew Hammer that Damien is in the process of destroying the Jewish clock, which would eradicate the Jewish calendar and Jewishness as we know it. The Hebrew Hammer nearly fails to save the day—the approach of Sabbath thwarts him, as the Sabbath is his kryptonite. Luckily, the day is saved by the Kwanzaa Liberation Front.

Next, Rahim and Carver pursue Damien to his North Pole lair, which is guarded with a stereotype alarm system, programmed to detect non-WASP tendencies. After battling all of Santa's henchmen (and, of course, employing as many stereotypes as possible), the Hebrew Hammer comes face to face with his nemesis. In peril of losing the battle, Carver turns to the nuclear weapon of the Jewish arsenal: he guilts Damien until the evildoer crumbles. The Hebrew Hammer has saved Hanukkah! We are left with this message of good cheer: "Merry Christmas, Niggers, and a Happy Jew Year!"

As a satire, this film leaves itself open for rigorous interpretation and criticism, yet its utility may best be understood within the vein of both Jewish humor rituals and its satiric form.

EXPLORING THE NATURE & FUNCTION OF HUMOR

Humor brings members of groups closer together and helps to define group identity. At the same time, it draws a clear distinction between those who are not members of a specific group. Nilsen posits that:

> When insiders tell such jokes, the jokes are tiny revolutions in chiding friends about the frailties to which human beings are prone. The insider is trying to expand the possibilities for group attitudes and behavior. But when outsiders tell the jokes, the effect is quite the opposite. Outsiders tend to focus on the group's most obvious characteristics and to imply that these characteristics belong to everyone in the group. As outsiders, they have little power to bring internal change, so the effect is to stereotype the group, thereby shrinking the options for thought and action. The insider expands the boundaries, while the outsider telling the same or a similar joke tightens the noose (p. 932).[1]

Jokes that are told about one's own group are considered more acceptable, palatable, and funny: jokes that are told by Others or outsiders about one's group generally are not. According to Boskin and Dorinson, "people have undoubtedly always laughed at others who seemed 'distinct' to reassure themselves and to blunt the threats implicit in differences. Ethnic slurs in joking form have reflected the tensions of social difference in America.[2] Robinson and Smith-Lovin note that "an individual will use and appreciate humor when the objects of the humor are in categories to which the individual do not belong…people enjoy humor that targets members of groups with whom they do not empathize.[3] For instance, for a joke to be defined as true Jewish humor, it must come from Jews: "*Jewish jokes* are only those which are told by Jews to other Jews. Non-Jews tell *jokes about Jews*."[4] Koller, quoted in Silberman-Federman, further explains that any joke about Jews, but not *from* Jews is anti-Semitic: "A Jewish joke then is both developed and defined by Jews, while an anti-Semitic joke is manufactured and presented by non-Jews."[5] This ritualized humor, understandably, can be the source of misunderstanding and the cause of even greater tensions; humor can easily be seen as purposefully widening the gap between groups, though this might not be the intent. Nilsen shares an anecdote that demonstrates this occurrence:

> At a humor workshop on our campus a woman told how her parents had told her never to laugh at ethnic jokes. When she arrived at college as a freshman, her assigned roommate happened to be Jewish. While the two of them were getting acquainted, some of the roommate's friends from high school dropped in and told the latest Jewish jokes. The woman was proud that she didn't laugh, but the next day she was called in by the head resident and told that her roommate didn't feel comfortable and wanted a change. The roommate had concluded that the woman was Anti-Semitic and hadn't laughed because she accepted the characters in the jokes as accurate and therefore not funny.[6]

While silence as a reply to ethnic jokes may be just as dangerous and volatile as laughing at the joke, the looming issue is about the I-Other dialectic at work in humor rituals. It is critical to understand that the content of the joke is just as important as the source. Again, the most hurtful and unacceptable kind of ethnic humor is arguably that which emanates from an Outsider.

Because humor is a ritualized means both of uniting and maligning certain ethnic groups, it can be used as a tool for establishing power hierarchies and social control. Boskin and Dorinson[7] note that ethnic humor originated as a function of social class, rooted in feelings of White superiority and antagonism, and was used as a weapon by the haves against the have-nots. According to hierarchy-building theories of humor, individuals higher (or aspiring to be) in social hierarchy employ more humor than those of lesser status or power. Groups that have more social power than others tend to belittle other groups to maintain or improve their status. Groups with less power, it seems, tend to belittle themselves and the stereotypes ascribed to them in order to gain power. The authors further opine that higher-status groups use humor to keep lower-status groups low. It is also imbued with the ideology of the dominant social class. For example, in the United States, the pervading notions of competition and "survival of the fittest" emerge out of a capitalist and individualist instinct in which persons thrive at the top at the expense of others who are on the bottom of the class structure. Hence, the majority of ethnic jokes are about those who exist at the lower rungs due to their social positionality. One of the interesting dimensions of *The Hebrew Hammer* is that the humor is not steeped in economic but rather social and religious disadvantage. It is purely about structural inequalities related to ethnic politics and religion rather than what Blaxploitation films explored as racist vulgarities uncovered in the systemic exclusion of Blacks—which of course led to a lack of privilege and opportunity in every area of Black American life. So, clearly the struggles are different and therefore the put-downs and innuendos must also be different.

Humor, which may be used either to raise or subvert groups, can be a barbed and vicious weapon whose wounds can be inflicted so deeply that it takes many years of recuperation and healing to undo the harm. The only effective counter-weapons are deflection and/or diffusion. Without these, it flourishes mainly when there is tension between or within groups.[8] According to Boskin and Dorinson,[9] humor is delivered through bared teeth with the intent to either control or cause conflict. Robinson and Smith-Lovin refer to humor as "a socially acceptable form of aggression."[10] Grotjahn says that "wit is decidedly not a sign of gentle love, but of undisguised hostility."[11] Mintz quotes Boskin as saying "humor is one of the most effective and vicious weapons in the repertory of the human mind."[12] Gordon[13] feels that laughter is born out of hatred and is basically savage. While that seems harsh, if not misguided, Mintz[14] opines that ethnic humor in particular is often used as an expression of hostility and superiority, and can be seen as either fostering or softening that hostility. It is clear that humor may also be cathartic for insiders; however, when used by outsiders to castigate marginalized group members, it is counterproductive. Lowe,[15] in line with Boskin's and Dorinson's earlier comment that humor is used by those aspiring to raise themselves in the social hierarchy, asserts that humor is a weapon of liberation. Comedy is a ritual means of stepping outside of the dominant culture and attacking it. In this light, Lowe quotes Langston Hughes: "Since we have not been able to moralize them out of existence with indignant editorials, maybe we could laugh them to death with well-aimed ridicule."[16] Obrdlik[17] notes that people whose lives are marked by social uncertainty find refuge in making and spreading jokes about their oppressors.

Nilsen[18] refers to the attacking of out-groups as the "darker side" of ethnic humor. This sense of humor also works in reverse—groups often augment their identity on "humorous" stereotypes that are ascribed to them by others.[19] Ethnic humor stems from a sense of being a member of an in-group. Apte, quoted in Lowe, notes that "ethnic humor seems basic in human societies, and stems from 'ethnocentrism, ingroup adulation, outgroup resentment, prejudice, and intolerance of the life-styles of others.'"[20]

The root of ethnic humor, according to Boskin and Dorinson[21], is stereotypes. These stereotypes are taken to heart by the maligned groups. They are used in mocking self-description and used as a means of attack against detractors. Boskin and Dorinson further their commentary on the uniting influence of stereotypes in ethnic humor by mentioning that "conflict, which is implicit in a variety of forms—satire, irony, sarcasm, parody, and burlesque—reinforces the in-group and weakens the out-group. Stereotypes figure prominently in most conflict humor."[22] The ritualized mocking of stereotypes and ascriptions not only became a hallmark for certain ethnic groups, it also catapulted their ethnic humor into the national limelight: "Mocking the features ascribed to them by outsiders has become one of the most effective ethnic infusions into national humor, particularly by Afro-Americans and Jews."[23] How have these avowed stereotypes become so integral to ethnic humor?

> Lawrence Mintz has pinpointed four stages in the [humor development] process: the first featured critical humor that targeted the out-group; the second involved self-deprecatory humor; the third stressed realism; and, finally, the fourth stage reversed the first stage as the oppressed minority gained revenge by assaulting the majority culture.[24]

Avowing to stereotypes as a ritualized method of strengthening one's own group at the expense of one's detractors has been much discussed in literature reviewing Jewish humor. According to Juni and Katz,[25] the Jewish joke is an attempt to equalize the attacker's hold over the "other." Instead of fleeing from aggression, victims adapt by joining with the aggressor to persecute themselves. Quoting Grotjahn, the authors note "aggression turned against the self seems to be an essential feature of the truly Jewish joke. It is as if the Jew tells his enemies: 'You don't need to attack us. We can do that ourselves and even better.'"[26] Humor is determined by survival strategies—it is a disarming tactical maneuver.

Agreeing with Juni and Katz, Silberman-Federman notes that modern American Jews use humor to protect themselves in a society in which they are the "other." She quotes Chaim Bermant as saying "the joke thus reveals the truth of the language of the Jews, that it is a weapon they use to defend themselves against the attacks of the Christian world."[27] Juni and Katz[28] consider this tactic analogous to the Abbot and Costello episode in which Abbot chases Costello with a bat, but when he catches him, Costello takes the bat only to hit himself in the head. Then, lying prostrate on the floor, Costello looks up at Abbot and says, "What are you going to do to me now?" Only by laughing at themselves do Jews become less vulnerable to the laughter and hostility of the other.

Humor is the primary means of self-protection and warding off anti-Semitism.[29] According to Juni and Katz,[30] self-directed humor is not only a discursive tactic for protecting oneself from one's aggressor, it can also be a tactic for gaining the upper hand. As noted previously, Jews (like African Americans) have gained a unique and privileged status as a funny "other." In addition, a victim who laughs instead of crying snatches victory from the attacker. Once Jews are able to laugh at themselves and in so doing ward off the blows of others, they can show up their attacker and, indeed, mock the entire world.

Similarly, African Americans have also responded to powerlessness and persecution with ritualized humor, avowal to ascribed stereotypes and self-mocking. According to Gordon:

American slavery provides the backdrop of tragedy against which African Americans developed their distinct form of humor, in which the material of tragedy was converted into comedy, including the absurd. This often included self-deprecation, as the slaves themselves were often the subjects of their comic tales. Self-deprecation continues to be a feature of African American humor, especially for exclusively Black Audiences.[31]

Like Jewish humor, African-American comedy is a reaction to society-at-large. They are both, at base, serious.[32] They both ritually self-protect and attack. African-American humor works as a safety valve to maintain dignity and capture power in the face of oppression. Gordon notes that games such as "playing the dozens" fulfill the need for a sense of power in the midst of misery. Boskin and Dorinson notes that Black humor is utilized to ward off punishment and retaliate quickly. It is a "type of control humor which is vital for the maintenance of a highly attuned and carefully sensitized community."[33]

Watkins maintains, "Since African-Americans have been inescapably engaged with the absurdity of America's racial arrangements for centuries, survival and sanity dictated that they adopt a comic view of society."[34] This perspective is enlivened in "playing the dozens," which America has come to know as "yo momma jokes." This ritualized game of insults was so much more than that. It functioned and has continued to function as a form of cathartic release that relies on verbal dexterity, sharp wit, innovative thinking, quick recovery and resilience, as well as small group participation.[35] Those who thrive in the game are considered masters at verbal jousting and at withstanding harsh invectives. They are quintessentially resilient and seemingly immune to ethnic humor though ethnic jokes, told by outsiders, are always provocative.

It certainly appears that both African Americans and Jews use humor in a ritualized fashion to protect themselves, attack the dominant culture, and maintain a sense of unity. Both ethnic groups use certain types of humor to accomplish these goals. Boskin and Dorinson note that "mocking the features ascribed to them by outsiders has become one of the most effective ethnic infusions into national humor, particularly by Afro-Americans and Jews."[36] Further, they mention that:

> Blacks and Jews shared the humor of the oppressed. Inwardly masochistic, indeed tragic, externally aggressive, even acrimonious, their humor generated several distinctive forms of expression such as gallows humor, the ironic curse, double meanings, trickster tales, and retaliatory jokes.[37]

It is with this recognition of the similarities among Jewish and African-American experiences that Kesselman constructs a cinematic narrative of a common oppressive condition built upon an absolutely ridiculous and unwarranted American social disregard for these two ethnic groups, among others. The film is a satire that tries to convince its audience through mergers of music, freedom fighters, and clothing style that relations between Blacks and Jews have been strained for far too long and for all the wrong reasons.

THE NATURE OF SATIRE

Satire is defined as "a literary work holding up human vices and follies to ridicule or scorn; or a trenchant wit, irony, or sarcasm used to expose and discredit vice or folly."[38] Satire is one of the oldest and most popular literary forms. When it is presented successfully, it is instructive, insightful, and brilliant. When done poorly or inadequately, it is solipsistic at best. In either case, satire is inherently about representations of identity. It invites audiences to probe more deeply to discover something unique about the character of human understanding but also to reveal cultural machinery at work. In its deconstruction of symbolically violent epistemes dormant within social norms, it takes the risk of being too subtle and believable that audiences overlook its form, or too overwhelming such that it upsets the balance of humor and overly implicates the audience. These two risks are especially present with satiric comedy films commenting on race and ethnicity that ethically challenge audiences to check socially derived assumptions and rotate hegemony in order to relieve it of its oppressive force. In order to accomplish this, as much as the content is meticulously crafted to evoke laughter, it must also recognize that it is imbued with the responsibility to point out truths about social reality and to do so with piercing accuracy. So, it is with these caveats about satire as a narrative form that we explore the film *Hebrew Hammer*.

As we reflect on the opening scene of the movie mentioned at the beginning of this chapter, clearly the severe portrayal of Mordechai's experience as a Jewish child may appear "over the top" since ethnocentrism is not always so blatant, yet it is important to remember that it is the job of satiric comedies like this one to use hyperbole to heighten the effects of everyday social idiocy and xenophobia directed toward marginalized group members. That is, in fact what makes this film appropriate as a text to examine in a book about dialogic ethics.

If "dialogic ethics" is about the need to build ethical capacity, collaborate on unified, core notions of character and connect who we say we are with our actual ethical practice, then the central question this study must examine is the extent to which *Hebrew Hammer* participates in this dialogue. Toward this end, this essay will also explore several stereotypical scripts embedded in Jewish and Black ethnic identities. The promotion of stereotypical cultural identities in widespread mass mediated contexts has already yielded a series of mainstream assumptions about race, ethnicity and culture. In each of these indelible iterations, consumers are left with distilled messages about how to perceive cultural others as ethnic caricatures. Essentially, we as consumers are engaged in an everyday disruption of a productive set of dialogic ethics and find ourselves as part of a dialectic where both producers and audiences are not given the option to comply with certain non-stereotypical scripts about ethnic bodies because those images are never presented. In this way, a Jewsploitation film is compelling for what it may potentially offer to audiences deprived of positive images of Jewish ethnic group members, yet it is also incumbent upon Kesselman to know and understand what Blaxploitation is before framing his theatrical work in this tradition.

WHAT IS BLAXPLOITATION?

The 1970s was an explosive period in Black filmmaking. Movies like *Sweet Sweetback's Baadasssss Song, Shaft, Superfly, The Mack, Cornbread, Earl & Me, Sounder, Cotton Comes to Harlem, Black Caesar, Mahogany, Coffy, Foxy Brown, Cleopatra Jones, Sparkle, Uptown Saturday Night,* and *Black Fist* represented a range of films of this era. Some of them were mainly comedy films featuring the likes of Richard Pryor while others gave rise to athlete-turned-actors like Muhammad Ali, Jim Kelly, Ken Norton and Jim Brown. Nonetheless, among them sprouted a separate genre that came to be known as Blaxploitation and was characterized by the coiffed afros, the gaudy jewelry, and the pimp clothing that is reminiscent of disco outfits.

The term blaxploitation refers to the exploitation of Blacks and Black images by Whites in films of the previous decade, the 1960s, rather than the manipulation and exploitation of Blacks within this genre. Blaxploitation is a term referring to the 1970s film genre that was designed to offer films for Black audiences exclusively developed by Black independent filmmakers; however the production of many of these films was not in the hands of Blacks at all. Beyond the handful of independently made films, MGM Warner Brothers, and Paramount Studios were coincidentally run mostly by Jewish executives. Virtually every film during this period with a wide distribution was backed by these motion picture companies who did so after having rejected Melvin Van Peebles' request for studio support of his film *Sweet Sweetback's Baadasssss Song.* Van Peebles' film was considered too radical for the time. This film, set in Los Angeles, was likely among the first to have an all-Black cast (with the exception of two dirty White cops). It has also been widely noted as the genesis of the Blaxploitation genre. Developed within a temporal context just after the Civil Rights movement when non-bourgeoisie Blacks were ever-conscious about not further entrenching the disempowered folks among them, the film assumes it has no right to dismiss the ghetto and all the trappings of a despondent lifestyle—drugs, prostitution, crime, etc. So, instead, it glamorizes them. "The [cinematic] elevation of the pimp/outlaw/rebel as folk hero"[39] essentially begins with Blaxploitation and with this film.

It is important to recognize that Blaxploitation is an intentionally anti-establishment genre. In retrospect or from afar one might think of the wildly clad bevy of film protagonists during this period as nothing more than a gallery of criminal misfits, pimps and prostitutes, and ghetto-dwelling savages trying to assume a position of authority within the underbelly of society just for the sake of having power. Yet, that would be a hasty generalization. While the characters are in fact presented this way, their roles are purposefully scripted this way in order to represent the kind of retaliation that cannot be controlled. No one controls the Superfly, the Mack, Shaft or Sweetback. Whether they embody the role of a drug kingpin, pimp, detective or whatever, they are not the docile, meek Black male protagonists of the 1960s whose first instinct is deference to Whites and "playing by the rules." Their characters develop their own rules and force the Man to deal with them on their terms. It compels the audience to side with the villain because the villain is presented as the true underdog who seems to have no other options available to escape the trap of a structurally disadvantaged lifestyle but to become the embodiment of the very thing the establishment despises and fears. It is direct message to White society that if White xenophobia and racism are rooted in this unfounded fear that Blacks are inherently violent, criminal, reckless, savage, intimidating and flawed just because of how they look, then since there is no way to interrupt that cycle without Blacks becoming a victim of it, they will fight back by being the quintessential object of White fear. It is the only domain where Whites lacked control over the Black body, but ironically these representations were so well aligned with White stereotypes about Blacks that White audiences curiously supported them wholeheartedly at the box office.

Film studios made millions of dollars and while all-Black casts benefited, Black images and representations on film both regressed and movie-going audiences in the 2000s still witness some of the residue and the indelible impact of these pathological images. The Blaxploitation hallmark stereotypes of the out-of-control buck and the lascivious Sapphire are so well received that Denzel Washington and Halle Berry won Oscars for their portrayals of a crooked cop in *Training Day* and a sexually charged working-class widow and mother. The Blaxploitation era did not as much initiate this line of stereotyping as much as significantly expand it and master it on film. This happened especially in Melvin Van Peebles' *Sweet Sweetback's Baadasssss Song.*

With no studio executive calling the shots on the film, Van Peebles chose to create an X-rated film with the main character Sweetback sketched as a sexually molested child turned sexually charged stud and badman who refuses to kowtow to Whites. The story unfolds with a Black man's death and detectives are looking for suspects, so Sweetback agrees to go to the precinct to be questioned. His willingness to be interrogated is interrupted when the racist White cops unnecessarily beat a young Black male, who we learn is a Black Panther, and so Sweetback quickly responds and kills the two cops. He then becomes a fugitive mostly harbored by folks within the Black community.

The movie sets the tone for this genre as there are multiple images of women as whores, men as studs and pimps, the main character as an outlaw and a proliferation of violence. The film has been praised for its audacity in saying what Blacks authentically felt about Whites. It also contains the familiar "reincarnations of all the sapphires and studs of yesteryear"[40] and the concomitant pathological representations of Blacks.

The conflicting nature of Blaxploitation films is rooted in how and why it should be celebrated. These films were bold, unafraid, energizing, empowering and supportive of Black actors and actresses. Blacks simply had only played in lead roles in which they were expected to "act White." Black audiences had become both used to and fed up with the servile, goofy, obsequious roles given to Blacks up until that point. They wanted to be themselves. They wanted to be employed while being themselves, and they wanted the kind of respect that White actors seemed to get without asking. This film set a precedent in this regard. Nonetheless, the other side of the conflict is that these films were also rather counterproductive in terms of getting Hollywood to see a side to the Black community that was non-pathological, a germ still pervasive in popular media today. The film did show a strong hero despite being akin to the brutal Black buck image, but that hero is misogynistic and a derelict. "The message of *Sweetback*," Melvin Van Peebles noted in a 1971 interview, "is that if you can get it together and stand up to the Man, you can win."[41]

After the *Sweet Sweetback's Baadasssss Song* proved lucrative, grossing nearly $15 million despite having limited release in small theaters and having been produced on a shoestring budget of less than $500,000 in a mere 19 days of shooting, the fledgling MGM studios immediately signed a deal to produce director Gordon Parks, Sr.'s film *Shaft*, which was later followed by two other installments—*Shaft's Big Score* and *Shaft in Africa*. Bogle notes, "This little picture [*Shaft*], which its studio, MGM, thought might make a little money, instead made a mint—some $12 million within a year in North America alone—and singlehandedly saved MGM from financial ruin."[42] Throughout the series the title character John Shaft (played by Richard Roundtree) was a renegade detective caught in the balance between the White world and the ghetto or a Black community to which he had allegiance.

In the original 1971 making of *Shaft*, the title character works alongside leaders of the Black Crime Mob and Black Nationals to fight against the White Mafia who are trying to blackmail the Black Crime Mob by kidnapping his daughter. *Shaft*, like all Blaxploitation films, is a film that grapples with a dual social consciousness, the principal ontological conflict of wanting to be accepted or treated justly in a White world while having a grounded sense of commitment to a suffering and always disadvantaged Black community. Additionally, Shaft's background music and lyrics, written by Isaac Hayes, gave us a hint of his predilection for women and his status as a stud: "he's the Black private dick that's a sex machine for all the chicks." This same line, incidentally, is the same one used in *Hebrew Hammer* to introduce the title character. We would be remiss, however, if we did not acknowledge that not all Blaxploitation films were male-dominated and geared toward the stud, mack, player image. In fact, a slew of films such as *Mahogany, Foxy Brown, Sparkle,* and *Coffy* introduced a Black heroine who was even more sexy and doubly brutal when compared to the male protagonists in other Blaxploitation films. The soundtracks complemented the edgy yet sensuous tenor to this genre.

The music in these films became extremely significant after Earth, Wind & Fire performed the score for *Sweet Sweetback's Baadasssss Song* and Isaac Hayes was awarded an Oscar for developing the score for *Shaft*. Every studio executive wanted this unique rhythmic sound seemingly most readily available among Black artists like Curtis Mayfield, Marvin Gaye, Quincy Jones, Staples Singers, Donny Hathaway, Aretha Franklin and others. The soundtracks were produced with the hope that they could achieve the fame and fortune of Hayes' LP. This was never repeated to the same magnitude. Yet, the audience excitement and energy in anticipation of these films were unprecedented and that is largely due to the new Black filmic images, the expected hero tactics, and the score. Even with this excitement, the NAACP, the Southern Christian Leadership Council, and the National Urban League protested these films due to their retrograde depictions of Blacks. The images of the oversexed, drug-using, pimps, whores and derelicts had outlived what little utility they may have had. Ultimately these civil rights organizations were successful in facilitating the end of this era of filmmaking that became increasingly more detrimental and surprisingly repetititous with each new film and yet it spanned the decade of the 1970s.

So, Kesselman's adaptation of the Blaxploitation genre was a complex decision. There are profound implications for this decision, and there are also formulaic missteps or omissions within *Hebrew Hammer* that say nothing of the Man enacting any kind of physical violence. In fact, the violence is characterized as principally ethnic, epistemic and perhaps ontological. The key questions that need to be asked of the film if it is to be considered true to form are *How have Jews been exploited previously? What is being fought for in the film? Is that which is being fought for a central facet of Jewish identity? Did the film help Jewish audience members retrieve agency over some long-stripped aspect of their community representations? Was the movie empowering to Jewish audiences? Does the film facilitate a mass movement toward expunging stereotypical images of Jews?* All these questions are easily answerable within the film. Clearly several of these questions reveal the mis-moves of the film. What Kesselman does not tell us is why he uses Blaxploitation to make the point he is trying to make when Blaxploitation was actually a retreat from Jews who wielded power in Hollywood; why he feels the need to transform the protagonist to look and act Black in the film; and why he is insistent upon likening the persecutory experiences of Blacks and Jews.

As has been discussed, the genre of Blaxploitation unavoidably carries with it certain problems and complications. What, then, does this genre communicate when it is co-opted by a different other as a means of presenting that group's disempowerment? Is it possible that the promises of providing a new discursive form and of yoking Jewish identity to Black identity override the shortcomings of this problematic genre?

In many ways, the usage of a prototypical Black genre to convey Jewish otherness makes sense, as neither group fits within the discourse of the majority in the United States. As Lerner and West put it, "Jews and Blacks are a pariah people—a people who had to make and remake themselves as outsiders on the margins of American society and culture…Both groups defined themselves as a people deeply shaped by America but never *fully* a part of America."[43] West goes on to posit that it is this othering that has brought about the tragicomic character of the Jewish and Black experiences, that which we see exhibited in Blaxploitation and *The Hebrew Hammer*.

The yoking of Blackness and Jewishness, on face value, may be seen as a positive. Not only does the melding of two othered groups present a louder voice and higher profile, it also demonstrates the diversity of prejudice in our society. Further, Blacks and Jews are oppressed for a common reason—the fact that neither lay claim to Whiteness. Karen Brodkin notes that, despite the generally "White" exterior of modern American Jews, most do not label themselves as white: "[Ethnoracial] assignment is about popularly held classifications and their deployment by those with national power to make them matter economically, politically, and socially to the individuals classified. We construct ethnoracial identities ourselves, but we do it within the context of ethnoracial assignment."[44] Jews tend to view themselves as a "White other," uncomfortable with the notion that they are part of the White majority.[45] This avowal of otherness comes in part from an unfortunate ascription: Brodkin notes that, "In time…'inferior' religious cultures became inferior races."[46]

Indeed, the shared unease at being pariah peoples has conjoined Blacks and Jews in other ways. The biggest outside supporters of the Civil Rights movement in the 1960s were Jews. The impetus for this, posits Goldstein, is that championing the rights of one disempowered group translates to the celebration of all minority groups: "Jews generally used Blacks and Black causes as surrogates for concerns that had become less immediate in their own lives, but to which they retained a strong emotional connection."[47] This support and empathy lead to the co-optation of other groups' discursive methods and successes. The leader of the radical Jewish Defense League, Meir Kahane, argues that "if Shirley Chisholm can walk around saying black problems come first for blacks—Beautiful! Right on! Black problems *do* come first for blacks…[and] Jewish problems must come first for Jews."[48]

Discomfort comes from equating Black and Jewish difference and inequality, however, as is done in *The Hebrew Hammer*. Lerner and West[49] note that Jews often take umbrage at the fact that Blacks lump them in the White oppressor, and Blacks tend to feel that Jewish life in America is facile due to the Jews' ability to pass and assimilate. Furthermore, historically there has been much misunderstanding between these two groups, with each consumed by who is the "most oppressed group." Goldstein argues that "in order to allay fears that they were an unstable racial element in white society, Jews often felt the need to assert a distinguishing line between themselves and the country's Black population. They hoped that by affirming the color line, they might help divert attention away from the problems raised by their own distinctiveness."[50] Brodkin agrees with this notion, and further problematizes it, noting that "ethnic pluralism gave rise to a new construction of specifically Jewish whiteness. It did so by contrasting Jews as a model minority with African Americans as culturally deficient."[51] Inventing African Americans as culturally deficient, Brodkin posits, makes Jews (and any other ethnic/racial group) seem exemplary.

Here, then, we begin to encounter the problems with *The Hebrew Hammer*. While it is true that in many ways African-American and Jewish relations are positive, Kesselman ignores the historical aspect of Jewish and Black relations in telling this tale of oppression. His apparent ignorance of this history is convenient, since it facilitates his interest in creating a unified voice for the oppressed and for attempting to strike a blow against the oppressor.

Kesselman's usage of a uniquely African-American genre to communicate American Jewishness is problematic. Not only does he use African-American culture to transmit Jewishness, he unifies the experience and the identities of these two groups. Clearly, Mordechai Jefferson Carver is appropriating key elements of Blaxploitation as a means of accessing and commenting on Black identity: Carver dresses as a pimp, drives an old Cadillac with his name on the license plate, and the like. Even his name bespeaks blackness; Mordechai Jefferson Carver is a thinly veiled play-on-words invoking the African-American cultural hero George Washington Carver. The naming of Kesselman's hero is a misstep in-and-of-itself; George Washington Carver was a botanist/teacher and inventor of many uses for the peanut who taught slaves self-sufficiency. His contributions to society were invaluable, but the homage to him is senseless. It would be akin to naming a Jackie Chan action hero after Eli Whitney or Thomas Edison. While Kesselman's aim is undoubtedly satirical, it reads again as if he is ignorant of Black culture. An homage that dishonors the group it is representing is not much of an homage at all.

While this Jewish Shaft has stereotypically Jewish characteristics, neuroses and tics, there is a clear attempt to demonstrate that his experience of suffering in a predominantly Christian society is akin to that experienced by Blacks. Kesselman does so by blending "typical" Jewish discourse with "typical" Black discourse. Here, we have Carver demonstrating that he is not White, but rather "colored": thus, he speaks using the idioms and discursive forms of Blacks. The Hebrew Hammer, when he is with Rahim, speaks in stereotypical Black dialect. When we first encounter Rahim, Carver refers to him as his "main man nigger," and when the White gentile man in the vicinity registers shock he is told that "we can call each other that." Carver is not merely speaking to a Black man; he is speaking *as* a Black man. Similarly, when he discusses Damien with Rahim he asks him, "Did you hear about this crazy-ass White boy?" The juxtaposition here accomplishes two ends: first, it demonstrates that Carver does not consider himself to be White; secondly, it unites Carver and Rahim as people who are "colored" in unity, or Black. Why is this so discomfiting? As noted in the earlier review of humor rituals, it is widely accepted that jokes told about a group *by* a group are useful and beneficial, whereas the same humor related by an outsider is bigoted. Carver is *not* a member of the Christian majority; he is an other. He is *not,* however, Black. Thus, operating within the structures of Black discourse does not create the sensation of united ethnic groups, it comes across as one ethnic group co-opting the discourse of another and speaking as an outsider.

Kesselman makes a college try at showing the unification of Jews and Blacks; for instance, mixing klezmer music with a 1970's era Black rhythm section does foster an acoustic semblance of two disparate parts making a unified whole, and it also maintains the underlying link to blaxploitation films that gave many R&B groups their first real breaks. The attempts at unification that are made elsewhere, however, are not as successful. When Mordechai and Esther escape the clutches of evil Christian children and are saved by the Jewish Underground Railroad leader Harriet Tubbleman, we again are presented with the unification of Jewish and Black persecution. Kesselman utilizes one of the predominant exemplars of Black escape and freedom from slavery to portray the getaway of two Jews from a demented Santa Claus. Naturally, the references are to Harriet Tubman (otherwise known as "Black Moses") and the Underground Railroad, which is a nickname for hush harbors where insurrectionist or runaway slaves could be offered safe refuge while fleeing from their slave masters.

By unifying the symbols, icons, discourse and signifiers of Black and Jewish oppression and by yoking Black and Jewish identity, Kesselman ignores the separate experiences of oppression encountered by these two minority groups. First, by doing so, he ignores a rich and at times troubled history of Jewish and Black interaction.

Jews and Blacks have not always strived for equality together; there has been intolerance, prejudice and separation involved. Regardless of the tension between the two groups, it is obtuse to equate the persecution of the two. Jews of the past century witnessed one of the worst atrocities to ever befall the world—but not here. Jews still remain the most persecuted religious minority in the United States.[52] Yet the Holocaust is not the same as slavery. Blacks are still persecuted more than any other minority in the United States.[53] Does this condone anti-Semitism, or make it any better than hate crimes against Blacks? Of course it doesn't. Additionally, Blacks are a visible minority, one that cannot easily assimilate or pass, whereas Judaism is closetable.[54] Again, does this mean that one type of hatred is worse, or more severe than the other? Of course it doesn't. But it *does* mean that the persecution of the two groups is not equitable, and that substituting a hero of one ethnicity for a hero of a different ethnicity is not effective. Additionally, putting his Jewish hero in the shoes of a Black hero raises one more issue: Kesselman seems to be equating Jewishness with race, a designation that Jews have been loathe to avoid since the Holocaust. *The Hebrew Hammer* misses its nail by conflating ethnic and racial prejudice; the two have had different impacts and casualties in American society, and lumping them together to form an overarching "racial" prejudice does no credit to the group whom he is striving to support.

Not only does Kesselman make a wrong turn by labeling Jews as a race, his employment of a Black genre as the backdrop to a Jewish film disrespects and disempowers Black identity. Black linguistic style merely becomes something to be co-opted, something that can be severed from a core Black identity. In having a central Jewish figure operate as would-be Black hero (with some additional stereotypes), Kesselman is making a mockery of Black discourse. Not only does he treat this discourse as something that is entirely co-optable, it becomes almost self-referentially prejudiced. Having a Jewish man utter the word "nigger" (and a Black man utter the word "kike") is not empowering; it is disrespectful and unethical. Further, Kesselman puts himself in a privileged position, one in which he has the capacity to speak for the other. This is a position that has been problematized oft before. For instance, Spike Lee condemned Stephen Spielberg's *The Color Purple* (1985) and *Amistad* (1997), making it clear "that any feelings of minority status on the part of a Jew did not make him eligible to impinge on the Black experience, which [he] felt should remain the artistic property of Black filmmakers."[55] Through his creation of *The Hebrew Hammer*, Kesselman merely hints at a (problematic) Black genre, turning it into a story of Jewish persecution at the hands of mainstream America. This juxtaposition of Black and Jewish identities yokes the two groups together, straining against the weight of persecution and hatred; it is, however, not a burden that is equally distributed. Blacks in this film are relegated to a secondary status and to a disembodied voice. As noted above, there has been a long history of minority groups denigrating African Americans to gain privileged status themselves. It is a shame that Kesselman makes this same miscue in an era when he certainly should have known better.

Kesselman's treatment of Jewish identity is also problematic and unethical for numerous reasons. One of the scenes in the film that best characterizes *The Hebrew Hammer's* presentation of Jewish identity occurs when, on his visit to the Jewish Justice League (JJL) headquarters, Carver must pass a battery of tests confirming that he is Jewish. The message conveyed by this scene is clear: in order to understand Jewishness (and, perhaps, the film), one must be an insider. To enter into the inner sanctum of the JJL, to have the privileged status to speak, one must be a Jew. Kesselman sets up an emic/etic dichotomy, portraying Jews as having an insider status, one which outsiders—Whites—cannot understand. This is troublesome because it widens a divide which, seemingly, Kesselman is attempting to bridge. His use of Blaxploitation demonstrates Jewish strength and links Jewish and Black suffering; it also, one would suppose, highlights a societal failing for its audience. Yet, by telling his audience that if they are not Jewish they do not belong and just do not get it, his message is automatically doomed to failure.

Kesselman is highlighting the aspect of Jewish ethnicity that is, as Steven M. Cohen and Arnold M. Eisen refer to it, connected to "all other communal or collective aspects of being Jewish: all manner of attachment to Jewish family members, neighbors, secular institutions, and the Jewish people worldwide."[56] This attachment to all Jews is fine; however, it does not allow for the inclusion of others. This is clear as we witness, for example, the scene at the headquarters of the Kwanzaa Liberation Front, where Carver and Rahim refer to each other as "nigger" and "kike," and register the shock of the White accountant. Here, White Christians are not included; they are reduced to "other" status. Theodore Reik tells us that Jewish humor has "the significance of reaching one's arms out to the other fellow"[57] Here though, Kesselman stands with his arms crossed, refusing entry to anyone who is not an insider and does not understand.

This emic, privileged position is not only harmful because of its exclusion of a gentile audience. It also prioritizes a certain type of Jewish identity at the expense of other Jewish identities. In the aforementioned scene where the Hammer must demonstrate his Jewishness, he must do so not only through obvious stereotypes, but through specific religious knowledge (naming six items on the Seder plate and stating his full Jewish name). The message communicated by this portion of this film is that if one does not know answers to Jewish trivia, is not able to play a musical instrument, etc., then one is not a Jew.

Similarly, the entire film is rife with very specific Jewish arcana, erudite knowledge that would only be familiar to a Jew steeped in Jewish lore. Some of these in-jokes include: the referential name "Hebrew Hammer," which refers to Judah Macabee (literally Judah the Hammer), the hero of Hanukkah; the names Esther and Mordechai, the Jewish saviors commemorated by Purim; the constant usage of Yiddish and Hebrew, etc. The information here is erudite; it is unreasonable to assume that the majority of Jews watching this film would understand the references. The film relies on "relevant discourse."[58] Jodi Cohen discusses how sociocultural identity is made relevant through text. If a text is pertinent to a certain audience, that audience frames the narrative differently than do other groups. She remarks that "relevant moments of meaning involve the spectators' social allegiances and the semiotic boundaries of the text."[59] By framing Jewishness as accessible only through relevant discourse, Kesselman demonstrates that only certain audiences are truly meant to "get" the film. This greatly reduces its scope and effectiveness.

In an even more troubling move, *The Hebrew Hammer* appears to be limiting the film to only certain types of Jews, thus enacting a politics of authenticity and essentialism. The notion of Jewishness as a privileged position, and as hierarchical, is visible at the official site of *The Hebrew Hammer*,[60] in which readers may take "The Jewish Confirmation Test," answer questions about Judaism (often involving stereotypes), and find out whether they are "Gentile," "Jew-ish," a "Member of the Tribe," or "Hard Hittin' Heeb." Here, the audience is presented with the notion that there are certain adequate and inadequate Jewish identities. Thus, those who do not know what a "latke" is or who Esther and Mordechai were are not truly Jews—they are only Jew-ish, or, heaven forbid, gentiles. *The Hebrew Hammer* practices exclusionism, letting only certain individuals hold claim to Jewishness.

This notion is also visible in the film in that every Jewish character is uniform; all of the Jews appear to be Orthodox. Every male Jew that we see is wearing a tallis, yarmulke, tefillin, and all of the other trappings of Orthodox Judaism. The representation of Jews in this film is only those who support a dogma; those who do not fit this depiction are excluded. Their voices are not merely ignored, they are silenced. Modern day American Jewish identity is no longer predicated on faith. While faith is certainly an optional element of that identity, it is not necessary. Modern American Jews now place greater importance on shared communal values, morality, rituals, and connection with other Jews, and it is these qualities that describe a "good Jew." Gerald Sorin argues that the thrust has changed from Judaism to Jewishness and from dogmatic religion to civil religion.[61] *The Hebrew Hammer* places Jewishness as an emic position, one which gentiles and non-religious Jews are not allowed to occupy.

Kesselman's privileging of Jewishness also seems to backfire, in that it demonstrates a rift between Jewishness and the mainstream, further relegating Jewishness to a pariah position. By purposively othering the Jews, Kesselman is not merely showing Jewishness as an unjustly disadvantaged position; he is showing it is ineffably different and separate. The scene in which this othering is most evident is that in which Mordechai and Esther attempt to pass as White, Christian, and, most notably, American. Both Mordechai and Esther, in this disguise, speak as if they are in "Leave It to Beaver," smile constantly, wear Jesus paraphernalia, mull over eating a bacon cheeseburger (a notoriously non-kosher food), and *carry American flags.* Here, it is highlighted that Jews do not approve of or understand the trappings of American culture. They do not eat the most popular food, and they do not talk like everyone else. Yet most important is that flag in Mordechai's hand. Why is that flag absent when Mordechai is not closeting his Jewishness? Because Jews are un-American, and not like "the rest of us." Christians, on the other hand, are patriotic, Kesselman argues, and have a love for their country—they share that love and affinity with other Americans. Jews do not. Rather than portraying Jews as a disenfranchised and sub-jugated other, Kesselman depicts Jews as willingly separating themselves. It is not America that does not choose them; *they* do not choose America. This strategic rhetorical move strikes a blow against that which Kesselman is fighting for: the right for Jews to be included. He shows us instead that Jews have that right; they do not choose it. So, unlike the message in Blaxploitation that power and control are inac-cessible and not an option, Kesselman falters as he shows viewers that Jews are only bereft of power when they choose not to have it. Arguably, an extension of that argument is that Jews, when they are being their Jewish selves, are not permitted access to power, but then Hollywood has already proven that claim incorrect.

This willing separation from the dominant, mainstream culture calls to mind Hannah Arendt's assessment of Jewishness. Arendt maintains that Jews have two options regarding their position in society: to be a "pariah," a conscious outsider who occupies a liminal position between the majority and the minority and is thus able to act "politically," or to be a "parvenu"—an assimilated Jew.[62] The pariah, Arendt argues, is the only Jew who can be a full-fledged member of society. Only a pariah may act politically, and in so doing distances him/herself both from Jews and from the mainstream. Kesselman seems to be taking a similar tack; he is acting as a pariah, separating himself from Jews while mocking the gentile majority. If understanding and acceptance are Kesselman's goal, he does damage by willingly sneering at inclusion.

The last overarching problem with *The Hebrew Hammer,* and the one that truly renders it as an unethical depiction of Jewish and Black identities, is its reliance on stereotypes. As with the genre upon which it models itself, the film represents ethnic/racial identity as a conglomeration of stereotypes, ones which generally are harmful to those they depict.

The list of stereotypes found within *The Hebrew Hammer* is long. Jews are greedy, unscrupulous, cheap, different, strange, weak, hysterical, neurotic, nervous, sensitive whiny, obsessed with food and sex (particularly of the oral variety), nagging, effemi-nate, impotent, argumentative, intellectual, sensitive, overly concerned with the successes of others, and mama's boys, and they have large noses, funny names, and speak differently. Because they are not the centrally located disempowered minority in this film, the Blacks within are not saddled with as many stereotypes, but they are there nonetheless. Blacks, according to the film, love rap and hip-hop, can't speak without swearing, adore basketball and watermelon, hate Whites, and are gun-toting, marijuana-smoking thieves.

Blaxploitation and Jewsploitation are prefaced in the notion of speaking *for* certain disempowered communities. The idea is that these identities are not adequately represented in mainstream media—and, indeed, in society as a whole—and thus these genres attempt to empower those communities, adequately representing the identities therein. Unfortunately, when this communication is performed largely through stereotypes, these identities are still relegated to the pit.

By having the Jewish characters exhibit "typical" attributes such as being money hungry, unscrupulous, neurotic, and weak, Kesselman only does them violence. Alan J. Spector notes that such humor might thus be categorized not as "ethnic" humor, but as "racist" humor:

> We find three criteria central to defining 'ethnic' humor as 'racist' humor. First, the ste-
> reotype must be negative. Second, if the target of the humor is an oppressed, subjugated,
> or otherwise subordinated group, the impact of that stereotype is significantly more potent.
> Finally, if the stereotype feeds into or reinforces a common fallacious stereotype of the
> group, the impact is all the more damaging because it can add to the subjugation of the
> targeted group.[63]

Rabbi Telushkin notes that: "The stereotyping inherent in much ethnic humor is worrisome. Far more often than most joke tellers will acknowledge, some hostile stereotypes are so negative as to do real damage to the ethnic group being mocked."[64] In a film that is supposedly reclaiming Jewishness and representing Jewish strength, such stereotypes only serve to cheapen the message. Interestingly, Kesselman appears to offer something of a pardon to Blacks within the film that he does not offer to the Jews. When Carver and Rahim are faced with the stereotype alarm, Carver warns his Black compatriot not to eat watermelon, dribble a basketball, or say "dawg." Rahim replies that he hates both watermelon and basketball. Here, Kesselman pokes fun at stereotyping. Yet then he has the Hebrew Hammer pick up a penny, setting off the alarm. While the alarm itself highlights the ridiculousness of stereotyping in society, Kesselman himself never appears able to free himself from its allure.

Stereotypes are also dangerous because they become accepted as fact not only by the outside group but by those being stereotyped as well. Stereotypes become avowed by Jews and force them into the discourse of the majority and lead to further self-mocking. As Sander Gilman contends, "Self-hatred arises when the mirages of stereotypes are confused with realities within the world, when the desire for accep-tance forces the acknowledgment of one's difference... One cannot escape these labels because of the privileged group's myth that these categories are immutable."[65] Spector argues that stereotypes also allow the majority to more easily victimize the minority: "If the stereotype reinforces what is a commonly held negative stereotype about a group, then that stereotype is helping to build a consensus of public opinion toward, at best, tolerance or indifference to oppression, and at worst, active participation toward that oppression."[66]

There is perhaps one positive that can be salvaged from *The Hebrew Hammer*'s abundant stereotypes, a positive which is self-referentially pointed to when the JJL Chief notes that few films have a positive, strong Jewish role model. The Hebrew Hammer is unarguably a stereotypical creation. He is also a hero. This hero sweats and whines when he finds out that everyone expects him to save Hanukkah. He breaks down after sex with Esther, becoming overly sensitive. He is waylaid by gentile vixens who coo that they have always desired the affections of a well-read and sensitive man. He is not a tough, hard, angry hero in the vein of Blaxploitation films. Perhaps this is a good thing. Instead of glorifying questionable traits—violence, lack of empathy, and a lack of roots, Kesselman presents us with an empathetic, sensitive, mama's boy who also kicks ass. This alternative heroism is perhaps what Lerner and West foresaw when they argue that a Jewish man becomes a man "by becoming a scholar, a reader of texts, or a scribe, someone who can act out his prowess in the realm of written words."[67] Kesselman offers us an alternative version of machismo, a trait in which Jewish men have long been stereotyped as lacking.

NOTES

1 Alleen Pace Nilsen, "In Defense of Humor," *College Education* 56 (1994): 932.

2 Joseph Boskin and Joseph Dorinson, "Ethnic Humor: Subversion and Survival," American Quarterly *37*(1) (1985): 81.

3 Dawn T. Robinson and Lynn Smith-Lovin, "Getting a Laugh: Gender, Status, and Humor in Task Discussions," *Social Forces* 80(1) (2001): 125

4 Nancy Jo Silberman-Federman, "Jewish Humor, Self-Hatred or Anti-Semitism: The Sociology of Hanukkah Cards in America," *Journal of Popular Culture* 28(4) (1995): 216

5 Ibid., 214.

6 Nilsen, "In Defense of Humor," 929.

7 Boskin and Dorinson, "Ethnic Humor."

8 Nilsen, "In Defense of Humor."

9 Boskin and Dorinson, "Ethnic Humor."

10 Robinson and Smith-Lovin, "Getting a Laugh."

11 Martin, Grotjahn. *Beyond Laughter* (New York: McGraw Hill, 1957).

12 Lawrence E. Mintz, "Humor and Ethnic Stereotypes in Vaudeville and Burlesque," *MELUS* 21(4) (1996): 24.

13 Dexter B. Gordon, "Humor in African American Discourse: Speaking of Oppression," Journal of Black Studies 29(2) (1998).

14 Mintz, "Humor and Ethnic Stereotypes."

15 John Lowe, "Theories of Ethnic Humor: How to Enter, Laughing," *American Quarterly* 38(3) (1986).

16 Ibid., 442.

17 Antonin J. Obrdlik, "Gallows Humor—A Sociological Phenomenon," *The American Journal of Sociology* 47(5) (1942).

18 Nilsen, "In Defense of Humor."

19 Boskin and Dorinson, "Ethnic Humor."

20 Apte, qtd in Lowe, "Theories of Ethnic Humor."

21 Boskin and Dorinson, "Ethnic Humor."

22 Ibid., 83.

23 Ibid., 97.

24 Ibid., 88

25 Samuel Juni and Bernard Katz, "Self-Effacing Wit as a Response to Oppression: Dynamics in Ethnic Humor," *The Journal of General Psychology* 128(2) (2001).

26 Ibid., 119.

27 Silberman-Federman, "Jewish Humor."

28 Juni and Katz, "Self-Effacing Wit."

29 Chaim Bermant, *What's the Joke?: A Study of Jewish Humor through the Ages London.* Weidenfeld and Nicholson, 1986; Bloom, Sam W. and Ilana Y. Zinguer, Inclusion and Exclusion: Perspectives on Jews from the Enlightenment to the Dreyfus Affair, (Leiden and Boston: Brill, 2003); Juni and Katz, "Self-Effacing Wit"; Silberman-Federman, "Jewish Humor."

30 Juni and Katz, "Self-Effacing Wit."

31 Gordon, "Humor in African American Discourse," 256.

32 Ibid.

33 Boskin and Dorinson, "Ethnic Humor," 91.

34 Mel Watkins, *On the Real Side,* (New York: Simon & Schuster, 1994), 567.

35 Michael L. Hecht, Ronald L. Jackson & Sidney A. Ribeau, *African American Communication: Exploring Identity and Culture,* (Mahwah, NJ: Lawrence Erlbaum Associates, 2003).

36 Boskin and Dorinson, "Ethnic Humor," 97.

37 Ibid., 90.

38 *http://www.m-w.com/cgi-bin/dictionary?va=satire*

39 Donald Bogle, *Toms, Coons, Mulattoes, Mammies & Bucks: An Interpretive History of Blacks in American Films,* (New York: Continuum, 2001), 236.

40 Ibid.

41 As qtd. in Bogle, *Toms, Coons, Mulattoes, Mammies & Bucks.*

42 Bogle, *Toms, Coons, Mulattoes, Mammies & Bucks,* 238.

43 Michael Lerner and Cornel West, *Jews and Blacks: Let the Healing Begin,* (New York: G.P. Putnam, 1995), 1.

44 Karen Brodkin, *How Jews Became White Folks and What that Says about Race in America,* (New Brunswick, NJ: Rutgers University Press, 2004), 3.

45 Eric L. Goldstein, *The Price of Whiteness: Jews, Race, and American Identity,* (Princeton, NJ: Princeton University Press, 2006); M. Hecht, R. Jackson, S. Ribeau, *African American Communication.*

46 Brodkin, *How Jews Became White Folks,* 54.

47 Goldstein, *The Price of Whiteness,* 198.

48 Ibid, 214.

49 Lerner and West, *Jews and Blacks.*

50 Goldstein, *The Price of Whiteness,* 3.

51 Brodkin, *How Jews Became White Folks,* 144.

52 FBI, 2004.

53 Ibid.

54 Michael L. Hecht, Sandra L. Faulkner, C.R. Meyer, T.A. Niles, Doug A. Golden, and Melanie Cutler. "Jewish American Identity: A Communication Theory of Identity Analysis of the Television Series 'Northern Exposure.'" *Journal of Communication* 52 (2002): 852–869.

55 Goldstein, *The Price of Whiteness,* 222.

56 Steven M. Cohen and Arnold M. Eisen, *The Jew Within: Self, Family and Community in America,* (Bloomington, Indiana: Indiana University Press, 2000), 102.

57 Reik qtd. in Bloom and Zinguer, *Inclusion and Exclusion,* 158.

58 Jodi R. Cohen, "The 'Relevance' of Cultural Identity in Audiences' Interpretations of Mass Media," *Critical Studies in Mass Communication* 8 (1991).

59 Ibid., 444

60 www.thehebrewhammer.com

61 Gerald Sorin, "Not by Ethnicity Alone: A Search for Meaning in American Jewish Identity," *Reviews in American History* 21 (1994).

62 Hannah Arendt, *The Jew as Pariah: Jewish Identity and Politics in the Modern Age,* (New York: Grove Press Inc., 1978).

63 Spector, Alan J. "Disney Does Diversity: The Social Context of Racial-Ethnic Imagery," in *Cultural Diversity and the U.S. Media,* ed. Yahya R. Kamalipour and Theresa Carilli, (Albany, NY: SUNY Press, 1998), 39.

64 Telushkin, Joseph, *Jewish Humor: What the Best Jewish Jokes Say About the Jews,* (New York: William Morrow & Company, Inc, 1992), 21.

65 Gilman, Sander L, *Jewish Self-Hatred: Anti-Semitism and the Secret Language of the Jews,* (Baltimore, MD: The Johns Hopkins University Press, 1986), 4.

66 Spector, "Disney Does Diversity," 41.

67 Lerner and West, *Jews and Blacks,* 64.

BIBLIOGRAPHY

Abrams, Nathan. "Triple Exthnics: Nathan Abrams on Jews in the American Porn Industry." *Jewish Quarterly,* 196 (2004). Found at *http://www.jewishquarterly.org/article.asp?articleid=38.*

Arendt, Hannah. *The Jew as Pariah: Jewish Identity and Politics in the Modern Age.* New York: Grove Press, Inc., 1978.

Bermant, Chaim. *What's the Joke?: A Study of Jewish Humor throughout the Ages.* London: Weidenfeld and Nicolson, 1986.

Bloom, James D. *Gravity Fails: The Comic Jewish Shaping of Modern America.* Westport, CT: Praeger, 2000.

Bloom, Sam W. and Ilana Y. Zinguer. *Inclusion and Exclusion: Perspectives on Jews from the Enlightenment to the Dreyfus Affair.* Leiden and Boston: Brill, 2003.

Bogle, Donald. *Toms, Coons, Mulattoes, Mammies & Bucks: An Interpretive History of Blacks in American Films.* 4th (ed). New York: Continuum, 2001.

Boskin, Joseph and Joseph Dorinson. "Ethnic Humor: Subversion and Survival." *American Quarterly* 37(1) (1985): 81–97.

Brodkin, Karen. *How Jews Became White Folks and What that Says about Race in America.* New Brunswick, NJ: Rutgers University Press, 2004.

Cohen, Jodi R. "The 'Relevance' of Cultural Identity in Audiences' Interpretations of Mass Media." *Critical Studies in Mass Communication.* 8 (1991): 442–454.

Cohen, Steven M. and Arnold M. Eisen. *The Jew Within: Self, Family and Community in America.* Bloomington, Indiana: Indiana University Press, 2000.

Gilman, Sander L. *Jewish Self-Hatred: Anti-Semitism and the Secret Language of the Jews.* Baltimore, MD: The Johns Hopkins University Press, 1986.

Goldstein, Eric L. *The Price of Whiteness: Jews, Race, and American Identity.* Princeton, NJ: Princeton University Press, 2006.

Gordon, Dexter B. "Humor in African American Discourse: Speaking of Oppression." *Journal of Black Studies* 29(2) (1998): 254–276

Grotjahn, Martin. *Beyond Laughter.* New York: McGraw Hill, 1957.

Hecht, Michael L., Sandra L. Faulkner, C.R. Meyer, T.A. Niles, Doug A. Golden, and Melanie Cutler. "Jewish American Identity: A Communication Theory of Identity Analysis of the Television Series 'Northern Exposure.'" *Journal of Communication* 52 (2002): 852–869.

Hecht, Michael L., Ronald L. Jackson, and Sidney A. Ribeau. *African American Communication: Exploring Identity and Culture.* Mahwah, NJ: Lawrence Erlbaum Associates, 2003.

Juni, Samuel, and Bernard Katz. "Self-Effacing Wit as a Response to Oppression: Dynamics in Ethnic Humor." *The Journal of General Psychology* 128(2) (2001): 119–143.

Lerner, Michael, and Cornel West. *Jews and Blacks: Let the Healing Begin.* New York: G.P. Putnam, 1995.

Lowe, John. "Theories of Ethnic Humor: How to Enter, Laughing." *American Quarterly* 38(3) (1986): 439–460.

Mintz, Lawrence E. "Humor and Ethnic Stereotypes in Vaudeville and Burlesque." *MELUS* 21(4) (1996): 19–28.

Neuman, Joshua, and David Deutsch. *The Big Book of Jewish Conspiracies.* Stamford, CT: Griffin, 2005.

Nilsen, Alleen Pace. "In Defense of Humor." *College Education* 56 (1994): 928–933.

Obrdlik, Antonin J. "Gallows Humor"—A Sociological Phenomenon." *The American Journal of Sociology* 47(5) (1942): 709–716.

Robinson, Dawn T. and Lynn Smith-Lovin, "Getting a Laugh: Gender, Status, and Humor in Task Discussions." *Social Forces* 80(1) (2001): 123–158.

Silberman-Federman, Nancy Jo. "Jewish Humor, Self-Hatred, or Anti-Semitism: The Sociology of Hanukkah Cards in America." *Journal of Popular Culture* 28(4) (1995): 211–238.

Sorin, Gerald. "Not by Ethnicity Alone: A Search for Meaning in American Jewish Identity." *Reviews in American History* 21 (1993): 190–194.

Spector, Alan J. "Disney Does Diversity: The Social Context of Racial-Ethnic Imagery," in *Cultural Diversity and the U.S. Media* edited by Yahya R. Kamalipour and Theresa Carilli, 39–51. Albany, NY: SUNY Press, 1998.

Telushkin, Joseph. *Jewish Humor: What the Best Jewish Jokes Say About the Jews.* New York: William Morrow & Company, Inc, 1992.

Watkins, Mel. *On the Real Side.* New York: Simon & Schuster, 1994.

Arendt, Adorno, and Benjamin

Response, Responsibility, and Commitment

G. L. ERCOLINI

The concept of cosmopolitanism, being a citizen of the world or inhabiting a worldly perspective, involves related concepts like being-at-home, belonging, and membership as well as the constellation of terms around homelessness, exile, and displacement. Narrative and memory connect to these concepts insofar as narrative, the submitting of a story to the public realm, helps to inscribe that story into public memory, which can offer—in at least some senses—a home, a place, a space. Furthermore, when the story is of a life, particularly at its end, some important questions to scholars in communication ethics involve how to respond, what responsibility is entailed, and the commitment that such a response articulates. These elements—narrative, homelessness, memory, responsibility, and commitment—form the contours of the elliptical relationship between Hannah Arendt, Theodor Adorno, and Walter Benjamin. All three were German intellectuals of Jewish descent fleeing Germany after the fall of the Weimar Republic. Only two of them, Arendt and Adorno, made it to America— Benjamin, captured at the Spanish border, committed suicide while in detainment. Arendt and Adorno, working in exile in America, both responded to the death of their friend with two different portraits, representing their differing commitments through the memory of Benjamin. Arendt's portrait of Benjamin represents her commitment to narrativizing life, and Adorno's essay demonstrates Adorno's commitment to a particular type of the intellectual. This chapter investigates those differing commitments through their portrayals of Benjamin after his death by placing Arendt and Adorno—hardly on friendly terms with one another—in context, looking to Arendt's portrait in *Illuminations,* Adorno's portrait in *Prisms,* and finally tracing-out the commitments demonstrated through their respective portraits of Benjamin.

ARENDT AND THE FRANKFURT SCHOOL

The connection between Hannah Arendt and the Frankfurt School is contested terrain. One aspect of this relates to the way in which the term "Frankfurt School" refers both to a literal school as well as a broader umbrella of theoretical and methodological issues concerned with a particular political and social context (anti-Semitism, fascism, and potentiality for emancipation) at a certain point in time (post-Weimar republic Germany and the escalation of World War II). In literal form, The Frankfurt School is the term for the Institute for Social Research at the University of Frankfurt, a program emphasizing sociological inquiry attendant to certain elements of Marxism, psychology, and empirical method. Hannah Arendt was never technically part of the Frankfurt School in its restricted sense, which included members Theodor Adorno, Max Horkheimer, Walter Benjamin, Herbert Marcuse, Eric Fromm, Leo Lowenthal, Friedrich Pollock, among several others. Perhaps more akin to an interdisciplinary program in social thought at the University of Frankfurt, the Frankfurt School in the technical sense constituted a particular program with affiliated faculty and so forth. The curious fact is that sometimes Arendt's name is included in what must be a broader sense of the term of the Frankfurt School as an approach, critical theory retrospectively under the wider aegis of the collective works of German Jewish intellectuals in exile in America escaping the escalating political and social conditions in Germany following Hitler's rise to power.[1]

Arendt's relation to the Frankfurt School in the restricted sense, therefore, is elliptical but also multiple. Both Arendt and the Freudian Marxist Herbert Marcuse studied with Heidegger at Freiburg. Several have noted Arendt's significant yet largely under-attributed influence on the second-generation Frankfurt School theorist of the public sphere, Jurgen Habermas.[2] Arendt was friends with literary and cultural critic Walter Benjamin, a cousin of her first husband Gunther Stern, and remained friends through her second marriage until Benjamin's death in 1940. When she was in Frankfurt in the early thirties, she was 'honored' in a student parody alongside Adorno, in "a skit in which the philosophical jargons of Theodor Adorno, Paul Tillich, and Hannah Arendt-Stern were elaborately parodied."[3] She had met other members of the Institute both in Germany and when it had been relocated in New York, its location in exile. Once one starts tracing the connections, they soon become numerous, and for good reason. Arendt and the members of the Institute for Social Research were both at some point affiliated with University of Frankfurt am Main, and as Jewish intellectuals who took refuge in America a matter of years apart. For the most part, although not members of the same immediate circles, their peripheral orbits crossed in many ways.

The relationship between Arendt and Theodor Adorno perhaps constitutes one of the most interesting and least-traced of these connections. While the edited collection *Arendt und Adorno* was published by Suhrkamp Verlag in 2003, not much work appears in English on the connection between the two thinkers. Most often, the two are compared/contrasted in terms of their approaches as contemporaries. For example, Albrecht Wellmer notes "Arendt's idea of this faculty of judgment, which for her was not least the faculty to perceive differences and to perceive the particular in its own right, has a deep affinity with Adorno's idea of nonidentifying thought."[4] Richard King draws together Arendt and the pair Adorno and Horkheimer under the thematic of writers who respond to anti-Semitism and racism "within the postwar 1945 universalist paradigm" and who had an "extra-academic impact."[5] Peter Uwe Hohendahl draws a comparison between the way in which both Arendt and Adorno approach Heinrich Heine's poetry, diverging on his symbiotic language.[6]

Accounts of their direct interaction are relatively sparse but characterized by antipathy on Arendt's part, for as the author of Arendt's standard biography Elisabeth Young-Bruehl notes, "Hannah Arendt was never sympathetic to the Frankfurt School Marxists."[7] On the other side of the equation, Arendt elicited nothing but silence from Adorno, at least from what has been made into public articulation. Direct reference to Arendt is largely absent in Adorno's work, his published correspondence, and correspondingly sparse in the secondary scholarship on Adorno.[8] Arendt's husband Gunther Stern had submitted his work on musicology for consideration towards a teaching position at the University of Frankfurt after initial encouragement by both Adorno and Horkheimer, the final product of which ultimately met with Adorno's objection. As Young-Bruehl notes, "this episode was only the first in a series which made personal sympathy unlikely."[9] Immediately after making Adorno's acquaintance, Arendt, not one to mince words, told her husband "Der kommt uns nicht in Haus! (that one's not coming into our house!)."[10] The direct contact between Arendt and Adorno is not much more extensive—but they did share a certain elliptical relationship through their mutual friend, Benjamin. Arendt's and Adorno's relationships with Benjamin provide an interesting avenue between them and also serve as a way in which both Arendt and Adorno demonstrate not only their commitments to Benjamin but also their broader intellectual and political commitments.

Benjamin's suicide in 1940 provoked a vitriolic response from Arendt, who attacks the Frankfurt School, particularly Adorno and Horkheimer, in response to Arendt's perception that the Institute was not meeting its responsibility in publishing Benjamin's manuscripts that had been delivered to their possession. Benjamin, who in 1933 fled Germany to Paris, was, in 1940, planning to emigrate to America, with an emergency visa arranged by Horkheimer, to rejoin the relocated Institute for Social Research. Benjamin, after crossing the French border into Spain, was detained. The border had just been closed that day and visas leaving the country were no longer honored. Facing the prospect of being returned to Germany the following morning, he took his own life. Before leaving, however, Benjamin had entrusted some of his extant manuscripts (including the famous, "Theses on the Philosophy of History") to his friend, Hannah Arendt, instructing her to deliver them to the Institute for Social Research in New York. She delivered them to the Institute's office[11] but after time passed, she becomes furious that the members of the Institute did not publish the manuscripts promptly. In a letter to her second husband Heinrich Blucher, she writes,

> I take it that the group of bastards…will simply suppress the manuscript…I was obligated to give it to them, knowing that Benji has sent them a copy which never arrived. Snubby, please, please say something. I'm all alone and so horribly desperate and frightened because they don't seem willing to print it. And so terribly furious that I could murder the whole lot of them…. We certainly won't be able to lecture them on loyalty to a dead friend.[12]

Arendt's initial response to the way in which the Institute failed to respond to the death and memory of Benjamin forms the initial angle of intervention of my study. This response calls attention to the question of how both Adorno and Arendt responded to the death and memory of Walter Benjamin and how these responses demonstrated their particular commitments and responsibilities toward him. The Institute did publish several essays of Benjamin's in the Institute's journal and Theodor and Gretel Adorno published a two-volume selection of his writings in 1955. In 1968, Hannah Arendt edited the first English translation of Benjamin's work, the collection of essays entitled *Illuminations*. Both Adorno and Arendt responded to the death of Benjamin and demonstrated a commitment to presenting his unpublished work. Not only did both Arendt and Adorno contribute substantial time and energy to making Benjamin's work available in a public capacity, both wrote essays about Benjamin's life and work. Arendt wrote an essay for *The New Yorker*, the same to be included in the volume *Men in Dark Times,* which is also the same essay that introduces her edition of *Illuminations,* all appearing within a year of 1968. Adorno wrote "A Portrait of Walter Benjamin," appearing in the collection of essays entitled *Prisms* published in the previous year. While noting Arendt's barbs at Adorno and the Frankfurt school in her essay (in part rejoinder to Adorno's characterization of Benjamin and as an extension of her polemic against how the Institute generally treated Benjamin), I am interested in the ways in which these two stories of Benjamin, these ways in which he is narrativized, demonstrate each of their respective commitments in a broader sense. The different ways Arendt and Adorno present Benjamin's story represent two different senses of commitment. Arendt's demonstrated commitment to Benjamin relates to the importance of narrativizing life and the importance of stories of life appearing in the public realm for remembrance. Adorno's demonstrated commitment to Benjamin is more of a reader-writer relationship, in some sense. Benjamin, long after his death, is still engaged in the work of Adorno and his influence is something that Adorno works through, both explicitly and implicitly, in his own work. In short, Arendt's commitment is to preserving the story, Adorno's to continuation of engagement under a particular conception of the intellectual.

ARENDT AND BENJAMIN

Arendt met Benjamin through her first husband but they became friends and associated much more frequently when she was in Paris with her second husband Heinrich Blucher. Gershom Scholem, in his account of his friendship in Benjamin, recounts that "In Berlin...I also met Walter's relative Gunther Stern (later Gunther Anders) and his first wife, Hannah Arendt, for whom Benjamin already seemed to represent a weighty intellectual authority—surely a rarity in those days."[13] As Arendt and Blucher left for Paris in 1933, Young-Bruehl describes that they "visited the literary critic Walter Benjamin whom they had both met but not known well in Berlin. Benjamin, a distant cousin of Stern's, was more at home in Paris than most of the refugee intellectuals."[14] The Bluchers and Benjamin met frequently, had discussions about philosophical and political matters, and became relatively good friends while they were all in Paris. Benjamin, although not holding any formal appointment, was an emerging figure informally on the French intellectual scene. Young-Bruehl recounts that "he was grateful for the few forums where French and émigré intellectuals met, like the *Institut pour L'Etude du Fascisme* where in 1934 he delivered his lecture 'The Author as Producer' to an audience that included Hannah Arendt."[15] They met, often with other intellectuals of Marxist sympathies, in Benjamin's apartment.

The three became relatively close, to the extent that Arendt in writing to Gertrude Jaspers, the wife of her much-adored mentor Karl Jaspers, retrospectively identifies "Benji" as "their best friend in Paris."[16] Even though Benjamin was a relation from Arendt's first marriage, Arendt and Heinrich saw much more of him and became closer to Benjamin than when she was married to Benjamin's cousin. Even in Arendt's absence, Blucher and Benjamin got along quite well. Blucher writes in a letter to Arendt on Sept. 15, 1937, "Yesterday I played chess with Benji for the first time and beat him in a long and interesting game. He was the perfect gentleman."[17] Not only was their relationship friendly and familial but always an intellectual exchange in a social context. In a letter to Jaspers, Arendt indicated that her study of *Rahel Varnhagen: The Life of a Jewess* was largely completed by goading from both Blucher and Benjamin, Arendt admitting "I completed it rather grumpily because Heinrich and Benjamin kept pestering me about it."[18] Herzog identifies the influence their social intellectual engagements had upon Arendt and that Arendt was quite influenced by the enigmatic and aloof yet charming Benjamin, particularly with regard to history and narrative.[19]

At the time that Benjamin was in Marseilles picking up the emergency visa arranged by the Institute for emigration to America, Benjamin, Arendt, and Blucher met up for the last time. Young-Bruehl describes the encounter, where Benjamin "entrusted to their care a collection of manuscripts, including the 'Theses on the Philosophy of History,' which he had hoped they would be able to deliver to the Institute for Social Research in New York. They had the honor of being their friend's messengers."[20] They were deeply affected by news of Benjamin's death, about which they learned in October of 1940 while still in France before the travel restrictions enabled them to leave for America the following year. In addition to the commitment Arendt assumes regarding his manuscripts, his work, and his story, Arendt writes the following poem about Benji, simply entitled "W. B:"

> *Dusk will come again sometime. Night will come down from the stars.*
> *We will rest our outstretched arms. In the nearness, in the distances.*
> *Out of the darkness sound softly small archaic melodies. Listening,*
> *Let us wear ourselves away let us at last break ranks.*
> *Distant voices, sadness nearby. Those are the voices and these are the dead*
> *Whom we have sent as messengers, ahead, to lead us to slumber.*[21]

ADORNO AND BENJAMIN

Adorno, enrolling at the University of Frankfurt in 1921, met Benjamin in 1923 through Adorno's family friend and early mentor, Siegfried Kracauer. Benjamin was, at that time, attempting to be considered for a teaching appointment at the University and submitted his *habilitationschrift* (monograph upon which such appointments were based) on German tragedy. While Benjamin did not get the formal appointment, he more or less remained in the circle of the Institute and, as related by Lorenz Jager, Adorno recounted that he "saw Benjamin very often, I would say at least once a week, probably more frequently during the whole of the time that he was living in

Frankfurt."[22] In the translation of Jager's biography of Adorno, the following brief but evocative reminiscence characterizes Adorno's view of their relationship.

> It is really quite difficult to speak of a 'purpose' in our spending time together, we spent time together in the very way that forty years ago intellectuals used to meet, simply in order to talk and in that way to tug a little at the theoretical bones that they were currently gnawing. That is how it was with Benjamin and me. I was very young, eleven years younger than he, and of the two of us I saw myself entirely as the one who took rather than gave. I know that I listened to him with tremendous fascination and would then sometimes ask him to explain things in more detail.[23]

The relationship between Adorno and Benjamin from 1923 until Benjamin's death could be characterized as one of intellectual engagement. Since Benjamin emigrated to Paris in 1933, a great deal of their relationship—punctuated by occasional visits—was largely epistolary, but intense, engaged, and sustained up until Benjamin's death.

According to Jager, "for both men, this was one of the most important relationships in their lives, and it was not free from tension."[24] Taking a cue from both Adorno's recollection and Jager's account, the relationship between Benjamin and Adorno in some ways resembles the mentor/prodigy configuration. Arendt describes Adorno as "his [Benjamin's] first and only disciple."[25] Hohendahl follows a similar characterization when describing how "Adorno came to follow the path of his older friend and mentor, who set out to reformulate the task of philosophy."[26] Along this line, the task of reconceptualizing philosophy is where Benjamin had a most significant influence, an influence that seemingly extended beyond Benjamin's death. Whether accurate or not, perhaps the mentor relation at least does some work, particularly when, at least according to Jay's account, "Adorno began in subtle ways to qualify some of the positions he inherited from Benjamin."[27] The lines of influence are perhaps more stunning and extensive—sometimes attributed, often not.

Benjamin and Adorno likely disagreed on more issues (on the emancipatory potential of mass culture, the value of Surrealism, the role of history, the function of materialism, the deployment of Marxist concepts, the role of experience, just to name a few examples) than they agreed upon, but only in the way that two thinkers so closely and intellectually engaged with one another could. Their extensive correspondence is replete with lively exchange, oftentimes stark divergence, and even heated critique. Henri Lonitz, editor of the correspondence between Adorno and Benjamin, notes that "the mutual critique which Adorno and Benjamin exercised upon each other's work during their years of emigration is worlds apart from the congealed form in which these crucial works have been first dissected and then clumsily recombined, received, interpreted, and 'transmitted' by those who have come afterwards."[28] While Adorno's critique of several elements in Benjamin's writing becomes evident, most extensively through their correspondence, it seems rather that the level of engagement, the careful attention, and the thorough reading each affords the other's work are far more revealing than many make of their relation. Others frame the relationship as Adorno intimidating and attacking the fearful, subservient, and accommodating Benjamin. In their sustained engagement with one another's work, the level of attentive reading is quite formidable in their exchange—perhaps more telling than whether substantively they agreed on content, which they often did not. Their form of exchange reflects a sustained and critical intellectual engagement of a personal nature.

Upon Benjamin's decision to commit suicide by morphine, his last words are to Adorno. After having taken the lethal dose on the evening of September 25, 1940, the night before the detainees were to be returned to Germany and likely forwarded to concentration camps, Benjamin leaves instructions for Henny Gurland, one of the fellow detainees, to relay his final thoughts to Adorno:

> In a situation with no escape, I have no other choice but to finish it all. It is a tiny village in the Pyrenees, where no one knows me, that my life must come to an end. I would ask you to pass on my thoughts to my friend Adorno and to explain to him the situation in which I have now found myself. I no longer have time to write all those letters I would dearly have written.[29]

Many speculate, following Arendt's account, that Benjamin's suicide made an impression on the border officials and thus they let the detainees travel to their destinations despite the border status. As with Arendt, Benjamin's suicide was "a deep personal blow"[30] to Adorno, and in some ways he continued his intellectual engagement with Benjamin long after his death—through his own work and through publishing Benjamin's work.

ARENDT'S "WALTER BENJAMIN: 1892–1940"

Arendt's essay on Benjamin, the introduction to the edited volume of Benjamin's work, *Illuminations,* tells a story of a man who is constantly plagued by bad luck, who is *sui generis,* and who is never at home. Arendt's story weaves elements of his life and writing together as if of the same dimension. The elements of bad luck, in Arendt's account, pervade Benjamin throughout his life in a way that he cannot help but recognize. Arendt frames Benjamin's luck through the childhood figure of Mr. Bungle, the hunchback who is always about when mishap occurs, and carries this sense through, evoking an underwritten pathos of misfortune. Yet, in Arendt's story of Benjamin, this sense of bungling misfortune is not out of a sense of pity for the one who is unaware or with a sigh in response to recklessness, but more with an ironic sensibility. Arendt explains that "one cannot say that he consciously disregarded due caution. On the contrary, he was aware that 'Mr. Bungle sends his regards' and took more precautions than anyone else I have known. But his system of provisions against possible dangers…invariably, in a strange and mysterious way, disregarded the real danger."[31] In one example, under the belief that Paris was under threat of being bombed, Benjamin relocated to Meaux, which, as Arendt explains, "was a troop center and probably one of the few places in France that was seriously endangered in those months of the phony war."[32] This bad luck pervaded the life of Arendt's Benjamin—persistent financial difficulties stemming from an outmoded idea of the subsidized man of letters, difficulty finding a stable and official academic appointment, only getting his due recognition posthumously, and the strange confluence of factors leading up to his suicide.

The circumstances of Benjamin's suicide serve as the most profound instance of the misfortune, bad timing, and inauspicious circumstances in which Benjamin persistently found himself. Arendt claims, "the immediate occasion for Benjamin's suicide was an uncommon stroke of bad luck."[33] Arendt amplifies the strange set of circumstances of bad luck at the Franco-Spanish border by emphasizing "a few weeks [later], the embargo was lifted again. One day earlier Benjamin would have got through without any trouble; one day later the people in Marseilles would have known that for the time being it was impossible to pass through Spain. Only on that particular day was the catastrophe possible."[34] Only at that particular moment—that very day—did the forces converge in such a way as to bring about the relatively improbable situation of being detained at the border and being sent back to Germany, to most likely an unimaginable fate as he was not only Jewish, but also an intellectual and, further, one with Marxist sympathies.

Arendt's Benjamin is also *sui generis,* thinking in an extraordinarily unusual and untimely capacity "incomparable to anything else."[35] While noting that Benjamin did not receive his due recognition during his lifetime except within a rather small circle, Arendt opens her essay with a discussion of the operation of posthumous fame, a fame belonging to "the lot of unclassifiable ones, that is, those whose work never fits the existing order nor introduces a new genre that lends itself to future classification."[36] Arendt's story along this axis, with persistent attention to the misfortune of 'Mr. Bungle sends his regards,' demonstrates how this singular brilliance of thought likewise served as the catalyst for misapprehension of his genius, particularly by Adorno and the other Institute members. Arendt holds little back in her attacks on Adorno and the Institute through the story of Benjamin and how he was treated in his association with them.

Adorno's well-known objections to some elements of Benjamin's thought, particularly the way in which Benjamin used Marxist concepts like dialectical materialism in less-than-rigorous and more whimsical deployments, serve in Arendt's account as a charge against Adorno. While she is grateful for the efforts of Horkheimer and the Institute in arranging for Benjamin's emergency visa to escape Nazi Germany, she disdainfully recounts her perception of the way in which the Frankfurt School members treated Benjamin. The Institute core members were invested in being "dialectical materialists and in their opinion Benjamin's thinking was 'undialectic,' moved in 'materialist categories which by no means coincided with Marxist ones,' was 'lacking in mediation' in so far as, in an essay on Baudelaire, he had related conspicuous elements within the superstructure...directly, perhaps even causally, to corresponding elements in the substructure."[37] Arendt continues by pointing out that "when Adorno criticized Benjamin's 'wide-eyed presentation of actualities,' he hit the nail right on its head; this is precisely what Benjamin was doing and wanted to do. Strongly influenced by surrealism, it was the attempt to capture the portrait of history in the most insignificant representations of reality, its scraps as it were."[38] So, where Adorno finds an undisciplined use and conflation of Marxist categories of analysis, Arendt finds a brilliant transformation and troubling of some of those concepts. Rather than misunderstanding metaphysics, history, and dialecticism, Arendt's Benjamin understood them and their limitations all to well—in fact so much so that in his unconventional use he transfigured those very concepts with an incomparable depth.

Arendt's Benjamin, finally, is one who is never at home—always a thinker in exile, in so many ways. His untimely meditations and his unusual way of thinking enabled one form of homelessness in that he never clearly fit into recognizable categories. In more than merely untimely thought, Arendt's Benjamin seemed out of sync with his time, a figure more suited to the 19th century Paris that captivated his attention so obsessively. Benjamin, in Arendt's story, had always envisioned himself as a man of letters, an independent and subsidized scholar released from the necessities of working for a living and able to flourish intellectually. However, things did not materialize in such a way for Benjamin, and he had to rely on a stipend from the Institute, always in need of assistance. Arendt describes that through the figure of Benjamin, "it was as if though shortly before its disappearance, the *homme de letters* was destined to show itself once more in the fullness of its possibilities, although—or, possibly because—it had lost its material basis in such a catastrophic way."[39]

Furthermore, in the context of the Jewish intellectual, another aspect of exile pervades Arendt's account of Benjamin. Not only did Benjamin, a Jew, take exile in Paris in 1933 from an increasingly hostile and dangerous Germany, but his complicated relationship with his status as Jew added another dimension to the ways in which Benjamin was always not at home. Arendt emphasizes the ways in which Benjamin's thought is indebted to Jewish mysticism—influenced by his long-time friend and renowned scholar of the Kabbalah, Gershom Scholem—and yet his unusual approach never placed him firmly in line with one influence, but as always in-between. Arendt describes the precarious in-between Benjamin inhabited regarding both Zionism and Marxism. In Arendt's conception, these ideologies offered two mutually exclusive options of resistance for the Jewish intelligentsia, "the two ideologies [that] faced each other with the greatest hostility."[40] Fully at home in neither of these positions, Arendt claims that "in a remarkable and probably unique manner, Benjamin kept both routes open for himself for years; he persisted in considering the road to Palestine long after he had become a Marxist, without allowing himself to be swayed in the least by the opinions of his Marxist-oriented friends, particularly the Jews among them."[41] Arendt identifies the broader perspective from which this intellectual homelessness emerged in the way in which Benjamin appreciated the negative aspects of different perspectives—the movement of critique against current conditions—but the positive aspect of ideology didn't interest him. Arendt observes, "he was quite young when he adopted this radically critical attitude, probably without suspecting to what isolations and loneliness it would eventually lead him."[42]

In a passage evoking Benjamin's bad luck, status as *sui generis,* and equivocal homelessness, Arendt explains, "Benjamin was forced into a position which actually did not exist anywhere, which, in fact, could not be identified and diagnosed as such until afterwards. It was the position on the 'top of the mast' from which the tempestuous times could be surveyed better than from a safe harbor."[43] Benjamin's unusual position—critically, socially, intellectually—in Arendt's account, constituted the base of his simultaneous brilliance and misfortune. Never at home, no matter when or where he went, Benjamin was untimely and rather otherworldly while simultaneously committed to the material and the everyday in its strangeness.

ADORNO'S "PORTRAIT OF WALTER BENJAMIN"

In Adorno's account, Benjamin is about what we are left with (and must come to grips with) in his writings. Adorno's Benjamin is captivating and enigmatic in part because of divided tensions throughout his work that provide the energy to his thought. Distinguished from Arendt's Benjamin, whose elements of life so very interspersed his enigmatic work, Adorno's Benjamin is a story of intellectual confliction on several levels but, ultimately, Adorno deals with the various ways in which Benjamin's thought functioned without the persistent emphasis on the biographical elements of the story that so interested Arendt. Adorno's story of Benjamin makes, if at all, sparse reference to biographical elements of Benjamin's life, the most notable of which opens the essay. Adorno begins: "the name of the philosopher, who took his own life while fleeing Hitler's executioners, has, in the more than twenty years since then, acquired a certain nimbus, despite the esoteric character of his early writings and the fragmentary nature of his later ones."[44] Adorno's account, therefore, after making its fleeting but dramatic nod to Benjamin's life, casts the story of Benjamin about the life of his thought—the way the thought took on a life of its own in how Benjamin was received. In Adorno's account, Benjamin's haunting and perplexing thought was at once constituted by a strange energy, a deeply divided and contradictory nature, and both exhibited and elicited an almost child-like awe.

Adorno's story of Benjamin interweaves an elusive vocabulary of energy throughout. In describing both the charge of Benjamin's thought and the attendant response resulting from it, Adorno indicates "a fascination of the person and of his work allowed no alternative other than that of magnetic attraction or horrified rejection. Everything which fell under the scrutiny of his words was transformed as though it had become radioactive."[45] The ways in which Benjamin's thought is thematized in accordance with both magnetic and radioactive forces align the thought with these recognizable and common natural forces that nonetheless still remain enigmatic and relatively little understood. Even further along these lines of everyday, pervasive, but still elusive forces, Adorno indicates Benjamin's "intellectual energy might be described as a kind of mental atomic fission."[46] Fission serves as a force of intervention resulting in a division, the process of which releases an almost unparalleled amount of energy, and characterizing Benjamin's thought in this manner indicates not only the force of his intervention into the everyday objects to which his keen eye is attuned, but furthermore with the release of such a powerful energy that pervades different dimensions of matter as to transgress several seemingly impermeable boundaries with an emission of a different order.

As emerging from the attributions of a strange energy—a radioactivity, a magnetic force both attracting and repelling, a process of fission, et cetera—Adorno's account of Benjamin persistently emphasizes the divisions, tensions, and contradictory forces that resonate in his thought. These deep divisions and contradictions almost serve as the engine providing the strange energy through some process of friction. In a somewhat similar vein as Arendt, Adorno identifies Benjamin's thought, both idiosyncratic and compelling, in its singularity. Adorno describes how "the subjectivity of his thought shrank to its own specific difference; the idiosyncratic movement of his mind, its singularity—something which, according to conventional philosophical mores, would have been held for contingent, ephemeral, utterly worthless—legitimized itself by giving his thought its compelling character."[47] Already divided and different from itself—a mental atomic fission—this strange caesura of mind produced an unconventional and almost unrecognizable, at least with regard to conventionality, kind of thought. This division against itself Adorno identifies as "ascetic forces counterbalanced an imaginative power kindled ever anew by each object. This helped Benjamin to develop a philosophy directed against philosophy."[48] This thought, divided against itself, produces a type of strange force that enables the move to a larger scale, but as isomorphic division—philosophy against itself.

Furthermore, division, paradox, and tension characterize not only Adorno's conception of Benjamin's mind, but also the ways in which "In the paradox of the impossible possibility, mysticism and enlightenment are joined for the last time in him…. It was nothing other than the explication and elucidation of this paradox, with the only means which philosophy had at its disposal, concepts, that drove Benjamin to immerse himself without reserve in the world of multiplicity."[49] Adorno's Benjamin is constituted by so many divisions, paradoxes, contradictions, and multiplicities, which produce an unusual, frustrating, and yet compelling character of thought. In some sense, Adorno's Benjamin is fascinating—in spite of, or even more so, in light of—the fact that one cannot help but respond in either valence.

Yet, at the same time as Benjamin was of piercing intellectual depth, Adorno's Benjamin is cast with a sense of the childlike. Most of this stems from Adorno's rejection of the types of hope in which Benjamin placed hope (over which Adorno diverged greatly), and thus for Adorno "everything that Benjamin said or wrote sounded as if though, instead of rejecting the promises of fairy tales and children's books with its usual disgraceful 'maturity,' took them so literally that real fulfillment itself was now a sort of knowledge."[50] Not only was the perspective with which Benjamin, in Adorno's account, replete with a certain type of wonder and promise that resonates more with children's stories (although, simultaneously, attuned to the catastrophe), Benjamin evoked a similar response in those to whom he appealed. Adorno explains, "anyone who was drawn to him was bound to feel like the child who catches a glimpse of the lighted Christmas tree through a crack in the closed door."[51] In a certain brilliance and luminosity of his thought, Adorno's narrativization almost infantilizes its very captivating force.

Adorno's portrait of Benjamin, perhaps most crucially, emphasizes his particular way of *seeing things:* his *perspective.* While Adorno attributes strange forces, emanating from several perplexing divisions, producing an almost childlike awe, to Benjamin in his account, what perhaps was most unusual and perplexing was his peculiar glance. Benjamin, although resisting facile categorization based on the content or genre of what he analyzed, perhaps is more consistent in not necessarily what he analyzed but how. Benjamin paid an unusually intense and focused attention not only to the overlooked minutiae but to the ostensibly esoteric, from which he was able to discern a complex set of resonances cutting through several layers. This way of viewing things not only characterized the approach admired by many but simultaneously becomes the point of controversy. Adorno identifies this other edge of the sword: "the true reason that he aroused hatred was that, inevitably and without any polemical intention, his glance revealed the ordinary world in the eclipse which is its permanent life."[52]

However, this line of characterization would be misleading if it did not attend to the particular way in which Benjamin's glance both extracted and hypostatized what was under scrutiny. As Arendt's account has pointed out, Adorno identifies (and resists) the static element in Benjamin's thought rather than movement or dialectics. On this point, the suspended and static status of the object affixed by Benjamin's perspective leads Adorno to write, "the glance of his philosophy is Medusan."[53] His glance, at once magnifying and fixing, in Adorno's account, is constituted in the unusual manner in which Benjamin surrendered himself to the object under study. Adorno identifies Benjamin's "incommensurability lies in the inordinate ability to give himself over to his object. By permitting thought to get, as it were, too close to its object, the object becomes as foreign as an everyday, familiar thing under a microscope."[54] Adorno's Benjamin in part exhibits a particular way of seeing things but goes beyond that through an orienting of the self towards what is under scrutiny.

Benjamin's unusual approach, in Adorno's account, generated a strange energy, a radioactivity resulting through fission, a series of enigmatic divisions that created a sense of almost childlike wonder, evident in both Benjamin's fascination with making-strange the ordinary but also in those attendant to his turns of mind. Adorno is both fascinated and frustrated by Benjamin's "capacity for continually bringing out new aspects, not by exploding conventions through criticism, but rather by organizing himself so as to be able to relate to his subject-matter in a way that seemed beyond all convention—this capacity can hardly be adequately described by the concept of 'originality.'"[55] Adorno's Benjamin, in short, is a force to which one must respond.

ARENDT'S DEMONSTRATED COMMITMENT

While Arendt writes few biographies in terms of the standard conception of the genre, one of her most consistent commitments across her works is to narrative. Given her few biographical enterprises—*Rahel Varnhagen* the most notable in this regard—her commitment to narrative is not to the form or genre but to the spirit of telling stories and submitting them to the human realm to take their own course. Stephen Browne identifies what is at stake in her commitment to narrative, in that "Arendt's reflections on the protection remembrance affords against the waves of time and transience; the perils of forgetting and its consequent destruction of hope, meaning, and motive for political life; and the disclosure of that life through speech and action represent three tightly braided themes with which the fabric of her thought is given its distinctive texture."[56] Stories must be told in order for us to remember. The realm of human relations, for Arendt, is both deed and word, both action and speech. Arendt's commitment to narrative in accordance with its function for memory and legacy does not merely serve as the constative content of her thought. Rather, in her commitment to preserving and presenting Benjamin's work and in her telling of his story, Arendt performs, enacts, and demonstrates this very commitment to which she is so devoted, particularly in *The Human Condition.*

In "The Web of Relationships and Enacted Stories" in *The Human Condition,* Arendt emphasizes the importance of stories in the web of human relations, the in-betweenness of human existence. She claims, "the realm of human affairs, strictly speaking, consists of the web of human relationships which exist wherever men live together…. Together they start a new process which eventually emerges as the unique life story of the newcomer, affecting uniquely the life stories of all those with whom he comes into contact."[57] This realm of the in-between, of inter-est, is where stories emerge and serve as the bulwark against oblivion and forgetting by preservation, perpetuation, and continuation. The realm of human relations is a tricky place—we cannot predict actions, and we cannot plan how things will appear in such a way as to determine the appearance. Through word and deed, humans appear to one another in the space of the political and, for Arendt, keeping this space open is, if radical reduction is permitted, her main political commitment.

While telling stories is about making lives appear in the public realm, the process of storytelling is not a volitional cognitive enterprise. The story serves as a making-appear in public, and that is about the extent to which control is a relevant factor in the process. Arendt explains, "it is because of this already existing web of human relationships, with its innumerable, conflicting wills and intentions, that action almost never achieves its purpose; but it also because of this medium, in which action alone is real, that it 'produces' stories with or without intention as naturally as fabrication produces tangible things."[58] Stories are not central for Arendt in the sense that many ascribe, based on the primacy of the authorial model, as conscious products of *homo faber.* Rather than revealing about their author, stories in the realm of human relations "tell us more about their subjects, the 'hero' in the center of each story, than any product of human hands ever tells us about the master who produced it, and yet they are not products, properly speaking."[59] Arendt's commitment to narrative is in accordance with the way in which stories disclose a "who" rather than inform us about a "what" by reducing a life to a certain form of ruling content. She provides a compelling example of this distinction in explaining that:

> *Who* somebody is or was we can know only by knowing the story of which he is himself the hero—his biography, in other words; everything else we know of his, including the work he may have produced and left behind, tells us only *what* he is or was. Thus, although we know much less of Socrates, who did not write a single line and left no work behind, than of Plato or Aristotle, we know much better and more intimately who he was, because

we know his story, than we know who Aristotle was, about whose opinions we are so much better informed.[60]

For Arendt, telling the story, submitting the "who" to the realm of human relations, is of far more importance in preserving memory and countering oblivion than the reduction of a life to a content. The story of Socrates tells us more about the disclosure of a "who" in the human realm than what we have of Aristotle since Socrates has a life story activated and submitted to the realm of memory and judgment.

In this particular function and operation of narrative lies Arendt's commitment to Benjamin. Arendt took seriously the obligation to ensure that Benjamin's story is told, however, her story in the essay "Walter Benjamin: 1892–1940" serves not merely as a summary of his thought in order to inscribe him in the annals of a long philosophical lineage of the *vita contemplativa*. On the contrary, Arendt's essay on Benjamin, by interweaving elements of his bad luck, *sui generis* status, and homelessness, incorporates elements of the life with the writing in such a way as to present his life and inhabiting the world to the public realm to be remembered, debated, discussed, and engaged. In other words, Arendt's commitment is to keep Benjamin alive and active rather than hypostatized and stagnant, relegated to a curious footnote if not to oblivion entirely. When Elisabeth Young-Bruehl introduces her biography of Arendt, she describes her rather Arendtian inspiration in her telling of the story of Arendt. She writes:

> the light from a person's work enters directly into the world and remains after a person dies. Whether it is large or small, transitory or enduring, depends upon the world and its ways. Posterity will judge. The light that comes from a person's life—spoken words, gestures, friendships—survives only in memories. If it is to enter the world, it must find a new form, be recorded and handed down. A story must be made from many memories and stories.[61]

This evocative passage, activating the Arendtian spirit in a story of Arendt, seems to get at the heart of Arendt's commitment to Benjamin in telling his story.

Given the important function of stories, it becomes clear that Arendt's commitment to telling Benjamin's story is about friendship and memory but not in the personal, sentimental, intimate variety. Arendt's demonstrated commitment to telling Benjamin's story, and her attendant attacks on Adorno and the Institute for failing to meet this obligation forthwith, demonstrate the political basis of friendship and responsibility. In her essay on Lessing, which serves as the introduction to the collection of essays entitled *Men in Dark Times,* a collection in which her story of Benjamin likewise appears—Arendt emphasizes this distinction. She explains:

> we are wont to see friendship solely as a phenomenon of intimacy, in which the friends open their hearts to each other unmolested by the world and its demands [following from Rousseau].... But for the Greeks the essence of friendship consisted in discourse.... In

discourse the political importance of friendship, and the humanness particular to it, were made manifest."[62]

This modality of friendship, distinguished from sentimental intimacy, characterizes the type of political commitment to Benjamin's story and memory demonstrated by Arendt. Arendt immediately enacted her commitment to telling the story of Benjamin upon news of his death, before she even left for New York to deliver the manuscripts. Young-Bruehl relates, "while they waited for their ship to Lisbon, the Bluchers read Benjamin's 'Theses' aloud to each other and to the refugees who gathered around them. They discussed and debated the meaning of his moment-to-moment messianic hope."[63] After delivering the manuscripts to the Institute office, Arendt became furious that the Institute did not publish the manuscripts immediately and in her mind "this confirmed her impression that the Frankfurt Institute members were not going to do what she thought they were morally obligated to do—publish Benjamin's manuscripts."[64] Arendt "never wanted to give Benjamin's manuscripts to Adorno, but she was bound by her friend's instructions."[65] Her commitment to telling the story of Benjamin, to taking action and submitting his life to the realm of human relations so as to be remembered, demonstrates her commitment to her political conceptions of narrative, memory, friendship, and responsibility. Arendt, herself stateless for eighteen years between leaving Germany and acquiring American citizenship, understood all too well the homelessness in which Benjamin always inhabited. While not fixing or abstracting Benjamin, she tells his story and, in a sense, affords him a home that perhaps he never found during his lifetime. She carries this commitment up until her death, for at that time she was working on the second volume of Benjamin's collected works entitled *Reflections.*

ADORNO'S DEMONSTRATED COMMITMENT

Adorno's relationship with Benjamin is of an altogether different register than Arendt's. Subsequently, and unsurprisingly, the commitment Adorno demonstrates in response to Benjamin differs altogether. Perhaps the two commitments differ to such a degree that enables both Arendt's attack on Adorno and the Institute for failing to demonstrate a certain type of commitment while simultaneously enabling Adorno's different commitment to be demonstrated in an altogether different manner. While Adorno is committed to publishing the works of Benjamin and telling Benjamin's story, as his essay "A Portrait of Walter Benjamin" illustrates, Adorno's commitment to Benjamin serves a different function than the Arendtian commitment to narrativizing the life for preservation. Adorno's telling of Benjamin's story demonstrates not only a commitment to a certain form of dialectical thought—to which he was invariably committed—but, I would argue more importantly, performs a commitment to continuing intellectual engagement with Benjamin long after he was gone. Adorno's commitment can be seen as continuing the intellectual engagement and rigorous exchange with Benjamin through his own writings, perhaps most notably in his essay on Benjamin. This commitment indicates not only a commitment to Benjamin but also to a certain version of the intellectual.

The profound influence Benjamin had on Adorno—even in, or perhaps especially, in the ways in which he diverged from Benjamin—indicates one way in which Adorno's commitment to Benjamin was continually demonstrated throughout his work. Concepts like negative dialectics and constellations become important for Adorno and the ways in which he itinerates these from Benjamin's thought demonstrate one form of commitment. Jager claims that "anyone who examines any of Adorno's later writings such as *Minima Moralia* will not fail to notice Benjamin's conceptual and stylistic influence. In this case, we may speak of a continuing conversation that not even Benjamin's death could terminate."[66] Jay also notes, "in the decade following Benjamin's suicide, which was a deep personal blow to Adorno, much of his work focused on the implications of these ideas, which were also embodied in the unfinished *Passagenwerk*[67] manuscript that came into his hands at the time."[68] These numerous lines of influence serve as one route through which Adorno demonstrates his vigilant commitment to Benjamin's thought and memory.

Along similar lines, the way in which Adorno consistently distances his own position from Benjamin's across his works can be seen to demonstrate something other than the standard explanation of Adorno's ungracious and polemical rejection of the former, but instead as an enactment of how Adorno is still working in relationship with and in response to Benjamin's thought. Given the extensive and involved role each played at several stages of their respective work, this sustained engagement with Benjamin can serve as a continuation of their intellectual engagement. Adorno, in retrospectively accounting for his relationship with Benjamin, indicated the tenor of their exchange as typical of the way in which intellectuals related to one another at that time.

In *Minima Moralia,* the work Jay identifies as influenced by Benjamin, Adorno consistently attends to the question of the intellectual. Subtitled "Reflections from Damaged Life," *Minima Moralia* is a Nietzschean-inflected collection of aphorisms about ethical concern with the "good life" in the catastrophe of "damaged life." In it Adorno distinguishes the particular version of the intellectual to which he is committed,

> Few things separate more profoundly the mode of life befitting an intellectual from that
> of the bourgeois than the fact that the former acknowledges no alternative between work
> and recreation…. The doctrine inculcated since Aristotle that moderation is the virtue
> appropriate to reasonable people, is among other things an attempt to found so securely

the socially necessary division of man into functions independent of each other, that it occurs to none of these functions to cross over to the others and remind each other of man."[69]

Aristotelian classification, along with a certain version of "work," has diminished the role of the professional intellectual to that of a specialist, and one whose thinking constitutes work in contradistinction to recreation. Intellectual activity has become professionalized, fragmented, and specialized. This current form of the intellectual does not align with our conception of those who we would consider "intellectual," for, as Adorno memorably puts it, "one could no more imagine Nietzsche in an office, with a secretary minding the telephone in an anteroom, at his desk until five o'clock, than playing golf after the day's work was done."[70] While the intellectual of Adorno's commitment involves "a cunning intertwining of pleasure and work leaves real experience still open, under the pressure of society," Adorno observes that "such experience is less and less tolerated. Even the so-called intellectual professions are being deprived, through their growing resemblance to business, of all joy. Atomization is advancing not only between men, but within each individual, between the spheres of his life."[71] For Adorno, circumstances have changed to the extent where joy, recreation, and investment have been stripped from the increasing professionalization of the areas once inhabited by intellectuals. For Adorno, the intellectual is less a formal or social category than a mode of habilitation, a mode of engagement, a way of being that demands the crossing of categories and distinctions, transgressions of which late capitalism is tolerating less and less.

From this version of the intellectual lies Adorno's relationship with and commitment to Benjamin. They related to one another as intellectuals and Adorno continues to engage Benjamin's thought—in both its fascinating and its frustrating elements—in his work. Adorno's essay on Benjamin, furthermore, demonstrates his commitment to continuing intellectual engagement—as a way of life, not as obligatory profession—with Benjamin. Adorno's account still responds to Benjamin's thought as if still working through the enigmatic, compelling aspects as well as the problematic aspects (his use of Marxist concepts without the appropriate rigor, his faith in the potential emancipatory potential of mass culture, his concept of history, his inattention to dialectics, etc.). Something persistently haunts Adorno in the thought of Benjamin that cannot be neatly excised by objections to the arigorous dialectical materialism. Adorno sees Benjamin's thought as attaining a strange "nimbus," as "radioactive," with certain charges, both attracting and repelling simultaneously. Adorno's account emphasizes his indebtedness to Benjamin through a careful and attentive engagement with his thought—mirroring the same careful and attentive engagement—that their seventeen years of correspondence also demonstrates. Adorno's story of Benjamin demonstrates a certain commitment to Benjamin—a commitment to a continuing philosophical engagement with his work—and one that resonates with his relationship with Benjamin.

CONCLUSION

Benjamin's legacy is unquestionable at this point in terms of influence and recognized depth. This legacy was not produced *ex nihilo,* resulting from merely the sheer brilliance of his thought. This transmission of this legacy was, indeed, a laborious enterprise. In part this legacy is handed down by both Arendt and Adorno, in different ways, attending to different Benjamins, demonstrating different commitments. As Young-Bruehl notes, "when Walter Benjamin's writings became available, many battles were fought over them."[72] Likely, with much approval from Arendt, his work, his life, and his story were made available in the public realm and subject to its unforeseeable consequences. Similarly, as Hohendahl notes, Adorno's essay "although… not without its critical barbs, directed largely at Benjamin's surrealist sympathies and his exaggerated hostility towards individual subjectivity…helped establish his importance as twentieth-century Germany's most original cultural critic."[73] Yet the stories and the works of Benjamin, produced by both Arendt and Adorno, tell as much about the particular commitments of both Arendt and Adorno as they demonstrate about their relationships with Benjamin. These respective demonstrated commitments to Benjamin not only help enable Benjamin to continue to be remembered and discussed as perhaps one of the most influential literary and cultural critics but also enact integral commitments: Arendt to narrativizing Benjamin's life, Adorno to framing Benjamin's intellectual engagement.

NOTES

1. Martin Jay describes, "Critical Theory was applied to the most pressing problem of the time, the rise of fascism in Europe. As Henry Pachter has pointed out, many émigrés without prior political interests or training were compelled by events to study the new totalitarianism. Psychologists like Ernst Kris examined Nazi propaganda, philosophers like Ernst Cassirer and Hannah Arendt probed the myth of the state and the origins of totalitarianism, and novelists like Thomas Mann wrote allegories of Germany's disintegration." Martin Jay, *The Dialectical Imagination: A History of the Frankfurt School and the Institute of Social Research 1923–1950* (Boston: Little, Brown and Company, 1973), 116.

2. Dana Villa R., *Arendt and Heidegger: The Fate of the Political* (Princeton: Princeton University Press, 1996), 4. Of further note, Habermas's essay on Arendt presents a sustained engagement with Arendt's concept of power in order to provide a point of distinction from Habermas's own emphases. This debt demonstrated through his distancing is put into sharp relief in the essay's

conclusion: "In order to ensure a normative equivalent between power and liberty, in the end she puts more truth in the venerable figure of the contract that in her own concept of a communicative praxis. So she retreats into the tradition of natural right." Jurgen Habermas, "Hannah Arendt: On the Concept of Power" in *Philosophical-Political Profiles,* Trans. Frederick G. Lawrence (Cambridge: Massachusetts Institute of Technology Press, 1983), 185.

3. Elisabeth Young-Bruehl, *Hannah Arendt: For the Love of the World,* 2ⁿᵈ Ed. (New Haven: Yale University Press, 2004), 82.

4. Albrecht Wellmer, "Hannah Arendt on Judgment" in *Hannah Arendt: Twenty Years Later,* Eds. Larry May and Jerome Kohn (Cambridge: MIT Press, 1996), 39.

5. Richard King, *Race, Culture, and the Intellectuals* (Washington, DC: Woodrow Wilson Center Press, 2004), 14–15.

6. Peter Uwe Hohendahl, *Prismatic Thought* (Lincoln: University of Nebraska Press, 1995), 112.

7. Young-Bruehl, *Hannah Arendt,* 80.

8. Ibid., 161. The absence of response on Adorno's part is somewhat puzzling, particularly since Arendt publicly criticized Adorno for changing his Jewish name Wiesengrund to his mother's Italian name, Adorno, and well as attacked him for praising a score dedicated to Hitler when he was writing freelance reviews in Nazi Germany before his emigration. The closest indication of a response does not come from Adorno himself, but from fellow Institute member Friedrich Pollock, the Institute's Assistant Director at the time, who "claimed that it was on *his* initiative that the name change took place," according to Martin Jay, *Adorno* (Cambridge University Press, 1984), 34. Young-Bruehl provides another small piece of the puzzle by at least accounting for Arendt's absence in Adorno and Scholem's collaboratively edited volume of Benjamin's correspondence when she explains "Hannah Arendt's own carefully preserved notes from him, written in the summer before his death, were not included in the volumes, for Scholem had severed his relations with her after the publication of *Eichmann in Jerusalem,* a book he despised" according to *Hannah Arendt,* 165. One can only speculate (perhaps speciously) Arendt and Adorno differed with regard to expressing antipathy toward one another: one with vitriol, one with silence.

9. Young-Bruehl, *Hannah Arendt,* 80.

10. Ibid.

11. According to Young-Bruehl, Arendt personally delivered the manuscripts to the Institute's office: "Alice Maier, the Institute's secretary and later Hannah Arendt's friend, received her and summoned 'Teddy' Adorno, who was amazed to find that Benjamin's manuscripts had survived. The writings, and particularly the 'Theses on the Philosophy of History,' came to play an important role in the intellectual development of the Frankfurt School," from *Hannah Arendt,* 166. Adorno's surprise likely refers to the fact that Benjamin's apartment was searched and his personal effects seized (a devastating blow, given his extraordinary penchant for collecting books) so Benjamin's preparations are the only reason why some of his papers survived.

12. Arendt, Hannah and Heinrich Blucher, *Within Four Walls: The Correspondence between Hannah Arendt and Heinrich Blucher, 1936–1968,* Ed. Lotte Kohler, Trans. Peter Constantine (New York: Harcourt, 1996), 72.

13. Gershom Scholem, *Walter Benjamin: The Story of a Friendship*, Trans. Harry Zohn (New York: Schocken Books, 1988), 191.

14. Young-Bruehl, *Hannah Arendt*, 115.

15. Young-Bruehl, 116.

16. Arendt, Hannah and Karl Jaspers, *Arendt/Jaspers Correspondence 1926–1969*, Ed. Lotte Kohler and Hans Saner, Trans. Robert and Rita Kimber (New York: Harcourt Brace Jovanovich Publishers, 1992), 41.

17. Arendt and Blucher, *Within Four Walls*, 39

18. Arendt and Jaspers, *Arendt/Jaspers*, 197.

19. Herzog, Annabel, "Illuminating Inheritance: Benjamin's Influence on Arendt's Political Storytelling" in *Philosophy and Social Criticism* 26 (2000): 1–27.

20. Young-Bruehl, *Hannah Arendt*, 162.

21. Young-Bruehl, *Hannah Arendt*, 161.

22. Lorenz Jager, *Adorno: A Political Biography*, Trans. Stewart Spencer (New Haven: Yale U P, 2004),65.

23. Ibid.

24. Jager, *Adorno*, 66.

25. Hannah Arendt, *Illuminations* Ed. Hannah Arendt, Trans. Harry Zohn (New York: Schocken Books, 1969), 2.

26. Hohendahl, *Prismatic Thought*, 218.

27. Jay, *Adorno*, 35.

28. Theodor Adorno and Walter Benjamin, *Theodor W. Adorno and Walter Benjamin: The Complete Correspondence 1928–1940*, Ed. Henri Lonitz, Trans. Nicholas Walker (Cambridge: Harvard University Press, 1999), 344.

29. Lonitz, Theodor W. Adorno and Walter Benjamin, p. 342.

30. Jay, *Adorno*, 36.

31. Arendt, "Walter Benjamin," 9.

32. Ibid., 7.

33. Ibid., 18.

34. Ibid.

35. Ibid., 3.

36. Ibid.

37. Ibid., 10. Perhaps this observation is now even more untimely given the developments after Arendt's essay. New readings of Marx, particularly by the autonomist Marxists reread Marx in such a way as to relate elements of the substructure and superstructure—a categorical division not to be troubled in traditional Marxist readings—and the way in which Arendt reads Benjamin's

here seems to provide at least some precursor to the way in which Marx is currently being reconceived.

38. Ibid., 11.

39. Ibid., 28.

40. Ibid., 34.

41. Ibid.

42. Ibid.

43. Ibid., 22.

44. Theodor W. Adorno, "A Portrait of Walter Benjamin," *Prisms,* Trans. Samuel and Shierry Weber (London: Neville Spearman, 1967), 229.

45. Ibid.

46. Ibid., 230.

47. Ibid., 229.

48. Ibid., 235.

49. Ibid., 241.

50. Ibid., 230.

51. Ibid.

52. Ibid., 232.

53. Ibid., 233.

54. Ibid., 240.

55. Ibid., 229.

56. Stephen H. Browne, "Arendt, Eichmann, and the Politics of Remembrance," *Framing Public Memory*, Ed. Kendall R. Phillips (Tuscaloosa: The University of Alabama Press, 2004), 50.

57. Hannah Arendt, *The Human Condition,* 2nd Ed. (Chicago: University of Chicago Press, 1998), 183–4.

58. Ibid., 184.

59. Ibid.

60. Ibid., 186.

61. Young-Bruehl, *Hannah Arendt,* xxxviii.

62. Hannah Arendt, "On Humanity in Dark Times: Thoughts about Lessing," Trans. Clara and Richard Winston, *Men in Dark Times* (New York: Harcourt, Brace, and World, 1968), 24.

63. Young-Bruehl, *Hannah Arendt,* 162.

64. Ibid., 166.

65. Ibid., 167.

66. Jager, Adorno, 66.

67. Also known as the "Arcades Project," this was the full-length work that Benjamin spent many years developing. It was not completed, but over one thousand pages of the manuscript exist. The "Arcades Project" was supposed to serve as Benjamin's masterpiece, in so many words.

68. Jay, *Adorno*, 36.

69. Theodor Adorno, *Minima Moralia: Reflections from Damaged Life*. Trans. E.F.N. Jephcott (London: Verso, 1974): 66.

70. Ibid.

71. Ibid.

72. Young-Bruehl, *Hannah Arendt*, 168.

73. Hohendahl, 49.

WORKS CITED

Adorno, Theodor W. "A Portrait of Walter Benjamin." *Prisms*. Trans. Samuel and Shierry Weber. London: Neville Spearman, 1967.

———. *Minima Moralia: Reflections from Damaged Life*. Trans. E.F.N. Jephcott. London: Verso, 1974.

———. "Philosophy and Teachers." *Critical Models: Interventions and Catchwords*. Trans. Henry W. Pickford. New York: Columbia U P, 1998. 19–35.

Adorno, Theodor and Walter Benjamin. *Theodor W. Adorno and Walter Benjamin: The Complete Correspondence 1928–1940*. Ed. Henri Lonitz. Trans. Nicholas Walker. Cambridge: Harvard U P, 1999.

Arendt, Hannah. *The Human Condition*. 2nd Ed. Chicago, Unversity of Chicago P, 1998.

———. "On Humanity in Dark Times: Thoughts about Lessing." Trans. Clara and Richard Winston. *Men in Dark Times*. New York: Harcourt, Brace, and World, 1968. 3–31.

———. "Walter Benjamin: 1892–1940." *Illuminations*. Ed. Hannah Arendt. Trans. Harry Zohn. New York: Schocken Books, 1969.

Arendt, Hannah and Heinrich Blucher. *Within Four Walls: The Correspondence between Hannah Arendt and Heinrich Blucher, 1936–1968*. Ed. Lotte Kohler. Trans. Peter Constantine. New York: Harcourt, 1996.

Arendt, Hannah and Karl Jaspers. *Arendt/Jaspers Correspondence 1926–1969*. Ed. Lotte Kohler and Hans Saner. Trans. Robert and Rita Kimber. New York: Harcourt Brace Jovanovich Publishers, 1992.

Browne, Stephen H. "Arendt, Eichmann, and the Politics of Remembrance." *Framing Public Memory*. Ed. Kendall R. Phillips. Tuscaloosa: The U of Alabama P, 2004. 45–64.

Habermas, Jurgen. "Hannah Arendt: On the Concept of Power." *Philosophical-Political Profiles*. Trans. Frederick G. Lawrence. Cambridge: MIT P, 1983. 171–187.

Herzog, Annabel. "Illuminating Inheritance: Benjamin's Influence on Arendt's Political Storytelling." *Philosophy and Social Criticism* 26 (2000): 1–27.

Hohendahl, Peter Uwe. *Prismatic Thought*. Lincoln: U of Nebraska P, 1995.

Jager, Lorenz. *Adorno: A Political Biography.* Trans. Stewart Spencer. New Haven: Yale U P, 2004.

Jay, Martin. *Adorno.* Cambridge: Harvard U P, 1984.

———. *The Dialectical Imagination: A History of the Frankfurt School and the Institute of Social Research 1923–1950.* Boston: Little, Brown and Company, 1973.

King, Richard H. *Race, Culture, and the Intellectuals.* Washington, DC: Woodrow Wilson Center Press, 2004.

Scholem, Gershom. *Walter Benjamin: The Story of a Friendship.* Trans. Harry Zohn. New York: Schocken Books, 1988.

Villa, Dana R. *Arendt and Heidegger: The Fate of the Political.* Princeton: Princeton U P, 1996.

Wellmer, Albrecht. "Hannah Arendt on Judgment." *Hannah Arendt: Twenty Years Later.* Eds. Larry May and Jerome Kohn. Cambridge: MIT Press, 1996. 33–52.

Young-Bruehl, Elisabeth. *Hannah Arendt: For the Love of the World.* 2nd Ed. New Haven: Yale U P, 2004.

■ ■ ■

The Reasonableness of Bias

LENORE LANGSDORF

> *...there is a primary listening which precedes our own speech...I*
> *hear the voices of others, of things, of the World long before I speak*
> *my own words...Phenomenologically the 'self' is modeled after the*
> *World which takes primacy in its first appearance...Things, others,*
> *the gods, each have their voices to which we may listen...Within*
> *auditory experience there is this primacy of listening...The*
> *'prelinguistic' is the philosophical counterpart to the 'pre-perceptual'*
> *bare sensation which, if found at all, is found by diverting one's ears*
> *and eyes from the objects.*[1]

Consider this world into which each of us is delivered—a world of objects and of the primacy of listening—in the phenomenological way of "diverting our ears and eyes" so that we may see more of what ("if found at all") usually is "seen, but not observed."[2] This way of doing philosophy requires us to suspend our everyday ways of seeing things, in the interest of observing what may escape our typical ways of attending to our surroundings. Typically, we *use* things, rather than *reflect* on their genesis and character, or on the possible consequences of taking them up within our historical, sociopolitical, and spiritual lives. Phenomenology, however, bids us to reflect on how "the things themselves" appear to those who encounter them. That is to say that we are not to consider things *in* themselves, apart from human involvement. Rather, phenomenological inquiry—and especially hermeneutic phenomenology, which I invite us to do here in relation to bias—examines any subject matter within its historical, social, and anticipated contexts. This is, as some phenomenologists say, an unnatural way of seeing, since it runs counter to both those typical ways of attending to objects and to positivistic modes of inquiry, which focuses on characteristics that are verifiable in direct perception or through logical deduction from what's perceptually present. A phenomenological mode of inquiry, in contrast, investigates any subject matter as a locus or node of meaning in a multi-dimensioned process of presence and absence. Longitudinally—which is to say, historically—understanding subject matters in their processual mode of being begins with a careful description of how they appear now. It also investigates their genesis in conditions that make them possible and the consequences that are likely to develop from their current situation. That description of past, present, and anticipated appearance extends into what I would call a correlative horizontal mode of inquiry, which studies any subject matter in relation to others that interact with it within all three temporal modes.

The phenomenology of bias that I propose here focuses on its genesis and place within the context of communication ethics. There are multiple possible avenues for investigating this phenomenon. Contemporary neuroscience research suggests that certain "mental muscles" may be instrumental in forming habitual behavior, including the development of dispositions for thinking about ethical and sociopolitical issues—the aspects of everyday life in which bias may be particularly evident.[3] Our everyday experience, along with a good deal of communication research, suggests that communicative interaction plays a role in reinforcing, and perhaps changing, those dispositions and the beliefs they support. Without either affirming or denying the intriguing contributions of neuroscience, I focus here on the contribution of communicative interaction.

We are all born listeners.[4] The listening newcomer emerges into an environment formed by (and quite literally, under) the voices of others. The newcomer typically cannot speak of that "primary listening," for it occurs at a place that Paul Ricoeur identifies as the "privileged point of perspective on the world which each speaking subject is"; a "point" at which the listener "is the limit of the world and not one of its contents."[5] The human being at this "privileged point" is an aesthetic work in progress, being shaped as the project of others.[6] The multiple voices of caregivers constitute that human being as it becomes a self. Yet we do not continue *only* listening for very long after separation from the other who delivers us into the world. While located within the center of that other (a mother), an emergent human being undergoes the voices and touches of constituting others but is able to interact only in rudimentary aural, chemical, kinetic, kinesthetic, and tactile ways. Birth is a delivery from that center; an expulsion from a space of activity, volition, and affect—but not simply by virtue of solitary effort. Typically, a literally emergent human being undergoes the will, intelligence, and affect of a mother and multiple others who are involved in this process of birth; of coming into one's own life. Among the initial independent acts we accomplish, as newborn human beings, is a cry, a sound that is interpreted by all around us as meaningful. At the moment of that initial utterance, our communicative abilities both decrease and increase, for as we are born, chemical interaction with our mothers' bodies is diminished and may then be lost, while aural, kinesthetic, kinetic, and tactile opportunities for communication grow and oral communicative interaction begins.

Young human beings are always already surrounded by others' stories, and only gradually are able to tell their own stories. Günter Grass's novel, *The Tin Drum,* provides an account of the genesis of one person's ability to tell his own story. The novel is about the life of Oskar Matzerath, who tells us of this very early memory:

> The moment I was born I took a very critical attitude toward the first utterances to slip from my parents…My ears were keenly alert…And what my ear took in my tiny brain evaluated. After meditating at some length on what I heard, I decided to do certain things and on no account to do other things.[7]

Although Oskar's story begins as receiver of the stories of others, he clearly is not a typical newborn. For he decides—earlier on than most of us—that his identity will rest in his own narrative. Most of us appear to move more slowly to that decision. Our earliest utterances are open to multiple and diverse interpretations by those around us. But, gradually, babbling and crying become wording; we become articulate enough to tell, and even insist upon, our own interpretations. All too typically, the story of human life is one in which the more we talk, the less we listen. But that takes us ahead of our story: We need to look at this process more carefully, if we are to uncover the genesis of bias and come to appreciate its value.

Early on, a human being's identity rests in stories told by others. As such—which is to say, as listeners—we are fragmented among the narratives we hear, dependent upon those other voices for our sustenance and survival. Gradually, reciprocity and reversibility of the "patient" and "agent" roles in these stories develop. Over a course of years after literal separation from the primary other and subsequent engagement in a process of being persistently and necessarily acted upon by others, a continual gathering and collecting of experiences enable me, as a unifying "I," to claim those experiences as my own. Listening, in itself, does nothing for the coherence of that multiplicity; does nothing to solidify "the voices of others, of things, of the World" as an identity—as my identity. Only as a living body begins to engage the resistance of others, begins to touch and be touched by—both literally and figuratively—the resistant (other-than itself) sources of those voices, do particular subject matters come to be delineated within the manifold presented to our senses. Correlatively, only by "diverting one's ears and eyes from the objects" can the reflecting phenomenologist uncover this particular form of life as one of active passivity—of requiring the care of others, of being acted upon by those others—as a condition for our being as agents with individual projects who interact with others.

The particularity of this kind of thing, a human being, rests in the fact that if we are to survive, our stories must be rooted in those of others. Very much unlike rocks and plants—and even somewhat unlike other forms of animal life—we must be the objects of others' care for a long period of time. Mothers and other producers of the conditions of living must produce their own sustenance and divert some portion of their productivity to these emerging agents, if we are to survive. By doing so, these producers of care keep us enmeshed in their narrative identities. In sum, others must be there, always already capable of acting in certain (caring) ways, in order that human beings, dependent upon and thus fragmented among their many sources, can engage in the lengthy process of coming to coherence by being delimited from, and thus other-than, their sources. We begin, as Ricoeur points out, in "indebtedness" to the other, and in many ways and to diverse degrees, we retain those debts.[8] To use an analogy to which we will return: these others, coming from their own places and living their own stories, provide the *warp* and *weft*—the *historicity* and *situatedness,* inevitable temporality and contingent cultural placement—in which new and distinctive agency comes to be.

Our mediated and gradual coherence as agents, then, is accomplished continually in communicative interaction that begins before most of us—who could not tell Oskar Matzerath's unusual story—can accomplish the mediations and evaluations needed for agency. This interaction begins as nonsymmetrical aural, chemical, kinesthetic, kinetic, and tactile communication that increases over time in the womb. After we are born listening, and only quite gradually, the world's communication with us by way of what we hear and what we feel is supplemented by what we can feel of the objects in the world, what particular others say and do not say to us, and what we can, and cannot, say in response. As listener, the voice of the other (the speaker) becomes part of the agent-in-formation; of what is not yet identifiable as an agent—in the sense of one who speaks and acts from a unique perspective. That agent comes into being within hearing, feeling, and understanding others' sayings and deeds. Typically, this aural-oral doubling—as both listener to, and creator of, sounds that are interpreted as meaningful—develops prelinguistically, in noises that others take to be evidence of a distinctive voice. It increases as we imitate the words of others and grows dramatically as those imitations combine in unique ways and begin to cohere into narratives in which we can say "I." That saying positions us as being active in a multiplicity of narratives and as affirming ownership of those narratives. Now I can create my own story from the perspective of my situation as speaker, addressing objects in my environment. But I still maintain myself as listener, belonging to an environment as the particular sort of thing who is addressed and affected by and gathers material for my story from, other speakers. Thereby I am able to respond to—and so in diverse ways come to be responsible for—other speakers.

We are unlikely to analyze this process in which human beings become agents, however, if we remain within the everyday, and perfectly common-sensical, pre-reflective perspective that presumes our own agency. Studying communicative interaction from that perspective encourages an individualistic orientation that takes communication to be an exchange of messages between agents, rather than primarily and persistently a doubled process: even as we become those who constitute stories, we constitute ourselves as the agents who tell those stories—and we do so in collaboration and competition with the stories of others. Although communication research has, for some time now, acknowledged that communication is a process, our primary focus has been on the formation and transmission of messages, and especially, on how that process can be improved so as to mitigate the separation (even, alienation) of human beings from one another. In other words, our project has been to analyze the process of communicating with the goal of avoiding "miscommunication"—and this is a good and even noble endeavor. It has led to research focused, in the work of diverse investigators, on one or more of four ontologically related objects: the rhetorical situation, the message, the rhetor, and the audience. Attention to those objects, however, has occasioned neglect of others. Communication theorists, as Kenneth Anderson noted, "rarely address ethical issues directly in terms of the role and function of communication in a society and for individuals"; rather, "pragmatic questions of effect, rather than ethical qualities, are the usual concern."[9]

Rob Anderson and Veronica Ross, in quoting Kenneth Anderson's observation in their textbook, note that philosophy offers "guidelines" for "ethical communication decisions."[10] They go on to discuss the motivation emphasis of duty-based principles of deontological ethics, the pragmatic (consequential) emphasis of teleological ethics, and the emphasis on equality among participants in egalitarian approaches—all of which presume individuals who seek to establish ethical relationships. All three approaches focus on abstract or generalized rules and reasons that may enable individuals to act more efficaciously in the service of duty, consequences, and equality. When Anderson and Ross turn to ethical theories that they find more amenable to a communication-based approach, they find that Martin Buber's focus on dialogue offers an alternative:

> …in his dialogic ethic, Buber saw what is uniquely human as the relations between persons, not the individualized persons themselves. Through concern for what he called the between,

or the relationship itself, each of us can become for other persons a unique 'you'…capable of being seen and respected in all our differences.[11]

Buber's emphasis on the relational character of dialogue, rather than on reasons, rules, or principles for choosing actions that lead to desired effects, exemplifies a phenomenological, in contrast to psychological, orientation toward communicative interaction. We need now to consider the importance of that distinction.

Ronald C. Arnett summarizes the basic difference in this way: "The 'between,' not the psyche, is at the heart of…Buber's dialogical perspective."[12] This orientation, Arnett goes on to explain, "rejects the psychologistic assertion that a human being is a set of owned potentials" and the correlative "possessive assumption that 'the meaning is in the person.'"[13] Buber's phenomenological understanding of human being begins, instead, in the "rhetorical situation 'between' persons,"[14] which I have explicated as a situation in which we are born listeners, delivered into communicative interaction that shapes and forms—the phenomenological term is "constitutes"—our individual being even as it constitutes the messages that are the more usual focus of communication research. Rather than behavioral assumptions of the primacy of the environment (what is outside of the individual) or humanistic assumptions of the primacy of the psyche (what is inside of the individual) phenomenology assumes the primacy of intentionality, understood as the directedness of communicative interaction. Calvin Schrag characterizes this directedness as a "rhetorical intentionality" that is intrinsically ethical:

> The distinctive stamp of rhetorical intentionality is that it reaches out toward, aims at, is directed to the other as hearer, reader, and audience. This intentionality illustrates not the theoretical reflection of cognitive detachment but rather the practical engagement of concrete involvement…. The rhetor…calls for deliberative action and reasoned judgment. Within this intentionality of engagement the ethical issue is unavoidably broached…. Rhetoric as the directedness of discourse to the other, soliciting a response, is destined to slide into ethics.[15]

Intentionality, then, is not a function of subjectivity or objectivity; rather, it is a characteristic of "the between" that Arnett emphasizes is crucial to Buber's conception of dialogue.

Arnett explains the "philosophical implications of intentionality" in this phenomenological sense as including "acceptance of a non-subject/object world view in which the meaning of a communication happening emerges 'between' persons, not in each person's internal perceptions or through environmental control."[16] Intentionality in this phenomenological sense, he remarks, is easily confused with the psychological sense of intentionality.[17] This may well be, as Arnett suggests elsewhere, because the assumptions of humanistic psychology (as in the work of Carl Rogers) rely on a "framework more kin to the American spirit of independence and freedom," while Buber's phenomenological approach "is not as culturally familiar."[18] The latter requires, Arnett notes, a "shift of emphasis from the self to the ontological reality of the 'between' in the rhetorical situation that is given life in dialogue."[19] In contemporary Euroamerican culture, which is strongly influenced by empiricism, relations (such as "the between") typically are assumed to have a different status within "ontological reality" than things, processes, or activities. Phenomenological research, as the study of how members of all of these categories appear to us, requires us to suspend belief in that assumption. We are then able to discover that relations have a distinctive, but not lesser, mode of appearance. Phenomenological investigation of "the between" reveals a framework of dependence and responsibility—in Ricoeur's terms, of "indebtedness" and "being-enjoined"—that reinforces the contrast between the "American spirit of independence and freedom" that Arnett identifies as the framework of Rogerian humanistic psychology and Buber's phenomenological orientation.[20]

Granted, we have here a philosophical orientation that "is not as culturally familiar" as those of humanistic or behavioral psychology. As in more everyday encounters with the unfamiliar, we have a choice to make: we can turn away from what is foreign, or we can investigate it with an eye toward whether it may be valuable in working with whatever concerns are at hand. If we choose the latter path—and I do so here—we typically seek to understand the foreign through linkage with what is already familiar. Often, we use analogical reasoning in order to transfer understanding from what's familiar to what's foreign. I take that path here in order to advocate understanding bias as both intrinsic to, and valuable for, understanding ethics as resident in "the between"; within communicative interaction, rather than within the psyche or established in an objective code or system of rules. This line of advocacy requires, first, the "shift of emphasis from the self to the ontological reality of the 'between' in the rhetorical situation that is given life in dialogue" which, Arnett emphasizes, is central to the difference between a phenomenological and psychological understanding of human being.[21] The second shift of emphasis if we are to use this unfamiliar way of understanding to study the nature of bias is to focus on how change and difference come to be in the ontological domain named "the between," rather than focusing on the producers or efficacy of messages. Behavioral psychology responds to that "how" question by seeking causes within a framework of scientific method. Arnett argues that humanistic psychology (as in the work of Carl Rogers) shares that framework (although with a pragmatic, rather than causal, orientation) in that it generates hypotheses that are to be tested.[22]

Phenomenological investigation eschews both causal and hypothetical reasoning in favor of accounts that focus on intentionality and emergent meaning. This approach requires "diverting one's ears and eyes" from the objects (as Don Ihde reminds us in our epigraph)—whether those be psyche or messages, cause or motivation, subjects/selves or objects/others. When I focus instead on the experienced meaningfulness of a situation as it's performed in the intrinsic directionality of communicative interaction, what appears is a multiplicity and fluidity within simultaneous processes of listening (or looking) and responding. What is generated in those processes are pliable and fluid moments of comprehension, dependent upon the particular doing and undoing of intentions that occurs as the unique positionalities of the discourse partners engage in a pattern that Calvin Schrag identifies as "convergence without coincidence." "Convergence," he argues in relation to the differences between rhetoric and philosophy, "presupposes something that makes a difference, something that comes between that which comes together."[23] Elsewhere, he finds that this same form of relation characterizes "the who of discourse," which "is not a 'thing,' a pre-given entity," yet is

> still a unity…secured not by an abiding substratum but rather by an achieved self-identity, acquired through a transversal extending over and lying across the multiple forms of speech and language games without coincidence with any of them. This transversal dynamics, effecting a convergence without coincidence, defines the unity, presence, and identity of the self.[24]

Schrag's emphasis on the persistence of multiplicity within unity expands upon Hans-Georg Gadamer's analysis of the "process of understanding" as one in which "a real fusing of horizons occurs—which means that as the historical horizon is projected, it is simultaneously superseded."[25] The condition for this process, Gadamer proposes, is that participants in communicative interaction "listen to tradition in a way that permits it to make its own meaning heard" as we interpret the significance of that meaning within our own situations.[26] Listening in this way, however, is not a smooth process of cumulation: "To think historically," he notes, "always involves mediating between those ideas [given by tradition] and one's own thinking. To try to escape from one's own concepts in interpretation is not only impossible but manifestly absurd. To interpret means precisely to bring one's own concepts into play."[27]

Yet interpretation also means the bringing of another's "own concepts" into play, and thereby interrupting any attempt to fuse horizons as a simple cumulation. Amit Pinchevski's reading of Emmanuel Levinas' focus on the radical otherness that we encounter in dialogue suggests that interruptions fuel the dynamic of superseding horizons and so prevent the collapse of convergence into coincidence. What those interruptions provide is a disruption of "one's own concepts" and an opening to those of others. Often, we label the latter prejudices, and typically, we evaluate interruptions negatively. Pinchevski's analysis, which I find is a useful basis for refining Gadamer's reconsideration of prejudices, rejects that negative evaluation.

Pinchevski follows Levinas in proposing "that the limit of communication is precisely what gives rise to communication as an ethical event."[28] He argues that much communication theory "presupposes a common foundation" that may "entail disregarding otherness" because of "the risk of seeing Others as variations of oneself."[29] He rejects that orientation as based on a conceptual linkage between communication and ethics "predicated upon the belief that better communication, understood as the exchange of ideas, knowledge, and information, upholds the possibility of over-coming strife, of promoting understanding, and thereby of creating greater harmony."[30] His intention, rather, is "to suggest a different conception of what might be implied in the term "ethical communication"; namely, "that the ethical possibilities in com-munication do not ultimately lie in its successful completion but rather in its inter-ruption."[31] Levinas' conception of alterity is basic to this alternative understanding. "It is precisely in the irreconcilable difference of alterity," Pinchevski asserts, "that Levinas founds the fundamental relationship with the Other" that is "the ultimate condition for communication."[32] Indeed, as Levinas writes: "if communication... bears the sign of failure or inauthenticity, it is because it is sought in fusion. One sets out from the idea that duality is to be transformed into unity."[33]

Rather than conceiving communication as an "exchange of knowledge" that will accomplish that unity, Pinchevski (following Levinas) proposes that we reject that priority of an epistemic goal in favor of acknowledging the priority of an ethical relationship of a peculiar kind: a "concern for the Other [that] is not a product of rational thought or calculation."[34] The nature of human subjectivity, he proposes, is "subjection to the Other."[35] This relation, I suggest, is the indebtedness that I have described in terms of beginning as listeners, dependent upon the stories of others with whom we only gradually come into verbal dialogue. That is, human beings begin as objects of concern.[36] That concern is expressed in communicating that approaches, addresses, and contacts the Other in order to signify difference from what has been said—which is to say, in order to relate to the Other on the basis of difference, rather than sameness; of dissensus, rather than consensus. Rather than transmitting information, this primal mode of communication interrupts all that has been said (as information) to and by the Other, and thus interrupts the Other's "own concepts." It presents the possibility of disrupting all that the Other has already judged, which is to say, all that the Other carries as prejudices in Gadamer's sense of the term—to which we will return presently. Simultaneously, this addressing is a responding to the Other—and so, disrupts "one's own concepts" as that very respond-ing bends one's concepts toward that response. Thus, as noted earlier, interruptions fuel the dynamic of superseding horizons and so prevent the collapse of convergence into coincidence.

This understanding of the positive value of interruption as addressing the Other and so presenting otherness, together with Schrag's concept of convergence without coincidence, inspires a refinement of Gadamer's concept of the fusion of horizons that enables us to appreciate the persistence of difference in any attempt to "transpose ourselves into a situation" thoroughly enough to listen to the Other with understanding.[37] This transposing, Gadamer proposes, "consists neither in the empathy of one individual for another nor in subordinating another person to our own standards"; rather, it requires that we "learn to look beyond what is close at hand—not in order to look away from it but to see it better."[38] This better sight, I suggest, is insight gained through "listen[ing] to the Other with understanding," rather than having empathy for or subordinating another.[39] That is, insight relies upon appreciating the diversity of horizons as constitutive of "the between" that's crucial in Buber's analysis of dialogue. For Gadamer, this broader view reveals that

> a hermeneutical situation is determined by the prejudices that we bring with us. They constitute, then, the horizon of a particular present…But now it is important to avoid the error of thinking that the horizon of the present consists of a fixed set of opinions and valuations…. Rather, understanding is always the fusion of these horizons supposedly existing by themselves.[40]

Gadamer proposes, therefore, that we acknowledge the prejudices that we bring with us as constitutive: "the prejudices of the individual, far more than his judgments, constitute the historical reality of his being."[41] Any attempt to "leave one's concepts aside," rather than bringing them "into play," relies upon "a naïve illusion."[42] Thus, Gadamer concludes, it is "necessary to fundamentally rehabilitate the concept of prejudice" from "the Enlightenment's discreditation of the concept" by delineating a category of "legitimate prejudices" as those justified by "reason"—without accepting "a mutually exclusive antithesis between reason and authority."[43]

Clearly, there are examples of words that can be rehabilitated insofar as they shed the negative connotations that have barred them from descriptive use.[44] However, within contemporary Euroamerican English usage—perhaps because of its strong association with "racial prejudice"—prejudice is a term that may well have gained an even more negative connotation than when Gadamer's term was rendered into English. Thus I propose that we use the term "bias" to designate those "legitimate prejudices" that can be justified by "reason." Both these and prejudices supported *only* by "authority" are pre-judgments that comprise the traditions "that we bring with us" into "a hermeneutical situation" that constitutes "the horizon of a particular present."[45] What, then, justifies some—those reasonable prejudices I call biases—as reasonable? My response to that question relies upon two distinctions. The first is made, although scarcely noticed, in everyday communicative practice; the second comes from contemporary ethical-political theory.

The everyday practice in which I've identified the first distinction is my students' classroom discourse, which often uses an unthematized distinction between bias and prejudice, or in Gadamer's terms, reasonable in contrast to authority-based prejudices. I find that students readily acknowledge their biases in regard to particular events, and typically will go on to say not only that they are biased, but that "everybody is," which is to say that people typically see a situation from a particular standpoint, position, or perspective. To be "prejudiced," however, is a condition that these same students shun: the usual distinction is that one cannot avoid being biased, and so it is appropriate to note that at certain points in a discussion, but one ought not be prejudiced. Bias thus seems an apt term for Gadamer's category of "legitimate prejudice" as that justified by "reason," but only if we associate what's "reasonable" as what appeals to culturally shared notions of what's fitting in a particular situation—which takes us to the second distinction.

Justification by appeal to culturally shared norms of what is fitting contrasts to notions of what's "rational," understood as that which is justified through well-formed arguments relying on formal or informal logic. Darrin Hicks identifies "reasonableness" as operative in the context of "public reason," which he defines as "the common"—*koinoi*—reason, understood as a means of formulating plans, putting ends in order, and making decisions accordingly, of the public in its capacity as citizens constituting a polity.[46] This is the context in which my students justify having "bias," but not "prejudice." As I have argued elsewhere,

> Close attention to the rhetorical efficacy of presenting multiple possibilities and preferences for taking actions, justifying beliefs, articulating feelings, and maintaining values in conversations reveals moments at which particular claims or positions are ratified by remarks such as 'that's reasonable.' I take such remarks to be explicit indications of partial, tentative, or provisional acceptance, in the sense of accepting that the claim or position is plausible in the context of the discussion—not, that its truth (in the demonstrable sense traditionally associated with 'logic') is thereby affirmed.[47]

To say that our biases are reasonable, then, is to say that they are justified in the experiences of everyday (which is to say, culturally, historically, and politically saturated) life that have been efficacious in constituting us as the persons we are. Reasonableness appeals to what is fitting—what seems to the participants in a situation to be fair and just—in a particular cultural, historical, and political context. Reasonableness thus contrasts to ratiocination, which appeals to the authority of absolute standards of true or false, good or bad.[48] Darrin Hicks' explication of this difference takes John Rawls' "disassociation of the true and the just" as correlative, respectively, to the rational and the reasonable. He quotes Rawls' assertion that "there is no thought of deriving one from the other" and goes on to argue for the value of conceptualizing "the reasonable as a distinct, basic, and freestanding ideal that can be used to evaluate whether or not our public justifications, and our actions in public deliberations, are fair and just."[49] Hicks concludes that "the ideal of reasonableness forms a basis for arguers' ethical and political conduct in public deliberations."[50]

My characterization of bias as reasonable rests on this categorizing of fairness and justice as matters of ethical, rather than epistemic, judgment. I associate reasonableness with Levinas' primal communication that presents the Other, rather than the more usual conception of communication as transmission of information, which is ultimately subject to rational determinations concerned with truth. For the latter, epistemic evaluations of truth or falsity are fitting; for the former, ethical evaluations of fairness and justice are fitting. Insofar as communication encompasses both human beings' primal approach, address, and contact with the Other and subsequent transmission of information, we need both modes of judgment. But that the two modes converge in our communicative practices is not to say that they coincide.

We can now take up this phenomenon of bias within the phenomenological orientation that redirects our attention away from the culturally familiar assumption of "naturally" independent human beings who initially present themselves as components of communication and toward communicative interaction itself. We begin, then, from the phenomenological description with which I began this chapter: human beings are constituted in the "between" that's easily overlooked when focusing on the objects that are in relation, but that I've identified as constituted in and by the very directionality of communicative interaction. The phenomenological sense of intentionality as directedness implicates meaning as residing in the multitude of relations that are constitutive of persons (but not "in" one or another person) rather than being prior (transcendent to) those relationships. Meanings, so understood, constitute the particular subject matters as what they are in particular situations. This does not mean that discourse creates things; rather, the meaningfulness of our discourse—how we attribute characteristics by means of our acting, speaking, and thinking—interprets the significance of the objects about which we speak as being thus-and-so, rather than otherwise.[51]

As I suggested earlier, and have argued elsewhere, communicative interaction is directed toward constituting both the subjects and the objects of that interaction.[52] More precisely, those subjects are both persons who constitute that interaction and objects who are constituted by it. Following out the implications of this doubled intentionality reveals human subjectivity as persistently in process; doing deeds and undergoing the consequences of those deeds, in response to the exigencies of particular situations—rather than in a rational mode that assesses responses in terms of universal standards.[53] In other words, intentionality constitutes the participants who communicate, even as intentionality constitutes the messages (products of those interactions) that inform those processual subjects and thus, so to speak, continue the constitutive spiral between self/subjectivity and other/objectivity.[54]

The intentional character of that "between" means that we are constituted within the communicated perspectives of others. Simultaneously, we constitute ourselves as distinct by virtue of the interpretations we make of others' stories, and the interpretations they make of our stories. In Ihde's words, "the 'self' is modeled after the World which takes primacy in its first appearance…Things, others, the gods, each have their voices to which we may listen." Or, in terms of my earlier description: we are born into a world shown and told to us by others who come from their own places, live their own stories, and anticipate the consequences of their actions. In that telling, showing, and acting, they provide the *historicity* and *situatedness*—the *warp* and *weft*—that we use to weave the stories that form our selves.

Let's now consider that weaving metaphor, which I borrow it from Schrag's concept of communicative praxis as an "interweaving" or "amalgam of discourse and action," more closely.[55] Schrag proposes that communicative praxis "proceeds by way of an appropriation of established patterns of custom and habit and a distanciation and critical engagement wherewith the established patterns are redescribed, modified, or straightway displaced."[56] Particular moments of communicative interaction rely upon those established patterns:

> Speaking is a creative act, at once a discovery of self and a self-constitution, but a creative act that takes place only against the background of a language already spoken, which has both a history and a formal structure, a language ensconced in the tradition, operating behind our backs, as Hans-Georg Gadamer would be wont to say.[57]

What's "already spoken" provides, then, the history and situatedness—the past and present; the warp and weft—of our own speaking.

We need to think now about how warp and weft are literally woven together. In the course of teaching courses in communication theory, persuasion, and rhetorical theory, I've often used these terms as metaphorical aids for explaining communicative praxis. Almost always, the initial response from students has taught me that my own early education, which included learning those terms, was quite different from theirs. I suspect that this experience of leaning on metaphors that don't work for our audience is a rather common one. "We live in a time in which the background narrative that gives meaning to our action cannot be taken for granted," Ronald C. Arnett and Pat Arneson write.[58] Thus, as they go on to say: "Teaching is often focused upon implementation strategies wherein students are deprived of an overt connect to the background narrative that the teacher tacitly assumes."[59] In this case of failed metaphorical explanation, the specific difference that stands in the way of an "overt connect" is my having learned to sew. If we're to appreciate the significance of the terms "warp" and "weft" for understanding bias as reasonable, we need first to be clear about their meaning. We can gain that clarity through some online research.

Marcy Tilton, in "Bias 101: Master the Tricks of Sewing Bias-Cut Garments with a Simple Style and Foolproof Fabric," explains that

> Grain refers to the straight and crosswise direction of the yarns making up a woven fabric, with bias running at any angle to the straight and crossgrains and the true bias running at a 45-degree angle to these grains… Garments appear softer and more fluid, have more stretch, and are more supple than those cut on the lengthwise or crosswise grain. The fabric also appears 'thinner' than the same fabric cut on the straight grain.
>
> Bias garments need more fabric than the same garment [when placed] on the straight grain, and are best cut one layer at a time so that grain doesn't distort. Working on the

bias requires a bit more time, a careful selection of fabric, as well as some alternative fitting and sewing techniques...[60]

Tilton concludes her article with this advice: "Bias garments don't wrinkle as easily as straight-grain garments do, but they can 'grow' on a hanger, so I always store them folded and flat."

Another article gives a more detailed vocabulary lesson. "Have you ever," Janet Wickell asks, "watched a weaver making fabrics at a loom, moving threads back and forth to form the fabric?" She continues:

> Long threads, called *warp* threads, are stretched on the loom and secured. They become the fabric's lengthwise grain, the threads that are continuous along the length of your yardage... More threads, called *weft* threads, are woven back and forth, perpendicular to the warp threads and along their entire length. These weft threads make up the fabric's crosswise grain... Selvages are the bound edges that run along each long side of the fabric. They are formed as the weft threads turn to change direction as the weaving process travels down the length of the warp... Pieces with edges cut parallel to either straight grain—the lengthwise or the crosswise—are less likely to stretch out of shape than pieces with edges cut along the bias...[61]

Everyday expressions like "don't get yourself stretched (or bent) out of shape" and "they threw away the pattern when they made her" can be helpful starting points for analogical reasoning. The analogy between garments cut on the bias and lives that don't follow what folk wisdom calls "the straight and narrow path" inspires extended comment, but space constraints allow for only a few highlights.

We are born into a particular history (the warp) that is in many ways quite rigid; stretched between a long ago past and a future, both of which are present to us as horizons. Those horizons are literally absent (given the nature of temporality) but are conceptually present as persistent and continually changing limits to our memories and anticipations. We are also born as the carriers of a thread of stories, a weft that moves through that history to create stories with particular textures. The end of any thread within that fabric is tied to the beginning of another; each of us begins as literally tied to the womb. The texture may be rough or smooth; individual lives appear (to those who live them as well as those who observe them) to proceed with difficulty or ease—so that we commonly say that someone had "a rough life" or "an easy time of it." If we now shift perspectives, so that we displace ourselves from any present moment in this weaving—which is to say, gain some reflective distance on that process—we can metaphorically locate ourselves as set within a texture that is, and yet is not, of our own making. Although traditional logic tells us that a thing cannot both be and not be in the same way at the same time, actual life teaches us that we often maintain contraries; in Martin Buber's phrase, life is lived as a "unity of contraries."[62]

From this more distanciated perspective, we can see that we are not simply a section of the fabric woven from history and situation. Rather, each of us is a story, analogous to a garment crafted by laying a pattern on that fabric. The garment which is my life may be placed on the straight grain or on the bias. The former is easier to construct; the latter enables greater flexibility—with the risk of excessive stretching that damages the attractiveness of the garment, or life, that has been cut on the bias. A behavioristic theory of human being presumes that individual lives are determined by their history and situation, analogously to garments that are cut along the length-wise and crosswise straight grain. Observation suggests, however, that human lives are more akin to garments cut on the bias: rather than simply accepting placement along the straight grain woven by history and situation, we craft our lives by cutting a transversal line across both historical record and cultural norms. No two garments may be cut from the very same section of fabric; no two lives may be placed at the same intersection of history and situation.

Thus, as my students say, we each have our own bias, and "everybody has one." The issue, then, is not whether we are biased, but whether our biases are reasonable; which is to say, whether they can be understood through the strategy of gaining insight by "look[ing] beyond what is close at hand—not in order to look away from it but to see it better."[63] What is "close at hand," in this metaphorical way of under-standing human being, is the warp and weft, the interweaving of history and situation that provides the same structure to all human lives. Insight looks beyond that same-ness to difference; specifically, to evaluating another's actions, beliefs, and values as fitting the biased placement of the pattern of an Other's life. Understanding a reason-able bias—whether my own, or another's—as one that accords with that placement is a condition for entering into communication with the Other. We may then go on to judge the truth of claims, but we do so in accord with standards of rationality rather than reasonableness.

NOTES

1. Don Ihde, *Listening and Voice: A Phenomenology of Sound* (Athens: Ohio University Press, 1976), 117–18.

2. I borrow this phase from Michael J. Hyde and Craig R. Smith, "Hermeneutics and Rhetoric: A Seen but Unobserved Relationship," *Quarterly Journal of Speech* 65 (1979): 347.

3. Matthew D. Lieberman and others, "Is Political Cognition Like Riding a Bicycle? How Cognitive Neuroscience Can Inform Research on Political Thinking," *Political Psychology* 24 (2003): 681–704.

4. The description of the listening self that follows borrows from an earlier discussion of inten-tionality in Paul Ricoeur's *Oneself as Another*. See Lenore Langsdorf, "The Doubleness of

Subjectivity: Regenerating the Phenomenology of Intentionality," in *Ricoeur As Another: The Ethics of Subjectivity,* ed. Richard A. Cohen and James L. Marsh (Albany: SUNY Press, 2002).

5. Paul Ricoeur, *Oneself as Another,* trans. Kathleen Blamey (Chicago: The University of Chicago Press, 1992), 51.

6. This use of "aesthetic" is polysemous; it evokes both artistry and varieties of sensory knowledge (in contrast to ratiocination) that Michael Gilbert calls "visceral and kisceral." (*Coalescent Argumentation,* Mahwah NJ: Lawrence Erlbaum, 1997) and Immanuel Kant identified as operative within "aesthetical judgment." (*Critique of Judgment,* trans. J. H. Bernard (New York: Macmillan, 1951).

7. Günter Grass, *The Tin Drum,* trans. Ralph Mannheim (New York: Pantheon Books, 1962), 46–47.

8. Ricoeur, *Oneself as Another,* 349.

9. Kenneth E. Anderson, "A History of Communication Ethics," in *Conversations on Communication Ethics,* ed. K. J. Greenberg (Norwood, NY: Ablex, 1981), 6.

10. Rob Anderson and Veronica Ross, *Questions of Communication: A Practical Introduction to Theory* (New York: St. Martin's Press, 1994), 263.

11. Anderson and Ross, *Questions of Communication,* 272.

12. Ronald C. Arnett, "Toward a Phenomenological Dialogue," *The Western Journal of Speech Communication* 45 (1981): 202.

13. Ibid., 203.

14. Ibid., 204

15. Calvin O. Schrag, *Communicative Praxis and the Space of Subjectivity (*Bloomington: Indiana University Press, 1986), 198–199.

16. Arnett, "Toward a Phenomenological Dialogue," 206–207.

17. Ibid., 206.

18. Ronald C. Arnett, "Rogers and Buber: Similarities, Yet Fundamental Differences," *The Western Journal of Speech Communication* 46 (1982): 358.

19. Arnett, "Toward a Phenomenological Dialogue," 211.

20. Ricoeur discerns a "demoralization of conscience" in Martin Heidegger's focus on Dasein's "ownmost potentiality-for-Being" (*Oneself as Another,* 348–51). Ricoeur advocates, in contrast, that "Listening to the voice of the conscience would signify being-enjoined by the Other" and thus, indebtedness to the Other, which calls for attesting that "I am called to live well with and for others in just institutions" (351).

21. Arnett, "Toward a Phenomenological Dialogue," 211 (as quoted earlier).

22. Arnett, "Rogers and Buber," 364.

23. Calvin O. Schrag and David James Miller. "Communication Studies and Philosophy: Convergence without Coincidence," in *The Critical Turn: Rhetoric and Philosophy in Postmodern Discourse,* ed. Ian Angus and Lenore Langsdorf. (Carbondale: Southern Illinois University Press, 1993), 126.

24. Calvin O. Schrag, *The Self After Postmodernity.* (New Haven: Yale University Press, 1997), 33.

25. Hans-Georg Gadamer, *Truth and Method*, second revised edition, rev. trans. Joel Weinsheimer and Donald G. Marshall (New York: Continuum, 2002), 307.

26. Ibid., 305

27. Ibid., 397

28. Amit Pinchevski, *By Way of Interruption: Levinas and the Ethics of Communication* (Pittsburgh: Duquesne University Press, 2005), 67.

29. Ibid., 69.

30. Ibid., 6

31. Ibid., 6–7.

32. Ibid., 71.

33. Emmanuel Levinas, *Proper Names*, trans. M. B. Smith (Stanford: Stanford University Press, 1969), 104; as quoted by Pinchevski, *By Way of Interruption*, 71.

34. Pinchevski, *By Way of Interruption*, 73.

35. Ibid., 74.

36. Pinchevski notes that "Levinas's version of ethical relation is more radical than Buber's"; specifically, Levinas "'criticizes the reciprocity and equality of the I-Thou' relationship in Buber (75). My analysis of the growth of reciprocity follows Buber rather than Levinas.

37. Gadamer, *Truth and Method*, 305.

38. Ibid.

39. *Webster's Third International Dictionary* defines insight as "the power or act of seeing into a situation or into oneself…of apprehending the inner nature of things."

40. Gadamer, *Truth and Method*, 306.

41. Ibid., 276–277.

42. Ibid., 396.

43. Gadamer, *Truth and Method*, 277. Gadamer's consideration of the question of just how we are to draw a line between positive (legitimate) and negative prejudices broadens into the question of how to assess the legitimacy of prejudice and authority. The "fundamental epistemological question for a truly historical hermeneutics," he writes, is "what is the ground of the legitimacy of prejudices?" (277). My discussion here sets this epistemological question aside, in order to focus on the ontology that underlies it, namely, the genesis and inevitability of bias ("legitimate prejudices").

44. The term "Methodist," as in The United Methodist Church, is one example of a term that has lost its originally negative connotations. The website of the Methodist Church of England explains the origin of the term in this way:

> 'Methodists' was originally a nickname applied to a revival movement in 18th century Britain, based within the Church of England and led by, among others, the brothers John and Charles Wesley…. Both brothers studied at the University of Oxford (at Christ Church) and John went

on to become a Fellow of Lincoln College, Oxford. In the early 1730s, a small group of students met regularly for Bible study and prayer, received Communion frequently and undertook works of charity; such devout behaviour was unusual in those times and they were soon ridiculed.

Other and more recent examples would be the term "black" to designate a person now more commonly referred to as "African American" or "person of color." In this case, the term has moved from negative connotations to preferred and then to relatively neutral status. The term "girl" for a female who is no longer a child also has a shifting history. For a time in the 1960s and 1970s, it was dispreferred for adult females by many in USAmerica, but it has regained substantial, if not universal, acceptability. Other terms, such as "Oriental," have shifted in the opposite direction. It was once used without evident negative connotations, but "Asian" is now preferred.

45. Gadamer, *Truth and Method*, 306.

46. Darrin Hicks, *Rhetoric & Public Affairs* 5 (2002): 241). Hicks goes on to say:

> Moral claims do not have to be completely verifiable, public reason does not demand the standards of scientific proof, but they should not contradict the claims supported by the best available evidence. When moral claims do not rest on empirical evidence they should at least be plausible. The arguments supporting public policies should not require citizens to ignore their experience or reject their beliefs unless they are supported by the most reliable and widely accepted methods of inquiry (242).

> "To be politically reasonable," he concludes, "means citizens are willing to collaborate with others in proposing fair terms of social cooperation and have the commitment to act on these terms, even if doing so means that they must accept less than what was hoped for" (243).

47. Lenore Langsdorf, "Reasonable Voices: Constituting What's Reasonable in Communicative Interaction," in *Arguing Communication and Culture,* ed. G. Thomas Goodnight (Washington, D.C.: National Communication Association, 2002), 114.

48. Darrin Hicks emphasizes that the reasonable is "political not epistemic"; it relies upon "virtues that are not intuitively derivable from the sorts of social intelligence needed to be rational." Rather, these are "distinct ideals." ("Reasonableness: Political not Epistemic," in *Arguing Communication and Culture,* ed. G. Thomas Goodnight (Washington, D.C.: National Communication Association, 2002), 106–07.

49. Darrin Hicks, "The Other Side of Reason: Reconstructing Reasonableness." Unpublished paper, 3. The embedded quotation is from John Rawls, *Political Liberalism* (New York: Columbia University Press, 1993), 51.

50. Ibid., 3.

51. The difference between the phenomenological concept of constitution and the more familiar concept of (social) construction—as in "the social construction of reality"—is that between blending elements so that they produce a novel phenomenon within which those elements lose their independent character, and assembling components so that they retain their independent character. As examples: constitution happens when we mix colors on a palette, bake a cake, or procreate via the merging of sperm with egg; construction happens when we build with bricks or boards, mount an exhibition of a photographer's work, or incorporate a geographic area as a township. As is generally the case in categorization, there are examples that frustrate easy classification—e.g., marriage, photo albums, tossed salads, and political entities.

52. Lenore Langsdorf, "Doubleness of Subjectivity," 42; also, Lenore Langsdorf, "In Defense of Poiesis: The Performance of Self in Communicative Praxis," *in Calvin O. Schrag and the Task of Phenomenology After Postmodernity*, ed. William McBride and Martin Beck Matustik (Evanston: Northwestern University Press, 2002).

53. John Dewey characterized this duality as "doing and undergoing" or "doing and suffering": "Experience is primarily a process of undergoing…[which] is never mere passivity…[it] is a matter of *simultaneous* doings and sufferings." He goes on to say that "experiencing *is* just certain modes of interaction…[it] means primarily not knowledge, but ways of doing and suffering." "The Need for a Recovery of Philosophy," in *John Dewey: The Middle Works*, 1899–1924, vol. 10, ed. J. A. Boydson. (Carbondale: Southern Illinois University Press, 1980), 8–9, 26. (original publication, 1917)

54. I speak of the "constitutive spiral" as the ontological counterpart of the more familiar "hermeneutic circle." The latter invokes the whole-and-parts interchange that, for a hermeneutic epistemology, leads to understanding a phenomenon. The former invokes the formation of subjectivity and objectivity within "the between." More traditional phenomenological language speaks of distinguishing the noetic and noematic poles of experience; that is, the philosophical position that "subject" and "object" are abstractions from a context that is always already marked by sedimented cultural, historical, social, and political meanings.

55. Calvin O. Schrag, *Communicative Praxis and the Space of Subjectivity* (Bloomington: Indiana University Press, 1986), 31, 33 *passim*.

56. Ibid., 63.

57. Schrag, *The Self After Postmodernity*, 16.

58. Ronald C. Arnett and Pat Arneson. *Dialogic Civility in a Cynical Age: Community, Hope, and Interpersonal Relationships* (Albany: SUNY Press, 1999), 60.

59. Ibid., 60.

60. Marcy Tilton, "Bias 101," *Threads Magazine* , http://www.taunton.com/threads/pages/t00007.asp (accessed February 15, 2007).

61. Janet Wickell, "Understanding Fabric Grain," http://scrapquilts.com/fabric_grain.html (accessed February 15, 2007).

62. As Ronald Arnett notes, "The unity of contraries assumes that many issues of importance have texture and depth that call together contrary perspectives, as in negotiating between…libertarian and conservative, profamily and procareer, and so forth." (Ronald C. Arnett, "Dialogic Civility as Pragmatic Ethical Praxis: An Interpersonal Metaphor for the Public Domain," *Communication Theory* 11 (2001): 316.)

63. Hans-Georg Gadamer, *Truth and Method*, 305.

WORKS CITED

Anderson, Kenneth E. "A History of Communication Ethics," in *Conversations on Communication Ethics*, ed. K. J. Greenberg, 3–19. Norwood NY: Ablex, 1981.

Anderson, Rob and Veronica Ross. *Questions of Communication: A Practical Introduction to Theory.* New York: St. Martin's Press, 1994.

Arnett, Ronald C. "Toward a Phenomenological Dialogue," *The Western Journal of Speech Communication* 45 (1981): 201–212.

Arnett, Ronald C. "Rogers and Buber: Similarities, Yet Fundamental Differences," *The Western Journal of Speech Communication* 46 (1982): 358–372.

Arnett, Ronald C. "Dialogic Civility as Pragmatic Ethical Praxis: An Interpersonal Metaphor for the Public Domain," *Communication Theory* 11 (2001): 315–338.

Arnett, Ronald C. and Pat Arneson. *Dialogic Civility in a Cynical Age: Community, Hope, and Interpersonal Relationships.* Albany: SUNY Press, 1999.

Buber, Martin. *The Knowledge of Man.* Edited by Maurice Friedman, Translated by Maurice Friedman and Ronald Gregor Smith. New York: Harper and Row, 1966.

Dewey, John. "The Need for a Recovery of Philosophy," in *John Dewey: The Middle Works*, 1899–1924, vol. 10, ed. J. A. Boydson, 3–48. Carbondale: Southern Illinois University Press, 1980. (original publication, 1917)

Gadamer, Hans-Georg. *Truth and Method*, 2nd rev. ed. Translation revised by Joel Weinsheimer and Donald G. Marshall. New York: Continuum, 2002. (original German publication, 1960)

Gilbert, Michael. *Coalescent Argumentation.* Mahwah N.J.: Lawrence Erlbaum, 1997.

Grass, Günter. *The Tin Drum.* Translated by Ralph Mannheim. New York: Pantheon Books, 1962. (original German publication, 1960)

Hicks, Darrin. "Reasonableness: Political not Epistemic," in *Arguing Communication and Culture*, ed. G. Thomas Goodnight. 104–112. Washington, D.C.: National Communication Association, 2002.

Hicks, Darrin. "The Promise(s) of Deliberative Democracy," *Rhetoric & Public Affairs* 5 (2002): 223–260.

Hicks, Darrin. "The Other Side of Reason: Reconstructing Reasonableness." Unpublished paper.

Hyde, Michael J. and Craig R. Smith, "Hermeneutics and Rhetoric: A Seen but Unobserved Relationship," *Quarterly Journal of Speech* 65 (1979):347–363.

Ihde, Don. *Listening and Voice: A Phenomenology of Sound.* Athens: Ohio University Press, 1976.

Kant, Immanuel. *Critique of Judgment.* Translated by J. H. Bernard. New York: Macmillan, 1951. (original German publication, 1790)

Langsdorf, Lenore. "The Doubleness of Subjectivity: Regenerating the Phenomenology of Intentionality," in *Ricoeur As Another: The Ethics of Subjectivity*, ed. Richard A. Cohen and James L. Marsh, 33–55. Albany: SUNY Press, 2002.

Langsdorf, Lenore. "In Defense of Poiesis: The Performance of Self in Communicative Praxis," in *Calvin O. Schrag and the Task of Phenomenology After Postmodernity*, ed. William McBride and Martin Beck Matustik, 281–296. Evanston: Northwestern University Press, 2002.

Langsdorf, Lenore. "Reasonable Voices: Constituting What's Reasonable in Communicative Interaction, in *Arguing Communication and Culture*, ed. G. Thomas Goodnight. 113–121. Washington, D.C.: National Communication Association, 2002.

Levinas, Emmanuel. *Proper Names*, trans. M. B. Smith. Stanford: Stanford University Press, 1969.

Lieberman, Matthew D. et al. "Is Political Cognition Like Riding a Bicycle? How Cognitive Neuroscience Can Inform Research on Political Thinking," *Political Psychology* 24 (2003): 681–704.

Methodist Church of Great Britain. "History of the Church,"http://www.methodist.org.uk/index. cfm?fuseaction=welcome.content&cmid=12 (accessed February 15, 2007).

Pinchevski, Amit. *By Way of Interruption: Levinas and the Ethics of Communication.* Pittsburgh: Duquesne University Press, 2006.

Rawls, John. *Political Liberalism.* New York: Columbia University Press, 1993.

Ricoeur, Paul *Oneself As Another.* Translated by Kathleen Blamey. Chicago: The University of Chicago Press, 1992. (original French publication, 1990)

Schrag, Calvin O. *Communicative Praxis and the Space of Subjectivity.* Bloomington: Indiana University Press, 1986.

Schrag, Calvin O. *The Self After Postmodernity.* New Haven: Yale University Press, 1997.

Schrag, Calvin O. and David James Miller. "Communication Studies and Philosophy: Convergence without Coincidence." In *The Critical Turn: Rhetoric and Philosophy in Postmodern Discourse,* ed. Ian Angus and Lenore Langsdorf, 126–139. Carbondale: Southern Illinois University Press, 1993.

Tilton, Marcy. "Bias 101," *Threads Magazine* http://www.taunton.com/threads/pages/t00007.asp (accessed February 15, 2007).

Wickell, Janet. "Understanding Fabric Grain," http://scrapquilts.com/fabric_grain.html (accessed February 15, 2007).

Dismissiveness and Dialogic Ethics

Rush Limbaugh and Public Dialogue

ROB ANDERSON AND KENNETH N. CISSNA

Rush Limbaugh was not employing a new rhetorical strategy when the powerful radio commentator dealt with a 19-year-old college student caller to his show on March 7, 2003. "Crystal" wanted to reply to Limbaugh's comments the previous day about her and a protest in which she had participated, and to ask him some questions. In an uncharacteristically lengthy exchange that Limbaugh's website later described as showing that Crystal was a "cliché-spouting" "know it all" "parroting" her professors and "uttering platitudes," the two discussed the pending Iraq war, which began only 13 days later, and its relation to such domestic issues as support for education.[1]

Two of Limbaugh's comments about this conversation caught our attention. First, Limbaugh's final utterance to Crystal at the end of their 20-minute conversation was "I'm sorry, but I am no clearer today understanding why you think the way you do than I was before I talked to you." For students of communication and public dialogue, this sentence seemed a sad commentary on a conversation, yet an intriguing one. Second, a day later, on the show's website, Limbaugh wrote, "I really tried to have a dialogue with Crystal, but it turned out to be impossible."[2]

Analysts and critics of public communication should listen carefully when powerful media figures point to occasions in which they attempted dialogue, but others simply would not cooperate. We attempted to do just that, by asking incisive questions: How did Limbaugh express his desire for dialogue? What did his young undergraduate interlocutor do—if anything—to subvert dialogue and call down the host's wrath (the site referred to Crystal's "mind full of mush")? What purposes, rhetorical and otherwise, were served by his style of reacting to her ideas and questions? Finally, does this interaction in any way represent a troubling trend? Limbaugh's rhetoric in this conversation invites analysis for many reasons, not least of which is that it so starkly lays out a tendency in contemporary public discourse that appears to be gathering momentum. In this essay, we explore this phenomenon, which we term *dismissiveness,* in order to chart some of its contours and, ultimately, its problematic relation to a dialogic ethic for public talk. We do not have space in this introductory essay to chart a more complete history of the phenomenon or how it plays out in various civic and political spheres.

Public figures have been dismissing, ignoring, or slighting others' arguments throughout the ages, for good reasons and bad. Nothing is new about claiming that opposition arguments are weak, and nothing is new about characterizing those arguments with venom, sarcasm, or withering critique. To discount another's points as not rising to the level of respectable reply also is not new; debaters in academic and parliamentary contexts, for example, have invoked the traditional concept of a *prima facie* case to indicate the threshold an argument must meet to merit a substantive reply. In recent years, however, our studies of power and ethics in public dialogue[3] have sensitized us in new ways to the rhetorical importance of an understudied and undertheorized phenomenon—in which communicators advertise that they need not reply to others. Specifically, the emergence of a polarized "argument culture" often concerned with seemingly intractable "moral conflicts" and media dramatization of public positions in bimodal and supposedly balanced this-or-that ways have all solidified the impact and frequency of the dismissive response in public discourse.[4]

To foreground *dismissiveness,* we first specify the phenomenon and chart its variants, especially as they relate to the potential for dialogic discourse. Second, we examine how dismissiveness functions as a rhetorical ploy in everyday popular culture, as we offer a close reading of the Limbaugh case study. Third, we suggest how a dialogic ethic that is especially alert to the dangers of dismissiveness can neutralize those dangers while retaining the advantages of vigorous, asssertive, and culturally inflected disagreement. Stated more straightforwardly, we (a) *define,* (b) *analyze* and *synthesize,* and, most importantly, (c) *illustrate* the ethical dimension of the dismissiveness phenomenon.

APPROACHING DISMISSIVENESS

In some ways, dismissiveness seems an unusual candidate to become an intellectual concept, in that it can be read as connoting a negative or deficit interpretation. Readers might rightly wonder what the opposite positive phenomenon would be, and whether scholars would be better advised, perhaps even more focused, to frame the problem from a more positive perspective. Yet a brief consideration of potential alternate terminology illustrates the problem.

CONCEPTUALIZING DISMISSIVENESS

Although "dismissive" and "dismissiveness" are common terms in the contemporary public vernacular, as search engines readily demonstrate, the concept of dismissiveness has no clear opposite. Is it the opposite of dismissiveness merely to notice something, to consider or engage it with due seriousness, or to value or prize it? And what of the dimension of time? While dismissiveness connotes an ongoing disdain, what positive concept as clearly indicates the maintenance of an ongoing interest in a person or issue? Is dismissiveness merely the opposite of confirmation, empathy, acknowledgment, or recognition?[5] Although all of these are in the conceptual ballpark, none seems to be a close enough fit for the dynamic of dismissiveness. As we show, part of the dismissive rhetor's approach is to engage and consider what is supposedly inadequate *while* arguing that it is not worth such consideration. Dismissiveness suggests a distinct semantic field apart from such concepts as confirmation, empathy, acknowledgment, and recognition, even though it is supported by similar connotations.

For us, at least, this is the core of the issue. We are concerned with the increasingly common social response of dismissing others or their arguments. To dismiss is not simply to erase, or ignore, or ridicule, or rebut someone or something. It is to recognize the person or argument, but recognize in such a way as to characterize the subject as beneath reply. It is represented as a recognition in spite of itself, from a rhetor who claims to have a large heart and desire for mutuality and listening, but who, unfortunately, is stymied by others. In such circumstances, dialogue may be—in fact, we suspect, often *is*—invoked as a kind of optimistic hope, but one supposedly made impossible by the insubstantiality of the other or the other's position.

By dismissiveness, then, we mean:

- Public discourse claims . . .
- About a topic of consequence . . .
- That state or strongly suggest . . .
- How some messages, persons, groups, or phenomena . . .

- Need not be, and will not be, acknowledged or taken seriously . . .
- Combined with a willful strategy of ignoring their implications . . .
- And a public assertion of the meaninglessness of the messages, others, or phenomena in question.

Thus, dismissiveness emerges as a particular rhetoric of listening—involving an intentional and proactive filter of disconfirmation and even dogmatism that essentially represents the dismissive speaker as situationally invulnerable to the entreaties of others: "I will not be reached," says the dismissing rhetor; "I am not available for this talk"; "I (and by extension, external auditors) need not attend to these [messages, others, or phenomena]"; and "I can assert this unambiguously."

Dismissiveness as we conceptualize it exists in an uneasy relationship with dialogic hopes for human communication, although this too is an issue rarely explored. In recent years, scholars from communication[6] and across the human studies[7] have reinvigorated the study of dialogue, including explorations of a number of different forms of a dialogic ethic.[8] Fortunately, no finalized definition of dialogue is necessary to point out that dialogue theorists have discovered significant conceptual overlaps in their studies. For example, recent communication-based studies of dialogue appear to stress that it exists primarily in particular moments of meeting rather than in extended ongoing relational states.[9] Earlier, we offered a brief synthesis that seemingly characterizes a variety of perspectives. "Dialogue," we wrote, "emerges as an issue concerning the quality of relationship between or among two or more people and of the communicative acts that create and sustain that relationship." Further, "reflects the attitudes participants bring to an encounter, the ways they talk and act toward one another, the consequences of meeting, and the larger context within which dialogue occurs."[10] We described eight characteristics that dialogic participants tend to create:

1. an *immediacy of presence* in which participants are available to one another in the here-and-now
2. a *genuineness and authenticity* that presume a thoughtful honesty on the part of all participants
3. a *recognition of "strange otherness,"* which involves a respect for the other and allows that even familiar others may surprise us
4. a *vulnerability* that allows all participants to be changed
5. caring about the other and about our relationships that results in a *collaborative orientation* toward the other
6. a *mutuality* in which participants interdepend, each defining and constructing self, other, and their talk simultaneously
7. a *temporal flow* that presumes historical continuity and immerses participants in a dialogic process

8. an element of surprise, or what we called *emergent unanticipated consequences*.[11]

These characteristics overlap with, and yet differ somewhat from, the definitions provided by Johannesen, Stewart, Arnett, and others.[12]

STYLES OF DISMISSIVENESS

If dismissiveness is a consequential phenomenon, how do we know it when we hear or see it? One obvious answer is that we may not. That is, to the extent that a dismissive response is a matter of listening style, inner dismissiveness may be cloaked to some extent by an outer rhetorical layer of sympathy, optimism, openness, and invitation. We can tell each other, for example, that we admire others who question our authority, but still react with minimal attentiveness to the actual questioning. We may say we want dialogue, but say it only because we have already decided that something approximating dialogue in the present circumstance will increase the chances that we obtain what we want. We may say "That's an interesting idea!" without any realistic intention at all of experiencing future interest in the idea or acting in ways congruent with such interest.

So dismissiveness, to be analyzed socially, must be heard or seen imperfectly in the refraction of its verbal and behavioral cues. Some rhetors may feel dismissed even though opponents fully consider their contributions but simply disagree with them. Ego-involvement is a constant danger whenever critics attempt to discuss the intentions or motivations behind public discourse. Nevertheless, we can focus on some relatively straightforward public instances of this interesting rhetorical approach. Many styles of dismissiveness are possible, but perhaps some can be identified by the contexts where we might hear the following:

- *I have the courage of my convictions, and I am certain about them. At least I'm honest about my [commitment; faith; fervor; etc.]:* In *Democracy and Disagreement*, Gutmann and Thompson analyze moral dogmatism and how public figures justify framing it at times in opposition to openness.[13] For example, former Secretary of Health, Education, and Welfare Joseph Califano, they write, once said about a public position, "I concluded that it was not sufficient simply to express my view clearly and consistently, but that it was also essential to communicate the certainty with which I held it. Any hedging would only encourage those who disagreed, to hope for a change that would not be forthcoming."[14] In other words, certainty and fervor justify a predecision not to change one's mind, and to listen for alternatives past that personal decision would be considered "hedging" or, perhaps, "flip-flopping."

- *We're right; you're wrong:* Related to the first style, of course, this approach states the dismissiveness more boldly, and with somewhat less self-congratulation. Although sometimes associated with political infighting (think of such hyper-partisans as Ann Coulter or James Carville), its tone can also be heard, for example, in some versions of inter-religious "dialogue" that amount to little more than occasions to compare how different the parties are, while implicitly colluding to bolster the barriers so thoroughly that no communicator is fundamentally open to change. At times, the dismisser will point out differences in background, beliefs, education, or experience that make the positions of the other unworthy of consideration. This attitude is different, of course, from nondismissive meetings in which the parties hold their basic positions, even strongly hold them, while still being vulnerable to dialogic surprises about others and their potential.

- *I will not dignify that accusation with a response:* Public figures, especially politicians, often respond to others' characterizations of them by avoidance or shifting the ground of disagreement, by claiming that the comment is an attack and that the vileness of the attack precludes any necessity of response. In fact, the rhetor implies that the other's comment is an outlandish and unjustifiable accusation, with any response simply serving to validate ("dignify") the criticism. Usually without proof, the rhetor casts him- or herself as victim of unfairness so obvious that an audience should be able to unmask it without further analysis. In other words, no dialogue is necessary.

- *Dialogue only slows us down:* Spokespersons for particular public positions will occasionally argue that because dialogue is difficult or time-consuming, it cannot be a worthwhile response to problems described as immediate and complex emergencies that demand the public's attention right now. Part of the problem here is that, as we and other scholars have noted, public and organizational dialogue can be a long and difficult process, and this reality has been used by powerful rhetors to deny the voice and just claims of others.[15]

- *Dialogue is a tool of the other side:* This can be heard in U.S. national politics, where activists sometimes announce that to have a conversation about an issue admits the validity of the issue, admits that there *is* more than one side, and that such an admission will damage their cause. Similarly, less powerful groups will sometimes insist that if they agree to talk with their more powerful counterparts that they will be co-opted into moving toward the others' positions.

- *They don't try to talk with me/us; why waste my/our time understanding them?:* This approach indicates that the rhetor has already decided which other communicators are, and are not, amenable to persuasion, which genuinely desire deliberation or dialogue, or which are even capable of absorbing the sophistication of one's arguments. Accusing the other of dismissiveness and nondialogic intent, as with Limbaugh's sarcastic claim that Crystal "knows it all" and won't participate in a conversation, is one form of this, as is Limbaugh's claim that Crystal has been duped by her professors and has failed to receive an education adequate to allow her to understand fully the issues of public life—money spent on her education, he claims, has been "wasted."

▪ *They are merely "playing politics" with this issue:* In this approach, the rhetor defines the other's motive as "political" (and thus, presumably, self-interested, narrow, unserious ["playing"], and thoroughly entrenched). The speaker will not typically cast self as adopting *another* political position, of course, but instead claims to operate "above" politics, in the rhetorical realm of reason, moral guidance, and pure motive. The attribution that the other, unlike one's self, is merely furthering a political aim is a way to dismiss engaging the other.

▪ *The evidence is not yet in:* In this approach, dialogue is deferred or delayed because of the presumption that a decision is *so* important that it must be based on a total awareness of the fullest possible range of facts. Of course, in most human affairs, absolute certainty is never obtained, and yet people, families, communities, nations must and do make choices and take actions. This position can be espoused by individuals who prefer inaction to action, or who prefer the status quo to considering a change.

▪ *That's the kind of comment I'd expect from [a liberal; a fundamentalist; a Russian; a Catholic; a Black woman; etc.]:* Such efforts to label the other not only are essentialist in the philosophical sense, and name-calling in vernacular speech, but they presume that one already knows what the other thinks or will say. Thus, they dismiss the other without ever hearing what the actual contributions might be. Cast in terms of our dialogic characteristics, the otherness is not "strange" (new, potentially surprising), but predefined. Any possibility for dialogic surprise is precluded by a dismissal of the other as just another [fill-in-the-blank].

THE PARADOX OF DISMISSIVENESS

Dismissiveness is not merely another tactic among many available to arguers. It is far more subtle, and far more threatening to genuine dialogue, than that status might imply because its power rests on an intriguing and somewhat subterranean paradox. Stated in everyday language, it develops something like this (from the standpoint of a dismissive interlocutor-in-conflict): "It's not simply that your position is weak, or that I disagree, or that you are wrong, or that you are unethical, or that you are ignorant or insensitive. *It is that you are actually beneath response.* Your points are self-defeating and patently absurd; they don't have the force necessary to stimulate reply. Yet I reply anyway, demonstrating my largess, my open-mindedness, my commitment to dialogue. I reply anyway, to dispense with the argument, characterizing it so that other audiences, less astute than I, will not be taken in." *The paradox: This is not worth reply, yet I reply—presenting myself as though in service to dialogue, in order to assist others.*

Dismissiveness in this public sphere sense does not emerge merely from a preestablished position of power ("I am important and have the authority to judge whether your ideas are worth response"), but simultaneously it establishes its own position of power beyond the interchange. As Limbaugh speaks to Crystal, he is also speaking beyond her, to a far larger audience that wants to know how he evaluates her. Clearly, it is not only conventionally powerful figures such as Limbaugh who are authorized to speak dismissively; students taking a difficult class can sometimes be heard to say: "This is worthless. The teacher is just spewing jargon. There's nothing here to study that common sense couldn't tell you"—thus currying favor with other students who are as yet unsure of the value of the distinctions or concepts. One can easily construct similar examples of faculty commenting on a message from university administration—or the administration commenting on the faculty; or management and labor; or developers and environmentalists; etc. Dismissiveness, in other words, is enabled by power at the same time as it enables or constructs it. It denies dialogue with the judged while it purports to represent more realistic or important dialogue with extended audience(s).

DISMISSIVENESS IN THE LIMBAUGH– CRYSTAL INTERCHANGE

Rush Limbaugh is, to say the least, a polarizing media figure. For 19 years he has had his own nationally syndicated radio show (and for 5 of those years he also had a regular television show). Perhaps more than anyone else over the past two decades, he has exemplified how to dramatize political involvement, almost always by exaggerating the moral differences between his favored "conservative" perspectives and the drawbacks of "liberal" ideology. Although others have followed his lead in developing generally far-right-leaning radio and television talk shows, he remains the prototypical conservative commentator in the U.S. Listeners are so devoted to his show that they call themselves, with no apparent irony, "dittoheads" as they listen for what they consider talking points to emphasize in their own water cooler and coffee shop conversations. Some listeners claim they listen only for the entertainment value of his trenchant and often witty commentaries, yet others clearly get much of their news about the world from Limbaugh. In one recent study, 27 percent of adults surveyed were found to consider Limbaugh not just an entertainer but a "journalist"; in the same survey, investigative reporter and editor Bob Woodward of the *Washington Post* was recognized as a journalist by only 30 percent.[16] Although liberals have attempted to demonize Limbaugh and his image,[17] some evidence suggests that negative aspects of Limbaugh's approach have been exaggerated by the mainstream media, and that such talk shows can contribute to a reinvigorated public sphere.[18] He has given voice to conservative citizens who felt underrepresented in American politics for many years. At the same time, most media commentators agree that he exemplifies and validates a strikingly confrontational rhetorical style in the recent media landscape.[19] Although his opponents on the left have tried to package their own versions of his show, they have been unsuccessful in emulating either Limbaugh's popularity or his impact.

Yet from an ethical perspective it is possible that Rush Limbaugh's contribution to the contemporary rhetorical tenor has profoundly altered the potential for the kind of public dialogue that could assist people in engaging in productive conflict, developing concertive mutual action across difference, or even, ultimately, producing consensus-based values. Conversation is the ostensible goal of the program, and this is in line with Jamieson's conclusion in *Eloquence in an Electronic Age* that political talk in the 20th century shifted from an oratorical to an interpersonal emphasis.[20] Yet it is political conversation with a vector; solidifying attitudes is still a prime goal. Limbaugh, therefore, doesn't produce his program with mutuality in mind; rather, he wants his side to prevail—to identify, defeat, and even humiliate what he believes to be morally deficient opponents. Journalist Anna Quindlen reported that in a recent speech Limbaugh "described the political polarization in this country as a war between good and evil" and said that "conservatives should not worry about dialogue with liberals; they should concentrate on defeating them."[21] Political scientists David Barker and Kathleen Knight's study of Limbaugh's political talk radio and public opinion revealed "an unmistakable pattern": When Limbaugh criticizes persons, groups, or ideas on at least half of his broadcasts, "regular listeners show a marked tendency to buy the Limbaugh message—displaying [more] hostility toward those items" than is explained by a host of other relevant factors. Further, they found that Limbaugh is more successful in mobilizing opposition to than support for someone or something.[22] Our goal in highlighting Limbaugh's polarizing style is not to refute or vilify him but to present a particular mini-case that illustrates the phenomenon of dismissiveness in a particularly representative way.

THE LIMBAUGH—CRYSTAL CONVERSATION

Recall from our introduction that Crystal was a 19-year-old student at the City University of New York (CUNY) who called to take exception to how Limbaugh characterized her on his show the previous day. We begin with a brief description of their interchange, with all quotes coming from our own transcript of the audio file that was available for a time on the show's website.

The call begins with Crystal wondering why Limbaugh's only response the previous day was to call her a "valley girl," which she says was "name calling." Limbaugh denies he called her a name and insists that "valley girl" is a "descriptive term" for how she sounded in the segment he played from an anti-war protest the day before. After replaying the clip from the previous day, Limbaugh identifies Crystal as "the third one, right?: 'we have reason to be concerned' [Crystal: "Yeah"]; 'the issue should be addressed'" and then, interestingly, Limbaugh adds "others were talking about how we could better spend this money on education and uh—."[23] Crystal then interrupts Limbaugh to defend what *others* had claimed: "Well, right, there have been severe budget cuts . . . especially in the CUNY schools here." She explains that some students are working two jobs and can't afford a tuition increase of $1400, before returning to the point of her call: the anti-war protest and Limbaugh's response of labeling her a valley girl. After Limbaugh says that "valley girl" was only a label for how she sounded, not what she said,[24] Crystal accepts that and asks Limbaugh now to "respond to what I was saying."

In a remarkable rhetorical move that is characteristic of much of the call, Limbaugh responds:

> Well, you were talking about "we have reasons to be concerned" and "issues should be addressed." I think that—in a nutshell—I am opposed to war, I don't like it any more than anybody else does, but I'm also a realist, and the idea that we are not spending enough on education is absolutely wrong and a joke. We are spending more than we need—.

Although initially responding to her expressed concern about the wisdom of initiating military action against Iraq, he shifts in mid-utterance to noting that "the idea that we are not spending enough on education is absolutely wrong and a joke," which was not the issue that Crystal called to discuss and avoids her request (which was to respond to what *she* said). Taken literally, Limbaugh has *agreed* with Crystal in being opposed to war, although, as we will see, this isn't, of course, true in this case. Apparently, Limbaugh did not hear—or has ignored—that she was talking about budget cuts in the CUNY system and increases to CUNY tuition rates, for he shifts direction to emphasize how the "federal budget [has never] once gotten smaller from year to year" and we're "spending more on education than we have ever in this country's history spent." Crystal, though, attempts to return their conversation to "how much we are going to be spending on this war," to which Limbaugh asks the first of his questions: "Let me ask you: Could you name the price for me for national security—what, what is a price that you would not pay—?" Crystal then asks him to define "national security," which at first Limbaugh declines to do because "we all know what we're talking [about] here when we talk about [Crystal: "No, we don't"] national security." Then he says he will define it "since you insist on being obstinate" (a phrase he repeats for emphasis). His definition consists of the question, "Have you ever heard of 9/11, September 11th?"

Although Limbaugh has hardly defined national security, Crystal says that she was in New York City on that day but objects that "Iraq is not connected to September 11th and that assertions to that effect are "speculations and accusations and suspicions." She concludes that it is "absolutely absurd what's going on right now." Limbaugh calls her objection "not true"—several times. Interestingly, although they have to this point been relatively civil—each receiving approximately equal time to talk, and each usually allowing the other to finish sentences and to make points—in one 25-word (and 13-second) utterance of Crystal's, Limbaugh attempts to interrupt her four times ("Nope," "Look that's—," "Crystal," and "Crystal" again). At this point, Limbaugh begins a speech of one minute 40 seconds. During the first 40 seconds or so, Crystal tries four times to respond, but Limbaugh continues talking and gets slightly louder. After her fourth attempt to enter the conversation, Limbaugh asks Crystal to "wait a minute, Crystal, wait a minute—now, listen to me once—just listen to me one time here," after which he continues for another minute to describe the relationship between al-Qaida, Iraq, and Saddam Hussein until he asks both Crystal and the radio audience to "Hang on a minute—we'll continue this after this time out," thus completing the first 7 minutes of their interchange.

After Limbaugh welcomes Crystal back to the show following the commercials, she tries to focus on national security and how "the Patriot Act 1 and 2, detention, special registration" are contrary to our espoused interests in defending liberty. Without responding to her, Limbaugh tells Crystal that he'd like to "ask you a couple of questions." The first is "Who are your intelligence sources? I want to know who it is that tells you this that has more credibility than Colin Powell and Condoleezza Rice." Crystal responds that she has read the transcripts of Powell's testimony before the United Nations, and she finds no proof there of a connection between al-Qaida and Hussein and Iraq, and asks Limbaugh to email his information to her because she'll read it, though Limbaugh twice interrupts her with "No, no." In seeming frustration, Limbaugh then says, "Crystal, wait, would you, would you please—can we [louder] get a conversation here instead of . . . ," and in a 45-second utterance he then asserts that she's proving that "we're wasting the money we've spent on your education." Limbaugh says that he's listened to Powell, trusts Powell and the admin-istration, and doesn't need that kind of proof. He then repeats his request that she tell him who "she trusts over this administration." Crystal says she doesn't "trust anybody," and that she's seen "no proof." For another minute, with Crystal attempting to re-enter the conversation four more times, Limbaugh makes his case for how dangerous Saddam Hussein and Iraq are. Crystal then objects that "There's no proof that he's resurrected a nuclear program there," to which Limbaugh says he's not talking about nuclear weapons and mentions Hans Blix, which Crystal seizes on to note that "Blix is not for war." "What does that have to do with anything?" Limbaugh asks, to which Crystal responds, "What it has to do with is that the man who is at the top of inspections is saying what we need is more time for inspections—not what we need is a military action."

At this point, Limbaugh confronts Crystal by suggesting she has hidden motives: "What's the real reason you oppose this country?" he asks. Crystal responds that she does not oppose the country, which Limbaugh immediately interrupts to say "Yes, you do. It is patently obvious that you oppose this country. You're not opposed to war, you're opposed to America." Crystal observes that Limbaugh is resorting again to name-calling and that she is "one of the most patriot [sic] people in this country." After Crystal suggests that "going to war with Iraq will only increase the current threat in this country," Limbaugh says she is a "walking cliché," and asks her another of his rhetorical questions: "In the basement of your house," he begins, "are six rattlesnakes." Crystal, laughing, responds, "I've heard your analogy," after which Limbaugh asks "What are you going to do about them?" Crystal replies, "How many rattlesnakes are you going to kill exactly? I mean, what are we talking about—we're talking about Iraq, and then what?"

Limbaugh declines to answer and says he is "trying to understand the way you think." Crystal then says "The way I think—" which Limbaugh interrupts to say "You will not answer any of my questions," and proceeds with another request: "Give me a rational argument for war." She starts to answer his question: "A rational argument for war is what they have been saying is that there are terrorist connections—" when Limbaugh again interrupts to say "No, no, you're not answering my question." After they argue for a bit (interrupting each other) about polling data and whether the majority of people in the U.S. and Britain favor or oppose the impending war, Limbaugh, continuing to talk over Crystal, directs his producer to "take her down, take her down a minute," cutting off Crystal's audio. Limbaugh then talks for three more minutes without interruption and without bringing Crystal back on the air. He says about Crystal, "You will not even listen. I don't know how in the world you learned anything—you know it all." "You won't answer any question I ask you. You are a walking cliché." She is, he says, "not courageous" and isn't even "practicing dissent." Instead, she is "mouth[ing] these platitudes and these clichés." She "see[s] evil," he proclaims, when she looks at "decency, and goodness, and character, and honor." He concludes this segment of the show with this comment about their interaction:

And it boggles the minds of those of us who try as hard as we can to understand why you think the way you do, and I'm sorry, but I am no clearer today understanding why you think the way you do than I was before I talked to you.

After another commercial break, Limbaugh returns for four minutes to take two additional callers who discuss Crystal and her call.

THEMES OF DISMISSIVENESS IN THE LIMBAUGH—CRYSTAL CONVERSATION

Limbaugh's conversational style provides vivid and public examples of rhetorical dismissiveness, its genesis and its consequences. We do not have the space—or need—in this essay to analyze the conversation line-by-line. Yet four themes emerge from our analysis of Limbaugh's near-prototypically dismissive attitudes and utterances; we have labeled them *name-calling, mischaracterizing, ground-shifting,* and *certainty.* All of these occur within the context of Limbaugh positioning Crystal's opinions for his listening audience, and within his own self-characterization that *he* is the one sincerely attempting "dialogue" and reasonable "conversation" in the presence of an interlocutor who refuses to listen.

Name-calling. Crystal's first contribution to the interchange, and surely a major motivation for phoning, was to draw attention to Limbaugh's calling her a "valley girl" the day before. She asks Limbaugh why he feels it necessary to engage in "name-calling" with people he disagrees with. He disagrees that he does this, stating that "valley girl" was not name-calling, but an accurate "descriptive term for the way you sounded in the bite": "I'm not calling you a name by calling you a valley girl." He is, however, deflecting attention from the content of her speech, and when she then asks him if he even recalls what she said, his answer provides no evidence that he does. Instead, he asks his producer to play the sound bite that was aired on the previous show. Later, after calling Crystal "obstinate" and asking her "What's the real reason you oppose this country?" (as one would ask a traitor), and just before labeling her three times as a "walking cliché" and once as a person who "mouths platitudes," when Crystal again objects to his name-calling, Limbaugh twice insists that he has "yet to call you a name."

After he asks the producer to "take her down" (cut off Crystal's side of the conversation), he takes two other calls supporting his treatment of her, during which time he denies that she is even talking for herself: she and other students who disagree with him are merely

. . . parroting what they've been taught by their professors, and their friends, whoever knows who else. It's all designed to make them feel good after they've said it. They think they are being worldly, bighearted, and uh open-minded instead of closed-minded and that sort of thing.

On his website, he was again drawn to dismiss by name-calling, repeating the "valley girl" and "walking cliché" labels, while asserting that she was "fixated on things she *claims* are 'name-calling'" (emphasis added). With no ear for the irony, Limbaugh then adds another label and further *ad hominem* attacks: Despite how much we're spending on education, he says, we get "tape recorders" like Crystal who can't "think" and are only "uttering platitudes." Crystal, the website says, has a "mind full of mush" and has "forgotten 9/11." We could not find even one instance where Crystal engages in similar name-calling behavior; by contrast, she attempts to answer each of the host's questions and attempts to keep the conversation focused on evidence and the issue of the advisability of the impending war with Iraq.

Mischaracterizing. In addition to denying using negative labels while referring to Crystal, Limbaugh mischaracterized her stated reasons for calling. While she attempted to focus on his characterization of her and on the war with Iraq, Limbaugh was quick to shift the subject to federal financing of education, which became the primary topic of his conversation with the first post-Crystal caller. This characterization continued on Limbaugh's website.

Another interesting ploy within the mischaracterization theme is to accuse the other of being disinterested in, or unprepared to participate in, a reasonable or rational dialogue. Limbaugh claims, while interrupting Crystal, that he wants her to listen better, when he's the one who more frequently interrupted. After characterizing Crystal's comments as "platitudes," and Crystal as being "sidetracked" about whether al-Qaida was connected to Iraq, he implores her to "wait a minute, Crystal—listen to me once"—as though she were the poor listener, even though *he'd* interrupted *her*. Later: "Wait . . ."—"can we get a conversation here instead of. . . ." He announces at one point, "You know what you're proving here is that we're wasting the money we've spent on your education." Still later: "You will not answer any of my questions," and right before he has his producer cut her off, he says you "won't answer any question I ask you," despite her remarkably direct responses on educational funding, the linkage between 9/11 and Iraq, trusting administration claims, and whether she wants to live with constant threat levels. The clearest instance of this ploy was heard when Limbaugh asks Crystal what a "rational argument for war" would be, evidently thinking she would flounder. She replies that a direct terrorist connection to Hussein and Iraq would justify war. But this is not, evidently, what Limbaugh wanted her to say. "No, no," he replied, "you're not answering my question." The website heading for part two of the show's audio segment was: "Listen to Rush try to get Crystal to answer a single question and listen for a second." Crystal supposedly was the stumbling block to dialogue: "I really tried to have a dialogue with Crystal, but it turned out to be impossible," he states on the website.

Ground-shifting. How, though, does Limbaugh characterize and engage the content of Crystal's claims? He ignores her specific and qualified comment about "severe budget cuts" and a "tuition hike" "especially in the CUNY schools here," in order to respond instead to something far broader: Calling himself a "realist," he asserts that "the idea that we're not spending enough on education is absolutely wrong and a joke. We're spending more than we need." He proceeds to discuss overall federal budget figures, as though he was responding to Crystal's point. He was off—twice. First, Crystal wanted to talk about the war, and was polite enough to respond when Limbaugh introduced this topic, and second, the concerns of Crystal's colleagues were with the cost of attending CUNY and not with federal funding for higher education. Another example: Crystal questions the "linkage" between Hussein and the 9/11 tragedy, after which Limbaugh shifts twice to how dangerous Hussein might be to the U.S. in the future: We have "nothing to fear from Hussein, correct?" As part of this strategy, he asserts (erroneously) that Japan and Germany weren't linked in World War Two, but we fought both anyway. As part of an interchange about the justification of the war, Limbaugh brings up the nuclear inspector Hans Blix, only to have Crystal remind him that Blix wasn't in favor of the war. "What does that have to do with anything?" he asks. He then doesn't reply to Crystal's cogent explanation that "the man who is at the top of inspections is saying what we need is more time for inspections. Not what we need is a military action—."

Certainty. When Crystal asks Limbaugh early in the call to respond to the substance of what she said, he shifted in mid-sentence from the impending war to education spending and said that "the idea that we are not spending enough on education is absolutely wrong and a joke." In response to Limbaugh's use of the term "national security," Crystal explicitly asks for his definition. He won't supply it: "We all know what we're talking about." Later, after Limbaugh introduces September 11th as the basis for his definition of national security and Crystal asserts that there is no proof that al-Qaida and Iraq are connected, Limbaugh interrupts her twice to say "No, not true" and "Not true." As he continues to expound on his view, he becomes louder and more insistent—he is unwilling to entertain any possibility that war against Iraq is not a good idea.[25] Ironically, while accusing her of "know[ing] it all" at "age 19," Limbaugh's rhetoric is far more dogmatic and certain. She also listens better than Limbaugh, does a better job of responding to him and his questions than he does to her, and interestingly, from our vantage point over five years later, she seems to have been largely right about her cautions related to the war and Limbaugh largely wrong.

DANGER SIGNALS AND A COSMOPOLITAN ETHIC OF NONDISMISSIVENESS

A dialogic ethic that can account for and also respond to dismissiveness must deal successfully with several issues. It should avoid a bland relativistic toleration of multiple viewpoints. It should remain open to the possibility that some moral conflicts—and ways of portraying them—are based on positions that are unlikely to change, at least in the short term. It should accommodate the potential for cultural presumptions that make meeting, much less dialogic deliberation, difficult. It should fit at least reasonably comfortably into contemporary media assumptions of multiple audiences and multiple publics. And it should offer an explanation of how the concept of caring must apply not only to the specific other(s) with whom we talk, but also to the specific ideas we talk about and the reciprocal and mutualized contexts we necessarily co-create, whether we intend cooperation or not.

In response to the problematic of dismissiveness, we offer a modest suggestion that could be called *an ethic of the clearing*. It is based on the relatively common perception that dialogue facilitators cannot make dialogue happen. No matter how skillful they might be, they cannot "do" dialogues for others as if they are presentations. And singly, they have no power to enforce an equivalent dialogic impulse on the part of others who feel equally implicated in a conflict context. Dialogue bears an uneasy relation to intention[26] and motivation because it cannot be forced; it is an outgrowth of possibility and ultimately surprise. But communicators can clear a space within which dialogic moments of meeting could emerge. The metaphor is not new for phenomenologists, for Rogerian psychotherapists, or for students of Zen spirituality. It implies the linkage of geographic, social, and psychological space. That is, communicators who are psychologically available for others' ideas have opened mental spaces for these ideas and are likely to facilitate physical spaces for their voices as well.[27]

The ethic of the clearing suggests a simple responsibility for conversation partners: What can I do to remove whatever impedes an open consideration of persons' meanings? Its impulse is the converse of the dismissive response, which asks instead (charitably phrased): How can I fill the interactional space with my own reasons, characterizations, and judgments that justify not-listening? To invoke the ethical stance of providing a clearing, talk show hosts would not have to forego offering their own opinions, nor would they have to hand over their programs to callers. The ethic of the clearing is an invitation to a form of conflict that matters, a form that might also produce more change than retrenchment.

Dismissiveness is such a common social reaction because its roots are found in the passionate way humans become committed to ideas and actions. At times we revile this tendency (you may think that your neighbor is way over the top when she calls the cops about your dog barking rather than talking with you), but we often revere it, too. People who stand fast, refusing to budge when they "know" they are right are often thought by their compatriots to have earned the right to dismiss opposition. Congenial listeners may respect not only the commitment itself but the passionate style with which the speaker believes it, feels it, and asserts it ("I will *never* talk with anyone who condones killing innocent people"; "we *never* negotiate with terrorists"). If dismissiveness is dangerous, and we think it is, it's because its threat is prosaic. It is so dangerous, in other words, not because it is uncommonly evil but because it is so commonly mundane and normal. Dismissiveness is symbiotic with the most foundational building blocks of our identities: our moral faith and religiosity, our cultural voices and how readily they can penetrate the babel of contemporary pop culture, our political beliefs, and our often intense ties to family expectations. Dismissiveness can spring from our perceived need to be ourselves, to assert and speak for ourselves, in a cultural milieu that (we think) too readily overlooks us. If we can't speak for ourselves, then we commission figures in media and public life to assert our interests, which they are certainly willing to do (usually for a price), and even do entertainingly.

Even more disturbingly, however, dismissal is readily experienced less benignly—not as an identity assertion but as an attack on the standing of another. Dismissiveness, as we have seen, is more than a matter of ignoring or putting down a person, group, or idea; it goes beyond disconfirmation or malacknowledgment to assert a rhetorical appeal to potential audiences designed to undercut their relation to the dismissed. It symbolically attempts to diminish the other person, persons, or ideas themselves—yet it also seeks to diminish that person's access to the audiences otherwise available to them for public discourse. Its sharpness of attack, in other words, is at precisely the rich point of dialogue itself: the connection *between* conversants' speaking and listening. It is as though the dismisser assumes the role of a rhetorically malevolent metacritic, seeking to comment upon the quality of another's speaker-audience connection and thus to undercut it.

Rush Limbaugh was not merely "against" Crystal and her ideas in his dismissiveness. His disagreement with her and her positions morphed rapidly into dismissal. Limbaugh presumed that she should not have access to "his" audience without his own fractionating commentary. He wanted her to speak, but only enough, and only in ways that verify the pre-existing judgment he had and to advertise his judgment to a potential audience. Stated another way, this was an interchange in which the audience was framed as *owned* by one of the interlocutors. Importantly, he argued that he *wanted* to have a "conversation" with her, a "dialogue" in fact, but that she would have no part of it. Through no fault of his own, in his portrayal, Crystal refused to become a suitable dialogue partner, becoming at various times the anti-dialogist transgressor, or the unwittingly ignorant dupe of her professors.

What can an ethic of the clearing offer in response? Dialogic communicators, we suggest, are under no obligation to agree with others or to suffer in silence when others oppose them. Dialogue, as we and a wide range of commentators have asserted, can and often should involve strong position-taking. Yet in response to the passionate and perhaps even unyielding position-taking of others, and in the face of the temptation toward dismissiveness, the metaphor of the clearing offers an interesting alternative.

Effective listeners don't just listen to what others have to say and recall it accurately; they are ethically and pragmatically bound to listen invitationally. In order to maintain others' choices in ways similar to Brown and Keller's interpersonal ethic,[28] such listeners should do what they can to create an open space in which the other's voice can be fully and realistically heard by oneself and an audience. We can't make dialogue happen. Much of dialogic potential, however, is found in what doesn't happen, by avoiding filling relational space with the second-order verbal violence of dismissing others.

In Wendell Berry's poem "The Return," a neighbor is a loud and obnoxious litterer, producing "—more rubbish in one night / than all the Shawnees made." The poet struggles with his relationship to

> *My neighbor and brother,*
> *a violent brainless man*
> *whom I must intelligently love*
> *although I do not, or become*
> *him, as he is.*[29]

In a relational context of potential dismissiveness, in other words, another choice emerges. And by taking that other alternative, dialogue has a future. It is not guaranteed, not necessarily pleasant, not even necessarily desired. The poet chooses not to portray the other in an end state of dismissal, however clear and even judgmental his estimate of the neighbor may be. But dialogue transcends judgment, including acts that invite potentially new aspects of relational context. Limbaugh started in judgment, and ended there too.

NOTES

1. The Limbaugh website (see *www.rushlimbaugh.com*) no longer contains the comments regarding the Limbaugh–Crystal call that we quote here and elsewhere nor the link to the audiofiles of the call. We accessed the site on March 10, 2003, at *http://www.rushlimbaugh.com/home/weekend_sites/weekly_review_030303_030703/content/crystal_knows_it_all_at_age_19.guest.html.*

2. It is possible, of course, that an assistant wrote that line, though we think that unlikely. Because much of the commentary on the website is written in the first-person singular and is entirely consistent with what Limbaugh said during the call, we attribute the comments there to the show's host.

3. Anderson, Dardenne, and Killenberg, 1994; Anderson and Cissna, 1997; Anderson, Cissna, and Clune, 2003; Cissna and Anderson, 1998, 2002; Hammond, Anderson, and Cissna, 2003.

4. Tannen, 1998; Gutmann and Thompson, 1996; Pearce and Littlejohn, 1997; Jamieson and Waldman, 2004.

5. For example, see, respectively, Cissna and Sieburg, 1981; Rogers, 1975; Hyde, 2005; and Taylor, 1992.

6. For example, Anderson, Baxter, and Cissna, 2004; Anderson, Cissna, and Arnett, 1994; Arnett, 1986; Arnett and Arneson, 1999; Cissna, 2000; Cissna and Anderson, 2008; Pearce and Littlejohn, 1997; Stewart, 1978.

7. For example, Grudin, 1996; Kogler, 1999; Nikulin, 2006.

8. For example, Arnett and Arneson, 1999; Habermas, 1992; Noddings, 1984.

9. For example, Baxter, 2004; Baxter and DeGooyer, 2001; Black, 2008; Cissna and Anderson, 1998, 2002; Poulos, 2008.

10. Cissna and Anderson, 1994, 15.

11. Ibid., 13–15; see also Anderson, 1994, 93–94.

12. Johannesen, 1971; Stewart, 1978; Arnett, 1992.

13. Gutmann and Thompson, 1996.

14. Ibid., 84.

15. Hammond, Anderson, and Cissna, 2003.

16. See the press release from the Annenberg Public Policy Center at *www.annenbergpublicpolicycenter. org/02_reports_releases/report_2005.htm*.

17. For example, Franken, 1996.

18. Capella, Turow, and Jamieson, 1996.

19. For example, see Appel, 2003.

20. Jamieson, 1990.

21. Quindlen, 2004.

22. Barker and Knight, 2000, 167, 168.

23. Crystal's two-sentence contribution to the montage of voices was this: "We have reason to be concerned and that's an issue that definitely needs to be addressed. However, I don't think that it calls for military action."

24. How that avoids the accusation of name-calling escapes us. Surely, to describe someone as a "valley girl" is name-calling by any standard. For our readers who didn't grow up in California, consider the entry for "valley girl" from that paragon of popular culture information, Wikipedia

(*http://en.wikipedia.org/wiki/Valley_girl*): The term originated in the 1970s and referred to "affluent young women living in the San Fernando Valley area of Los Angeles, California." The term, however, "morphed in the 1980s and 1990s to represent a more widespread and cartoonish stereotype of young women—typically characterized by a 'ditzy' or 'airheaded' personality, and unapologetically 'spoiled' behavior that showed more interest in shopping, personal appearance, and popular social status, rather than in any intellectual pursuit." We found her speech, both in the short audio clip and in the call, to be serious and focused, with no manifestations of the connotations of a valley girl by any definition.

25. That virtually all authorities now acknowledge that the evidence supporting the Iraq invasion was far less clear than its public portrayals has not influenced how certain Limbaugh continues to be even today about virtually everything he says on the air.

26. See Cissna and Anderson, in press.

27. See Spano, 2001.

28. Brown and Keller, 1979.

29. Berry, 1987.

BIBLIOGRAPHY

Anderson, Rob. "Anonymity, Presence, and the Dialogical Self in a Technological Culture." In Rob Anderson, Kenneth N. Cissna, and Ronald C. Arnett (Eds.), *The Reach of Dialogue: Confirmation, Voice, and Community*. Cresskill, NJ: Hampton Press, 1994. 91–110.

Anderson, Rob, Robert Dardenne, and George M. Killenberg. *The Conversation of Journalism: Communication, Community, and News*. Westport, CT: Praeger, 1994.

Anderson, Rob, and Kenneth N. Cissna. "Criticism and Conversational Texts: Rhetorical Bases of Role, Audience, and Style in the Buber-Rogers Dialogue." *Human Studies* 19 (1996): 85–118.

———. *The Martin Buber–Carl Rogers Dialogue: A New Transcript with Commentary*. Albany: State University of New York Press, 1997.

Anderson, Rob, Leslie A. Baxter, and Kenneth N. Cissna, Eds. *Dialogue: Theorizing Difference in Communication Studies*. Thousand Oaks, CA: Sage, 2004.

Anderson, Rob, Kenneth N. Cissna, and Ronald C. Arnett, Eds. *The Reach of Dialogue: Confirmation, Voice, and Community*. Cresskill, NJ: Hampton Press, 1994.

Anderson, Rob, Kenneth N. Cissna, and M. K. Clune. "The Rhetoric of Public Dialogue." *Communication Research Trends* 22.1 (2003): 1–37.

Appel, Edward C. "Rush to Judgment: Burlesque, Tragedy, and Hierarchical Alchemy in the Rhetoric of America's Favorite Talk Show Host." *Southern Communication Journal* 68 (2003): 217–230.

Arnett, Ronald C. *Communication and Community: Implications of Martin Buber's Dialogue*. Carbondale: Southern Illinois University Press, 1986.

Arnett, Ronald C. *Dialogic Education: Conversations between People and about Ideas.* Carbondale: Southern Illinois University Press, 1992.

Arnett, Ronald C., and Pat Arneson. *Dialogic Civility in a Cynical Age: Community, Hope, and Interpersonal Relationships.* Albany: State University of New York Press, 1999.

Barker, David, and Kathleen Knight. "Political Talk Radio and Public Opinion." *Public Opinion Quarterly* 64 (2000): 149–170.

Baxter, Leslie A. "Dialogues of Relating." In Rob Anderson, Leslie A. Baxter, and Kenneth N. Cissna (Eds.). *Dialogue: Theorizing Difference in Communication Studies.* Thousand Oaks, CA: Sage, 2004. 107–124.

Baxter, Leslie A., and Dan DeGooyer, Jr. "Perceived Aesthetic Characteristics of Interpersonal Conversations." *Southern Communication Journal* 67 (2001): 1–18.

Berry, Wendell. *Sabbaths.* San Francisco: North Point Press, 1987.

Black, Laura. "Deliberation, Storytelling, and Dialogic Moments." *Communication Theory* 18(2008): 93–116.

Brown, Charles, and Paul Keller. *Monologue to Dialogue: An Exploration of Interpersonal Communication* 2nd ed. Englewood Cliffs, NJ: Prentice-Hall, 1979.

Cappella, Joseph N., Joseph Turow, and Kathleen H. Jamieson. *Call-in Political Talk Radio: Background, Content, and Audience Portrayal in Mainstream Media.* Philadelphia: Annenberg Public Policy Center, 1996.

Cissna, Kenneth N. "Studies in Dialogue [Special issue]." *Southern Communication Journal* 65 2 & 3 (2000).

Cissna, Kenneth N., and Rob Anderson. "Communication and the Ground of Dialogue." In Rob Anderson, Kenneth N. Cissna, and Ronald C. Arnett (Eds.), *The Reach of Dialogue: Confirmation, Voice, and Community.* Cresskill, NJ: Hampton Press, 1994. 9–30.

———. "The 1957 Martin Buber–Carl Rogers Dialogue, as Dialogue." *Journal of Humanistic Psychology* 34 (1994): 11–45.

———. "Dialogue in Public: Looking Critically at the Buber–Rogers Dialogue." In Maurice Friedman (Ed.), *Martin Buber and the Human Sciences.* Albany: State University of New York Press, 1996. 191–206.

———. "Theorizing about Dialogic Moments: The Buber–Rogers Position and Postmodern Themes." *Communication Theory* 8 (1998): 63–104.

———. *Moments of Meeting: Buber, Rogers, and the Potential for Public Dialogue.* Albany: State University of New York Press, 2002.

———. "Public Dialogue and Intellectual History: Hearing Multiple Voices." In Rob Anderson, Leslie A. Baxter, and Kenneth N. Cissna (Eds.). *Dialogue: Theorizing Difference in Communication Studies.* Thousand Oaks, CA: Sage, 2004. 193–207.

———. "A Failed Dialogue? Revisiting the 1975 Meeting of Gregory Bateson and Carl Rogers." *Cybernetics and Human Knowing* 12 (2005): 120–136.

———. "Fresh Perspectives in Dialogue Theory [Special issue]." *Communication Theory* 17.2 (2008).

———. "Dialogic Rhetoric, Coauthorship, and Moments of Meeting." In Edda Weigand (Ed.), *Rhetoric and Dialogue.* Amsterdam: John Benjamins, in press.

Cissna, Kenneth N., and Evelyn Sieburg. "Patterns of Interactional Confirmation and Disconfirmation." In Carol Wilder-Mott and John H. Weakland (Eds.), *Rigor and Imagination: Essays from the Legacy of Gregory Bateson*. New York: Praeger, 1981. 253–282.

Franken, Al. *Rush Limbaugh Is a Big Fat Idiot and Other Observations* New York: Delacorte Press, 1996.

Grudin, Robert. *On Dialogue: An Essay on Free Thought*. Boston: Houghton Mifflin, 1996.

Gutmann. Amy, and Dennis Thompson. *Democracy and Disagreement*. Cambridge, MA: Harvard University Press, 1996.

Habermas, Jürgen. *Autonomy and Solidarity: Interviews with Jürgen Habermas* (Rev. ed.; P. Dews, Ed.). London: Verso, 1992.

Hammond, Scott C., Rob Anderson, and Kenneth N. Cissna. "The Problematics of Dialogue and Power." *Communication Yearbook* 27 (2003): 125–157.

Hyde, Michael J. *The Life-Giving Gift of Acknowledgment: A Philosophical and Rhetorical Inquiry.* West Lafayette, IN: Purdue University Press, 2005.

Jamieson, Kathleen H. *Eloquence in an Electronic Age: The Transformation of Political Speechmaking.* New York: Oxford University Press, 1990.

Jamieson, Kathleen H., and Paul Waldman. *The Press Effect: Politicians, Journalists and the Stories that Shape the Political World.* New York: Oxford University Press, 2004.

Johannesen, Richard. "The Emerging Concept of Communication as Dialogue." *Quarterly Journal of Speech* 57 (1971): 373–382.

Kogler, Hans-Herbert. *The Power of Dialogue: Critical Hermeneutics after Gadamer and Foucault* (Trans., Paul Hendrickson). Cambridge, MA: MIT Press, 1999.

Nikulin, Dmitri. *On Dialogue*. Lanham, MD: Lexington Books, 2006.

Noddings, Nel. *Caring: A Feminine Approach to Ethics and Moral Education*. Berkeley: University of California Press, 1984.

Pearce, W. Barnett, and Stephen W. Littlejohn. *Moral Conflict: When Social Worlds Collide*. Thousand Oaks, CA: Sage, 1997.

Poulos, Christopher N. "Accidental Dialogue." *Communication Theory* 18 (2008): 117–138.

Quindlen, Anna. "The Elephant in the Room." *Newsweek* 72 (2004, April 8).

Rogers, Carl R. "Empathic: An Unappreciated Way of Being." *Counseling Psychologist* 5 (1975): 2–10.

Spano, Shawn. *Public Dialogue and Participatory Democracy: The Cupertino Community Project.* Cresskill, NJ: Hampton Press, 2001.

Stewart, John. "Foundations of Dialogic Communication." *Quarterly Journal of Speech* 64 (1978): 183–201.

Tannen, Deborah. *The Argument Culture: Moving from Debate to Dialogue*. New York: Random House, 1998.

Taylor, Charles. *Multiculturalism and the Politics of Recognition*. Princeton, NJ: Princeton University Press, 1992.

■ ■ ■

Afterword

KATHLEEN GLENISTER ROBERTS AND RONALD C. ARNETT

Communication Ethics: Between Cosmopolitanism and Provinciality is the second volume to emerge from the National Communication Ethics Conference. Just as this book followed another, others will follow this project. This afterword is more a foreword for ongoing projects stimulated by our colleagues. We offer deep thanks to each one of our colleagues and those interested in the questions of communication ethics not only for their scholarship but for the heuristic energy that they provide for so many. We are the fortunate recipients of that heuristic energy. Out of this conference comes the next book by Kathleen Glenister Roberts, again looking at the question of cosmopolitanism, engaged from a critical stance that asks whether or not cosmopolitanism is simply modernity masquerading under another garb. She begins to examine the gaps and ethical questions in the philosophical notion that all humanity is of a single moral community. Such questions will be ongoing, but the hermeneutic entrance into the question of cosmopolitanism is: simply whether or not it is modernity and its monologues attempting to rise once again?

Ronald C. Arnett pursues the issue of provinciality further in two projects: (1) *Communication Ethics Literacy: Dialogue and Difference* (with Janie Harden Fritz and Leeanne Bell) (Sage, 2009) that unites provinciality and a multiplicity of goods in communication ethics, and (2) a project on Hannah Arendt, *Communication Ethics in Dark Times*. Both projects go to *local soil,* examining the consequences of human lives caught in the midst of narrative disruption, in the midst of ground withdrawn from their feet. Communication ethics and provinciality keep the ground under our feet.

In the words of Edith Stein, an afterword becomes the foreground of pragmatic recognition. She states that there is no final answer, "however, I leave the answering of this question to further investigation and satisfy myself here with a 'nonliquet,' 'It is not clear.'"[1]

NOTES

1. Stein, *On the Problem of Empathy* in Sister Teresa Benedicta of the Cross (ed.), *The Collected Works of Edith Stein,* Vol. 3. (Washington, D.C., ICS Publications, 1989), 118.

Contributors

CHITRA AKKOOR is a doctoral student in Interpersonal Communication at the University of Iowa. Her research interests sit at the interstices of interpersonal relationships and culture, specifically in the contexts of migration and diaspora. Some of her ongoing research projects include the study of marital and parent-child communication among Asian Indian immigrants in the United States and Germany, the competing discourses of authenticity and adaptation at a Hindu temple, and the negotiation of identity among other diasporic populations in Germany.

ROB ANDERSON, Professor of Communication at Saint Louis University, studies and teaches at the intersection of interpersonal communication and media studies. He is especially interested in problems of public dialogue, contemporary cultural criticism, communication ethics, Taoist philosophy, and the university as an interactional system. His 11 books include *Dialogue: Theorizing Difference in Communication Studies; Moments of Meeting; The Martin Buber–Carl Rogers Dialogue: A New Transcript with Commentary; The Reach of Dialogue;* and *The Conversation of Journalism.*

PAT ARNESON is Associate Professor in the Department of Communication & Rhetorical Studies at Duquesne University. Dr. Arneson's work examines issues of human communication from philosophical perspectives. Her research interests include rhetoric, philosophy of communication, interpretive approaches to research, interpersonal communication ethics, and educational assessment. She has published over 25 book chapters, journal articles, or research reports. She is editor of *Perspectives on Philosophy of Communication* (2007) and *Exploring Communication Ethics: Interviews with Influential Scholars in the Field* (2007). She is co-author with Ronald C. Arnett of *Dialogic Civility in a Cynical Age: Community, Hope and Interpersonal Relationships* (1999).

RONALD C. ARNETT is chair and professor in the Department of Communication & Rhetorical Studies at Duquesne University. He is the author of *Communication Ethics Literacy: Dialogue and Difference* (Sage, 2009) with Janie Harden Fritz and Leeanne Bell as well as *Dialogic Confession: Bonhoeffer's Rhetoric of Responsibility* (2005), for which he received the Religious Communication Association 2005 Scholar of the Year Award and the Everett Lee Hunt Award for Outstanding Scholarship; *Dialogic Civility in a Cynical Age: Community, Hope, and Interpersonal Relationships* (with Pat Arneson, 1999); *Dialogic Education: Conversations About Ideas and Between Persons* (1992); *Communication and Community* (1986), for which he won the Religious Speech Communication Association Book Award; and *Dwell in Peace: Applying Nonviolence to Everyday Relationships* (1980). He is coeditor of *Communication Ethics in an Age of Diversity* (with Josina M. Makau, (1997) and *The Reach of Dialogue: Confirmation, Voice, and Community* (with Rob Anderson and Kenneth Cissna, 1994).

LESLIE BAXTER is F. Wendell Miller Distinguished Professor of Communication Studies at the University of Iowa. Her research focuses on dialogic communication in personal, social, and familial relationships. She is the recipient of the 1995 Berscheid/Hatfield Award for Mid-Career Achievement by the International Network on Personal Relationships and the 2002 Legacy Theory Award by the Communication Theory Interest Group of the Central States Communication Association. She has published over 100 articles and book chapters in addition to 5 books. Her book *Relating: Dialogues and Dialectics* (with Barbara Montgomery; Guilford, 1996) received the G.R. Miller Distinguished Book Award from the Interpersonal Communication Division of the National Communication Association. She also is a past president of the Western States Communication Association.

CLIFFORD G. CHRISTIANS is the Charles H. Sandage Distinguished Professor and a Research Professor of Communications at the University of Illinois-Urbana. He holds joint appointments as a Professor of Journalism and a Professor of Media Studies. He has been a visiting scholar in the Department of Philosophy at Princeton University, a research fellow in social ethics and also a visiting scholar in ethics at the University of Chicago, and a Pew fellow in ethics at Oxford University. He is the author or co-author of *Responsibility in Mass Communication; Jacques Ellul: Interpretive Essays; Teaching Ethics in Journalism Education; Good News: Social Ethics and the Press; Media Ethics: Cases and Moral Reasoning* (7th ed.); *Communication Ethics and Universal Values;* and *Moral Engagement in Public Life: Theorists for Contemporary Ethics.* His forthcoming authored or co-authored books are *Journalism in Democracy: Normative Theories of the Media; Keywords in Critical and Cultural Studies; Handbook of Mass Media Ethics;* and *Ethical Communication: Moral Stances in Human Dialogue.*

KENNETH N. CISSNA is professor and chair, Department of Communication, University of South Florida. His research emphasizes dialogue and public dialogue, including such books as *The Reach of Dialogue; The Martin–Buber–Carl Rogers Dialogue; Moments of Meeting: Buber, Rogers, and the Potential for Public Dialogue;* and *Dialogue: Theorizing Difference in Communication Studies,* and the monograph "The Rhetoric of Public Dialogue." He edited the *Journal of Applied Communication Research* and the *Southern Communication Journal,* and is past president of the Florida Communication Association and Southern States Communication Association.

G. L. ERCOLINI, currently a doctoral candidate at The Pennsylvania State University in Communications Arts and Sciences, is presently teaching communication courses at the University of South Carolina. While her work has ranged from such seemingly diverse subjects as Kenneth Burke, Stanley Kubrick, and rhetoric in and of the Enlightenment, her approach is unified by a sustained and persistent attention to questions concerning agency and subjectivity and their relation to the study of rhetorical theory and history.

WALTER R. FISHER is former Director of the Annenberg School of Communication, University of Southern California. He is past president of the Western Communication Association, editor of *The Quarterly Journal of Speech* (1984–86) and the *Western Journal of Communication* (1976–78). He has been recognized as a distinguished teacher and scholar by the National Communication Association, the Western Communication Association, and several universities. Most prominent among his publications is his book *Human Communication as Narration: Toward a Philosophy of Reason, Value, and Action* (1989). Now Emeritus Professor, he continues to explore the reconstruction of reason and ethics in communicative transactions.

PAT J. GEHRKE is Assistant Professor of Communication in the Department of English at the University of South Carolina, where he teaches graduate and undergraduate seminars in contemporary rhetorical theory, communication ethics, and rhetorical pedagogy. His work has been published in *Philosophy and Rhetoric, The Quarterly Journal of Speech, Philosophy Today, Critical Studies in Media Communication,* and numerous other journals.

RONALD L. JACKSON II is Associate Professor of culture and communication theory in the Department of Communication Arts & Sciences at the Pennsylvania State University. He is author of eight books including the recent *African American Communication: Identity and Culture* (with Michael Hecht and Sidney Ribeau, 2003), *Scripting the Black Body: Identity, Discourse and Racial Politics in Popular Media* (2006), and *Black Pioneers in Communication Research* (with Sonja Brown Givens 2006). Author of almost four dozen articles, chapters and reviews, Dr. Jackson has developed two theories coined "cultural contracts theory" and "black masculine identity theory." He is currently working on a 3-volume *Sage Encyclopedia of Identity* (with psychologist Michael Hogg) for Sage Publications while continuing his successful book series for SUNY Press on the politics of identity negotiation.

CHRISTOPHER LYLE JOHNSTONE is Associate Professor of Rhetoric and Basic Course Director in the department of Communication Arts and Sciences at the Pennsylvania State University. He received his bachelor's degree in Rhetoric from the University of California at Davis, and his Ph.D. in Communication Arts from the University of Wisconsin, Madison. Professor Johnstone's research and teaching interests concentrate on classical rhetorical theory and practice, philosophy and rhetoric, and communication ethics. His scholarship in these areas has been published in both regional and international journals, as well as in the *Quarterly Journal of Speech, Philosophy and Rhetoric,* and *Advances in the History of Rhetoric.* His essays have appeared in several edited books and in the *Encyclopedia of Rhetoric.* Professor Johnstone has served on the editorial boards of the *Quarterly Journal of Speech, Philosophy and Rhetoric,* the *Southern States Speech Journal, Rhetoric Society Quarterly,* and *Communication Quarterly.*

LENORE LANGSDORF is a professor in the Speech Communication Department at Southern Illinois University, Carbondale. Her research and teaching interests focus on philosophy of communication/rhetoric, hermeneutic phenomenology, process philosophy, critical theory, and critical constructionist investigation of communication in relation to class, ethnicity, gender, and identity. She is co-editor of a number of publications, including *Phenomenology, Interpretation, and Community* (with Stephen H. Watson and E. Marya Bower, State University of New York Press, 1998), *Reinterpreting the Political: Continental Philosophy and Political Thought* (with Stephen H. Watson and Karen A. Smith, State University of New York Press, 1996), and *Recovering Pragmatism's Voice: The Classical Tradition, Rorty, and the Philosophy of Communication* (with Andrew R. Smith, State University of New York Press, 1995).

JAMIE MOSHIN is scholar who works at the intersection of race, identity, whiteness, ethnicity and discourse. His work focuses in particular on the representation of American Jewishness; his master's thesis (from the Pennsylvania State University), investigated the representation of Jewishness in humorous films about the Holocaust, and he is currently at work on a Doctoral Dissertation (at the University of Washington) on the Jewish appropriation of African American rhetorical devices and discursive identifiers.

KATHLEEN GLENISTER ROBERTS is Associate Professor of Communication & Rhetorical Studies at Duquesne University and President of the Pennsylvania Communication Association. She teaches and conducts research in rhetoric and philosophy of intercultural communication, specifically in the areas of alterity, cosmopolitanism, and narrative. Dr. Roberts is the author of *Alterity and Narrative: Stories and the Negotiation of Western Identities* (2007) and nine essays in refereed journals such as *Communication Theory, Argumentation and Advocacy, Communication Quarterly, Text and Performance Quarterly,* and *The Howard Journal of Communications.* She has been a PFF Fellow, a Richard Dorson Fellow, and a recipient of the Presidential Scholarship Award from Duquesne University.

JOHN STEWART graduated from Pacific Lutheran University and Northwestern University. He completed his Ph.D. at the University of Southern California in 1970 and accepted a position as Director of the Basic Interpersonal Communication Course at the University of Washington. Since his 1978 article on the "Foundations of Dialogic Communication" in the *Quarterly Journal of Speech,* his scholarly and instructional writings have attempted to clarify the insights of dialogue philosophers and extend them to enhance dialogue practice in families, friendships, classrooms, and organizations. He spent 32 years at the University of Washington, teaching undergraduate and graduate philosophy of communication, theory, interpretive research, and interpersonal courses and serving as Graduate Program Coordinator. In

2001, he joined the University of Dubuque as Vice President for Academic Affairs, where he continues to teach undergraduate and graduate communication courses.

Index

Adorno, Theodor: A rendt-Benjamin-Adorno relationship, 215–216; and Benjamin, 220–222; demonstrated commitment, 219, 231–234; and the Frankfurt School, 216; and Heine's poetry, 217; "Portrait of Walter Benjamin," 218, 225–228

African Americans, 194–195, 202, 205, 258n44. *See also* Blacks

Agathon, 163, 166

Ali, Muhammad, 197

alienation, 52, 94, 245

Allport, Gordon, 111, 112

Al Qaeda, 109

American Indian. *See* Native American

anthropology, philosophical, 5, 11–13, 17, 113

Apel, Karl-Otto, 144

Appadurai, Arjun, 94, 98

Appiah, Kwame Anthony: *Cosmopolitanism: Ethics in a World of Strangers,* 107–109; cultural ancestry of, 90; on globalization, 48; the local element, 112–113; in support of Nussbaum, 60

Arendt, Hannah: Adorno-Benjamin-Arendt relationship, 215–216; assessment of Jewishness, 207; and Benahib, 90; and Benjamin, 219–220; criticism of Adorno, 235n8; demonstrated commitment, 219, 228–231; on enlarged mentality, 3, 83; and the Frankfurt School, 215–219; insight on fear, 77; student of Heidegger, 18n5; "Walter Benjamin, 1892–1940," 222–225

Aristotle, 11, 49, 60, 141, 229–230

Armstrong, Karen, 59–60

Arneson, Pat, 1, 131, 135

Arnett, Ronald C.: on Buber's dialogical perspective, 246–247; on community, 123; on dialogic civility, 131; further projects, 285–286; on "hope within limits," 135; on the "unity of contraries," 259n62

Critical
Jntercultural
Communication
Studies

General Editor, Thomas K. Nakayama

Critical approaches to the study of intercultural communication have arisen at the end of the twentieth century and are poised to flourish in the new millenium. As cultures come into contact—driven by migration, refugees, the internet, wars, media, transnational capitalism, cultural imperialism, and more—critical interrogations of the ways that cultures interact communicatively are needed to understand culture and communication. This series will interrogate—from a critical perspective—the role of communication in intercultural contact, in both domestic and international contexts. This series is open to studies in key areas such as postcolonialism, transnationalism, critical race theory, queer diaspora studies, and critical feminist approaches as they relate to intercultural communication, tuning into the complexities of power relations in intercultural communication. Proposals might focus on various contexts of intercultural communication such as international advertising, popular culture, language policies, hate crimes, ethnic cleansing and ethnic group conflicts, as well as engaging theoretical issues such as hybridity, displacement, multiplicity, identity, orientalism, and materialism. By creating a space for these critical approaches, this series will be at the forefront of this new wave in intercultural communication scholarship. Manuscripts and proposals are welcome that advance this new approach.

For additional information about this series or for the submission of manuscripts, please contact:

Dr. Thomas K. Nakayama
Hugh Downs School of Human Communication
Arizona State University
P.O. Box 871205
Tempe, AZ 85287-1205

To order other books in this series, please contact our Customer Service Department:
(800) 770-LANG (within the U.S.)
(212) 647-7706 (outside the U.S.)
(212) 647-7707 FAX

Or browse online by series:
www.peterlang.com